GCE A2 Level

A2 Level for **OCR**

Applied

Business

Catherine Richards • Rob Dransfield

Neil Richards • Karen Hough

www.heinemann.co.uk

✓ Free online support
✓ Useful weblinks
✓ 24 hour online ordering

01865 888058

Heinemann Educational Publishers
Halley Court, Jordan Hill, Oxford OX2 8EJ
Part of Harcourt Education

Heinemann is the registered trademark of Harcourt Education Limited
Text © Catherine Richards, Rob Dransfield, Neil Richards, Karen Hough, 2006

First published 2006

10 09 08 07 06
10 9 8 7 6 5 4 3 2 1

British Library Cataloguing in Publication Data is available from the British Library on request.

10-digit ISBN: 0 435352 91 1
13-digit ISBN: 978 0 435352 91 2

Edited by Rosalyn Bass and Chris Goddard
Typeset by Tek-Art, Croydon, Surrey
Original illustrations © Harcourt Education Limited, 2006
Cover design by Pete Stratton
Printed in the UK by CPI Bath
Cover photo: © Corbis/Chuck Savage
Picture research by Natalie Gray

Acknowledgements
The authors and publishers are grateful to those who have given permission to reproduce
material. Every effort has been made to contact copyright holders of material reproduced in this
book. Any omissions will be rectified in subsequent printings if notice is given to the publishers.

Text acknowledgements
BT (British Telecom) p**316**; Barclays Bank p**97**; Comet (the Comet logo is a registered trademark
owned by the Comet Group plc) p**329**; Investors in People p**333**; LOVEFiLM p**77**; Marks
& Spencer p**110**; Microsoft product screenshot reprinted with permission from Microsoft
Corporation p**177**; Office Cakes p**58**; Paultons Park p**80**; Royal Bank of Scotland p**97**; Wave 105 FM
p**173**

Photo acknowledgements
Alamy Images/CapitalCity Images p**149**; Alamy Images /Chloe Johnson p**314**; Alamy Images/
David Greggs p**302**; Alamy Images/Mike Stone p**364**; Alamy Images/Patrick Blake p**211**; Alamy
Images/Photofusion p**190**; Alamy Images/PHOTOTAKE inc p**310**; British Airways p**260**; Corbis
p**349**; Corbis/Cameron p**1**; Corbis/Eva-Lotta Jansson p**101**; Corbis/Liewig Media Sports p**180**;
Corbis/John B Boykin p**281**; Corbis/Philippe Lesage p**10**; Corbis/Thierry Tronnel p**266**; Corbis/
Zefa p**297**, **343**; easyJet p**56**; Empics/PA p**348**; Getty Images/Eyewire p**123**; Getty Images/Iconica
p**105**; Getty Images/Imagebank p**53**; Getty Images/PhotoDisc p**47**, **325**; Harcourt Education
Ltd. Mark Bassett p**175**; iStockPhoto/Lisa Gagne p**135**; Natalie Gray p**14**, **184**; NOKIA p**154**;
Photolibrary p**191**; photos.com p**93**, **249**; Report Digital/Andrew Ward p**382**; Rex Features p**33**,
45, **171**, **195**, **272**, **373**, **392**; Rex Features/Toivanen p**235**; TopFoto/The Image Works p**158**; TopFoto
UPP p**182**; Virgin Trains p**339**

Websites
Please note that the examples of websites suggested in this book were up to date at the time of
writing. It is essential for tutors to preview each site before using it to ensure that the URL is
still accurate and the content is appropriate. We suggest that tutors bookmark useful sites and
consider enabling students to access them through the school or college intranet.

Contents

Introduction   v

Unit 9 Strategic decision-making   1

9.2.1	Mission statements, aims and objectives	3
9.2.2	Business planning, strategy and decision-making	7
9.2.3	Financial business planning	23
9.2.4	Human resource planning	32
9.2.5	Integrated marketing planning/strategy	41
9.2.6	Contingency planning and crisis management	44

Unit 10 A business plan for the entrepreneur   53

10.2.1	Reasons for construction of a business plan	55
10.2.2	Information within a business plan	58
10.2.3	Appropriate research for a business plan	95
10.2.4	Business plan templates	97
10.2.5	Constraints that impact on implementation	99

Unit 11 Managerial and supervisory roles   105

11.2.1	The business context within which the report will take shape	107
11.2.2	Planning how to gather information for the report	133
11.2.3	Researching into the business context and analysis of the information that is collected	134
11.2.4	Production of a report	143
11.2.5	Evaluation of the factors which can influence the environment in which a manager/supervisor performs her/his role	145

Unit 13 Promotion in action   149

13.2.1	Devising a strategy	151
13.2.2	The environment within which the strategy will take shape	154
13.2.3	Planning the strategy	156
13.2.4	Researching of the strategy and analysis of the information that is collected	160
13.2.5	Producing a plan of action	169
13.2.6	Internal and external influences on promotional activity	185

059265

Unit 14 **Constructing a financial strategy** 195

14.2.1 Devising a strategy 197
14.2.2 The business context within which the strategy will take shape 198
14.2.3 Planning the strategy 200
14.2.4 Strategic research 239
14.2.5 Analysis to inform strategy 239
14.2.6 Evaluation and recommendations 244

Unit 15 **Launching a new product or service in Europe** 249

15.2.1 Devising a strategy 251
15.2.2 The business context within which the strategy will take shape 252
15.2.3 Planning the strategy 279
15.2.4 Research of the strategy and analysis of the information that is collected 280
15.2.5 Production of a plan of action 291
15.2.6 Evaluation of the strategy 292

Unit 16 **Training and development** 297

16.2.1 Devising a strategy 299
16.2.2 The business context within which the strategy will take place 300
16.2.3 Planning the strategy 318
16.2.4 Research of the strategy and analysis of the information that is collected 322
16.2.5 Production of a plan of action 328
16.2.6 Evaluating effectiveness 336

Unit 17 **Business Law** 343

17.2.1 Sources of law 345
17.2.2 Law of contract 352
17.2.3 Business formation 364
17.2.4 Business dissolution 374
17.2.5. Employment protection 378
17.2.6 Health and safety legislation 383
17.2.7 Consumer protection legislation 386
17.2.8 Intellectual property rights 390

Glossary 399
Index 405

Introduction

This book is designed to support the OCR Applied Business Single and Double Award courses and help you succeed on the second year of your studies, known as A2 Level.

Like the OCR AS Applied Business books, this book is designed to welcome you to the practical world of business by providing material about the business world that exists around you.

Throughout the book you will be presented with information that will encourage you to think about theories relating to business, take part in practical activities and thinking sessions as well as using hints and tips to help you produce high-level work towards your final marks at A Level.

This book provides enough unit support material for you to complete your OCR Single or Double award A Level by finishing the A2 year.

The units

There are ten units in the OCR A2 specifications. Some are mandatory and some are optional, as categorised below (units in italics are not featured in this book):

Mandatory units for both the Single and Double Award
Unit 9 Strategic decision-making (externally assessed)
Unit 10 A business plan for the entrepreneur

Optional units for both awards
Unit 11 Managerial and supervisory roles
Unit 12 Launching a business on-line
Unit 13 Promotion in action
Unit 14 Constructing a financial strategy
Unit 15 Launching a new product or service in Europe
Unit 16 Training and development

Additional mandatory units for the Double Award
Unit 17 Business Law (externally assessed)
Unit 18 Managing risk in the workplace (externally assessed)

To complete your OCR Single Award A Level, you need to study the two mandatory units, 9 and 10, and choose one optional unit from the list above – a total of three units.

To complete your OCR Double Award A Level, you will need to study the two mandatory units, 9 and 10, and choose three optional units from the list above, plus Unit 17 – a total of six units.

This gives you a varied choice of units from which you can select within this book. Make sure you check with your teacher which ones you are going to do as a class to ensure you are working on the right ones!

Features of this book

Each unit begins with an introduction which gives background information and links to the assessment process. There is a list of additional resources at the end of each unit to help you research, update and extend your knowledge.

Other features of the units are:

Key terms are printed in bold and explained on the page. These terms, and other terms you need to know, can be found in the comprehensive **glossary** at the end of this book.

Theory into practice applies business theories to current business practice.

Think it over encourages you to think more deeply about what you have learned.

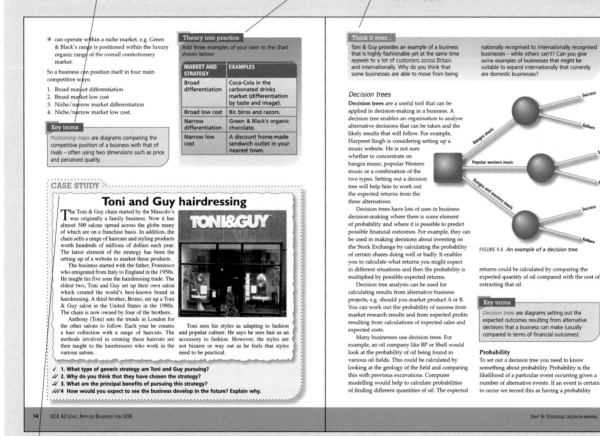

Case studies have been chosen to be up to date and interesting so they are relevant to you.

Most case studies have **differentiated questions** to allow you to work at the level you are best able to. The levels are indicated by one to three ticks:

✓   These questions are for everyone. They check knowledge and understanding.

✓✓   These questions are more challenging and require some analytical skills.

✓✓✓ These are the most challenging questions and involve recommendations, conclusions and judgements. If you want higher grades, you need to be able to answer these questions.

Unit assessments occur in Units 9 and 17 which are externally assessed. Case study material tests your learning in the unit.

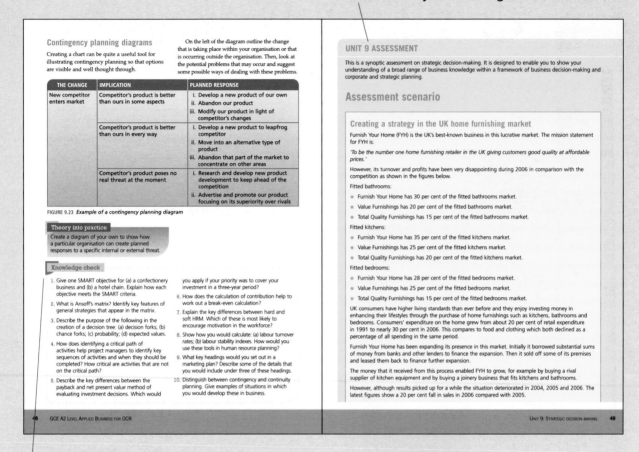

Contingency planning diagrams

Creating a chart can be quite a useful tool for illustrating contingency planning so that options are visible and well thought through.

On the left of the diagram outline the change that is taking place within your organisation or that is occurring outside the organisation. Then, look at the potential problems that may occur and suggest some possible ways of dealing with these problems.

THE CHANGE	IMPLICATION	PLANNED RESPONSE
New competitor enters market	Competitor's product is better than ours in some aspects	i. Develop a new product of our own ii. Abandon our product iii. Modify our product in light of competitor's changes
	Competitor's product is better than ours in every way	i. Develop a new product to leapfrog competitor ii. Move into an alternative type of product iii. Abandon that part of the market to concentrate on other areas
	Competitor's product poses no real threat at the moment	i. Research and develop new product development to keep ahead of the competition ii. Advertise and promote our product focusing on its superiority over rivals

FIGURE 9.23 *Example of a contingency planning diagram*

Theory into practice

Create a diagram of your own to show how a particular organisation can create planned responses to a specific internal or external threat.

Knowledge check

1. Give one SMART objective for (a) a confectionery business and (b) a hotel chain. Explain how each objective meets the SMART criteria.
2. What is Ansoff's matrix? Identify key features of general strategies that appear in the matrix.
3. Describe the purpose of the following in the creation of a decision tree: (a) decision forks; (b) chance forks; (c) probability; (d) expected values.
4. How does identifying a critical path of activities help project managers to identify key sequences of activities and when they should be completed? How critical are activities that are not on the critical path?
5. Describe the key differences between the payback and net present value method of evaluating investment decisions. Which would

you apply if your priority was to cover your investment in a three-year period?
6. How does the calculation of contribution help to work out a break-even calculation?
7. Explain the key differences between hard and soft HRM. Which of these is most likely to encourage motivation in the workforce?
8. Show how you would calculate: (a) labour turnover rates; (b) labour stability indexes. How would you use these tools in human resource planning?
9. What key headings would you set out in a marketing plan? Describe some of the details that you would include under three of these headings.
10. Distinguish between contingency and continuity planning. Give examples of situations in which you would develop these in business.

UNIT 9 ASSESSMENT

This is a synoptic assessment on strategic decision-making. It is designed to enable you to show your understanding of a broad range of business knowledge within a framework of business decision-making and corporate and strategic planning.

Assessment scenario

Creating a strategy in the UK home furnishing market

Furnish Your Home (FYH) is the UK's best-known business in this lucrative market. The mission statement for FYH is:

'To be the number one home furnishing retailer in the UK giving customers good quality at affordable prices.'

However, its turnover and profits have been very disappointing during 2006 in comparison with the competition as shown in the figures below.

Fitted bathrooms:

- Furnish Your Home has 30 per cent of the fitted bathrooms market.
- Value Furnishings has 20 per cent of the fitted bathrooms market.
- Total Quality Furnishings has 15 per cent of the fitted bathrooms market.

Fitted kitchens:

- Furnish Your Home has 35 per cent of the fitted kitchens market.
- Value Furnishings has 25 per cent of the fitted kitchens market.
- Total Quality Furnishings has 20 per cent of the fitted kitchens market.

Fitted bedrooms:

- Furnish Your Home has 28 per cent of the fitted bedrooms market.
- Value Furnishings has 25 per cent of the fitted bedrooms market.
- Total Quality Furnishings has 15 per cent of the fitted bedrooms market.

UK consumers have higher living standards than ever before and they enjoy investing money in enhancing their lifestyles through the purchase of home furnishings such as kitchens, bathrooms and bedrooms. Consumers' expenditure on the home grew from about 20 per cent of retail expenditure in 1991 to nearly 30 per cent in 2006. This compares to food and clothing which both declined as a percentage of all spending in the same period.

Furnish Your Home has been expanding its presence in this market. Initially it borrowed substantial sums of money from banks and other lenders to finance the expansion. Then it sold off some of its premises and leased them back to finance further expansion.

The money that it received from this process enabled FYH to grow, for example by buying a rival supplier of kitchen equipment and by buying a joinery business that fits kitchens and bathrooms.

However, although results picked up for a while the situation deteriorated in 2004, 2005 and 2006. The latest figures show a 20 per cent fall in sales in 2006 compared with 2005.

Knowledge check questions at the end of each unit test your learning of key points.

This course will put you in good stead for progression on to a higher education course in business or will help you to develop your skills for business that will assist you in the world of work.

Good luck with your studies!

Catherine Richards
Rob Dransfield
Neil Richards
Karen Hough

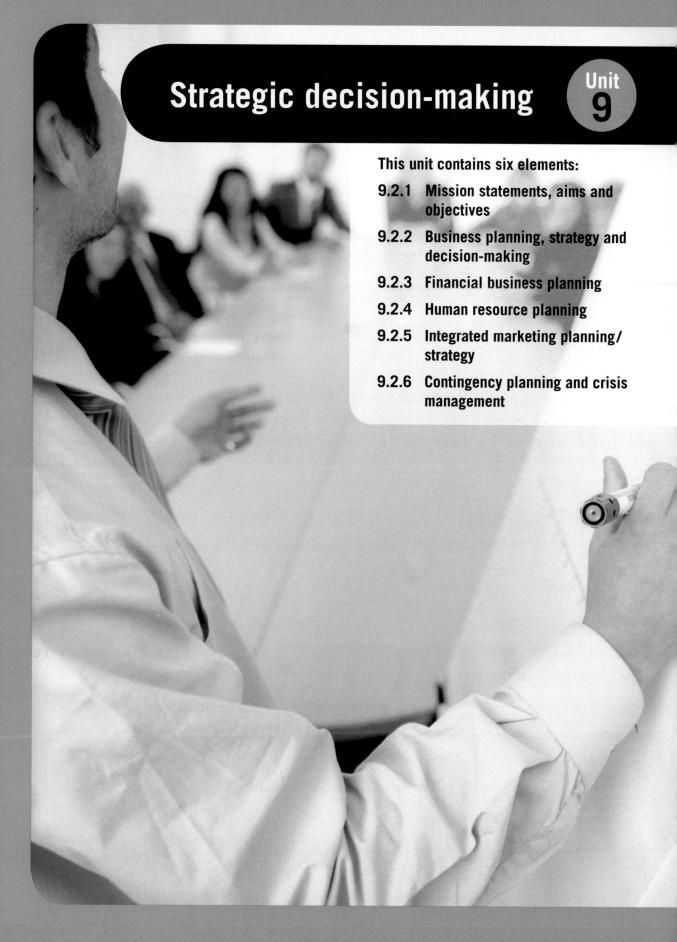

Strategic decision-making

This unit contains six elements:

9.2.1 Mission statements, aims and objectives

9.2.2 Business planning, strategy and decision-making

9.2.3 Financial business planning

9.2.4 Human resource planning

9.2.5 Integrated marketing planning/strategy

9.2.6 Contingency planning and crisis management

Strategic decisions are the big decisions that businesses make. Strategies affect the whole of the organisation rather than small parts of it. Typically, strategic decisions involve substantial resourcing issues. For example, an organisation like British Airways may decide to expand into new markets such as China or an organisation such as Cadbury-Schweppes may decide to cut out some of its old products and focus on new product lines. These are strategic decisions and this unit looks at how important decisions like these are made.

As strategy involves the whole organisation, it involves all aspects of running a business, including finance, marketing and human resource management.

This unit brings together all the various elements that you have been studying on this course. You will have an external assessment that covers all of the mandatory units in an integrated way. The mark that you get for the external assessment will be your mark for the unit.

9.2.1 Mission statements, aims and objectives

Aims and objectives

All organisations need to have a sense of direction. This direction is given by **aims** and **objectives**.

* The aim is the overall goal that you are trying to achieve. It may be set out in fairly general terms.

* Objectives tend to be more specific. They break down the overall aim into more focused targets.

For example, the aim of a supermarket chain may be to be:

'the best supermarket chain which consistently sets the standards for high-quality produce, service and customer satisfaction'.

Everyone involved in the organisation can understand this aim. However, they will want to have clearer guidance about what this end purpose entails which is why the organisation needs objectives such as:

* to be the market leader

* to increase sales by 5 per cent a year

* to have the industry leading profit margins

* to provide the highest levels of customer satisfaction in the industry.

If you look at these objectives you can see that they are SMART:

* specific
* measurable
* attainable
* realistic
* time-constrained.

They are specific because they set out in clear terms what the target is, i.e. market leadership, increased sales, leading profit margins, highest customer satisfaction. You can see that these objectives are easy to understand and to communicate.

Key terms

Aim is the overall purpose – a superordinate goal for a plan or organisation.

An *objective* is a more specific target to be achieved. A clearly defined set of corporate objectives provides measurable goals in achieving the overall aim or purpose of an organisation.

They can also be measured, e.g. through market share, value of sales, profit margins and customer satisfaction surveys.

The objectives need to be attainable and realistic given available resources and the state of the market. There is no point in setting objectives that can't be attained as this will be demotivating and lead to a loss of confidence in the company. In addition, they shouldn't be set too low so that they are too easily attained.

The objectives also need to be set to a time period, e.g. to increase sales by 5 per cent in 2007 or to have the highest profit margins every year.

Strategic activities

We can think of businesses having a cycle of strategic activities as shown in Figure 9.1 below. Figure 9.2 shows how this will work in practice, using Ryanair as an example.

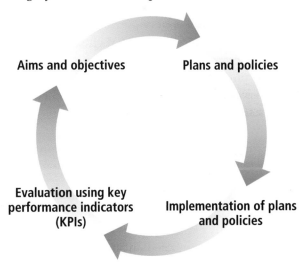

Aims and objectives → **Plans and policies** → **Implementation of plans and policies** → **Evaluation using key performance indicators (KPIs)** →

FIGURE 9.1 *Cycle of strategic activities*

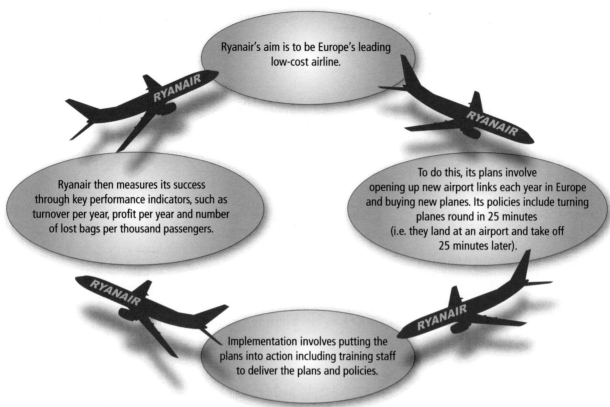

FIGURE 9.2 *Ryanair's cycle of strategic activities*

Mission statement

Business strategists recognise superordinate goals as being one of the key elements of a successful business. A superordinate goal is another name for an aim. An aim is superordinate because it encapsulates all of your objectives.

Businesses typically express their superordinate goals in terms of a mission statement which sets out the purpose of an organisation. For example, the mission statement of Newcastle United Football club starts out by saying that:

> *'the club seeks to play attractive football and to win Trophies'*

Anyone reading this mission would know what Newcastle United was all about. You would expect the club to buy exciting players and to employ coaches who concentrated on attacking football.

The mission statement of UGC cinemas is:

> *'We have one major goal: to captivate the public.'*

Immediately you get a feel for the priorities of the organisation and how you would expect it to operate.

The mission of Pfizer (the largest pharmaceutical company in the UK) is:

> *'Pfizer's corporate mission is to become the world's most valued company to patients, customers, colleagues, investors, business partners and the communities where we work and live.'*

You can see from the Pfizer mission statement that the emphasis is on respecting and listening to all of the various stakeholder groups.

The mission statement gives a feel for the culture of the organisation (typical patterns of behaviours within an organisation). For example, the mission statement of Kingston upon Hull City Council is:

> *'The Council will strive to secure a positive and sustainable future for the City. This will be achieved through decisive leadership, consultation, the development of inclusive and meaningful partnerships and the support of active and empowered communities.'*

Theory into practice

In a group, choose an organisation that you and one or two other students know something about. Individually create a mission statement for the organisation.

Your mission statement should:

- set out the purpose of the organisation
- give a feel for the culture of the organisation and the importance of stakeholders.

When you have created the mission on your own, share ideas with the group. See if you can produce a group mission statement. If possible, compare your mission statement with the actual mission statement of the organisation. Carry out an Internet search to see if the mission is available.

Now create five SMART objectives for your chosen organisation. Remember that these objectives should line up with the mission of the organisation.

Vision

The **vision** sets out what the organisation can become. You will often hear business and political leaders state, 'I want to share my vision with you.' The vision sets out an ideal future for an organisation which, it is to be hoped, can be grounded in reality. A vision is a long-term aspiration of a leader for his or her firm that can be described to colleagues and that will urge them on.

One way of distinguishing between mission and vision is:

✳ a mission sets out why a firm exists, its role in life

✳ a vision is a view of what the firm could become, imagining a desired future.

Key terms

Vision is a future directed statement setting out what an organisation is and what it is trying to achieve.

Taking account of the views of stakeholders

Today we live in what the Labour government terms a '**stakeholder society**'. A stakeholder society is one in which the views of everyone are taken into account and in which we all have rights and responsibilities. Businesses also apply this stakeholder model.

In the 1990s, Sir John Collins the chairman of Shell introduced the concept that businesses need to earn a licence to operate. What he meant was that successful businesses need to secure the approval of all of their stakeholders – it is society that gives business a licence to operate. You can see how this would relate to an organisation like Shell in Figure 9.3 below.

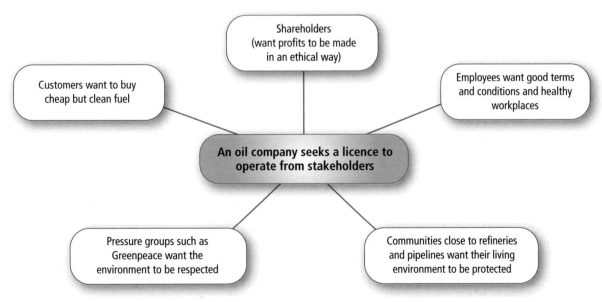

FIGURE 9.3 Securing approval of stakeholders

As shown in Figure 9.3, all of the stakeholder groupings exert pressure on the company and, as a result, the aims and objectives which the organisation is able to establish involve a compromise between the interests of various stakeholder groups. Of course, those stakeholder groups with most power and influence will be able to put most pressure on the organisation to ensure their own objectives are given priority.

Triple bottom line

Businesses traditionally sought to make a profit on the **bottom line**. However, today most organisations recognise the need to develop a triple bottom line (Figure 9.4).

CASE STUDY

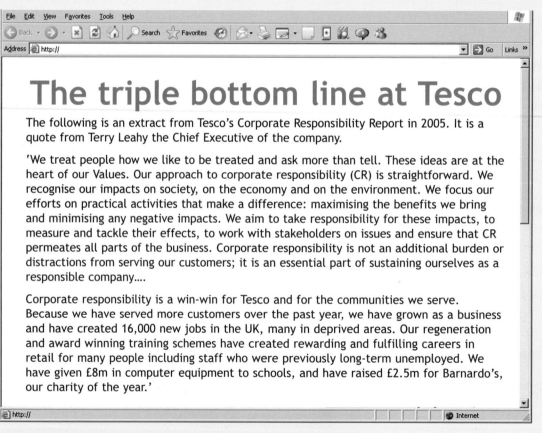

The triple bottom line at Tesco

The following is an extract from Tesco's Corporate Responsibility Report in 2005. It is a quote from Terry Leahy the Chief Executive of the company.

'We treat people how we like to be treated and ask more than tell. These ideas are at the heart of our Values. Our approach to corporate responsibility (CR) is straightforward. We recognise our impacts on society, on the economy and on the environment. We focus our efforts on practical activities that make a difference: maximising the benefits we bring and minimising any negative impacts. We aim to take responsibility for these impacts, to measure and tackle their effects, to work with stakeholders on issues and ensure that CR permeates all parts of the business. Corporate responsibility is not an additional burden or distractions from serving our customers; it is an essential part of sustaining ourselves as a responsible company....

Corporate responsibility is a win-win for Tesco and for the communities we serve. Because we have served more customers over the past year, we have grown as a business and have created 16,000 new jobs in the UK, many in deprived areas. Our regeneration and award winning training schemes have created rewarding and fulfilling careers in retail for many people including staff who were previously long-term unemployed. We have given £8m in computer equipment to schools, and have raised £2.5m for Barnardo's, our charity of the year.'

✓ 1. How can Tesco's be said to be operating a triple bottom line?

✓✓ 2. What do you understand by a 'win-win' approach?

✓✓ 3. To what extent is Tesco able to develop a stakeholder approach in creating objectives and strategies?

✓✓✓ 4. What factors are likely to limit the ability of an organisation to develop a true stakeholder approach to objective setting?

TRADITIONAL FINANCIAL BOTTOM LINE	NEW SOCIAL BOTTOM LINE	NEW ENVIRONMENTAL BOTTOM LINE
*	*	*
To make a profit	To make a contribution to society	To show respect for the environment

FIGURE 9.4 *The triple bottom line*

9.2.2 Business planning, strategy and decision-making

You need to use strategic planning tools and models to aid business decisions and create a strategic direction for a business. You need to know about the following planning tools and models:

* Ansoff's matrix
* **Porter's generic strategies**
* decision trees
* critical path analysis.

Key terms

Porter's generic strategies mean typical competitive positions that business can take to win market share. These positions are based on either seeking to be the low-cost producer or the provider of products that are different from those of competitors.

General strategies

The aims and objectives of an organisation are the goals that it is seeking to achieve. The strategies are the means to achieve these ends. In choosing a strategy an organisation has to consider the fit between the resources available to it and alternative plans that it wants to carry out. For example, there is no point in planning to expand in a major way unless you have the financial resources to do so. However, if you do have the resources then it might make sense to expand.

Currently Ryanair's strategy is to expand. It is able to do this because it has millions of euros in cash balances, and it is making operating profits of about 30 cents in the euro (2006).

In the same way, Tesco is able to expand both in the UK and in the United States because it is the market leader. Almost £1 in every £7 spent in this country is spent at Tesco (2006) and it has operating profits of 6 pence in the pound (2006).

There are a number of general strategies that a business can employ as shown in Figure 9.5.

Key terms

Diversification means broadening out to produce a variety of goods and services rather than engaging in narrow specialisation.

As well as general strategies, businesses adopt competitive strategies. Competitive strategies are all about how a business positions itself in relation to the competition. For example, is the business seeking to gain high levels of sales by offering lower prices than rivals? Alternatively, is it seeking to provide a quality good or service which is sold at a premium price?

GENERAL STRATEGY	WHAT IS INVOLVED
Growth	Expanding what you already do well. For example, Tesco is currently expanding the number of stores that it builds in prime locations. It makes sense to do so because this increases turnover at the expense of the competition.
Multinationalisation	Expanding into more and more countries in order to benefit from growing markets. For example, more and more UK companies are expanding into China and India which are fast-growing economies.
Diversification	Expanding into new product areas and product lines. For example, Apple expanded beyond its home computer and desktop range to add iPods to its list of products.
Retrenchment	Sometimes it makes sense to cut back on product lines that are less successful to focus on your most successful lines. For example, in 2006 Unilever cut back its frozen foods division.

FIGURE 9.5 *General business strategies*

Business tools

A number of business tools are helpful in planning market positions.

Ansoff's matrix

Igor Ansoff defined strategy in terms of the relationship between the organisation and its environment: 'The positioning and relating of the firm or organisation to its environment in a way which will assure its continued success and make it secure from surprises'.

This section therefore sets out to outline the sorts of general positioning that an organisation can take to create an appropriate fit between strategy and the organisational environment. It starts off by examining some of Ansoff's ideas about choosing a growth strategy that takes account of the product and market influences.

In developing a portfolio strategy (a portfolio of products and services on which to focus), an organisation can choose a number of alternatives to generate ongoing growth as shown in Figure 9.6.

Key positioning strategies

There are four key strategies open to the firm.

Market penetration

This involves selling more of the same product to the same types of people. This is possible either by increasing market share at the expense of others, by developing a **competitive advantage**, or by growing the total market size.

For example, Ryanair has increasingly dominated the low-cost airline market in Europe by offering new routes and competing effectively to get customers to and from their destinations on time.

> **Key terms**
>
> *Competitive advantage* is the advantages that you have over rivals usually related to having lower costs or more exciting and different products and services.

	EXISTING PRODUCT	NEW PRODUCT
Existing market	Market penetration	New product development
New market	Market development	Diversification

FIGURE 9.6 *Ansoff's product-market expansion grid*

Product development

This involves a company exploiting the strength of its relationship with customers and using its creative ability to develop new products suited to their needs. Supermarkets are a good example of this. They have gradually moved away from simply selling groceries to selling a wide range of other products including household goods, clothes, petrol, computers and even cars.

Market development

New customers can be more difficult to develop than products, but where an organisation has significant product strength this can be a good opportunity for growth. Examples can include selling to export markets or a different customer type. Lucozade, a high-energy drink, was originally sold to speed recovery from illness, but the company developed a new market among sports people.

Diversification

Diversification involves developing new expertise both in terms of product and markets and is the highest risk alternative. Often companies, rather than develop their own expertise, will buy another company to achieve their objectives. For example, Ford Motor Company acquired the Kwik-Fit replacement car tyre and exhaust fitting company.

Matching the strategy with the environment

Ansoff's matrix outlines a range of ways in which organisations can seek to position their strategy in relation to their environment. There are a number of strategies available to create an appropriate position.

> ### Key terms
>
> *Ansoff's matrix* is a diagram setting out the positions that a company can take to fit its strategy to the business environment.

Growth

The Ansoff matrix is essentially concerned with growth strategies. Growth is one of the most frequent strategies that an organisation considers. In thinking about growth it needs to examine the external environment. For example, is there going to be enough growth in the market to warrant expansion? Will the organisation be able to outcompete the competition?

Growth is illustrated by the spread of a number of high-profile coffee shops such as Starbucks and Costa Coffee. In a very short period of time they have expanded in the UK to dominate many city centre locations, motorway service stations, airport lounges etc.

Theory into practice

Identify the Ansoff positioning strategy in each of the following case studies and explain why you have classified each case the way you have.

Case study 1: We are all familiar with the Mars bar in its chocolate bar form. This was a standard product that had been around for many years. Technologists at Mars then came up with the bright idea of developing Mars ice creams.

Case study 2: The drinks manufacturer AG Barr claims that only two people know the recipe for Scotland's most famous drink and renowned hangover cure Irn-Bru. The ingredients of the orange concoction have remained a secret since Glasgow's Barr family started making the drink in 1901. Even when Robin Barr, now the chairman of AG Barr, handed over the chief executive post to Roger White at the start of 2004, he did not pass on the magic formula and remains one of the two people who know it. The identity of the other person has never been revealed for 'security reasons'. In March 2006, the company launched a new Irn-Bru drink branded as Irn-Bru 32. It is the first major extension of the Irn-Bru brand since a diet version entered the market in 1980. The company invested £3m in making an Irn-Bru energy drink 'with a twist'.

Case study 3: MFI, the national chain of furniture stores, acquired Howden's Joinery, which fits kitchens, bathrooms and bedrooms.

Case study 4: The pressure that Britain's top supermarket groups are putting on their high-street rivals was spelt out by a report in March 2006 which showed that their sales of non-food products has doubled since 2001. Sales of clothing, footwear and entertainment products has almost doubled in the last five years.

Lakshmi Mittal

Another organisation that has grown rapidly in recent years is Mittal Steel. This steel manufacturing company is owned by Lakshmi Mittal, the UK's richest person. Mittal Steel own steel companies across the globe.

Stability

Stability is always an important strategy for an organisation. Stability makes sense when an organisation has experienced previous periods of rapid growth. The organisation then needs to establish clear systems and procedures that enable it to consolidate its position. For example, although the Virgin group is seen as a dynamic organisation which frequently moves into new areas, it also believes in consolidating new businesses once they are established. Virgin believes that once it has gone through a period of rapid expansion, for example moving into insurance, or into Virgin Cola, it needs to establish these lines before moving on to new things. This would involve ensuring that all systems within a new business venture are customer driven and based on quality performance.

Many organisations will seek stability at times when the environment gets a bit rocky. A useful analogy can be drawn with the piloting of an airplane. When the pilot hits a bad patch of weather, then all efforts will be focused on stabilising the airplane.

Profitability

Seeking profit is always an important ingredient of strategy, particularly in organisations in which shareholders are the key stakeholders and where the shareholders' perception of the organisation is influenced by the profit. Although organisations like to take a longer-term view on profits, where shareholders are influential (and where shareholders can switch their shareholding easily) organisations are also forced to consider the shorter and medium term. Market share is often an important driver of profitability.

Efficiency

Efficiency is important when organisations are competing with each other to keep costs down. An obvious example is in the rivalry between supermarket chains. Costs here can be kept down by having efficient distribution and computer systems and by having just the right stock that customers want to buy so nothing goes to waste. You can imagine how important efficiency is in high-street clothes retailing.

Market leadership

Many companies will pursue a strategy designed to give them market leadership because they know that should they win the lion's share of the market then the profits will follow. The market leader is best able to manage the external environment because profits can be channelled into securing ongoing competitive advantage.

Market leadership is both a short-term, medium-term and long-term strategy. By winning market leadership, organisation's rivals will always be coming from a catch-up position and will be hampered by disadvantages, particularly in areas related to technology and marketing.

Theory into practice

Here is a list of market leaders. In each case, identify the market in which they have the leadership:

- Intel
- Google
- Microsoft
- Tesco
- Vodafone
- Cadbury-Schweppes
- British Airways.

Gaining market leadership

Britain's most famous chocolate maker Cadbury's overtook Mars as the world's leading confectioner in 2006. A century after it began producing Dairy Milk bars at Bournville in Birmingham, the company revealed it had overtaken its great rival, leaving Swiss-based Nestlé in third place.

The news came amid a backlash against unhealthy snacks such as chocolate bars which prompted Cadbury's to print keep-fit tips on wrappers. Instead of its more traditional brands, it was the organic Green & Black's range which boomed in the UK, with sales up by half since Cadbury's bought it in 2005.

Around the world it was sugar-free chewing gum which enabled Cadbury's to overtake Mars. Overall, Cadbury's was able to gain market share in 17 out of 20 confectionery markets.

It is a far cry from the firm's beginnings in 1824 when John Cadbury opened up his tea shop in Birmingham and began producing cocoa and drinking chocolate as a sideline. The first Cadbury's milk chocolate was produced in 1897, and by the 1920s bars such as Flakes and Crunchies had established it as Britain's market leading chocolate brand.

✓ 1. Why is it important for Cadbury-Schweppes to become the global market leader in confectionery products?

✓✓ 2. What advantages would they gain from being the market leader in 17 out of 20 confectionery markets?

✓✓ 3. What effect would Cadbury's market leadership have on rivals?

✓✓✓ 4. How could Cadbury's seek to build on this market leadership?

Survival

The well-known business writer, Peter Drucker stated that:

'It is the first duty of a business to survive. The guiding principle of business economics, in other words, is not the maximization of profits; it is the avoidance of loss. Business enterprise must produce the premium to cover risks inevitably involved in its operation. And there is only one source for this risk premium: profits.'

Drucker referred to the 'required minimum profit' as representing for the business enterprise 'at the very least the profit required to cover its own future risks, the profit required to enable it to stay in business and to maintain intact the wealth producing capacity of its resources'. He sees businesses as being there fundamentally to serve customers and to innovate in order to progress and develop.

Mergers and acquisitions

Mergers and **acquisitions** are another key strategic route for the organisation, enabling a change in positioning in an existing marketplace or movement into new marketplaces. The organisation needs to look at its resources and its objectives and match its strategies to these. Merging with another organisation often provides the best way to grow. For example, Mittal Steel recognised that to be successful in the global steel industry you need to grow to a large size. It seeks to be the biggest in the market. This was exemplified in 2005 by the acquisition of a huge previously state-run steel enterprise in the Ukraine in 2005.

Porter's generic strategies

The American business writer, Michael Porter identified a number of general strategies that businesses can adopt to gain competitive advantage.

His analysis was based on the study of lots of different businesses. From his analysis he identified two main competitive positions that will be successful:

* being the low-cost producer
* differentiating your products from rivals.

How do you become the low-cost producer?

The answer is to dominate your market so that you can produce on a large scale. When you produce on a very large scale your costs per unit are very low. Provided your costs per unit are lower than your rivals you will be able to sell at pricing points that are lower than theirs – you outcompete them. Look at the following three examples.

Example 1: Coca Cola is the best selling carbonated drink in the world (although sales have started to fall in a number of countries because of concerns about healthy diets). As Coca-Cola sells such vast quantities of the product some of its unit costs are extremely low. For example, the unit cost of producing the Coca-Cola can is extremely small.

Example 2: Intel provides 70 per cent of the microchips that go into our computers. They dominate the world market. As a result their costs per microprocessor are extremely small enabling the company to make large revenues.

It then uses the profit generated by these revenues to invest in better and better microchips to keep ahead of the competition.

Example 3: One pound out of every £3 spent on groceries in this country is spent at Tesco (2006). Although Tesco typically only makes profit margins of 6 pence for every £1 of sales, there are an awful lot of 6 pences. Tesco is able to plough this back into the business. At the same time it is able to offer good-quality produce at lower prices than its rivals.

How do you differentiate your product from rivals?

Differentiation is the process of making your product different from the competition. There are all sorts of ways of doing this, e.g. by offering a higher specification product, a better designed product, more extras, more attractive packaging, better advertising and promotion etc. For example, people buy iMacs because they offer better design features, look more attractive and offer superior multi-media applications than many rival products.

There are all sorts of other ways of differentiating your product including:

* a better location for a hotel or restaurant
* more gizmos in a motor vehicle, or better green credentials
* more attention to detail, e.g. through customer service in a hairdressing salon
* better parking facilities and shorter waiting times to see a film in a cinema.

All of these factors and many more are differentiators. Differentiated products can typically be sold for higher prices, while continuing to attract customer loyalty.

We can illustrate Porter's generic strategies by using a **positioning map**. The differentiated products appear at the top right-hand corner of the map. The low cost/high volume sales products appear at the bottom left. In the market for hotel accommodation chains hotels like the Ritz and the Hilton position themselves in the differentiating segment of the map offering high levels of customer service and high price. In contrast, hotel chains like Travelodge position themselves at the low price/low level of service section of the map (Figure 9.7).

In this example we would describe the Ritz and Hilton as having upmarket positions. In contrast we would describe Travelodge as having a downmarket position. All of the hotels give the customers what they want – and they all have a competitive advantage in their sector of the market.

Porter developed his analysis further by suggesting that there are four main strategies that businesses can take to achieve competitive advantage. The extra dimension to his analysis is that a business:

✳ can operate within the broad market as a whole, e.g. the confectionery market

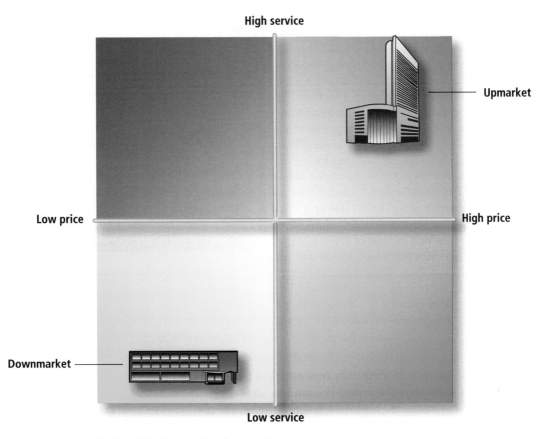

FIGURE 9.7 *Example of a positioning map*

✳ can operate within a niche market, e.g. Green & Black's range is positioned within the luxury organic range of the overall confectionery market.

So a business can position itself in four main competitive ways:

1. Broad market differentiation
2. Broad market low cost
3. Niche/narrow market differentiation
4. Niche/narrow market low cost.

CASE STUDY

Toni and Guy hairdressing

The Toni & Guy chain started by the Mascolo's was originally a family business. Now it has almost 500 salons spread across the globe many of which are on a franchise basis. In addition, the chain sells a range of haircare and styling products worth hundreds of millions of dollars each year. The latest element of the strategy has been the setting up of a website to market these products.

The business started with the father, Fransesco who emigrated from Italy to England in the 1950s. He taught his five sons the hairdressing trade. The eldest two, Toni and Guy, set up their own salon which created the world's best-known brand in hairdressing. A third brother, Bruno, set up a Toni & Guy salon in the United States in the 1980s. The chain is now owned by four of the brothers.

Anthony (Toni) sets the trends in London for the other salons to follow. Each year he creates a hair collection with a range of haircuts. The methods involved in creating these haircuts are then taught to the hairdressers who work in the various salons.

Toni sees his styles as adapting to fashion and popular culture. He says he sees hair as an accessory to fashion. However, the styles are not bizarre or way out as he feels that styles need to be practical.

✓ 1. What type of generic strategy are Toni and Guy pursuing?
✓✓ 2. Why do you think that they have chosen the strategy?
✓✓ 3. What are the principal benefits of pursuing this strategy?
✓✓✓ 4 How would you expect to see the business develop in the future? Explain why.

Toni & Guy provides an example of a business that is highly fashionable yet at the same time appeals to a lot of customers across Britain and internationally. Why do you think that some businesses are able to move from being nationally recognised to internationally recognised businesses – while others can't? Can you give some examples of businesses that might be suitable to expand internationally that currently are domestic businesses?

Decision trees

Decision trees are a useful tool that can be applied in decision-making in a business. A decision tree enables an organisation to analyse alternative decisions that can be taken and the likely results that will follow. For example, Harpreet Singh is considering setting up a music website. He is not sure whether to concentrate on bangra music, popular Western music or a combination of the two types. Setting out a decision tree will help him to work out the expected returns from the three alternatives.

Decision trees have lots of uses in business decision-making where there is some element of probability and where it is possible to predict possible financial outcomes. For example, they can be used in making decisions about investing on the Stock Exchange by calculating the probability of certain shares doing well or badly. It enables you to calculate what returns you might expect in different situations and then the probability is multiplied by possible expected returns.

Decision tree analysis can be used for calculating results from alternative business projects, e.g. should you market product A or B. You can work out the probability of success from market research results and from expected profits resulting from calculations of expected sales and expected costs.

Many businesses use decision trees. For example, an oil company like BP or Shell would look at the probability of oil being found in various oil fields. This could be calculated by looking at the geology of the field and comparing this with previous excavations. Computer modelling would help to calculate probabilities of finding different quantities of oil. The expected

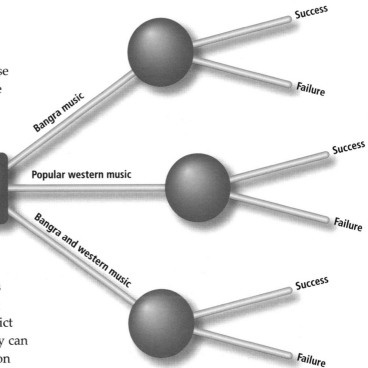

FIGURE 9.8 *An example of a decision tree*

returns could be calculated by comparing the expected quantity of oil compared with the cost of extracting that oil.

Key terms

Decision trees are diagrams setting out the expected outcomes resulting from alternative decisions that a business can make (usually compared in terms of financial outcomes).

Probability

To set out a decision tree you need to know something about probability. Probability is the likelihood of a particular event occurring given a number of alternative events. If an event is certain to occur we record this as having a probability of 1 – in other words there is a 100 per cent chance that it will happen. For example, the probability that the world will keep spinning on its axis tomorrow is 1.

If there are two equally good football teams playing in the Cup Final then there is a 50:50 chance that team A will win, and a 50:50 chance that team B will win. In this example we would represent the probability of team A winning as 0.5.

* A probability of 1 represents a certainty.

* A probability of 0.9 represents a nine in ten chance of an event happening.

* A probability of 0.8 represents an eight in ten chance of an event happening.

In setting out decision trees we need to be able to work with probabilities. In your decision trees you will want to work out:

* the probability of an event happening

* the financial outcome resulting from that event happening.

To work out the expected financial return from a particular event happening you need to multiply the probability of it happening by the expected financial return.

For example, if there is a 0.5 probability of an investment earning £100,000, then it would be reasonable to expect £50,000 from making this investment.

$0.5 \times 100,000 = £50,000$

The investment could make £100,000 or it could make zero but the average figure expected to receive using probability is £50,000.

A decision tree consists of the following factors.

* Decision points: represented by squares placed at points at which decisions have to be made.

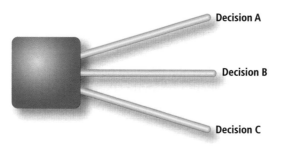

* Chance nodes: represented by circles. At these points there are different possible outcomes resulting from decisions that can be made, e.g. the decision may lead to success or failure.

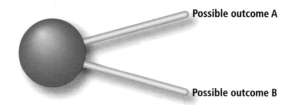

* Probability: the probability of a particular event occurring is expressed as a numerical value on the decision tree. The values used are between 0 (absolutely no chance of an event happening) and 1 (absolute certainty that it will happen). For example, if there is a 0.7 chance of success, there is a 0.3 chance of failure.

* Expected values: these are the financial outcomes of the decisions that have been made, e.g. if a firm is faced with a decision that has a 0.5 chance of making a £50,000 profit and a 0.5 chance of making a £20,000 loss then:

expected value = $0.5 \times 50,000 + 0.5 \times -20,000$
= $25,000 - 10,000 = 15,0000$.

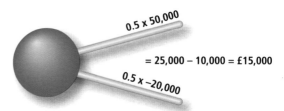

Look at another example of how a business would make a loss from making a particular decision. If a firm has a 0.3 chance of making a profit of £300,000 and a 0.7 chance of making a loss of £300,000 then:

expected value = $0.3 \times 300,000 + 0.7 \times -300,000$
= $90,000 - 210,000 = -120,000$.

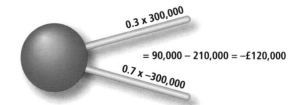

Theory into practice

A confectionery and sweet manufacturer is deciding which of three products to develop. Market research has identified the following information.

- There is a 0.1 chance that Sugar-free chewing gum will be a success leading to profits of £2m. However, there is a much higher chance of 0.9 that the product will fail leading to a loss of £200,000.

- There is a 0.5 chance that Healthybars will be a success leading to profits of £400,000 per year.

However, there is a 0.5 chance that it will fail leading to an annual loss of £200,000.

- There is a 0.6 chance that Liquidtabs will be a success leading to profits of £600,000. However, there is a 0.4 chance that they will lead to a loss of £200,000.

Set out a decision tree to illustrate which product should be developed. Read the following instructions to help set out your decision tree.

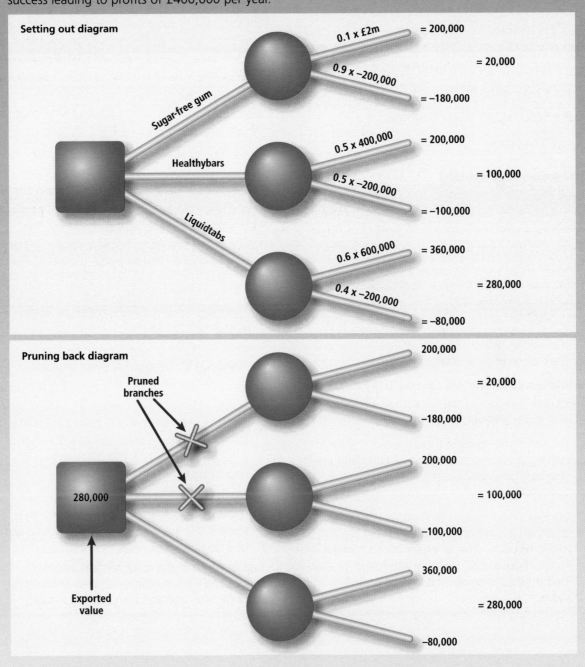

Setting out diagram

Sugar-free gum	0.1 x £2m = 200,000
	= 20,000
	0.9 x −200,000 = −180,000
Healthybars	0.5 x 400,000 = 200,000
	= 100,000
	0.5 x −200,000 = −100,000
Liquidtabs	0.6 x 600,000 = 360,000
	= 280,000
	0.4 x −200,000 = −80,000

Pruning back diagram

Pruned branches

200,000
= 20,000
−180,000

280,000

200,000
= 100,000
−100,000

Exported value

360,000
= 280,000
−80,000

1. Put in the decision fork at the start of the diagram. Initially this is left blank – there is nothing in the middle of it.

2. Draw three lines going from this fork to three chance forks that represent the three alternatives you can make. Label each of the lines with the names of the alternatives, in this case the products that could be made.

3. From the chance forks, draw another two lines which represent success or failure. Along these lines or at the end of these lines, put the calculations based on multiplying the probability × the expected financial outcome.

For example, for Sugar-free chewing gum the calculations will be as follows:

$0.1 \times £2m = £200,000$ (success)

$0.9 \times £200,000 = -180,000$ (failure)

This would therefore yield a result of $£200,000 - £180,000 = £20,000$

Carry out the same process for each of the three alternatives to tell you which of the options creates the highest expected value i.e. option 3 would give an expected value of £280,000.

You can now prune your tree back. Work backwards across the diagram from right to left and cut off branches A and B by putting an X through them. Then put the expected value of £280,000 in the decision fork at the start of the diagram.

Remember to first work across your diagram from left to right. And then work back from right to left.

Theory into practice

Set up decision trees based on the information below.

1. A textile company is considering locating in the East Midlands. It has calculated the following figures in relation to three alternatives.

   If it sets up in Derby there is a slim chance of only 0.2 of making a profit, but the profit would be a substantial £2m per annum. However, there is a 0.8 chance of making a loss of £1m per annum.

   If it sets up in Nottingham there is a 0.6 chance of making a more modest profit of £1m per year and a 0.4 chance of making a loss of £200,000.

   If it sets up in Leicester there is a 0.8 chance of making an even smaller profit of £800,000 per year, but only a 0.2 chance of making a loss of £100,000.

   Set out a decision tree to illustrate the above, and then prune back the tree to show the expected value. Give an explanation of why it might choose to set up in an alternative location to that which provides the highest expected value.

2. A business is deciding which of three machines to invest in. It will choose the machine which yields the highest expected value over a four-year period. Which of the following should it go for? Illustrate your answer by drawing a decision tree and then pruning it back.

   - Machine A has a 0.3 chance of making profits of £2m a year for three years and then £1 million in the final year.
     It has a 0.7 chance of making a loss of £100,000 in all four years.

   - Machine B has a 0.5 chance of making zero profit in the first year and then £2m a year for the next three years. It has a 0.5 chance of making a loss of £150,000 per year in all four years.

   - Machine C has a 0.1 chance of making a profit of £5m in all four years. However, there is a 0.9 chance that it will make a loss of £1m in all four years.

   Explain which of the machines you would choose and why. Illustrate your answer by setting out a decision tree and then pruning it back.

Critical path analysis

When coordinating a business plan, it is important to map out the tasks that must be carried out and perform them in a planned sequence. For instance, when launching a new product, market research should be carried out before the advertising campaign is prepared, adverts must be created prior to the launch, etc. These events can be linked as shown in Figure 9.9, where A must be completed before B can be started:

FIGURE 9.9 *Activities taking place in sequence*

However, in many cases activities do not have to take place in sequence; they can be carried out simultaneously. For example, the advertising could be prepared at the same time as the promotional campaign is designed. Figure 9.9 shows that before you prepare the advertising and design the promotional campaign you must carry out the market research, but you can carry out the advertising and promotional preparation at the same time (Figure 9.10).

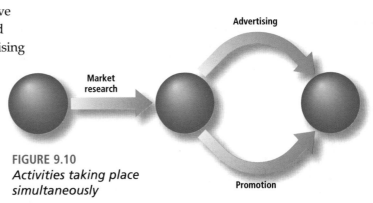

FIGURE 9.10
Activities taking place simultaneously

Building up a critical path diagram

Critical path analysis involves the setting out of a diagram which includes a critical path (Figure 9.11). Typically you would use a colour to highlight the critical path.

The diagram sets out:

* the sequence of activities involved in carrying out a project
* the time taken to carry out each activity
* the critical path i.e. the sequence of activities which are most crucial because delays to them will delay the completion of the project as a whole.

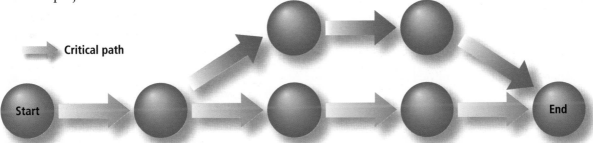

FIGURE 9.11 *Critical path diagram*

Key terms

Critical path is the path of arrows showing the most important activities involved in executing a plan. They are critical because they need to be completed on time.

Critical path analysis is a means of identifying the critical path of activities that are required to be completed to finish a project on time. Critical activities are ones that must be completed in sequence on time.

Once the critical path has been identified, it becomes possible for project managers to keep a close eye on this sequence of activities to make sure that tasks are being completed on time. If problems arise it may be possible to plough extra resources into activities along this path.

A critical path diagram consists of a series of **nodes** which are points in time when one or more activities must start or finish. These are represented as circles. The node contains three elements. The top shows the number of the node in a sequence e.g. 1, 2, 3.

The first node is node 1. The bottom half of the node is split into two parts. The left-hand part shows the earliest time you can start an activity. For example, Activity A which is the first activity in a project could be started at the beginning of the project which is Day 0, so 0 is inserted in the bottom left of the node. The bottom-right segment of the node represents the latest finish times which will be explained later.

Earliest start time ──▶ 0 | LFT ◀── Latest finish time

You can now start to draw a simple sequence of activities (Figure 9.12):

* A can start at the beginning of the project and takes 2 days
* B can start at the beginning of the project and takes 16 days
* C cannot start until A is finished and takes 8 days
* D will follow B and C.

Note that the length of the arrows does not represent the length of the time to do an activity – it is simply a drawing device to join up the nodes. The length of time taken to carry out an activity is shown by a number written under each activity.

The **earliest start time (EST)** we can start Activity C is after 2 days because we must complete A first. The earliest time you can start activity D will be after 16 days.

You can now put in the **latest finish times (LFT)**. This is the latest time you can finish an activity if the project is to be completed on time.

In the simple diagram shown in Figure 9.12 the critical path is along the B arrow. This is because it is the longest period to get to the third node (16 days). The A, C route is not critical because it would only take 10 days (A=2 and C=8). The latest time to get to node 3 is therefore 16 days. You fill this in the bottom right hand part of node 3.

The latest finish time (LFT) for activity A is 8 days. This is because C also takes 8 days and node 2 must be reached by day 8 or the A, C route would hold up the project. This tells managers that although the A, C route is not critical they must still keep an eye on it to make sure that activities along that route finish by the latest finish times allowable. The problem is that some activities that are not critical are not given a high enough priority so time is wasted on them. Working out the latest finish time for each activity helps us to keep a good eye on progress.

You can now work back across the diagram filling in the latest finish times in each node along the diagram.

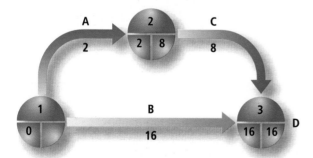

FIGURE 9.12 *A simple sequence of activities*

> ## Key terms
>
> *Node* is a point in a critical path diagram showing the earliest and latest times that particular activities can finish and start.
>
> *Earliest start time (EST)* is the earliest time that an activity can start.
>
> *Latest finish time (LFT)* is the latest time that an activity can finish if a project is to be completed on time.

Ravi has set out a simple critical path for opening his health food shop. First of all he sets out the important activities, how they are sequenced and the time they take to complete.

ACTIVITY	SEQUENCE	TIME DURATION
Apply for loan	A (starts project)	2 weeks
Loan accepted, sign paperwork	B follows A	1 week
Buy shop	C follows B	12 weeks
Decorate	D follows C	1 week
Advertise	E follows C	3 weeks
Put in fittings	F follows D	1 week
Display stock	G follows D, E and F	1 week
Official opening of shop	H follows G	1 week

Ravi then draws up a critical path diagram.

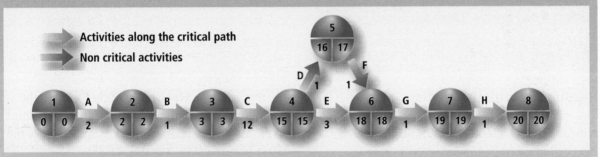

FIGURE 9.13 *Critical path diagram for health food shop*

- Working from left to right in Figure 9.13, the first node shows the start of the project.
- Activity A takes 2 weeks so the earliest start time shown (EST) in node 2 is 2 weeks.
- Activity B takes 1 week. The EST in node 3 is therefore 3 weeks.
- Activity C takes 12 weeks. The EST in node 4 is therefore 15 weeks.
- Activity D (decorating) takes 1 week and follows C. The EST for node 5 is therefore 16 weeks.
- Activity F (putting in the fittings) follows D and takes 1 week.
- Activity E can be carried out at the same time as D and F. It takes longer than the two of them put together as it takes 3 weeks (compared with 2 for D and F). So if node 6 is drawn there must be an EST of 18 weeks. This is because the earliest time to get to the node is based on the sequence A, B, C, E (2 + 1 + 12 + 3 weeks).
- Activity G follows E and F and takes 1 week.
- Activity H follows G and takes 1 week.
- The latest finish times (LFTs) show the latest time that a stage needs to be completed to get the project finished on time. If G is not finished by the 19th day, the project won't be finished by the 20th day. If E is not finished by the 18th day, G will not be able to start on the 18th day, and so on.

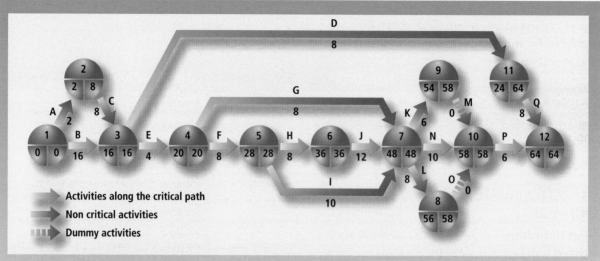

FIGURE 9.14 *Critical path diagram for a project with 12 nodes*

Figure 9.14 shows the number of days required to finish a project with 12 nodes. Note that the two activities drawn in dotted lines are 'dummy activities' which do not use up time or resources. The critical path is shown by the orange arrows going down the centre of the diagram. These are activities which take place in sequence and represent the longest sequence of activities to complete the project. It is essential that these activities are carried out on time.

Explain the figures in the nodes showing the latest finish times. Start at the end of the project and work backwards, towards the left of the diagram.

Reading the critical path diagram

You can work out the earliest times along the critical path, which is the earliest time that the next activity in the sequence can start. Using Figure 9.14 as an example:

* B takes 16 days so the earliest time we can get to node 3 is 16 days.

* E takes 4 days so the earliest you can get to node 4 is 20 days.

* F takes 8 days so the earliest you can get to node 5 is 28 days.

* H takes 8 days so the earliest you can get to node 6 is 36 days.

* J takes 12 days so the earliest you can get to node 7 is 48 days.

* N takes 10 days so the earliest you can get to node 10 is 58 days.

* P takes 6 days so the earliest you can get to node 12 is 64 days.

The earliest times can be transferred to the critical path diagram as shown in Figure 9.14.

You can then work backwards filling in the latest times that activities must start. For example, in Figure 9.14 because activity P takes 6 days the latest you can start it is the 58th day.

Slack time

When a node is not linked to the critical path then the latest time shown in the node may be different to the earliest time. This is because there is not so much pressure to complete activities on time. The difference between the latest time and the earliest time is referred to as 'slack time'. Even though there may be slack time in carrying out an element of a project, it is important to start well in time rather than wait until the last possible moment to start the activity.

In Figure 9.14, for example, you can see that there is some slack time in node 2. The earliest that activity A finishes is 2 days. The latest activity C must start is 8 days so there is 6 days of slack time.

Slack time is defined as the amount of excess time available to reach any particular event. Another way of looking at this is that slack is the number of days (or weeks) that the latest allowable time (L) exceeds the earliest possible time (T) an event can be reached. It can be calculated by subtracting the T time from the L time at each event.

Theory into practice

Calculate the total amount of slack time that is shown in Figure 9.14.

Planning activities using the critical path diagram

Using the critical path construction methods outlined you can calculate the total production time for production projects or total time taken to complete other types of projects, e.g. managing a research project, constructing a computer program etc. The network diagram also identifies the schedule of activities that need to be performed. It gives a clear visual tool to plan activities.

For planning activities that require critical path analysis, software packages such as Microsoft Project can be invaluable. They highlight the times certain resources need to be employed, including the specific responsibility of the project team members. As well as helping to solve the problem, the software facilitates the effective communication of the plan.

9.2.3 Financial business planning

As we have seen, typical strategies for business include growth within the home market and growth overseas. In order to grow, a business needs to invest. In order to make investment decisions it is important to be able to calculate the risk and return on alternative investment opportunities. For example, a business might want to compare:

* the return on investing in China or India

* the return on buying a high-quality manually operated machine, or a state-of-the-art automated machine

* the return on building a factory in Stoke-on-Trent, Glasgow or Liverpool.

Organisations need to have some means of weighing up the returns on investment projects.

Appraising investment projects

In this section we examine ways of appraising investment projects using three main methods:

* accounting rate of return

* payback

* net present value.

Theory into practice

1. Draw a critical path diagram to illustrate the following.
   * Task A must be carried out at the start of the project and is expected to take 30 days.
   * Task B must also be carried out at the start of the project and is expected to take 15 days.
   * Task C follows B. Duration 30 days.
   * Task D follows A and C. Duration 15 days.
   * Taks E follows C. Duration 10 days.
   * Task F follows E. Duration 14 days.
   * Task G follows both A and C. Duration 7 days.
   * Task H follows D, F and G. Duration 14 days.
   * Once H is completed the project is finished.
   * The project must take no longer than 83 days.

2. Draw a critical path diagram to illustrate the following.
   * A and B start at the beginning of the project. A takes 12 days and B takes 6 days.
   * C follows A and B and takes 10 days.
   * D follows C and takes 3 days.
   * E can be carried out at the same time as D and takes 4 days.
   * F follows E and can be carried out at the same time as D and takes 3 days.
   * Follows F, E and D to complete the project and it takes 5 days.

Accounting rate of return

Business performance is measured by its return on capital employed, so it makes sense to appraise proposed strategic projects on the same basis. This is widely referred to as the accounting rate of return (ARR).

Accounting rate of return =

$$\frac{\text{Average annual profits}}{\text{Average capital employed}} \times 100\%$$

Illustrating accounting rate of return

A project requires immediate cash payments to purchase fixed assets that have lives of four years with no residual value. The assets depreciate at a fixed rate of £6,000 a year. Assets depreciate over time – they become less valuable due to wear and tear and because they go out of date. If they depreciate at £6,000 a year they will have no value in the accounts at the end of the fourth year. Workings are shown for project 1:

Project cash flows

Year	Project outlay and inflows	
		(£)
0	Cash outflow on fixed assets	-24,000
1	Net cash inflow	6,000
2	Net cash inflow	6,000
3	Net cash inflow	8,000
4	Net cash inflow	8,000

You can now show the profit in each of the years. This is measured by the cash inflow – the **depreciation** charge.

Year	Annual profit
1	0
2	0
3	2,000
4	2,000

Key terms
Depreciation is the fall in the value of a fixed asset over time.

Average capital employed can be calculated. Capital means the value of the fixed assets. To get an average of this value over the period you need to set out the value of the capital at the start and the value at the end and divide by two.

Residual value is the remaining value of an asset after it has been fully depreciated.

Key terms
Average capital employed is the average value of the capital employed in a business over a period of time.

Average capital employed =

$$\frac{\text{Capital at start} + \text{Capital at the end}}{2}$$

Average capital employed = £12,000

You can therefore work out the accounting rate of return.

Accounting rate of return =

$$\frac{\text{Average annual profits}}{\text{Average capital employed}} \times 100\%$$

Accounting rate of return = $\frac{£1,000}{£12,000} \times 100\%$

$$= 8.3\%$$

Theory into practice

A company is considering two projects. Using the accounting rate of return (ARR) approach, decide which is the better investment.

	Project A	Project B
	£	£
Initial investment	-10,000	-20,000
Year 1 cash receipts	+4,000	+9,000
Year 2 cash receipts	+5,000	+9,000
Year 3 cash receipts	+5,000	+12,000
Year 4 cash receipts	+4,000	+10,000
Total cash receipts	+18,000	+40,000
Profit over 4 years	+8,000	+20,000
Average annual profit	+2,000	+5,000
Initial investment	10,000	20,000
Accounting rate of return	?	?

Payback

The purpose of the payback method is to establish how quickly the investment cost can be repaid. The shorter the **payback period**, the better the project. Payback recognises the importance of the timing of returns on investment. Often it is helpful to get the money you invested back as quickly as possible. For example, if you were a property developer investing £1m you want to get your £1m back as soon as possible from selling finished houses. It might be better to invest in a development that recoups your £1m in a couple of years but only doubles your money in that period, rather than one which triples your money but over a three year period.

Key terms

Payback period is the length of time required to payback an original investment assuming that the investment is depreciated in a straight line.

We all know the value of having money now. When we invest it, it gets locked into a project for a period of time which can be seen as a sacrifice. So often it makes sense to invest in something that pays back quickly.

Using this method, for example, if there were two investment possibilities that both cost £15,000 you could select an alternative as shown in the illustration below. Project A repays the initial cost by the end of Year 4, whereas Project B does not repay until the end of Year 5. On this basis, you would choose Project A.

	Project A	Project B
	£	£
Initial cost	-15,000	-15,000
Year 1 cash receipts	+3,000	+1,000
Year 2 cash receipts	+3,000	+1,000
Year 3 cash receipts	+4,000	+3,000
Year 4 cash receipts	+5,000	+3,000
Year 5 cash receipt	+3,000	+10,000

The essential feature of the payback form of capital appraisal is that it takes timing into consideration. This can be of special value to firms with liquidity problems where early returns of funds is of primary importance. For businesses where capital equipment is constantly being changed, the payback method can provide a rough guide to the extent of the risk.

The main criticism is that it does not take into account the timing of cash flows. Instinctively you know that £1 in the hand today is worth more than a promised £1 for receipt on some future date. This is because there is a time value of money that allows for:

* a risk that unforeseen circumstances will prevent us receiving the amount expected

* a sacrifice in not being able to use the money now.

The time value of money is often represented by a composite annual percentage rate, e.g. bank deposit rates include amounts to cover the time value of money.

Net present value

The time value of money is considered by the appraisal technique known as the discounted rate of return.

Consider a sum of £100 that is invested in a savings account that returns interest at 10 per cent per annum. Assuming that the interest is left in the account at the end of each year, the savings account balance at the end of each of the next four years will be:

Year	Interest @ 10% pa £	End of year £
0		100.00
1	10.00	110.00
2	11.00	121.00
3	12.10	133.10
4	13.31	146.41

Using an interest rate of 10 per cent, £100 today is worth £110.00 in one year's time, £121.00 in two years and so on. It can also be said that £110.00 in one years time is worth £100 today and £121 in two years time is also worth £100 today. It is also possible to say that £133.10 in three years time has the same value as £146.41 in four years time. This can be demonstrated by restating the values in today money, i.e. they are both worth £100 today invested at 10 per cent per annum.

This provides a valuable tool for valuing cash flows that occur at different times over the life of a business project. By reducing all future cash flows to a common measure, comparisons can be made between projects. The total of all cash flows restated in today's money terms is called the net present value (NPV).

The NPV of a future cash flow is found by multiplying it by a discount factor. The size of the factor depends on the discount rate used (cost of capital) and the number of years that it is discounted for. The easiest way of finding a discount factor is to look it up in an NPV table.

For example, cash in 4 years' time discounted at 10 per cent should be multiplied by a factor of 0.6830. Over 4 years this gives a total of £146.41. The relationship of present value to final value is 146.41 / 100.00 = 0.6830. Using mathematical notation:

$$\text{NPV discount factor} = \frac{1}{(1 + r)^n}$$

Where r = discount rate
n = number of years

The following NPV table uses figures from the earlier illustration for ARR but this time discounted at a rate of 10 per cent per year.

						INTEREST RATE						
Year	5%	6%	7%	8%	9%	**10%**	11%	12%	13%	14%	15%	20%
1	0.9524	0.9434	0.9346	0.9259	0.9174	**0.9091**	0.9009	0.8929	0.8850	0.8772	0.8698	0.8333
2	0.9070	0.8900	0.8734	0.8793	0.8417	**0.8264**	0.8116	0.7972	0.7831	0.7695	0.7561	0.6944
3	0.8638	0.8396	0.8163	0.7938	0.7722	**0.7513**	0.7312	0.7118	0.6931	0.6750	0.6575	0.5787
4	0.8277	0.7921	0.7629	0.7350	0.7084	**0.6830**	0.6587	0.6355	0.6133	0.5921	0.5718	0.4823
5	0.7835	0.7473	0.7130	0.6806	0.6499	**0.6209**	0.5935	0.5674	0.5428	0.5194	0.4172	0.4019

Year		Cash flow (£)	Discount factor	Present value (£)
0	Cash outflow – investment	-24,000	1.0000	-24,000
1	Net cash inflow	6,000	0.9091	5,455
2	Net cash inflow	6,000	0.8264	4,958
3	Net cash inflow	8,000	0.7513	6,010
4	Net cash inflow	6,000	0.6830	5,464
				-2,113

FIGURE 9.15 *Example of an NPV table*

Projects with positive net present values provide financial returns in excess of the cost of capital. Negative net present values highlight project that fail to provide adequate financial returns and should be discarded.

Where a choice has to be made between projects competing for limited finance, the projects with the highest net present value should be given priority.

Theory into practice

Supercolour Printers Ltd currently has to turn work down because it has insufficient print capacity. A new printing press would cost £400,000 but would enable £500,000 worth of additional work each year to be processed. Annual running costs will be two operatives at £25,000 each and materials amounting to £100,000.

1. Calculate the payback period.

2. Calculate the net book value, assuming the company policy is to discount four years of cash flows at 20 per cent per annum.

3. Calculate the accounting rate of return assuming the printing press is depreciated over four years.

Supercolour Printers has another investment opportunity. Currently, the work of cutting out card from printed sheets has to be done out-of-house. To do the work in-house requires a die-cutting machine that would cost £300,000. Although the machine would cost £100,000 a year to run, it would erase the annual cutting charges of £325,000.

4. Calculate the payback period.

5. Calculate the net book value based on a 20 per cent discount rate.

6. Calculate the accounting rate of return.

7. Unfortunately the company does not have sufficient financing facilities to fund both the printing press and the die-cutting machine. Which investment opportunity should the company pursue, based on the numbers presented here?

Once you have carried out your calculation you can check your answer here:

1. Annual cash flows from extra sales will be:

£500,000 (revenue) – £50,000 (wages) – £100,000 (material) = £350,000.

Payback period

Year	Cash flow £	Cumulative cash flow £
0	-400,000	-400,000
1	350,000	-50,000
2	350,000	300,000

The payback period is clearly longer than one year but less than two.

Payback period: 1 year + 52 weeks × $\frac{50,000}{350,000}$

= 1 year and 7.4 weeks

2. Net present value:

Year	Cash flow (£)	Factor	Net present value (£)
0	-400,000	1	-400,000
1	350,000	0.8333	291,655
2	350,000	0.6944	243,040
3	350,000	0.5787	202,545
4	350,000	0.4823	168,803
	1,000,000		506,045

A positive NPV of £506,045 satisfies the company's investment criteria.

3. Accounting rate of return:

Annual profits =
Sales revenue – wages – materials – depreciation

£500,000 – £50,000 – £100,000 – $\frac{£400,000}{4}$

= 250,000

Average capital employed = $\frac{£400,000}{2}$

= £200,000

Accounting rate of return:

$\frac{\text{Average annual profits}}{\text{Average capital employed}} \times 100\%$

$= \frac{£250,000}{£200,000} \times 100\%$

=125%

4. Benefits come in the form of annual cost savings. Savings £325,000 less £100,000 running costs.

Payback period:

Year	Cash flow £	Cumulative cash flow £
0	-300,000	-300,000
1	225,000	-75,000
2	225,000	150,000

The payback period is again longer than one year but less than two.

Payback period –

1 year + 52 weeks × $\frac{75,000}{225,000}$

= 1 year and 17.3 weeks

5. Net present value:

Year	Cash flow (£)	Factor	Net present value (£)
0	-300,000	1	-300,000
1	225,000	0.8333	187,493
2	225,000	0.6944	156,240
3	225,000	0.5787	130,208
4	225,000	0.4823	108,518
	600,000		282,459

A positive NPV of £282,459 satisfies the company's investment criteria.

6. Accounting rate of return:

Annual profits improvement =
Cutting costs sales revenue – running costs – depreciation

$$= £325,000 - £100,000 - \frac{£300,000}{4}$$

$$= £150,000$$

Average capital employed: $\frac{£300,000}{2} = £150,000$

Accounting rate of return =

$$\frac{\text{Average annual profits}}{\text{Average capital employed}} \times 100\%$$

$$= \frac{£150,000}{£150,000} \times 100\% = 100\%$$

7. Evaluation:

	Printing press	Die-cutting machine
Payback	1 year, 7 weeks	1 year, 17 weeks
Net present value	£506,045	£282,459
Accounting rate of return	125%	100%

The printing press would appear to provide the best financial return, as measured by all three appraisal techniques. Although the die-cutting machine provides good returns, the printing press gives a shorter payback period, a higher net book value and a higher accounting rate of return. On a purely financial basis, investment should proceed with the printing press.

Break-even analysis

Calculating the **break-even point** of a business is important in **strategic decision**-making. For example, in deciding whether to open up a new overseas venture it is helpful to know how long it will take to break even.

Typically businesses don't just want to break even. They want to go well beyond the break-even point to make substantial profits. Just as with the payback investment appraisal method, break-even helps us to understand how long it takes to create secure margins within the business.

The break-even point is the point at which sales levels are high enough not to make a loss, but not high enough to make a profit. In other words, sales revenues just cover costs. In order for a business to survive, it must know how many units it needs to sell to break even.

> ### Key terms
> *Break-even point* is the point at which the revenues earned by a business exactly match the costs.

You can calculate break-even in the following way:

$$\text{Break-even point in sales units} = \frac{\text{Fixed costs}}{\text{Contribution per unit}}$$

Where contribution per unit =
Selling price – variable cost

Fixed costs are costs that are incurred however little or much the business produces or sells. For example, the fixed costs of a chocolate factory will include heating and lighting, rent and rates, management salaries etc.

Variable costs are the costs that vary with sales or production. For example, a variable cost in a chocolate factory would be the cost of the cocoa and sugar that goes into the chocolate mix.

Contribution is the difference between the selling price of an item and the variable cost. For example, if a typical chocolate bar costs 50 pence and includes 25 pence of variable cost. Then contribution = 50 – 25 = 25p per chocolate bar. Another way of looking at this is to say that each chocolate bar made contributes 25 pence to paying off the fixed costs.

If the fixed costs of the chocolate factory are £2 million per year, then 8 million chocolate bars would need to be sold to break even. (You would need the contributions of 8 million chocolate bars to pay off the £2 million of fixed costs.)

Example of break-even analysis

In order to raise finance for her car repair business, Kirsty Jones is preparing a business plan to present to her bank manager. She wants to show how many customers she needs to attract each week in order to break even. Fixed costs are estimated to be £400 a week and a typical repair at £120 will incur material costs of £40.

Contribution per customer = £120 − £40 = £80

Break-even point $= \dfrac{£400}{£80}$

= 5 customers per week

Sales value at break-even =
number of customers × sales price
= 5 × 120 = £600

A good way of identifying the break-even point is to use a graph or chart. The chart in Figure 9.16 illustrates Kirsty Jones' break-even.

Customer numbers	Fixed cost £	Variable cost £	Total cost £	Sales value £
2	400	80	480	240
4	400	160	560	480
6	400	240	640	720
8	400	320	720	960

The first step in constructing the chart is to quantify costs and revenues at different volumes of sales.

The next step is to plot fixed costs, total cost and sales revenue against business activity, in this case, numbers of repairs.

The point at which the lines for sales revenue and total cost intersect is the break-even point.

At sales volumes to the left of the break-even point, the vertical gap between sales and total cost lines represents the loss made. To the right of the break-even point, the gap between the two lines represents profit.

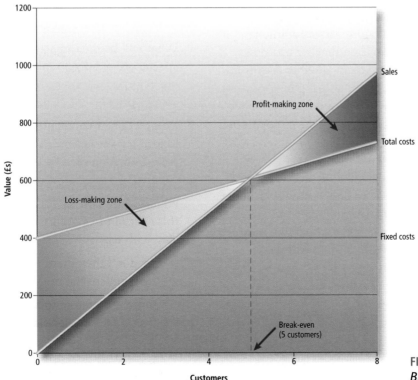

FIGURE 9.16
Break-even chart

Quantitative and qualitative decision-making

Much of the analysis in this section has been of a quantitative nature. The implication has been that you can use numbers to judge the best strategies to take. The options that produce the best numbers are the ones to choose. However, in the real world we don't always have the numbers that we require so there is a role for qualitative decision-making. Qualitative decision-making involves deciding on the best possible decision by using other criteria than simple numbers, using judgement, intuition and previous experience.

For example, in making an investment decision to build a new factory you don't know exactly what the impact will be on the local community or the knock-on effects on employment and other social indicators in the area. You therefore have to make decisions on what you perceive to be the best option. You can also canvas opinions of those involved in decision-making processes (stakeholders) by asking them whether they think decision A is better than decision B. They may not be able to tell you how much decision A is better than B but they will inform you which they think is the better decision.

In the same way, senior managers in an organisation can make qualitative decisions, such as this is the 'right thing to do' because it is 'better for the people concerned'.

You must be cautious about giving too much power and authority to quantitative decision-making or you would always be swayed by the quantitative market researchers and financial accountants.

In recent years, the company Reckitt-Benckesir has been very successful. It produces a range of household and pharmaceutical goods ranging from Cillit Bang (drain cleaner) to Disprin. The company uses intuition as well as detailed research in bringing new products to market. The company believes that you can only go so far with quantitative approaches. In addition, you need to use a common-sense knowledgeable awareness of your market and business environment.

Quantitative and qualitative factors

Decisions made on the weighting given to quantitative and qualitative factors can be illustrated by taking the example of special order decisions. Special order decisions are decisions about whether to accept or reject special product orders at prices below normal market prices.

A special order is a one time non-recurring order. For example, a new customer may request that you make up a large order for them. One way of approaching the special order is to use quantitative techniques, e.g. calculate prices, quantities, costs and contribution. You can calculate break-even and profit margins by using quantitative techniques.

However, the wise manager may also employ qualitative techniques. For example, qualitative considerations would include:

* What will be the impact of us offering a special order price to this new customer on our regular customers. Might they also want a special price?

* What will be the potential of the new order to lead to new sales? If this is the case then a price reduction may be beneficial.

* What is the customer's ability to maintain a relationship with us. If they are going to take this special price order then we want them to stay with us.

* If they don't then there will be little point in giving them special prices.

It is important therefore to always think about qualitative aspects of decision-making.

1. You supply wedding dresses to overseas customers. A customer in China asks you for a quote on a special price to supply 100 dresses to them. What quantitative and what qualitative factors do you take into account before quoting a special price?

2. What qualitative factors are the most important in special order decision-making?

3. What quantitative factors are the most important in special order decision-making?

4. Evaluate one other situation in which qualitative decision-making relating to financial decision-making would be important.

Special order decisions

The quantitative and qualitative dimension of special order decisions can take into account many factors as shown in the following example.

A business making greetings cards set up last year and has just started to break even. It advertises cards over the Internet as well as to retail chains. As a result of its Internet presence it has recently attracted overseas interest.

The company is able to produce 10,000 cards a month. It sells the cards at an average price of £1 mainly to small retailers. The variable cost of producing each card is 50 pence and the business has overheads of £4,000 per month.

A Chinese company has asked to have a special order made up for them whereby they would buy 5,000 cards for two months only. Should the firm take up that order, bearing in mind its size and the possibility of getting repeat business with this company?

Currently, each card contributes 50 pence to paying off overheads. The firm is breaking even when it sells 8,000 cards in a month. So it is making profit on 2,000 cards at 50 pence a time with a monthly profit is £1,000.

The Chinese company would buy 5,000 cards but only at 40 pence each. If the business sold 5,000 cards to China in a particular month at 40 pence each, they would make £2,000 from doing so but they would only have 5,000 other cards to sell at 50 pence each. This would give them

a further £2,500 with a monthly profit in those two months of £500 (a fall in profit of £500). In quantitative terms it would not make sense to take on the order. However, the business has to make the qualitative decision taking into consideration factors such as:

* would this lead to repeat orders?

* would making up bulk orders to China help to reduce costs?

* would it be good practice to turn away existing customers for two months?

Quantitative and qualitative decisions therefore go hand in hand.

A business supplies teapots to Indonesia. It sells 8,000 a month and is left with unused capacity of 2,000 (with orders it could make another 2,000). Each teapot is sold for £20. The cost of producing each teapot is £12. The business has monthly fixed costs of £48,000. The firm has had a request to supply 5,000 extra teapots to a firm in Malaysia at a price of £25. The costs of distribution to Malaysia will be the same as to Indonesia. The Malaysian special order is for a trial period of three months only. What factors should the business take into consideration in deciding whether or not to make up the special order?

Business decisions and the wider business environment

Financial decisions must always be made against a background awareness of what is happening in the broader business environment. For example, investment decisions in this country typically are based on the level of business confidence. If business people feel confident in the following areas, they will be prepared to invest:

* demand in the economy is growing

* inflation is under control

* the world market is healthy

* optimism and consumer expenditure is growing.

Of course, expected rates of return on investment projects reflect this level of optimism/or pessimism. Each month the Confederation of British Industry (CBI) carries out a survey of business confidence in this country. The level of business confidence reflected in this survey correlates very strongly to levels of investment in the UK economy. It is therefore very important to consider what is happening in the wider environment when making business decisions. For example, a business will want to know what is the current level of interest (price of borrowing money) and general level of demand in the economy before engaging in investment decisions.

Cost benefit analysis

Cost benefit analysis (CBA) is another decision-making technique that is used for strategic decision-making. Cost benefit analysis involves weighing up the costs against the benefits of projects. CBA is used for public sector decision-making activities such as building new roads and other building and environmental projects as well as some private sector activities.

For a project to take place then the benefits must outweigh the costs. Typically, two major different types of costs and benefits are identified.

Private benefits are ones which accrue to the decision maker, for example a business making a particular decision. Social benefits are ones which go beyond the decision maker, e.g. impacts on customers/employees/the community etc.

Private costs are costs to the decision maker, for example the cost of investing in a project and ongoing project costs. Social costs are the impacts on wider society.

A major difficulty of cost benefit analysis is the attachment of monetary values to costs and benefits. For example, how do you measure the loss of value to the community and to nature when you build on a green field area?

Some aspects of cost benefit analysis are best carried out through quantitative analysis, but qualitative considerations should also be involved in decision-making. In other words again, it must be considered whether option A is better or worse than option B, who thinks this is the case and what is the evidence on which they base their judgements?

9.2.4 Human resource planning

You need to understand human resource planning at a number of levels:

1. Human resource development as strategy. Organisations need to have a clear strategy in relation to the relationships that they build with their people. Increasingly human resource management is seen as a strategic function of a business, reflected in mission statements, business plans and policies.

2. Human resource planning as a means of making sure that the organisation has people with the right skills for the right jobs.

3. Human resource development implementation particularly through personal development plans.

4. Human resource planning and evaluation tools, such as measuring employee satisfaction and labour turnover rates. Using these key performance indicators of employee satisfaction enables the organisation to keep a check on how successful its strategies are.

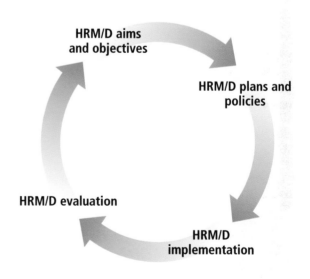

FIGURE 9.17 *Human resource planning cycle*

Aims and objectives

In planning a strategy for an organisation, it is important to place a strong emphasis on the people aspects of that strategy. What is required is:

✱ inclusion of human resource aims in the vision or mission of the organisation (see pages 4–5) which shows a commitment by top managers to give this priority to people

✱ creation of sets of policies and plans which are all about human resource

✱ development, e.g. equal opportunities and diversity policies and plans, training and development schemes, appraisal schemes etc.

People are the most important resource of any organisation. This is truer today than ever before. Most people today are involved in service industry which means they come into direct contact with customers either on the end of the phone, communicating by e-mail or through face-to-face contact.

Three of the UK's ten largest companies are banks (HSBC, HBOS and Barclays) and modern banking is based on personal contacts, direct phone links (often to call centres), and electronic communications. Britain's third largest company (by market capitalisation) is Vodafone which is a company built on a range of person-to-person links. The success of these businesses depends on having highly motivated employees that are prepared to take some responsibility for building good links with the stakeholders that they come into contact with.

A travel agency comes into direct face-to-face contact with customers

McDonald's

An example of an organisation that most people are familiar with and where employees are in daily contact with customers is McDonald's.

Human resource strategies must lie at the heart of an organisation. A useful place to look for evidence of this is in a mission or vision statement. McDonald's vision statement is:

- 'We will be the best restaurant experience ... by far!
- We will be people focused and customer driven ... passionately!
- We will inspire people with our can do attitude ... always!'

All McDonald's employees receive training in a range of aspects of working for the company, e.g. relating to health and safety, interacting with customers, appraisal systems and many other areas.

A strong emphasis in the training is on customer service which McDonald's refer to as hospitality. McDonald's define hospitality as 'doing whatever it takes to make customers feel welcome and leave with a smile by ensuring outstanding Quality Service, Cleanliness and Value'.

They believe that little touches make the difference such as:

- helping a customer to take their tray to a table
- opening doors
- setting up a high chair
- treating children as stars
- looking for magic moments i.e. opportunities to do something special for a customer.

McDonald's believe that to deliver their vision they need highly motivated managers who are able to motivate teams of employees. The emphasis in management is on creating the tone of making sure that McDonald's is a fun place to work.

McDonald's believes that 'good managers are the engines behind the restaurants ... combining energy, ideas and flexibility, ... with a commitment and appetite for hard work'.

McDonald's seeks to promote managers who have team-building skills. McDonald's also believe that managers should know when to delegate responsibility to other team members.

Whilst McDonald's has its critics, it also has its supporters. As an organisation, it carries the Investors in People Award and in 2005 was placed in The Times Top 100 graduate employers.

✓ 1. **What is your overall view of McDonald's? Do you think they are people-focused? What evidence would you cite to support your view?**

✓ 2. **Why do McDonald's set out that they are people-focused in their vision statement?**

✓✓ 3. **Why is it important to put an emphasis on human resource management in** a vision or mission statement? Using the Internet, find other examples of companies that put an emphasis on human relations in their vision/mission statements.

✓✓✓ 4. **What would McDonald's need to do to make their vision of people management a reality?**

Human resource management

McDonald's provides an interesting example of an organisation that places an emphasis on people in its superordinate goals (its vision statement). Other organisations also emphasise the human side of things. For example, the mission statement of Levi's is:

'We all want a company that our people are proud of and committed to, where all employees have an opportunity to contribute, learn, grow and advance based on merit, not politics or background. We want our people to feel respected, treated fairly, listened to and involved. Above all we want satisfaction from accomplishments and friendships, balanced personal and professional lives, and to have fun in our endeavours.'

The modern concept of human resource management (HRM) is that it is a strategic function of an organisation. As a strategic function, HRM should be a part of everything that people (particularly managers) do in the organisation. Taking this view, all managers should see themselves as people managers.

There are two approaches to human resource management – a hard and a soft approach as shown in Figure 9.18 below.

Human resource plans

Another aspect of human resource planning is to link plans for people into the overall corporate strategy of the organisation. For example, if the generic strategy of the organisation is to grow from an organisation employing 10,000 people to one employing 50,000 and embracing new sets of technologies, then human resource planners need to think about:

* how to recruit the extra 40,000 people
* how to make sure that the organisation has people with the right knowledge and skills to work with the new technologies.

Human resource planners need to keep an inventory of:

* current human resource requirements of the organisation
* future human resource requirements of the organisation
* current human resource capabilities of members of the organisation
* the age profile of members of the organisation
* turnover of employees within the organisation
* training and development plans of members of the organisation.

This is a very detailed process. A starting point is to ask the question: what are going to be the requirements of the organisation next month, next year, in two years time and in five years time?

You can then tackle the question: to what extent are we able to meet these requirements from training and development programmes within the organisation?

HARD HRM	SOFT HRM
With a hard HRM approach, people are valued. However, they are valued for what they can contribute to an organisation. Managers will employ motivational techniques with people to get the best out of them in order to make the organisation successful.	With a soft HRM approach, people are valued in their own rights. Managers employ motivational techniques to help people to develop. With soft HRM the emphasis is on development as well as training. Development is all about finding out about the needs of individuals and then helping them to meet personal objectives. The individual benefits as well as the organisation. Soft HRM places much more emphasis on the needs of individuals. It is often referred to as human resource development (HRD).
Training people to meet organisational objectives is an important part of hard HRM.	

FIGURE 9.18 *Hard and soft approaches to human resource management*

Assuming that a gap is identified between the requirements and what can be provided within the organisation, then the question arises: how can we recruit, train and develop new staff to meet our requirements?

Figure 9.19 below shows how successful human resource planning involves matching up the supply of labour available to a business with the organisation's demand for human resources.

Rosemary Harrison in her book *Human Resource Development in a Knowledge Economy*, (Palgrave Macmillan, 2003) describes the relationship between development and business objectives in the following way:

'Developing people as part of an overall human resource strategy means the skilful

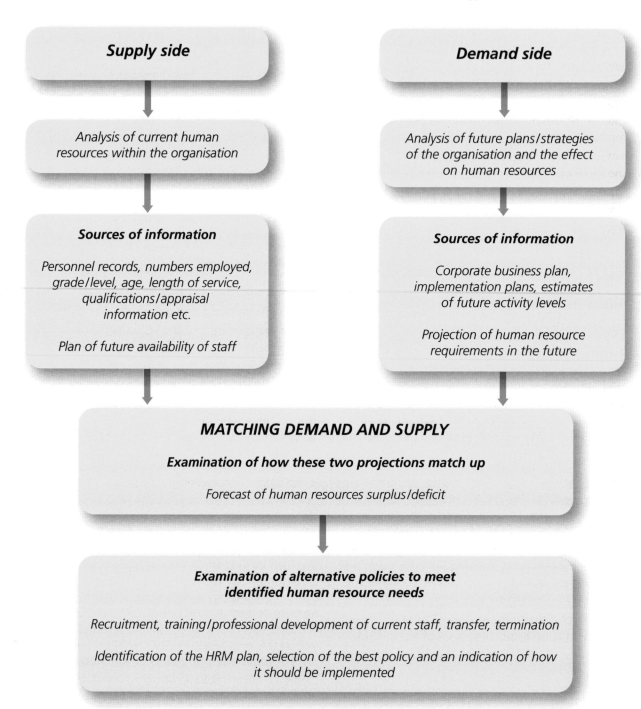

FIGURE 9.19 *Matching up labour with demand for human resources*

provision and organisation of learning experiences, primarily but not exclusively in the workplace, in order that business goals and organisational growth can be achieved.

Such development must be aligned with the organisation's vision and longer-term goals in order that, through enhancing the skills, knowledge, learning and innovative capability of people at every level, the organisation as well as the individual can prosper.'

The implication is that training and development needs to be closely allied with the purpose and objectives of the organisation. The organisation and the individual are able to grow together through a clear sharing of objectives. Personal development involves identifying ways in which the individual can become more knowledgeable and skilful while developing appropriate attitudes in a way that helps them to work with the organisation to achieve shared objectives.

Implementation of human resource plans

Personal development plans

In recent years, increased emphasis has been placed on personal development plans (PDPs) as a vehicle to enhancing motivation and commitment in the workplace. It is a live and current document owned by individual employees. It is a plan that is agreed upon between an employee and often a coach or mentor setting out development targets. The plan will regularly be reviewed. It will identify development opportunities both within and beyond the workplace.

There is increasing emphasis on individuals taking responsibility for their own development, recognising their own strengths and weaknesses and taking control of their own futures through PDPs.

Where the PDP can be linked to organisational objectives through the appraisal process then there can be a shared focus on achieving individual and organisational objectives at work.

A PDP might have four separate sections:

1. Needs arising from performance, identified through appraisal.
2. Needs arising from potential new requirements in the current role for example because the nature of the job is changing.
3. Needs arising from career aspirations.
4. Needs arising from aspirations for personal development.

You can therefore see that personal development planning lies at the heart of human resource strategy implementation. It provides the means by which a soft human resource approach can be delivered within the organisation.

Theory into practice

Draw up a simple PDP following the key points shown below and complete it in relation to your present work.

- PDP for (name)
- My current strengths at work are (think about the aspects of your job that you do well. In addition, list the skills that you do particularly well, e.g. communicating with others, working in a team, helping others etc.).
- My current weaknesses at work are (identify what you find difficult and skill deficiencies).
- The areas for development that I will be focusing on in the next two months will be (include details for areas that you will be focusing on, success criteria and when will this be done by – don't list more than five areas).

Organisation objectives

Organisations are best able to achieve their objectives when there is a direct link between the needs of the individual and the needs of the organisation. If we start with the premise that it is individuals within the organisation that achieve good things rather than the organisations themselves, we can see that if individuals are developed and perform better, the organisation also benefits.

FIGURE 9.20 *Different levels of organisational needs*

The organisation's objectives are determined by balancing the interests of a range of stakeholders, e.g. shareholders, employees, customers, etc. Most organisations today set out their purpose in the form of a mission statement and a set of supporting objectives.

Organisational level needs are concerned with identifying any weaknesses in an organisation in terms of having personnel with the appropriate knowledge, skills and attitudes. Training and development can then be planned and targeted to address these needs.

Departmental needs can be brought in line with organisational needs so that all departments are pulling in the same direction. Jobs can then be designed to best enable the organisation to meet its objectives, and a training needs analysis and a training plan makes it possible to enable the organisation's human resources to work effectively in helping the organisation to succeed.

Performance in any job depends on a complex set of factors. One set of factors is applying a given 'body of knowledge' and a range of skills associated with the job or occupation. This is true whether the job is working on the checkout in a supermarket, working as an apprentice bricklayer or as a senior manager of a chemical manufacturing company. Thus, it is possible to specify what any individual needs to know and understand, and to be able to do if successful performance in the job or occupation is to be possible. Such a specification constitutes training needs at the level of job or occupation. The specification is independent of any particular individual and it identifies what all individuals need to know and to be able to do if they wish to work successfully in the job or occupation.

Identifying individual training needs follows from the job/occupation level. Any individual employee will possess knowledge, skills and attitudes some of which will be relevant to performing in the job or occupation. However, it is unlikely that they will possess all the knowledge, skills and attitudes (KSA) required at the job-occupation level.

Therefore, individual training needs can be thought of as the gap between the KSA required by the job and the KSA currently held by the individual employee.

FIGURE 9.21 *Comparing current skill levels with required levels*

At an individual needs level the present abilities of each member of staff need to be assessed against the standards needed to carry out their work effectively. Individual needs within the organisation can be met through appraisal and personal development planning.

Evaluating your human resource strategy

Surveys

The most common way of evaluating human resource strategies today is to use employee satisfaction surveys. These are questionnaires that are filled in anonymously.

Typical questions will include:

* How long have you been working for the company?

* Would you say that you:
    a. enjoy your work more than at the same time last year?
    b. enjoy your work at the same level as the same time last year?
    c. enjoy your work less than at the same time last year?

* What aspects of your work do you particularly enjoy?

* What aspects of your work do you dislike?

* What improvements would you like to see to working conditions?

You can see that some of these questions can be analysed by quantitative techniques. Others are more qualitative in nature.

Carrying out an employee satisfaction survey enables an organisation to monitor employee relations and human resource strategies over time.

When organisations construct employee satisfaction surveys they will work with consultants who have worked with a number of companies. The consultants will meet with focus groups of employees to discuss the sorts of questions that should go into the questionnaire.

Labour turnover

In addition to employee satisfaction surveys, firms will use a number of other instruments to monitor employee satisfaction.

An obvious indicator of satisfaction is the labour turnover rate. The labour turnover rate (sometimes referred to as wastage) is measured by:

$$\frac{\text{Number of staff leaving in a time period}}{\text{Average number of staff employed in that time period}} \times 100$$

For example, if a hospital employed a nursing staff of 400 but found that 100 nurses left during the year, the wastage rate would be:

$$\frac{100}{400} \times 100 = 25\%$$

Such information is used to predict likely turnover in the future, to see if there is a need to examine in detail the reasons for the high turnover and to find out if there is a need to recruit new staff to replace those leaving.

While the labour turnover index is useful, as with most statistics it needs to be considered alongside other factors. For example, are there particular areas of the organisation where the rate of leavers is high? The leavers' length of service should also be taken into account: are the most experienced people leaving or people with relatively little experience?

Labour stability index

As well as the wastage rate, some organisations make use of a **labour stability index**. This provides an indication of the tendency for employees with long service to remain with the organisation, thus linking the leaving rate with the length of service:

$$\text{Stability Index} = \frac{\begin{array}{c}\text{Number of staff leaving} \\ \text{with more than} \\ \text{one year's service}\end{array}}{\begin{array}{c}\text{Number employed} \\ \text{one year ago}\end{array}} \times 100$$

For example, if a Premier Division football club (first team players only) had 44 employees at the start of the season who have been with the club for over a year and during the season 11 experienced players were transferred out, then the labour stability index would be:

$$\frac{11}{44} \times 100 = 25\%$$

> ### Key terms
>
> *Labour stability index* is a measure of how long employees stay with their employees or how stable the labour retention rate is in a particular workforce.

Absenteeism and sickness rates

Other indicators of employee satisfaction are absence and sickness rates. The absence rate can be calculated as:

$$\frac{\text{Number of days of absence}}{\text{Total number of working days}} \times 100$$

The sickness rate can be calculated as:

$$\frac{\text{Number of days of sickness}}{\text{Total number of working days}} \times 100$$

Both of these are represented as percentages.

The techniques outlined above provide easy to measure and monitor approaches for evaluating a human resource strategy. However, it is important to balance quantitative with qualitative measures of performance.

CASE STUDY

Shelbourne School

Shelbourne School is a small rural comprehensive school. For much of the 1980s and 1990s it retained most of its staff who were happy to work in a caring and supportive atmosphere. Many staff had children who attended the school and they had confidence in the headteacher. Results were good and parents were happy with performance.

However, during the early 1990s the Conservative government created new performance measures using league tables so that schools were required to meet certain standards related to numbers of A–C passes at GCSE, SATs results and A level results. Comparisons were made between one school and another. The implication was that while Shelbourne School was above the national average using these indicators, some people suggested it could do better, including the Chair of Governors.

Eventually in 2000, the existing head felt she was being pushed out and so took early retirement. A new dynamic head came into the school to drive up standards and to make changes that would raise Shelbourne's GCSE pass rate in the A–C category from 55 per cent to 65 per cent of pupils. The emphasis was to be on putting more staff time into students who might achieve only three or four A–C passes but, with greater staff support, could be pushed into the five A–C grades category.

The table below shows the staff wastage rate during the time of the transition to the new head (who managed to raise the GCSE pass rate to 57 per cent by the summer of 2006).

	1998	1999	2000	2001	2002	2003	2004	2005	2006
Number of staff employed	100	100	100	100	99	98	97	96	95
Number of staff leaving	1	0	1	3	5	10	12	10	14

✓ 1. Calculate the wastage rate in each of the years shown. What has been happening to the wastage rate?

✓✓ 2. What possible explanations could you give for the changes in the wastage rate?

✓✓✓ 3. Do you think that the wastage rate reflects well on the school?

✓✓✓ 4. What other means could have been employed to gauge employee satisfaction? Which of these would have been the most effective measure of the human resource strategy?

Productivity

A further way of assessing the effectiveness of human resource strategy is by exploring measures of **productivity**.

Productivity can be used to measure the contribution that a range of inputs make to production or output. For example, the impact on production of using a new machine could be measured by the units of output produced in a given period of time, e.g. an hour.

Productivity can also be used to measure labour productivity. This can be measured by dividing the output produced in a given time period by the number of labour hours that went into making that output. This figure could then be monitored over a period of time to see if labour productivity is rising.

$$\text{Labour productivity} = \frac{\text{Number of units of product}}{\text{Number of hours of labour time}}$$

To make comparisons, the figure for labour productivity can be changed to units of output per hour, per minute or even per second.

If the amount of units produced one week were 100 and only 90 were produced the week before, labour productivity has increased. Employees can monitor how labour productivity responds to human resource initiatives such as paying higher wages or giving employees better working conditions.

As well as measuring labour productivity in terms of physical units, it can also be measured in terms of sales revenue:

$$\text{Labour productivity} = \frac{\text{Value of output (£s or pence)}}{\text{Number of hours of labour time}}$$

Key terms

Productivity is the output or revenue that can be achieved within a given time period using given resources.

Think it over...

Labour productivity can be measured in terms of both the physical number of units of output that can be produced in a given period of time and/or the value of how much can be produced in a given period of time expressed in money. Which of these measures do you think would be more useful for measuring productivity and why?

9.2.5 Integrated marketing planning/strategy

Marketing planning is the process of:

* establishing marketing objectives that fit with the organisation's strategic plan

* setting out in a plan how these objectives will be achieved.

Marketing is an integrated process involving a number of elements such as carrying out detailed market research, targeting appropriate segments of the market, choosing an appropriate marketing mix, understanding the nature of the competitive environment, etc.

Marketing strategy needs to be planned against the background of changes in the organisational environment.

Marketing objectives need to be built into the organisation's strategy and tactical thinking. It is concerned with:

* establishing objectives and allocating resources to meet these – a clear plan of action must be set out

* setting out ways of evaluating performance against marketing targets – this should be done prior to implementing the plan

* assessing the position and performance of the organisation in the various markets in which it operates, including strengths and weaknesses in each of these markets.

Marketing plan

The key to creating a marketing plan is to construct a document that is easy to follow and which has practical use. Above all, it should show that you know who your customers are and that you have created the strategies and tactics that will enable you to satisfy these customers.

Firstly, the question that the plan should address is: what are our marketing objectives?

Once the objectives have been established, the following questions need to be addressed:

* Who are our customers?

* What are the markets that we are operating in?

* Which segments of that market are we operating in so that we can target our customers?

* What position will we take in each of these markets, e.g. upmarket, downmarket?

* How will we communicate with our customers?

* How will we make sure that we provide them with the appropriate marketing mix?

* Who are our competitors and how will we beat them?

* What are our strengths and weaknesses and what are we doing about them?

* How will we measure our marketing progress? (In other words how will we evaluate the success of our marketing plan?)

The marketing plan provides an organisation with a road map setting out the route that they intend to take to achieve marketing success.

Here is a useful guide to what to include in your marketing plan:

---

1. Introductory overview. A brief summary of the plan. This should give a brief preview of the plan in just a few sentences. Explain the goals to be achieved and any key assumptions that you make in the plan (e.g. the assumption that the market will grow at 10 per cent per annum based on previous years growth figures). Outline the major steps that will be taken to achieve the goals.

---

2. The vision or mission of the organisation. Describe the vision/mission and explain how marketing will help to achieve this vision. For example, if the vision is to be the leading e-tailer of Bangra music in the UK, show that your market research and attention to customer requirements will help you to achieve this vision.

---

3. Objectives. Set out clearly what your marketing objectives are. A number of these objectives are likely to be quantifiable (remember SMART objectives on page 3). For example, your objectives might relate to market share, market growth, new product development etc.

---

4. An outline of your market. This should be a descriptive section setting out the needs identified through your market research. Show that you have carried out detailed market research to give a clear picture of your market. A SWOT analysis is helpful here. This analysis shows the internal strengths and weaknesses of the organisation, its brands and its products. The opportunities and threats lie in the external environment. For example, new opportunities lie in expanding and new markets. These opportunities might result from economic and social trends such as rising standards of living or changes in demographics such as rising numbers of older people. Other opportunities might result from legal changes, e.g. changes in environmental laws creating a demand for environmentally friendly products. Threats can also result from economic, social and political factors. Threats will also come from the actions of competitors.

---

continued ▶

5. Market segmentation. You need to show that you have an understanding of what is happening in the overall market in which you are operating. In addition, you need to understand how that market is broken down into segments and which of those segments you will be targeting. For example, if you produce probiotic yoghurt, not only do you need to show that you understand what is happening to yoghurt as a category, but you also need to explain what is happening in the probiotic yoghurt segment, e.g. who buys probiotic yoghurt, how often they make purchases, the key factors that drive their purchasing patterns, what flavours they like etc.

6. Sales targets. Sales targets are an essential part of marketing planning. Market research helps you to establish appropriate sales targets. These sales targets lie at the heart of business budgeting processes. Sales targets help to establish sales revenue expectations, production budgets, materials requirements budgets etc. It is important to clarify the assumptions around which sales targets are built, e.g. how much the market grew last year, the percentage of the market controlled last year, how big the market will be next year etc.

7. Products and services. Describe and define each of your products and services. Explain how they meet the requirements of your market.

8. Advertising strategy. So far you have described your market and its segments and the products and services that you will provide. You now need to show how you are going to communicate messages about your products and services to each of the targeted markets. In particular you need to show how your advertising messages will help you to gain an advantage over rivals.

9. Distribution channels. Describe the various ways in which you will distribute your goods and services to end consumers. Show how these distribution methods fit with the preferred requirements of your customers.

10. Competitor analysis. Set out who your competitors are. A good way of doing this is to draw a positioning map to show your position in the market and how this relates to your customers. A positioning map is typically drawn using the two most significant dimensions of competition in your marketplace. One of these dimensions is usually price. Explain the main strengths and weaknesses that you have relative to the competition.

11. Marketing tactics. Your marketing strategy needs to be backed up with some key tactics. For example, you should explain how you will communicate with your customers. What tactics will you employ, e.g. sales promotions, direct leafleting of customers, cinema advertising, advertising in the national and local press, etc.

12. Marketing budgets. You need to set out in numbers a marketing budget. This should consist of columns showing time periods, e.g. months of the year and rows showing the various marketing expenses, and totals.

13. Resource availability. You need to briefly describe the resources that you have available to support the marketing plan. These resources will include marketing personnel (who and how many), and the marketing budget (how much has been allocated to marketing activities).

14. Measurement/evaluation. Right from the start you need to create measures to judge the success of your marketing efforts. These are sometimes referred to as metrics (measures). Useful metrics include consumer awareness of products/advertising campaigns. These can be measured, for example by asking a sample of 100 people if they have heard of a product, or whether they can associate a particular advert with your product. Other way of measuring the success of a marketing initiative is an increase in sales following an advertising campaign/product launch.

15. Keys to success. Set out the most important factors that the success of your plan will depend on.

16. Brief conclusion.

Creating a marketing plan for a budget, environmentally friendly car

Figures produced by the insurance company Direct Line showed that in 2006 the cost of owning a car was almost the same as having a mortgage:

Monthly cost of running a new car

Finance	£46
Service, repair and upkeep	£61
Fuel	£94
Road tax	£15
Insurance	£63
Parking	£54
Breakdown recovery	£29
Depreciation	£149
Total	**£511**

Monthly cost of a £100,000 mortgage at 5% interest over 25 years

	£579

A typical middle range model such as a Ford Mondeo will set you back £511 a month, while the average home loan repayment is just £68 more at £579 a month.

Direct Line showed that the total cost of motoring has gone up by more than 55 per cent over the past 20 years. In contrast, home loans have become cheaper, with much lower interest rates and about 800,000 borrowers remortgaging every year to get a better deal.

Create a marketing plan for a new hybrid type small environmentally friendly car to be launched by a Japanese car manufacturer producing in Britain. A hybrid is a car that uses both petrol and an electrically charged battery. The battery charges up while the car is running on faster roads. The car switches to run on the battery when in congested areas.

Show that you can create an integrated plan that will enable the new hybrid car to be successful. The car is much smaller than other cars, and is easy to park. It is a two seater with storage space for shopping and other items.

9.2.6 Contingency planning and crisis management

You need to be able to evaluate the options available for an organisation if the strategic direction they pursue proves to be incorrect, or the external environment has changed to the point that a radical reassessment of strategy may be required. 'What if…' analysis, crisis management and **contingency planning** need to be considered for any business plan. In your assessment for this unit you are likely to be provided with a dynamic external environmental change, which may require some **proactive approach** or at least a short-term **reactive approach.**

A proactive approach is when managers plan strategies ahead of events. Managers seek to take control of the situation by thinking ahead, for example they create market plans, financial plans and human resource plans for the growth of a company. In creating these plans they anticipate the likely state of the economy and the market.

In contrast, a reactive approach is one where managers react to changes which usually take place in the external environment. These are unforeseen changes, such as the arrival of a new competitor, a sudden downturn in the economy, a sudden change in consumer buying patterns etc.

Successful managers are ones who can both:

* shape change (proactive management)

* react appropriately to unforeseen changes (reactive management).

Contingency planning is different from continuity planning. They are both a form of proactive planning. Continuity planning seeks to prevent disasters from happening by removing potential causes. In contrast, contingency planning is for when disaster does strike, it seeks to find solutions so that recovery can take place.

Proactive approach is a planned approach anticipating change. Doing something rather than waiting for a change to happen before taking action.

Reactive approach means responding to change rather than planning for change – sometimes referred to as 'firefighting'.

Contingency planning means making plans in case the unusual happens.

CASE STUDY

Scenario planning at Shell

Shell, the oil and gas company, provides one of the best examples of how to go about contingency planning. In the early 1970s the world was taken by surprise, by a number of oil crises caused by oil producing countries grouping together to push up the price of oil.

As one of the world's major oil producers, Shell decided that they would never be caught out by such uncertainty again and as a result they developed scenario planning. Scenario planning involves thinking out all of the possible changes that could take place in a business' external environment including political changes involving events such as wars, economic changes such as widespread inflation or the crash of the stock market, environmental changes such as global warming.

Shell grouped together all the worst possible situations to create 'worst case scenarios'. These would be situations of multiple 'bad events'. They then examined alternative scenarios, e.g. 'the most likely scenario', the 'best case scenario' etc. What strategic planners then had to do was to create appropriate responses to these situations. Scenario planning involves envisaging a range of possible situations and devising corporate strategies to deal with each of these situations.

✓ 1. Why do you think scenario planning is important for an oil company?
✓ 2. What other types of businesses should use scenario analysis planning?
✓✓ 3. What would be 'the worst case scenario' for an oil company? What sort of responses would you think would be appropriate for dealing with this situation?
✓✓✓ 4. Devise a 'worst case scenario' and a 'most likely scenario' for a company of your choice. Explain how the strategy that the company would pursue would be different in each case.

Steps in creating a contingency plan

There are all sorts of crises that may affect a business. Typically these crises are associated with change. There are two main types of change that create crises situations:

* changes that are external to the organisation, for example, a new competitor comes into the market, the market changes, buying patterns by consumers change, economic conditions change, etc.

* changes that are internal to the organisation i.e. the organisation introduces a change process.

There are several steps that can then be taken to create a contingency plan (see Figure 9.22). The purpose of the contingency plan should be to enable the organisation to quickly and efficiently resume normal working after some form of crisis resulting from external or internal change.

Contingency planning should therefore be ideally seen as a proactive process. There should be plans for dealing with a crisis should one occur. This relates to all sorts of businesses, not just those in which risks are greatest or where there is a public outcry when things go wrong. However, we can learn a lot from examining the contingency planning approaches of organisations with higher than average health and safety and environmental risks such as nuclear power generators, oil companies etc.

---

1. Carry out a risk assessent of your business. The purpose of the risk assessment is to identify possible risk areas. For example, these may relate to products, e.g. competition arising, processes, e.g. processes that become out of date, people (people leaving your organisation that are difficult to replace) etc.

2. Identify the impact on the business of each of these risks occurring. What will be the effects? What are the chances of each of these risks occurring? Rank the risk and probability of occurrence.

3. Identify alternative solutions to risks that are likely to occur. Come up with a range of solutions. These need to be well researched.

4. What is the cost of each solution? What is the benefit of each solution? Try to identify solutions which have the greatest net benefit i.e. benefit – cost = net benefit.

5. Create an action plan for dealing with crises. Who will be responsible for managing each aspect of the action plan? These contingency plans should be set out on paper. In some situations, simulated contingency plans should be practised. Obvious examples of where simulations would be necessary include threats of a terrorist attack on buildings and installations or some sort of spillage or leak that is hazardous to the environment.

6. Establish a training programme which will enable the implementation of the contingency plan. A trained team is required to implement the contingency plans.

7. Make sure that people know what to do if the contingency plan has to be implemented.

8. Carry out an assessment of the adequacy of the contingency plan. It is often helpful to ask independent assessors to carry out this task.

FIGURE 9.22 *Template for creating a contingency plan*

Oil spillages

Oil spillages are usually given high-profile coverage in the media. As a result, oil companies have spent more time and money on contingency planning than most. Many people are affected by oil spillages. For example, the clean up when an oil tanker damages its hull involves a range of agencies, companies and governments in the clear-up operation. The spillage may affect the environment, fisheries, industry and recreational activities.

Contingency planning typically involves a tiered response:

- Tier 1 occurs when spills are small and involves local clear-up operations.
- Tier 2 affects a wider area and should be covered by a local plan.
- Tier 3 involves a much bigger regional disaster and involves regional, national and international agencies in the clean-up operation.

At each of these levels the contingency plan should contain two key elements.

1. A policy document setting out the overall plan. There should be clear objectives to inform the plan. The strategy should set out who should take responsibility for what and give an overall framework. The strategy should cover:
   - risk assessment
   - resources at risk and priorities for protection
   - response strategies
   - organisation and responsibilities
   - equipment

   - resources and manpower
   - communication and control
   - training exercises and updating of plans.

2. An operational or action plan setting out the key steps to be involved in a clean-up operation.

✓ 1. What sorts of businesses is contingency planning most important in and why?

✓✓ 2. Should contingency planning and crisis management be seen as a proactive or a reactive discipline? Explain your answer.

✓✓ 3. What is the relationship between strategy and tactics in contingency planning?

✓✓✓ 4. If you were creating a contingency plan for a specific business (choose one) which areas would you include in your plan? Explain your choice relating this to the context of the business that you chose to examine.

Contingency planning diagrams

Creating a chart can be quite a useful tool for illustrating contingency planning so that options are visible and well thought through.

On the left of the diagram outline the change that is taking place within your organisation or that is occurring outside the organisation. Then, look at the potential problems that may occur and suggest some possible ways of dealing with these problems.

THE CHANGE	IMPLICATION	PLANNED RESPONSE
New competitor enters market	Competitor's product is better than ours in some aspects	i. Develop a new product of our own ii. Abandon our product iii. Modify our product in light of competitor's changes
	Competitor's product is better than ours in every way	i. Develop a new product to leapfrog competitor ii. Move into an alternative type of product iii. Abandon that part of the market to concentrate on other areas
	Competitor's product poses no real threat at the moment	i. Research and develop new product development to keep ahead of the competition ii. Advertise and promote our product focusing on its superiority over rivals

FIGURE 9.23 *Example of a contingency planning diagram*

Theory into practice

Create a diagram of your own to show how a particular organisation can create planned responses to a specific internal or external threat.

Knowledge check

1. Give one SMART objective for (a) a confectionery business and (b) a hotel chain. Explain how each objective meets the SMART criteria.

2. What is Ansoff's matrix? Identify key features of general strategies that appear in the matrix.

3. Describe the purpose of the following in the creation of a decision tree: (a) decision forks; (b) chance forks; (c) probability; (d) expected values.

4. How does identifying a critical path of activities help project managers to identify key sequences of activities and when they should be completed? How critical are activities that are not on the critical path?

5. Describe the key differences between the payback and net present value method of evaluating investment decisions. Which would you apply if your priority was to cover your investment in a three-year period?

6. How does the calculation of contribution help to work out a break-even calculation?

7. Explain the key differences between hard and soft HRM. Which of these is most likely to encourage motivation in the workforce?

8. Show how you would calculate: (a) labour turnover rates; (b) labour stability indexes. How would you use these tools in human resource planning?

9. What key headings would you set out in a marketing plan? Describe some of the details that you would include under three of these headings.

10. Distinguish between contingency and continuity planning. Give examples of situations in which you would develop these in business.

This is a synoptic assessment on strategic decision-making. It is designed to enable you to show your understanding of a broad range of business knowledge within a framework of business decision-making and corporate and strategic planning.

Assessment scenario

Creating a strategy in the UK home furnishing market

Furnish Your Home (FYH) is the UK's best-known business in this lucrative market. The mission statement for FYH is:

'To be the number one home furnishing retailer in the UK giving customers good quality at affordable prices.'

However, its turnover and profits have been very disappointing during 2006 in comparison with the competition as shown in the figures below.

Fitted bathrooms:

- Furnish Your Home has 30 per cent of the fitted bathrooms market.
- Value Furnishings has 20 per cent of the fitted bathrooms market.
- Total Quality Furnishings has 15 per cent of the fitted bathrooms market.

Fitted kitchens:

- Furnish Your Home has 35 per cent of the fitted kitchens market.
- Value Furnishings has 25 per cent of the fitted kitchens market.
- Total Quality Furnishings has 20 per cent of the fitted kitchens market.

Fitted bedrooms:

- Furnish Your Home has 28 per cent of the fitted bedrooms market.
- Value Furnishings has 25 per cent of the fitted bedrooms market.
- Total Quality Furnishings has 15 per cent of the fitted bedrooms market.

UK consumers have higher living standards than ever before and they enjoy investing money in enhancing their lifestyles through the purchase of home furnishings such as kitchens, bathrooms and bedrooms. Consumers' expenditure on the home grew from about 20 per cent of retail expenditure in 1991 to nearly 30 per cent in 2006. This compares to food and clothing which both declined as a percentage of all spending in the same period.

Furnish Your Home has been expanding its presence in this market. Initially it borrowed substantial sums of money from banks and other lenders to finance the expansion. Then it sold off some of its premises and leased them back to finance further expansion.

The money that it received from this process enabled FYH to grow, for example by buying a rival supplier of kitchen equipment and by buying a joinery business that fits kitchens and bathrooms.

However, although results picked up for a while the situation deteriorated in 2004, 2005 and 2006. The latest figures show a 20 per cent fall in sales in 2006 compared with 2005.

As a result, a strategic review of the company has been introduced. The main focus of the review is likely to be a closure of at least 20 of the 200 stores that the company owns in different parts of the country. However, this may only be the start. Eventually up to 100 stores may have to be closed. An alternative strategy that the company is considering is to open a new flagship superstore which will sell a much wider range of upmarket kitchens, bathrooms and bedroom furniture.

One of the main problems that the store faces is that it operates at the downmarket end of the market. However, despite offering relatively cheap kitchens, bathroom and bedroom furniture it has tried to target more affluent customers. FYH has tried to move a little bit upmarket and has raised its prices. However, this put off its traditional customers. At the same time, more affluent customers were not impressed by the furniture as they preferred furniture from more upmarket rivals. Upmarket kitchen brands require a lot of investment and FYH had not invested significant sums in this area.

At the same time competition from DIY chains intensified. DIY chains want to carry out the whole project from building the new extension on a house to a new kitchen.

Despite these problems FYH still has 20 per cent of the home furnishing market. FYH now wants to concentrate on the UK market. In the past it invested in kitchen and bathroom companies in France, Germany and the United States. These have now been sold off.

FYH's main rivals are Value Furnishings (VF) which seeks to provide cheap affordable furniture for the mass market, and Top Quality Furnishings (TQF) which has carved out a niche for itself by offering service over price. TQF realise that they couldn't compete by price alone, so they try to compete on service, both by offering a more personalised design-based service and by delivering goods free of charge.

Additional information about the economy

At the same time FYH is reviewing its strategy in 2006 there has been some quite pleasing news about the state of the economy. The inflation rate in the economy is very low at 2 per cent and unemployment in the economy is almost at the full employment point. Living standards are rising and the economy is growing at a steady rate.

An economist advising FYH had this to say about the level of risk in the economy. 'So where do the risks lie? Well of course there is always the possibility of catastrophe – another terrorist atrocity, meltdown in the Middle East, a pandemic of avian flu or a sudden acceleration in climate change. Yet these are risks that are always with us and by their very nature are largely unpredictable. We can put in place crisis management plans to confront them should the worst come to the worst, but it would be pointless trying to predict them.

Then there is the risk that Europe's still-fragile economic recovery won't continue as predicted. This seems a rather more potent cause for concern than the possibility of a human variant of avian flu, for Europe has a long and distinguished history of stalled economic recovery.'

Questions about case study material

Section A

1. What is meant by a stakeholder? (2 marks)

2. Identify four possible stakeholders in Furnish Your Home. (4 marks)

3. Conflict may occur between stakeholder groups at FYH. Show how conflict may occur between two stakeholder groups should FYH decide to reduce the number of retail outlets it operates in the UK. (6 marks)

4. Explain how FYH's strategy has altered in recent times. (4 marks)

5. Explain how FYH's strategy has been influenced by its external environment. (4 marks)

6. State two business objectives that FYH may be seeking to achieve. (4 marks)

7. Draw a positioning map that compares the position of FYH and its competitors. (5 marks)

8. Explain how FYH's mission statement might need to be adjusted if it is to change its competitive position. (5 marks)

Section B

9. Evaluate FYH's current strategy in relation to Porter's generic strategy model. (8 marks)

10. Compare the generic strategy being adopted by FYH and compare this with the generic strategy of its two main rivals. (6 marks)

11. In your view which firm has the best strategy given the current market situation? (6 marks)

12. If FYH decides to go ahead with the option of setting up a new flagship store it will need to know what key steps will be required to put this into practice. A preliminary assessment has been carried out which yielded the following steps:

ACTIVITY	WHAT IS INVOLVED	TIME IN MONTHS
A	Carry out market research	6
B	Carry out financial analysis	2
C	Identify an appropriate store location	3
D	Apply for planning permission	6
E	Select appropriate contractors	3
F	Prepare site for development	3
G	Select and recruit employees	4
H	Train employees	4
I	Promote and advertise the store	3
J	Prepare launch campaign	2

a. Complete the diagram by entering the number of each node, the earliest start time for each node and the latest finish time for each node on the network. (6 marks)

b. Make a list of the sequence of the activities along the critical path. (8 marks)

c. After how many months will the store be ready to open? (2 marks)

d. Explain how critical path analysis will enable managers to supervise and control the project once it has started. (4 marks)

13. FYH is also considering investing in improving some of its smaller stores by giving them a facelift. It is going to pilot this investment project in a small store in the Midlands. The company has a strict policy on investment decisions that: the investment must have a return on capital (ARR) which exceeds 10 per cent. At the end of the life of the investment project the fixed assets purchased for the facelift, that is, the initial costs, will have a zero residual value (in other words the stores would need a complete new facelift). FYH has £50,000 of internal funds available for the project and the cost of capital is 10 per cent.

The expected cash flow from the project is shown below:

Year	Cash flow from refurbishment project (£)
Initial costs 0 (present)	(50,000)
1	19,000
2	19,000
3	18,000
4	9,000
5	

In your view should the company go ahead with the refurbishment project? Show your working.

(6 marks)

14. Are there any qualitative factors that the organisation should take into consideration as well as the quantitative ones in making this financial decision? (5 marks)

Section C

15. Using both quantitative and qualitative data, justify a recommendation as to whether FYH should cut back and close existing stores, and whether it should open a new flagship store. (25 marks)

16. Explain how contingency planning will enable FYH to deal with a sudden fall in consumer spending resulting from a fall in living standards in this country. (10 marks)

Total 120 marks.

Resources

To find practical examples of the strategies that companies have and are developing, carry out specific searches. For example, to find out more about Toni and Guy search www.toniguy.com

Alternatively, for a larger company like Shell, try www.shell.com. On this site you will find useful information such as Shell Global Scenarios to 2005.

To find out about specific aspects of strategy, carry out a search linking the name of the company and the specific aspect that you want to research e.g. **Amazon and vision**, or **Nike** and **objectives**.

To find out more about key theories outlined in this unit, do an Internet search for:

* 'Michael Porter home on the web'

* 'Michael Porter's big ideas'

* 'Business world according to Peter Drucker'

* 'Thought leaders, Michael Porter'.

Books

Dransfield, R. (2003), *Corporate Strategy*, Heinemann, Oxford

Dransfield, R. and Coles, M. (2003), *Accounts Made Easy*, Nelson Thornes

Websites

www.aloa.co.uk

www.tutor2u.net

A business plan for the entrepreneur

This unit contains five elements:

10.2.1   Reasons for construction of a business plan

10.2.2   Information within a business plan

10.2.3   Appropriate research for a business plan

10.2.4   Business plan templates

10.2.5   Constraints that impact on implementation

Introduction

This mandatory unit outlines issues that any **entrepreneur** could face when planning for their future. Business planning is very important for all businesses as it helps them work out what they want in the future and how they are going to measure their success.

Successful business planning uses skills that you have already acquired at AS level including marketing, people and finance to see how they influence one another.

Business planning is also about considering what is happening outside the business and the influence that external factors can have. As you study this unit, you will need to be thinking about an idea to use for your business plan and be able to analyse all the elements that may affect that business in practice.

You will need to spend time screening your business ideas before you finally select or reject your ultimate business idea. You will need to choose a business idea that interests you but is not unmanageable. Suitable business ideas could be an Internet café, sandwich delivery service or coffee shop.

> **Key term**
>
> An *entrepreneur* is someone starting their own, often risky, business.

10.2.1 Reasons for construction of a business plan

When setting up in business it is sometimes easy to concentrate only on the day-to-day running of the business rather than what is going to happen in the future, which can lead to problems or even bankruptcy.

A business plan is a 'living document' that considers and puts into a written form details about where the business wants to end up in the future. As the business or external factors change, so too does the business plan.

A business plan cannot guarantee the success of a business but it can help an entrepreneur to get a realistic picture about what is happening and how things may affect the success of their idea, such as where to get funds and who potential competitors might be.

The business plan is a planning tool that gives the entrepreneur something to work from. This is because the plan gives details about all the essential elements of that business including:

* a description of the business
* its products or services
* its **aims** and **objectives**
* its marketing plan
* its financial predictions.

Key terms

The *aims* are the purpose of a business, what it works towards.

The *objectives* are the list of plans that a business uses to achieve its aims.

Giving businesses a clear picture of the various stages they need to go through in order to be successful

A business plan helps coordination during the first stages of setting up the business. This may include choosing the overall aims of that business or the type of ownership the business is likely to have. The business plan may be vital in order to get financial help from banks or other funding institutions. The plan allows entrepreneurs to also consider the more practical side of the skills needed by staff and the location of premises.

Setting goals and objectives for the business, in both the short and long term

Setting goals for the business in the longer term can help the entrepreneur really think about what they want to achieve by considering their **unique selling point** (**USP**) or niche in the market. These goals are also known as aims that the business is working towards. Many organisations produce a written statement of their aims known as a Mission Statement.

To be successful, the business needs to be offering something different from the competition or be the only business that is offering that product or service in the area. Opening a new business is not always about thinking of a new concept or invention, but a way of doing something different that will attract people to buy your services rather than those of your competitors.

Key terms

The *USP (unique selling point)* is what makes that product or service different to others.

easyJet

Well-known organisations rely on good business planning

easyJet is a classic example of good business planning and demonstrates how important it is to make the most of opportunities and influences as they arise. Founded in 1995 by Stelios Haji-Ioannou, easyJet has gone from a one-route operator to being one of the largest airlines in Europe.

easyJet did not offer a new service as such because air travel already existed. However, in 1997 after the market was deregulated it was able to start offering flights to destinations of the airline's choice at prices chosen by them. This was a big change in terms of external influences as governments heavily influenced when and where flights went before deregulation.

In addition to choosing their destinations and prices, easyJet really helped to establish the concept of low-cost. They adopted this in all areas of the business by extensively using the Internet for bookings and operating as a ticketless airline to reduce administration costs. They also decided not to provide free meals on flights which also significantly reduced costs but at the same time allowed them to make money on board by providing these services at an additional cost if required.

The Easy group of companies has now expanded through more business planning into other budget areas including cinemas, car hire, cosmetic products and even a cruise ship.

For more information access easyJet's website www.easyjet.com.

✓ 1. What concept did Stelios choose for his airline and how did this differ from other airlines?
✓✓ 2. Describe two advantages easyJet are likely to have experienced through good business planning and how these directly relate to the success of easyJet.
✓✓✓ 3. Judge the extent to which good business planning was the key factor that contributed to easyJet's success.

Theory into practice

You will need to produce a list of possible ideas that you could consider for your business plan. Consider the uniqueness of each idea – is it offering something different from your competition? What is your unique selling point?

Once the aims have been set, the organisation has an idea of where they are heading but smaller steps are needed to help achieve them. These steps are the list of plans that a business uses to achieve its aims and are called objectives.

The aim of a business might be to make a profit so the corresponding objectives could be to increase sales through additional advertising or to cut staffing costs.

If these objectives are SMART (Specific, Measurable, Agreed, Realistic and Time-constrained) they can be used as a gauge to work out whether the business is being run as predicted by the plan or if changes need to be made in order for things to be put back on track.

Ensuring the monitoring and reviewing of progress is made more straightforward

An entrepreneur cannot measure progress without having something to measure that progress

against and this is why planning is so important.

The Green Bean Organic Coffee Shop Ltd has the objective of achieving £200,000 turnover by the end of 2008. Using this objective the entrepreneur can calculate how likely it is that this will happen. If the shops have a sales turnover of £100,000 by November 2007, what else needs to be done to increase the turnover? Is the figure of £200,000 realistic or should adjustments be made to projected turnover and potential profit figures?

The opposite can of course happen too. Is turnover higher than expected and if so what might be causing this? Should the predicted annual turnover by 2008 be increased to £300,000? Measurement allows changes to be made.

Persuading other stakeholders to, for example, finance a business, both as it is starting up and then as it is growing

One of the most common reasons why any entrepreneur will produce a business plan is to persuade others to invest in the business. A **stakeholder** is anyone who has an interest or is affected by the business including the entrepreneur themselves, their business partner or a lender such as a bank or building society.

Funding the business could also be through **venture capitalists** that look for small businesses to invest in, grants from business organisations or loans from family or friends. Stakeholders can also be the local community or council. If your business is likely to have an impact on the local community, such as a nightclub or festival event, these stakeholders would need to be persuaded that they would not be adversely affected.

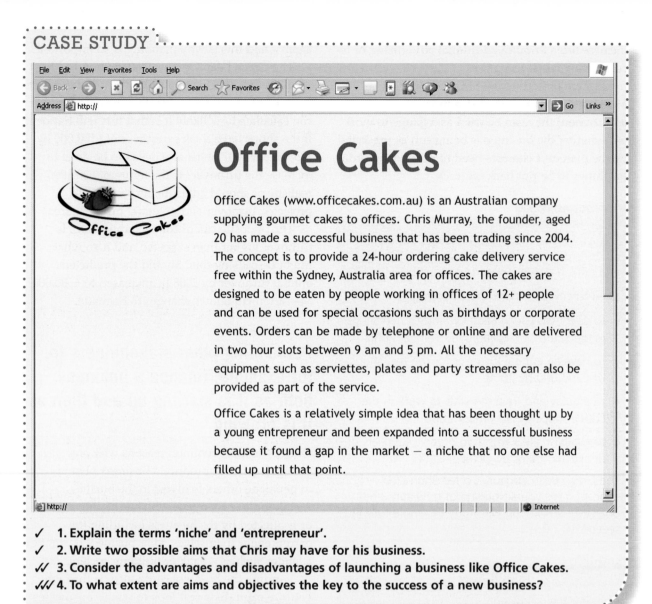

Office Cakes

Office Cakes (www.officecakes.com.au) is an Australian company supplying gourmet cakes to offices. Chris Murray, the founder, aged 20 has made a successful business that has been trading since 2004. The concept is to provide a 24-hour ordering cake delivery service free within the Sydney, Australia area for offices. The cakes are designed to be eaten by people working in offices of 12+ people and can be used for special occasions such as birthdays or corporate events. Orders can be made by telephone or online and are delivered in two hour slots between 9 am and 5 pm. All the necessary equipment such as serviettes, plates and party streamers can also be provided as part of the service.

Office Cakes is a relatively simple idea that has been thought up by a young entrepreneur and been expanded into a successful business because it found a gap in the market — a niche that no one else had filled up until that point.

✓ 1. Explain the terms 'niche' and 'entrepreneur'.
✓ 2. Write two possible aims that Chris may have for his business.
✓✓ 3. Consider the advantages and disadvantages of launching a business like Office Cakes.
✓✓✓ 4. To what extent are aims and objectives the key to the success of a new business?

Theory into practice

Now consider your own business plan:

- What will be the gap in the market that you could fill?
- What will be unique about your business?
- Is this a new business that has not been done before or an adaptation of an existing idea?
- What is the reasoning behind your choice of business enterprise?

10.2.2 Information within a business plan

The next stage of business planning is actually producing the document itself. Business plans are usually divided into five key sections:

* preliminary information
* marketing plan
* production plan
* financial plan
* human resource plan.

Each section needs to be completed in full and combined together to provide a real idea of what the enterprise is about. When completing your business plan it is a good idea to make use of appendices. Put research data from each of your sections at the back of your business plan making clear reference to it under the relevant section.

Preliminary information

This section deals with the information that needs to be presented first. Figure 10.1 gives you an idea of the type of information that should be included and why.

TYPE OF INFORMATION	DESCRIPTION	FACTORS TO CONSIDER
Name	The name of the enterprise which may also give specific details about what the enterprise actually does, such as Bob's Bicycle Hire.	<ul><li>Gives the right impression of the business from the start.</li><li>Not liable to go out of fashion.</li><li>If you are going to trade in Europe, does it mean anything in another language or can it be translated?</li><li>Is it easy to spell?</li><li>Does anyone already have it?</li></ul>
Mission statement	The mission statement gives details of the aims of the business, its purpose and values. For example, Oxfam works with others to overcome poverty and suffering.	<ul><li>What is its purpose – why does it exist?</li><li>What is involved in the actual business itself?</li><li>What does the business stand for or value, for example does it value ethical or green issues?</li><li>Profit or not-for-profit business?</li></ul>
Location	The location of the business is extremely important as it gives detailed information to potential stakeholders, including investors, about where the business is going to operate from and why that location is important.	<ul><li>What is the image of the area?</li><li>Is it expensive to locate in this area and if so are these additional costs justified?</li><li>What is the competition in the area?</li><li>Supplier location?</li><li>Potential customer location?</li><li>Will customers visit the location or will the business be run online or remotely?</li><li>Is the business located in an area of social deprivation and will it be entitled to government grants?</li></ul>
Physical size of business	The physical size of the business is important as it influences the type of location that is needed and the initial investment needed.	<ul><li>Is the equipment needed to run this business large?</li><li>Is the business run from home or a purpose built factory?</li><li>Is a lot of storage space required for stock or can **JIT** production techniques be used?</li></ul>

continued ▶

TYPE OF INFORMATION	DESCRIPTION	FACTORS TO CONSIDER
Type of business ownership	The type of ownership needs to be described within the business plan so the elements of risk and **liability** can be explored.	• Sole trader? • Partnership? • Limited company (Ltd)? • If the liability of the business is unlimited, for example a sole trader, which assets do you as an entrepreneur own – house or car?
Goals and objectives	The mission statement outlines the long-term purpose of the business and what it wants to achieve but the preliminary information should also contain details about the goals that the business wants to achieve over a specific period of time and the objectives that support those goals.	Two of the objectives for the Green Bean Organic Coffee Shop are: • to open two Organic Coffee Shops in the South of England by November 2006 • to have an annual turnover for the two shops of £200,000 by 2008. You will need to consider what your goals are for your business and how these can be broken down into objectives that can be measured.

FIGURE 10.1 *Preliminary information within a business plan*

Key terms

JIT is the process known as Just in Time.

A *liability* is the extent to which a person or business is responsible for debts.

Theory into practice

Using Figure 10.1 to help you, write a draft of the preliminary information part of your business plan. You may not be able to complete it in full but it will start to focus your ideas.

Ask a critical reviewer to look at each section of the plan and give you some feedback on ways you could improve it.

- Is your information clear?
- Does it make sense?
- Are your objectives SMART?

Marketing plan

Marketing is an essential part of the business plan because it allows the business to make informed judgements about the level of demand for its products and services. Predicting the right level of sales can make a huge difference to the success of the business as it will allow the right levels of stock or provision of services to be planned for.

Before you do your **primary research** you will need to look at the section on **secondary research** to consider the size of the market that you are thinking of entering, what kind of market share you would like to attract and how that market is segmented. By identifying a **target segment** within a market your market research is more likely to be valid and specifically relate to the product or service that you wish to offer.

Use of primary data in market research

Primary data is very important to an enterprise as it allows them to find out general market information as well as being able to focus on specific information that they want to know about their product or service and the likelihood of it being purchased. The purpose of the research will affect which method of data collection is chosen. The main uses of primary data are to:

* work out whether or not there is a place for a new product or service in a market

* judge the position of an existing product or service in a market and to see if changes need to be made to increase its volume

* estimate potential profitability

* gauge trends in the market to estimate future growth or decline

* work out how to be more competitive and enhance features of the product to increase its unique selling point (USP).

Key terms

Primary research is research that is collected at first hand, also sometimes called field research.

Secondary research is research that has been collected by someone else, also sometimes called desk research.

A *target segment* is a specific part of market that has been chosen to be marketed to.

Primary data is particularly useful, if done correctly, because you know how up to date and reliable it is. It is also tailored to the individual needs of your business and only data that is appropriate to the business plan will be collected. The five main methods of collecting market research are:

* observation

* experimentation

* surveys

* questionnaires

* focus groups.

The choice of method is critical because it will influence the type of data that is supplied and how useful it is to the business. There will also be a cost implication for each method including physical costs, such as paper, photocopying, postage or time costs (the product may need to be launched quickly to beat competitors).

The type of data that needs to be collected is important, whether it is qualitative or quantitative.

Qualitative research collects information about why people act in the way that they do, including their motivation, judgements and opinions. The following questions are examples of qualitative research questions.

* Why do you like the shape of this product?

* How does price affect your decision to buy a product?

* What influence does reputation have on your decision to buy?

* What is your opinion of the company name 'Green Bean Organic Coffee Shop' – what image does it portray?

Quantitative research is much more concerned with facts and figures that can provide statistical judgements. This information provides a picture of what is happening but not reasons as to why consumers feel the way they do. Choosing the right questions is also very important. If you ask the wrong questions you will get the wrong information and it is likely to be costly and time-consuming to repeat any areas of the research. The questions in Figure 10.2 are examples of quantitative research questions.

Do you drink coffee?				Yes		No
How often do you drink coffee per day?	1	2	3	4	5	6
How much would you pay for a cup of coffee?	£0.50–£0.99		£1.00–£1.49		£1.50–£1.99	

FIGURE 10.2 *Examples of quantitative questions*

	STRONGLY AGREE	AGREE	HAVE NO OPINION	DISAGREE	STRONGLY DISAGREE
I prefer to buy coffee that is organically produced.					
Price is really important to me when buying coffee.					

FIGURE 10.3 *An example of Likert scaling*

GREEN BEAN ORGANIC COFFEE									
	1	2	3	4	5	6	7	8	
Strong									Weak
Value for money									Expensive
Smooth									Bitter

FIGURE 10.4 *An example of semantic scaling*

Questionnaire design

If you opt to use a questionnaire for your primary research you will need to consider how your questions are structured. Three different methods of asking questions are outlined below.

Likert scaling

Your **respondents** should tick which box they think accurately describes their response to the statement (Figure 10.3).

> **Key term**
>
> A *respondent* is a person who has taken part in primary research e.g. answered a questionnaire.

Semantic scaling

Semantic scaling requires respondents to indicate their opinions by putting a cross or tick in the relevant box based on the scale of 1 to 8 (Figure 10.4).

Ranking

Ranking requires respondents to place features in order of importance (with 1 being the most important) as shown in Figure 10.5.

	RANK 1 TO 5
Price	
Taste	
Brand name	
Organically produced	
Aroma	

FIGURE 10.5 *An example of ranking*

Sampling

The most accurate method of collecting data for primary research is to collect data from all the consumers of a particular product or service. This group of people is known as the population. However, this is likely to be so expensive and time-consuming that the benefit of doing the research would be outweighed by the costs. To allow market research to go ahead a business needs to research a sample of people who are thought to represent the whole market. This activity is known as sampling. There are five main types of sampling that could be used within the research plan (Figure 10.6).

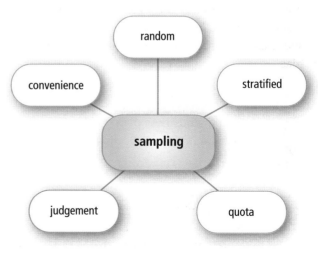

FIGURE 10.6 *Different types of sampling*

Random sampling

This is when a random sample to be researched is taken from the whole population. Each person should have an equal chance of being chosen to complete the research. Statistical calculations will then be made to map the findings of the sample group to the whole population to try to work out likely levels of demand. It is important to get the sample size right when considering using random sampling – too small a sample may not be statistically representative but too large a sample is likely to be very expensive.

Stratified sampling

This is when the population to be researched is divided into different groups such as their socio-economic status or where they live. A random sample is then taken from each of the groups to give a representative picture of what is happening in the whole market.

Quota sampling

This is when a quota is decided before the market research takes place so that a specific quota of sub-groups is taken, for example 50 women aged 20–26 and 50 men aged 20–26. When the market researcher has got 50 responses for each group, they have completed their quota. This method of research is used commonly because it is cheaper and quicker than other methods but may not be as accurate as random.

Judgement sampling

This is when the sample is deliberately chosen. It is most commonly used in small-scale industrial market research. However, as the sample is specifically chosen it may be liable to **marketing bias.**

> **Key term**
>
> *Marketing bias* occurs in results that reflect a way of thinking that may not be truly representative of the whole sample.

Convenience sampling

Like judgement sampling, the sample in convenience sampling is chosen based on how easy it is to get responses. The researcher will go to an area such as a specific road or outside a shop to collect the data. This means that it may be liable to bias as there is not an equal chance of being chosen and it may not be representative of the population as a whole.

> **Theory into practice**
>
> Thinking back to your business plan consider:
>
> - what type of primary data will you need to collect?
> - which research method will you use to collect that data?
> - how will you justify why this is the best method to use?
> - what are the advantages and disadvantages of using that method?
> - which method of sampling may be appropriate to use.

Use of secondary data in market research

Most businesses will want to do secondary research before they do primary research so they can get an idea of what is happening in the area that they are likely to locate or the market in which they are trying to enter. It is cheaper than primary research so it can avoid a lot of time and money being spent on an idea which has either already been done or is not workable.

Secondary research is information that has been collected and published by someone else. It is useful to a business because it exists already and can provide information about what is happening in a market. Businesses can make use of two sorts of secondary data: data available within the business such as sales records, invoice payments and loyalty cards or data available outside the business such as marketing reports, newspapers or websites. Some examples of different sources are listed in Figure 10.7. You will need to conduct secondary research in the relevant areas for your business idea.

Newspapers, magazines and trade journals	Newspapers such as *The Times, The Independent* or *The Telegraph* *The Economist* *Fashion Extras* *Stationery Trade Review*
Consumers' associations	Which? www.which.net Trading Standards www.tradingstandards.gov.uk National Consumer Council www.ncc.org.uk
Market research companies	Mintel www.mintel.com Dun and Bradstreet www.dnb.com/uk Mori www.mori.com CIM www.cim.co.uk
Government statistics	www.ons.gov.uk www.dti.gov.uk www.statistics.gov.uk www.oecd.org
National and international agencies	World Bank, International Monetary Fund, International Trade Centre and International Labour Organization
Competitors information	Websites, catalogues and published accounts
Other	Banks, building societies, yellow pages, websites

FIGURE 10.7 *Examples of secondary data sources*

Secondary data is useful for a business because it gives information about a range of products and services that are already available in a market and any changes affecting that market (Figure 10.8).

Secondary research is very useful but also needs to be considered carefully. One of the first things to consider is how reliable the data is and what **methodology** was used (this is the way that the data was collected), whether or not the data is up to date and the purpose for which the information was collected in the first place. The research should be as objective as possible so that

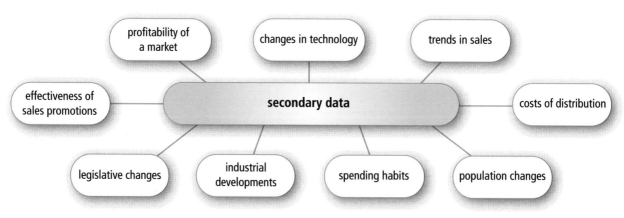

FIGURE 10.8 *Uses of secondary data*

it reflects the true picture of what is happening rather than what the business wants to happen.

Factors affecting the demand for a product or service

Lots of different things can affect the demand for a product or service.

* *The quality of the product or service.* Is it for a specialist niche market or a more budget quality mass-produced market, e.g. the difference between a unique hand-made wedding dress or an off-the-shelf one from a department store?

* *The product range it is part of and its image.* Is the product part of a brand or associated with an image, e.g. clothing or accessories?

* *Is it essential or a luxury?* Demand for a luxury product may be affected by other factors, e.g. is it something that is linked to a season or is it associated with festivals such as Christmas, Ramadan or Diwali?

* *The lifestyle of potential customers.* Is the product or service related to a particular lifestyle such as a sporty, healthy living or associated with a hobby or interest? The popularity of that activity could influence demand, e.g. in 2005 when England won the Ashes, products and services associated with cricket increased in demand.

* *The income of potential customers.* What is happening in the national and local economies can affect income, e.g. if interest rates are high, people's living costs such as their mortgage and loan payments will be high and they will have less money available to spend. Redundancies in the local area may reduce the amount of money being spent as consumers become less confident about the future.

* *The level of service available when purchased and after purchase.* After-sales service can be as important as the sale itself. Does the product or service come with a guarantee, how long for and what is available?

* *The level of availability and how the product is distributed.* Is it high-street based or available online? Is the service provided at times that suit the customer?

* *The level and type of competition.* Who are the competitors and what power and tactics do they use? Are they a large multinational or a smaller enterprise and what makes a customer buy a product from your business rather than another?

Methods of identifying and analysing competition

The competition that your business is going to face could make the difference between a business being successful or not successful. Make sure that in your research you answer the following questions.

* How big is the market?

* How many competitors are there?

* Which type of products do your competitors sell?

* What is the market share for each competitor?

* What level of quality are competitors' products?

* What is brand loyalty like amongst competitors?

* Are there any new products being launched or that have been launched?

* How do your competitors distribute their products?

* Which type of advertising promotions do your competitors use?

* What are your competitors' pricing strategies?

One way of identifying gaps within a market and where competitors are placed is to use a market map. A market map uses two scales within it and you can choose different measurements in order to compare businesses within the same market. The two measurements used for comparison are quality and price.

High quality

Valet
Master

Individual
Hand-Washed
Motors

Shiny Vehicles

Superior Motor Clean

Roller Wash

Speed
Clean

Cheap And Easy

**Low
price**

**High
price**

Self-Service Wash

Low quality

FIGURE 10.9 *An example of a market map for car washing businesses*

The market map in Figure 10.9 shows there are many car washing competitors in the mid- to low-priced section with mid- to high quality but few in the high price/high quality section and low price/low quality. These two areas may identify gaps that could be exploited by the business.

By completing a market map for your business, it is possible to identify strategies adopted by your competitors. Each competitor is placed within a relevant part of the market map. If a section of the market map is very full it is likely that part of the market is very full so you will either need to come up with a unique selling point for your business or consider targeting your business in another area of the market. Equally, it is important not to enter an area of the market where there would not be a demand for your product or service.

Theory into practice

Produce a market map for the market that your business is in and decide which measurements are important to monitor, such as price or quality. How many other businesses are in the same market your business is in?

Use of marketing models
SWOT analysis
SWOT refers to strengths, weaknesses, opportunities and threats. Applying a SWOT analysis (Figure 10.10) to your marketing plan can help you to identify any possible pitfalls in your research as it attempts to identify what is good about your marketing plan and what is not so good.

SWOT analysis is a tool that examines influences on a business with strengths and weaknesses (internal) and opportunities and threats (external).

Strengths	Weaknesses
relate to what is good inside the business	relate to areas that are a problem inside the business
Opportunities relate to issues that are external to the business e.g. areas where the business could expand or develop	**Threats** relate to issues that are external to the business that may limit its performance

FIGURE 10.10 *SWOT analysis*

Remember that, like any other business tool, a SWOT analysis is only as good as the information you put in to it. Try to remain objective at all times and consider how an outsider would view your business. The opportunities and threats deal with what is happening outside your business and could identify gaps in the market that should be filled or the threat from your competition in terms of brand loyalty or predatory pricing.

Using the information you have collected to date, produce a basic SWOT diagram to analyse your marketing plan. Update it regularly as and when you collect additional information.

PEST analysis

PEST refers to political, economic, social and cultural and technological factors.

PEST analysis is a business tool that looks at external influences on a business.

*   *Political, legal and fiscal influences.* These influences relate to changes in government, tax policies, regulations and international trade agreements. A change in the level of Value Added Tax (VAT) can have a huge influence on the pricing of a product and its potential profitability. Changes in legislation, regulations and policy will affect the way the business is run, for example changes in health and safety regulations will mean that the business will need to enhance their provision in these areas.

*   *Economic.* These factors influence the demand for products due to changes such as in interest rates, unemployment, inflation or exchange rates. A rise in interest rates is likely to affect the amount of disposable income that a potential consumer has and therefore demand may fall. A decrease in interest rates is likely to have the opposite effect. Changes in disposable income can increase demand substantially for more luxury goods. Exchange rates work in a similar way in that the number of tourists visiting the UK is affected by the strength of the pound. A strong pound will make it much more expensive for tourists to come to the UK and spend money on products or services.

*   *Social and cultural.* These influences relate to anything to do with society including changes in consumer tastes and fashions, the number of births, the age of the population, education, ethnic mix, lifestyle or levels of crime. Any influence affecting the way people live could have an effect on the demand for a product.

*   *Technological.* Over the past twenty years there have been enormous changes from a technological perspective. Technology has changed the way we use our bank, do our work, shop, for example online, and the way that products are made with an increased use in technological production. This can lead to greater efficiency and therefore potential **economies of scale**.

Economies of scale is the process whereby individual unit costs decrease as production goes up. There are a number of different types including purchasing and technical economies.

File   Edit   View   Favorites   Tools   Help

Back   Search   Favorites

Address http://   Go   Links »

eBay

eBay has revolutionised the way that auctions are carried out. Started in 1998 in America, eBay was designed to bring together buyers and sellers to an online market place. Unlike traditional auctions or garage sales, eBay directly evolved through changes in technology and access to the Internet. Moving from traditional auctions to online access has resulted in changes to the way that buyers and sellers behave:

- buyers and sellers can be in their own homes whilst trading
- trading can take place 24 hours a day
- trading can take place over a number of days or weeks rather than a short timeframe, providing the potential for increased interests and bids
- removal/distribution costs are reduced as the object for auction does not have to be transported to an auction room
- trading can be seen as fun, more like a hobby or interest
- extensive use of automated payments are made potentially reducing costs
- it attracts people of all ages.

The length of time taken from registration to sale or purchase is very short through using online forms. Registration takes minutes and from that point onwards buyers and sellers can start to trade. eBay hasn't just stayed within the world of collectibles or items that are usually bought and sold second hand but has always allowed people to trade new goods and for virtually anything to be traded online.

http://   Internet

✓ 1. What difference has technology made for eBay?

✓✓ 2. Describe two threats that you can think of that might affect eBay in the future from a technological point of view, outlining their limitations.

✓ 3. Can you think of any other businesses or markets that have been revolutionised by technology?

✓✓✓ 4. Consider the extent to which your business idea might be affected by technological developments.

Ordering shopping online with arrangements for home delivery and self-service checkouts are a complete transformation. Mobile phones have now gone from just being used as a telephone to being used as a form of mini lap top. Technological change may happen very quickly and can transform an industry including its marketing methods, e.g. the use of Internet marketing rather than traditional methods, such as radio and television advertising.

Ansoff matrix

Applying tools such as the **Ansoff matrix** to your marketing plan will also allow you to make judgements about your strategy and gauge success. The Ansoff matrix matches strategies for existing and new products to existing and new markets. It outlines suitable strategies for these products and markets. Each strategy is described in more detail following this table.

	EXISTING PRODUCT	**NEW PRODUCT**
Existing market	Market penetration	New product development
New market	Market development	Diversification

Before drawing up your Ansoff matrix, you will need to work out which of these strategies your business is aiming for.

✳ Market penetration is when a business tries to gain more control of an existing market. It might do this by reducing prices to encourage more people to buy its goods or services.

✳ New product development is when new products are sold to existing markets, for example camera mobile phones replacing ordinary mobile phones.

✳ Market development requires existing products to be sold in new markets. An example of such a strategy is selling breakfast cereals as diet foods or as evening snacks. This is a new market for this product.

✳ Diversification is when an existing firm offers a new product in a new market. There are lots of examples of businesses that have adopted this

kind of strategy. Tesco, for example, traditionally known for its supermarket operations has diversified into credit cards and insurance. Whitbread diversified into health and leisure by operating David Lloyd Leisure Centres.

Consider the usefulness of tools like Ansoff within your business plan. Ansoff can be very useful as a planning tool to give entrepreneurs ideas for strategies for their business but has also been thought as too simplistic because it does not take into account any of the support structures needed to successfully implement a strategy. Ansoff only gives ideas but does not necessarily make follow-up happen.

Product life cycle

Another useful marketing model is the product life cycle. This shows the potential stages for a product or service and how strategies can be used to extend their lives. After the product has been researched and developed there are four key stages in its life (see Figures 10.11 and 10.12). Extension strategies can be used to extend maturity to avoid the product going into decline.

Each stage of the product life cycle is labelled and gives an idea of where the product is in its life time, a bit like a human life.

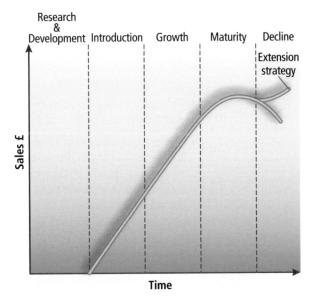

FIGURE 10.11 *An example of a product life cycle*

STAGE	FEATURES
Research and Development	• Research stage. • The marketing plan is being prepared. • Costs are high. • Not launched yet so no sales.
Introduction	• Product is launched on to the market. • Price will be set to reflect the type of product. • Promotion and awareness of the product. • Maybe a monopoly in the market. • Sales are low and costs high. • Products may get withdrawn at this stage.
Growth	• Customer awareness increases and sales and profits start to rise. • Rising profits mean other businesses start to take an interest in the product. • Costs of manufacturing may still be high as investment is made, for example, in machinery or equipment. • Competitors costs will be less and they may try to push down prices by offering the product more cheaply to gain market share. Their success will depend on brand loyalty.
Maturity	• Sales continue to rise but the rate at which they rise starts to become less steep. • Highly competitive. • Mass market and weak brands often disappear at this stage as they cannot compete. • Promotion to try and maintain market share so money will be spent on reinforcing the brand image or packaging. • Extension strategies will be planned for at the end of this stage or at the beginning of the decline stage. • Profits are still good.
Decline	• When a product's sales start to fall and profits also fall as a result, the product is in the decline stage. • A product may go into decline because it is not offering what customers now want or it has been made out of date due to technology. • Some businesses will stop their marketing to cut costs and allow the product to keep slowly declining but will still make some profits between then and when it is finally withdrawn. This may be because it is a product that is part of a range or is a spare part for another product and will continue to be made for a while. • If a product is likely to damage the business' reputation it will be withdrawn earlier. • Some products will have extension strategies launched to start to increase sales again, for example by changing the product's design or use.

FIGURE 10.12 *Stages of the product life cycle*

The product life cycle is useful when considering the marketing strategy for your business. You may be considering offering a new product, in which case the product may need to have time spent on research and development before it is launched. Alternatively it may be launched and then grow rapidly before reaching maturity. At the end of maturity, products are either given extension strategies in order to increase sales again or will go into decline. The product life cycle gives a guide to the pattern of a product's life but what it can't do is demonstrate how long each part of the life cycle will last. Kit Kat has been in maturity for a number of years and underwent a number of extension strategies in the late 1990s.

CASE STUDY

Kit Kat

KIT KAT IS THE BEST selling confectionary bar produced by Nestlé. Since it was officially launched with the name Kit Kat in 1937, sales continued to be good and the product remained in the maturity stage of the product life cycle for many years competing with other big sellers such as Dairy Milk from Cadbury.

However in the late 1990s, although Kit Kat was still one of the top selling confectionary bars in the UK, sales had started to drop and Nestlé were facing the reality that Kit Kat was potentially starting to move towards the end of the maturity stage and into decline.

Whilst Nestlé continued to produce the traditional variety of Kit Kat, they also began to consider other forms of Kit Kat as extension strategies to boost sales. Kit Kat Chunky was launched and targeted to the 12–20 age market. Sales and market share increased and Kit Kat Chunky became popular in its own right. Additional extension strategies have been used by Nestlé to continue to strengthen the brand both in the UK and abroad. In the UK, new versions have been made using white chocolate, orange, mint, vanilla, strawberry, lime, white yoghurt and lemon and Caramac, to name but a few, and other varieties have been produced for other countries including green tea and melon. As a result of these strategies Kit Kat has not gone into decline.

✓ 1. What do you think has helped Kit Kat to remain as Nestlé's top selling confectionary bar?
✓✓ 2. Consider how the product life cycle can be used to help with business planning?
✓✓ 3. Discuss where in the product life cycle your business plan's product is likely to be – is it a new product being launched or is it an adaptation of an existing product?
✓✓ 4. Which stage of the product life cycle relates to your product – growth or maturity?
✓✓✓ 5. What are the possible weaknesses of using a model like the product life cycle for your product and to what extent do you think such a model has implications for your business plan?

Extension strategies may include:

* increasing the use of a product
* encouraging the use of the product on more occasions
* reducing the price
* adapting the product, e.g. improved product or new packaging
* introducing promotional offers
* changing the image of the product
* targeting new markets for existing products
* adapting the product into new forms e.g. washing powder becoming washing liquid or capsules.

The product life cycle can be applied to your business idea to help plan the stages that the product or service will need to go through in its life time. It may also give a business some idea of the likely capacity and funding they will need at any of the given stages. Planning for the stages can also influence the pricing strategy as prices may be planned to be higher at the introduction and growth stages and then reduced during maturity. It does have limitations in terms of its usefulness though because it is impossible to gauge how long a product will stay in one of these stages and therefore planning can be difficult. The length of time it stays in any one part of the cycle will depend on:

* competitors
* technological change
* economic influences.

It can also be difficult to work out the exact point on the product life cycle where the product lies, for example when a product moves from growth into maturity. In addition, there might be a temporary drop in sales during maturity but this may not mean the product is in decline. This can cause difficulties for the business because if they see a drop in sales and believe a product is entering the decline stage of the model, they are likely to withdraw money from the marketing budget and therefore sales will drop further and the product will definitely enter the decline stage.

All product life cycles will look different, so if a business has more than one product it will have more than one product life cycle. It is not possible to draw conclusions from one and then map them to the other.

Boston matrix

The **Boston matrix** helps decision-making using portfolio analysis. A portfolio is a collection of products or services that a business offers and the analysis looks at the position of these products or services in their relevant markets. The Boston matrix looks at the market share and growth in which a business operates. There are four categories within the Boston matrix and these are known as Star, Question Mark, Cash Cow and Dog (Figure 10.13).

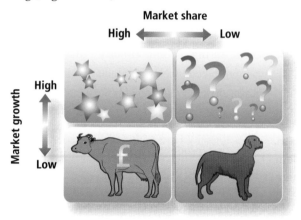

FIGURE 10.13 *An example of a Boston matrix*

To complete a Boston matrix, a business will map where its products go in order to see how balanced its portfolio actually is. Each category within the matrix has its own features and benefits.

* Stars are products with high market share in a high-growth market. They generate lots of sales but often need lots of money to be spent on them as the market is growing as well. Stars are destined to become the cash cows of the future.

* Cash cows are products with high market share in a low-growth market. They generate lots of sales and profits from these products are used to help fund question marks or stars. Within the product life cycle, these products are in the maturity stage.

* Question marks (also known as problem children) are products that have low market share in a high-growth market. They need lots of money to be spent on them if they are going to become stars. New products usually start off as question marks and then either grow market share and become stars or have low market growth and then become dogs.

* Dogs are products with low market share and low growth (in decline on the product life cycle). They may have been cash cows or question marks before they moved to the dog category. Businesses want as few dogs as possible because they add little to the portfolio. Sometimes dogs are retained by a business as they are still making some low sales that might attract customers to buy other products that they make.

By analysing their portfolio a business can try to concentrate on having a higher balance of stars and cash cows. Stars require lots of investment, so balancing those with cash cows is important so that there is money available to support them. This reduces the risk to the business as there is a balance between money available for development and profits to be able to support that development. Such planning also helps the business to have good cash-flow.

Key terms

Ansoff matrix is a marketing tool to help businesses plan for growth.

Boston matrix is a tool that is used to manage product portfolio development.

Choice of product or service and its distinctive features

Within your marketing plan you will need to be able to make sure that you consider all the elements of the marketing mix and its four Ps (product, price, place, promotion).

Applying models such as the PEST, SWOT or Ansoff means that the business has a realistic idea about who they are competing against and identifying reasons why customers would like to buy their products rather than those of their competitors – trying to establish their USP.

Price of products/services

You will need to carefully consider the pricing strategy you are going to use and justify why you have used it giving judgements as applicable. The price of a product has a huge influence on whether or not people buy a product.

Price elasticity and income elasticity (Figure 10.14) will affect the level of demand. It gives detailed information about the relationship between price or income and the level of sales.

When considering the price of the product it is worth bearing price and income elasticity in mind because if you need to change your price for any reason, e.g. in response to competition or as a result of increasing costs, you will need to forecast what effect this might have on your business. Both price and income elasticity may be important when considering the pricing strategy for the business because you might decide to enter the market with a low price (price penetration) and then increase the price later on. You will also need to consider general trends in income and their effect.

PRICE ELASTICITY	INCOME ELASTICITY
$\dfrac{\text{\% change in sales demand}}{\text{\% change in selling price}}$	$\dfrac{\text{\% change in sales demand}}{\text{\% change in income}}$
If a change in selling price results in a high change in demand a product is said to be price elastic.	If a change in income results in a high change in demand a product is said to be income elastic.
If a change in selling price has little effect on demand a product is said to be price inelastic.	If a change in selling price has little effect on demand a product is said to be income inelastic.

FIGURE 10.14 *Price and income elasticity*

Some different pricing strategies that could be considered are shown in Figure 10.15 below.

Price skimming	A high price will be used to enter the market and profits skimmed off. This means that the business makes a lot of profit before competitors can enter the market. This type of strategy is often used by businesses dealing with new technology.
Price penetration	A low price is used to enter the market and build up customer loyalty. Once customers have increased their loyalty the price also increases.
Competitive pricing	This is when the price reflects what the competition are doing and is priced competitively.
Psychological pricing	Prices like £1.99 seem psychologically cheaper than £2.00 even though there is only 1p difference.
Cost-plus pricing	Adding an additional amount to the cost of the product means that profit per product is easier to work out. However it may not take into account the demand for that product.
Price discrimination	Price discrimination is when a different price is charged, usually for a service, for purchasing at a different time. For example, fares on trains for travel after 9.00 am in the morning are significantly cheaper than before 9.00 am but the service is essentially the same.
Predatory pricing	Predatory pricing is when the price is deliberately low in order to put the competition out of business and may result in a price war.

FIGURE 10.15 *Pricing strategies*

Theory into practice

Choosing a pricing strategy for your business will need a lot of care and consideration. At A2 level you will need to identify your chosen strategy, justify why you have used it and outline the possible advantages or disadvantages of using such a strategy.

Research and complete the following table to help you with your ideas:

PRICING STRATEGY	ADVANTAGES	DISADVANTAGES	APPLICABLE TO MY BUSINESS
Price skimming			
Price penetration			
Competitive pricing			
Psychological pricing			
Cost-plus pricing			
Price discrimination			
Predatory pricing			

Methods used to promote products/services

Promotion of your service will need to be outlined in your marketing plan. You will need to consider your work on promotion for AS level including advertising and sales promotions. How will your promotion strategies encourage customers to buy your products or services rather than those of your competitors?

How products/services will be distributed to consumers

Finally outline your distribution to consumers. How will the product reach your customer? Choosing the right method of distribution will affect the likely success of the business. It must be offered at the right place at the right time for the consumer. Consider which of the following options would be right for your business.

* direct to the consumer
* through a retail outlet
* through a wholesaler
* through an agent.

> **Theory into practice**
>
> You will need to ensure that you have considered all of the possible issues related to the marketing of your business by constructing a checklist. The checklist should include:
>
> * the choice of product or service and what makes it distinctive from others
> * the price of the product or service
> * methods used to promote the product or service
> * how products or services will be distributed to customers.

Production plan

Production isn't just about producing a physical product, it can also refer to the way that a service is performed. The way that something is made or performed will influence the final product/service offered, e.g. budget or expensive, high or low quality.

You will need to consider five key elements of your production plan and apply them to your business idea:

* quantity
* equipment/plant/machinery
* quality
* different stages of production
* timing.

Quantity to be produced

Quantity of production is very important as your business might produce few highly branded high-quality goods or services, e.g. one-off wedding dresses or it might offer higher quantities of lower-priced services, e.g. car washes for £5. The amount of production will also link in to financial issues that you have learned at AS level including economies of scale and **capacity utilisation.** As a reminder, capacity utilisation is the measurement as a percentage of how many units the organisation is actually producing as a percentage of what it could produce. The higher the capacity utilisation the more efficient the business is likely to be as production is as high as possible. Time must be allowed though for machinery breakdown and working to a high capacity utilisation will only work if there is a demand for the product.

> **Key terms**
>
> *Capacity utilisation* is the extent to which a business makes use of the maximum amount they can produce (its capacity).

One way a business can reduce its average costs is by increasing its level of output. Output represents the amount a firm can produce and will depend upon the firm's capacity (its maximum level of output).

If a firm increases its level of output it may be able to reduce its average costs as fixed costs such as rent do not change when output changes. The more products or services a business can buy in bulk the cheaper the price the business needs to pay due to discounts. This means that as more units are made the cost to make each individual unit falls. This is known as economies of scale.

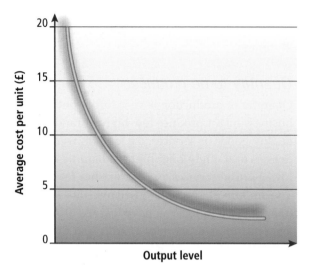

FIGURE 10.16 *Average cost at different levels of output*

Figure 10.16 shows that as the firm increases its level of output its average costs will fall. The reason why average costs fall as the output or scale of the firm is increased is because the firm is able to benefit from economies of scale. Economies of scale reduce costs and reduce the cost per unit as more are made. This does reach a maximum point where the costs have been reduced as much as possible before they will start to go up again as a result of diseconomies of scale.

Economies of scale fall into a number of categories.

✳ *Technical economies*. These enable the business to make use of automated equipment as many more units can be produced by machines than if they were done by human labour only. This is only feasible when the fixed costs of the machine can be spread thinly over many units of output.

✳ *Specialisation*. This is possible because the production process can be divided up and

people whose skills exactly match the job requirements can be recruited. Staff can then be trained and become highly effective at carrying out their limited task, e.g. production or customer service.

✳ *Purchasing*. These economies result from discounts obtained by buying supplies of materials and components at lower unit costs. This lowers the cost of making each unit.

✳ *Financial*. These economies stem from the lower cost of capital charged to large firms by the providers of finance. Banks charge lower rates of interest and equity investors are more willing to accept low-dividend yields from bigger firms.

Plant, machinery and equipment required

The plant, machinery and equipment required will need to be planned alongside the finance plan. This is because finance affects the investment possible. If your business is online you may not need premises for customers to be able to visit but you may need some form of **call centre** to answer calls instead. You will also need to consider hardware and software to run your site, hosting costs and security measures. If the business offers a service it may take place in the client's home, for example a window cleaner.

Key terms

A *call centre* is a customer service centre where calls are handled by telephone operators.

Theory into practice

Produce a full list of plant, machinery and equipment required using spreadsheet software such as Excel to provide details of what is needed. Work out a figure of money that you think you might need, which can also be used as part of your finance plan.

Online DVD rental service

www.lovefilm.com was launched in March 2004 and is now Europe's leading online DVD rental service carrying over 70,000 titles. The concept behind the service is that customers can rent DVDs online and have them delivered to their door by first class post.

The film is then allocated to that customer until they decide to return it and then another will be sent to them. Customers have lists of films that they wish to rent and these are held on their user account — as a film is returned a new film is sent out immediately so the amount of time spent being delivered or received is kept to a minimum.

Lovefilm's main resources are its website, a help centre where operators can respond to queries from customers by telephone and email and a huge warehouse where the DVDs are stored. In fact in May 2005 Lovefilm outgrew their warehouse and had to move to larger premises to cope with the demand for over 160,000 DVDs to be distributed every day!

✓ **1. Describe the different types of economies of scale that Lovefilm may benefit from.**

✓✓ **2. Analyse the advantages and disadvantages to Lovefilm of only allowing customers to access their services by website, phone and email rather than face to face.**

✓✓✓ **3. Lovefilm relies on postal delivery by Royal Mail. Judge the impact and relevance of Royal Mail's resources on Lovefilm's business.**

Quality levels required and means of assuring targeted quality

Quality depends on the type of product or service that you are offering and the image that your business is aiming for. Some services require a minimum level of quality and can result in Health and Safety issues if these are not met e.g. a central heating engineer must be CORGI registered. If someone attempts to work on a central heating boiler without this registration they should be prosecuted for breaking the law. Poor quality service could lead to dangers potentially resulting in an accident or even death.

The desired final quality of your product or service will be influenced by the raw materials or equipment used, for example a restaurant may serve high-quality meals made from the best ingredients or lower-quality meals made from value-style products

Working out ways to ensure that quality is maintained at the desired level is important. This can be done in lots of different ways (Figure 10.17).

Quality assurance	This is where employees are empowered to accept or reject the quality of a product and aims to get the product right the first time
Quality control	This is when products are inspected at the end of the process and those that are not up to standard rejected. Quality control can also be used for services by using mystery shopper or customer feedback schemes.
Total quality management (TQM)	This is the idea that everyone is responsible for quality and should seek to make improvements. This includes feedback from customers, employees and suppliers.
Kaizen (continuous improvement)	This is the Japanese idea of continuous improvement, that everyone (including the accountant, cleaner or administrator) is responsible for looking for ways to improve the product or service.

FIGURE 10.17 *Maintaining quality*

The method chosen to control quality within your business will depend on the level of tolerance allowed for that product or service (how important it is that the product or service is offered correctly the first time and how many defects are expected/allowed for in a given sample). For service industries it may be more acceptable to have more errors made by an organisation offering keyboarding services than a sandwich bar serving food to the public that may cause food poisoning.

Think it over...

Consider the tolerance levels that you think would be acceptable in the following professions:

- hairdresser
- clothes manufacturer
- mechanic
- surgeon.

Quality standards

Quality standards are also important when considering quality within your business. You may consider applying for quality marks such as ISO EN 9000 if this could be used as a good marketing tool for your business.

Products and services certified for ISO EN 9000 are able to add the BSI log displayed on their products to show they are quality assured and certified by the British Standards Institution (BSI).

The main benefits for businesses of having BSI certification is that consumers know that products or services should conform to specified requirements. Consumers know they should be dependable, reliable and maintainable. Health and safety, including a range of legal and regulatory requirements, must have been followed by the business which in turn should make employees feel happier and safer in their jobs. A motivated and safe workforce should lead to higher productivity and potential for sales leading to more profits!

Benchmarking

Benchmarking means measuring the performance of the business against the best performers in the industry. The aim of benchmarking is to learn what is the best practice in order to improve performance. This is useful in service and product based organisations. For services you may be able to set the expected quality levels based on the benchmarking for your industry, for example by measuring your expected performance against others, e.g. level of expected customer complaints.

Different stages of production for the product or service

There will be different stages of production for the product or service offered depending on the production method chosen. See Figure 10.18.

An example of the different stages of production for a web design service is as follows:

Stage 1 – receive customer enquiry

Stage 2 – meet to discuss requirements

Stage 3 – produce quote to send to customer for approval

Stage 4 – customer approves and sends deposit

Stage 5 – website produced

Stage 6 – draft shown to customer for approval or any adaptations

Stage 7 – final website given to customer for hosting

Stage 8 – final payment taken from customer and feedback on process

Stage 9 – follow up maintenance and quality check at later date.

Quality can be highlighted and emphasised at all stages of the process and training used to support those stages from making sure that the customer is dealt with appropriately when calls are received through to the actual production of the site itself.

Timing of production to meet customer needs

Timing is crucial! Will there be variations in demand for your product or service that will affect levels of stock needed or availability of staff? If the business is seasonal, e.g. ice cream making, what happens to the timing of production in the summer compared to the winter? Are there other services that can be offered in the winter?

PRODUCT	SERVICE
Job production – production of a one-off product to order, e.g. a handmade cake.	Is this a one-off service or can it be offered to more than one person at more than one time?
Batch production – a limited number of products are made and the method changed to make a number of another type of product.	What kind of resources are needed to offer this service: human, equipment?
Flow production – raw ingredients go in at the start of the process and then the product goes through each stage before it is completed at the other end (very expensive for a new business).	What kind of training is needed before this service can be offered?
Where is quality checked – raw materials, during production, at completion, at distribution point?	How can quality be maintained and checked?

FIGURE 10.18 *Issues related to production methods*

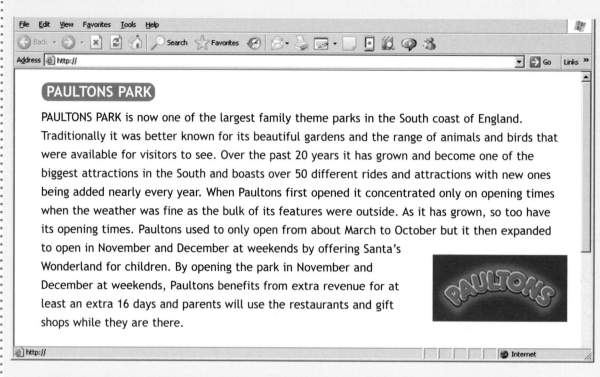

PAULTONS PARK

PAULTONS PARK is now one of the largest family theme parks in the South coast of England. Traditionally it was better known for its beautiful gardens and the range of animals and birds that were available for visitors to see. Over the past 20 years it has grown and become one of the biggest attractions in the South and boasts over 50 different rides and attractions with new ones being added nearly every year. When Paultons first opened it concentrated only on opening times when the weather was fine as the bulk of its features were outside. As it has grown, so too have its opening times. Paultons used to only open from about March to October but it then expanded to open in November and December at weekends by offering Santa's Wonderland for children. By opening the park in November and December at weekends, Paultons benefits from extra revenue for at least an extra 16 days and parents will use the restaurants and gift shops while they are there.

✓ 1. How has Paultons Park increased its output by making use of seasonal changes?

✓✓ 2. What are the advantages and disadvantages for staffing and resource levels of opening throughout the year?

✓✓✓ 3. Make recommendations to Paultons Park on further changes that could be made to increase customer numbers at different times/seasons giving analysis and judgements about your choices.

Theory into practice

In small groups, think of businesses in your area that offer seasonal services. What do they do in the winter? Produce a wall display analysing the different options that they use and make recommendations for different ways they could make use of spare capacity during their quiet months. Remember, some businesses may have their busy times during winter and have spare capacity during the summer.

There may be demand variations between evenings and mornings for your business or certain days may be busier than others, for example restaurants are more likely to be busy on a Friday or Saturday night rather than a Tuesday.

You will need to consider differing levels of demand from potential customers.

Your customer might be another business rather than the final consumer of the product. If you are manufacturing T-shirts you may supply them to retail outlets rather than selling them direct yourself. Timing of production as a supplier is extremely crucial to make sure that the final end user of the product can get access to it via your distributor. Getting it wrong can mean you have too much or too little stock.

If there is too much supply and not enough demand you may need to reduce your price, for example by having a sale. If you don't have enough supply, prices can increase as people offer more money than the priced goods. Online auctions can increase the chances of this happening.

Live8

During the Live8 concerts of July 2005 to 'Make Poverty History', 150,000 tickets were freely distributed via text to start with and then a further 55,000 offered free from other locations including theatres and cinemas. The tickets themselves had no face value at all so were virtually free apart from the cost of a text message, if ordered that way, of £1.50.

Demand for these tickets far outstripped supply and tickets began to be exchanged illegally on the black market and via Ebay for up to £700. Ebay was criticised in the media and by Sir Bob Geldof (one of the key Live8 organisers) for allowing such a practice to take place as people were making money out of an event that was supposed to raise awareness of poverty in Africa. The basic issue that became evident as a result of these inflated prices was that there were a lot more people demanding tickets than could be supplied and therefore the price went up.

✓ 1. Describe the impact of insufficient supply on Live8 ticket prices.

✓✓ 2. Considering the case of Live8 and the extremely high demand for tickets, produce a case for and against pricing the tickets at £20 per person.

✓✓✓ 3. Make recommendations to the Live8 committee about whether or not future tickets for concerts should be free or payable giving justified reasons for your thinking.

Financial plan

This is probably one of the most important and difficult parts of your business plan so it needs careful attention.

Sources of finance

The most important aspect of your financial plan is where you are going to get your money. Possible sources are outlined in Figure 10.19.

Banks	Banks are able to offer loans, business accounts and overdraft facilities based on the business plan. Interest is payable based on the predicted risk. Some security will need to be provided e.g. assets, such as a house.
Building societies	Building societies are also able to offer loans, business accounts and overdraft facilities based on the business plan. Interest is payable based on the risk of the venture. Some security will need to be provided e.g. assets, such as a house.
Venture capitalists	These are people who invest in new and up-and-coming risky ventures usually in return for a share of the ownership.
Friends or family	Money from friends and family may either be invested in the business in exchange for limited shares or paid back as a loan – often at a lower rate
Savings	Using savings in the bank/building society means that no interest is paid but savings may take time to build up if you haven't got any already.
Government grants	These are available from the EU, national government and local government. A grant is money that is given to an entrepreneur that doesn't have to be paid back and the amount of that money will depend on where it is coming from. For more information see www.businesslink.gov.uk/.
Prince's Trust	If you are between 18 and 30 you can apply for a low-interest loan or other services such as free legal advice or discounts. More information is available at the Prince's Trust website (www.princes-trust.org.uk).

FIGURE 10.19 *Sources of finance*

Complete the table below. Are there any other methods of finance that you could use?

SOURCE OF FINANCE	ADVANTAGES	DISADVANTAGES	SUITABLE FOR MY BUSINESS
Banks/building societies			
Venture capitalist			
Friends or family			
Savings			
Government grant			
Prince's Trust			

When choosing the method of finance for your business you will need to consider:

* the type of ownership that you have chosen, e.g. sole trader or limited company

* whether or not your business is a profit or not-for-profit business

* short-term needs, e.g. start up or longer term e.g. for a lease for ten years

* projected sales figures and likely payback time

* the cost of finance dependent on risk – small businesses usually have high interest rates as they are more risky to invest in.

Many small businesses suffer from problems with finances in their first few years and lots fail. It is important for small businesses to consider issues regarding their financial arrangements, for example a small business will need to consider the effect of funding on their ownership if they have to give some ownership rights to the investors. This can lead to potential problems in terms of who is running and/or owning the business (divorce of ownership and control).

Budgets, including estimates of start-up and working capital

A budget is a financial plan used to make predictions, set targets and control expenditure. You will need to demonstrate that you can understand budgeting by explaining and justifying the **start-up budget** and **working capital** needed for the business.

Start-up budget

The start-up budget gives details about the initial money that is needed by the business to start trading. This money is needed to get things moving in the first place. For a service business such as the Sunshine Cleaning Company shown in Figure 10.20, start-up funds are needed to buy cleaning products, a van, uniforms, insurance, leaflets and advertising to name but a few. The budget start-up costs may be set at £5,500 to give some flexibility in terms of how much individual items cost. Sometimes it may be possible to spread some of these costs over the first few months. For example the van or computer may be bought on hire purchase so monthly payments could be made over the first few months to avoid such a high initial outlay.

COST	£
Cleaning materials	200
Van	2,000
Overalls	200
Computer	1,500
Launch advertising	500
Website build and initial hosting	600
Mobile telephone	75
	5,075

FIGURE 10.20 *An example of a start-up budget*

You will need to think about everything your business is likely to need and then produce a start-up budget. As your business is a new business you will need to conduct research into the market and your competitors as you will not have accounts from previous years. Your budgets need to be realistic and represent what is likely to happen rather than what might happen in an ideal world. So be critical of your figures and if your budgeted sales revenue figure appears too high then it probably is! You will need to consider budgets for different areas of your business including production, human resources, marketing and so on.

You will also need to consider how many months to budget for. Businesses may budget for the next three months, six months or over a year. You will need to consider and justify which one of these timescales is most relevant for your business.

Sales budget

When you are producing your budget you will also need to consider whether or not it will need stock and budget for it. Figure 10.21 gives the sales budget for three months for Creamy Cakes Ltd.

	OCT	NOV	DEC
Sales revenue (£)	4,500	4,500	5,500

FIGURE 10.21 *Example of a sales budget*

Creamy Cakes Ltd buys in cakes in bulk from a cake manufacturer to sell to the general public. These figures are predicted sales revenues that the cake shop expects to get each month for its first three months of trading. Sales budgets can give overall budget predictions as shown or they can also break down the sales budget into different sections. For example, a beauty therapist may produce a sales budget based on the estimated different treatments they expect to provide (Figure 10.22). By breaking down each product or service it is much easier to carry out variance analysis when the business is up and running.

SALES REVENUE (£)	OCTOBER	NOVEMBER	DECEMBER
Nails	400	500	700
Waxing	200	200	300
Massage	75	100	150
Skin tanning	100	100	150
Total	775	900	1,300

FIGURE 10.22 *Example of a sales budget broken down into different services*

Produce the following budgets for your business idea.

- Sales.
- Production – how much does it cost to produce your product or offer your service?
- Marketing – how much will you spend on promotion?
- Human resources – how much will you need to pay out for staff?
- Overheads – which overhead costs do you have such as rent or insurance?
- Purchasing – which materials do you need to buy to produce your product or service

BUDGET TOTALS	OCTOBER
Sales revenue (£)	4,500
Purchasing	(800)
Marketing	(400)
Human resources	(2,900)
Overheads	(1,000)

FIGURE 10.23 *Example of a summary budget (first month of trading)*

Using a familiar spreadsheet package, produce a budget sheet for each of the areas relevant to your business e.g. purchasing and sales. Calculate a total budget sheet using formulae to help you.

Summary budget

When you have produced each individual budget you are then able to bring those budgets together to produce a form of summary budget. A summary budget for Creamy Cakes Ltd is shown in Figure 10.23. Each of the individual budgets feeds into the summary budget so you can see the overall picture. The sales revenue figure shown earlier forms part of the sales revenue budget – money coming in. The figures in brackets show money that is budgeted to be paid out.

Working capital

Working capital is the day-to-day money needed to pay the bills and for the business to remain trading. It is the difference between the current assets (cash and debtors due to settle their accounts and stock) that the business has and its current liabilities (the debts that must be paid in the short term).

> Working capital = current assets – current liabilities

Figure 10.24 gives an example of how to calculate working capital. In this case the working capital figure is £4,600 – £3,600 = £1,000.

CREAMY CAKES LTD	CURRENT ASSETS (£)	CURRENT LIABILITIES (£)
Cash	4,000	
Debtors (people that owe you money)	500	
Stock	100	
Creditors (people that you owe money to)		1,600
Bank loan		2,000
Total	4,600	3,600

FIGURE 10.24 *An example of how to calculate working capital*

It is important to estimate how much working capital is needed by the business in order to make sure it can continue trading. Within your budget you will need to make sure that money is available to pay for fuel, raw materials and wages by budgeting for how much working capital you are likely to need.

Working capital needs careful management within a business – too much working capital will mean that the business has lots of cash available that is not being used to its best ability. This means there is an interest cost to the business as this money could have gained interest from alternative investments. On the other hand, not enough working capital in the business means that your business won't be able to pay its bills and may become insolvent.

Factors that influence how much working capital your business has include:

* the level of sales – high sales means that money needs to be available to buy more purchases

* trade credit – the time offered by suppliers to pay for purchases e.g. one month or two months and whether or not that payback is with or without interest

* payment time – the amount of time that it takes to get payment from customers

* the level of inflation in the economy i.e. if levels are high then working capital needs to be higher to allow for price and wage increases.

Working capital is extremely important to new businesses because it is likely that large amounts of start-up expenses are paid out before any income starts to come in. At the start of the business sales figures may be low and credit deals by suppliers may be more difficult to negotiate. On top of this other costs such as marketing to make customers aware of the product or service are usually high.

Large businesses may make things more difficult for small businesses by negotiating long payment periods. For example, if your business is offering a window cleaning service to a large company, that company may negotiate payment after 14 days. This means that money will be spent at least two weeks before payment is received. It is quite common for debtors to still fail to settle invoices within the time negotiated so there needs to be extremely careful cash-flow management.

Theory into practice

Look at the budgets for the two companies shown below.

CHOCCO DESSERTS LTD	
Bank	200
Creditors	400
Loan from bank	2,000
Debtors	750
Stock	600
Cash	300

ICE SNAX LTD	
Bank	500
Creditors	200
Loan from bank	750
Debtors	300
Stock	1,000
Cash	250

* Work out the working capital figure for each business.

* What recommendations would you make for each business?

Look back at your budgets and business plan so far – consider the level of working capital that you might need and the implications for your type of business.

Simple cash-flow forecasts

Cash-flow forecasts show how money flows into and out of the business. Planning for money coming in and going out ensures the best possible use can be made of the business' resources. The cash-flow forecast can be used in a number of ways:

* to highlight times when outgoings are larger than income and therefore an overdraft may be needed

* to provide evidence on which a lender can base their decisions to lend money
* to outline targets for the business to work to
* to plan and outline future expansion implications
* to allow the business to undertake benchmarking against competitors.

Producing a cash-flow forecast requires you to use your budgeted figures that you have already produced and add them into the cash-flow forecast to see when cash deficits may be a problem or when surpluses are likely to arise and may be invested elsewhere. The cash-flow forecast for Bouncing Castles Ltd shown in the following exercise illustrates how the forecast is produced.

Theory into practice

Bouncing Castles Ltd is a new business hiring out bouncy castles for children's parties and fetes. They plan to start trading on 1 May.

* Small castles cost £250 to buy, bouncing slides cost £300 and large castles cost £400. Bouncing Castles Ltd has found a supplier and agreed to buy three of each type on one month's credit during their first month of trading.

* Each castle whether small or large needs approximately £8 for petrol per day. Repairs and other maintenance are expected to cost £5 per castle per month – this includes washing.

* The castles will need to be delivered to homes and schools by van. A suitable van is to be purchased in May costing £2,000. The cost of

tax, maintenance, insurance and fuel for the van is estimated to be £200 per month.

* Only one person is to be employed by the business at a cost of £850 per month.

* Advertising is going to be £100 per month for the first three months and then reduced to £50 per month.

* When the castles are not being used they are to be stored in a lock-up costing £100 per month.

* The hire rate for the castles is £55 per day for a small castle, £60 per day for the bouncing slide and £70 for the large castle. The castles can be used both outside in gardens and inside in halls or homes during the winter months.

Bookings are expected to be as follows.

	SMALL CASTLE	BOUNCING SLIDE	LARGE CASTLE
May	6	10	3
June	10	12	6
July	16	16	10
August	24	20	16
September	10	12	6
October	10	12	6

The cash-flow forecast for six months for Bouncing Castles Ltd is shown below:

	MAY	JUN	JUL	AUG	SEP	OCT
Receipts						
Bank loan	5,000					
Booking receipts	1,140	1,690	2,540	3,640	1,690	1,690
Total receipts	6,140	1,690	2,540	3,640	1,690	1,690
Payments						
Bouncy castle purchase	2,850					
Van purchase	2,000					
Castle petrol costs	152	224	336	480	224	224
Castle repairs and maintenance	75	75	75	75	75	75
Van running costs	200	200	200	200	200	200
Wages	850	850	850	850	850	850
Advertising	100	100	100	50	50	50
Rental of lock-up	100	100	100	100	100	100
Bank loan payment	175	175	175	175	175	175
Total payments	6,502	1,724	1,836	1,930	1,674	1,674
Receipts – payments	(362)	(34)	704	1,710	16	16
Balance b/f	0	(362)	(396)	308	2,018	2,034
Balance c/f	(362)	(396)	308	2,018	2,034	2,050

Produce your own cash-flow forecast for your business using your knowledge from AS level and the example shown for Bouncing Castles Ltd to help you.

Break-even forecasts

Break-even formula

Break-even gives the point at which costs are equal to sales revenue. The break-even point (BEP) can be worked out with the following break-even formula.

$$BEP = \frac{\text{fixed costs}}{\substack{\text{unit contribution} \\ \text{(selling price – variable cost per unit)}}}$$

Calculating break-even allows a business to work out how many products they need to sell before they can actually start to make a profit.

Margin of safety

The margin of safety (MOS) can also be calculated in order to allow the business to work out the amount of units by which sales can fall before the business starts to make a loss. This is calculated with the following formula.

MOS = actual sales in units – BEP in units

Break-even chart

A break-even chart enables a business to identify the following:

* break-even point in sales units and sales revenue
* margin of safety

* amount of profit or loss made at different levels of sales
* the effect of changes in fixed costs, variable costs and selling prices.

The chart displays the revenue and costs at future levels of output and enables the user to identify the break-even point. In Figure 10.25, the break-even output level is 50,000 units. This is when costs = revenue. The margin of safety is 15,000 units. This is the amount of units that the business is making over the break-even output.

Using a break-even chart it is also possible to work out the contribution that a product or service makes to fixed costs. This is worked out in the following way.

Unit contribution = selling price – variable cost

This is useful as it allows individual products or services to be viewed in terms of how much they contribute towards overall overhead costs or indeed if they have a negative contribution and might be losing the business money.

Profit can also be worked out by multiplying the margin of safety by the unit contribution. This is useful when comparing different products or services within the business.

Benefits of break-even analysis

1. It can provide very quick results for display either by hand or on a computer.
2. It can be used to help investors decide whether or not to invest in a small business.
3. It allows small businesses to forecast what might happen to their business if sales go down or costs go up.
4. It is easy to apply with a minimum amount of training needed.

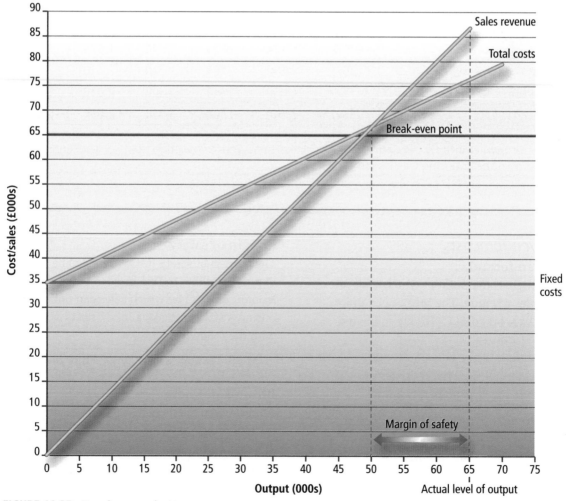

FIGURE 10.25 *Break-even chart*

Limitations of break-even analysis

1. It can oversimplify the situation in terms of pricing as often businesses will offer different prices to different customers, e.g. discounts or trade prices.

2. It is only useful for a short amount of time as both costs and prices may be changing rapidly.

3. It is only as useful as the data that is put into it in terms of future costs and sales.

4. It does not take into account economies of scale (as more products are made the cost per unit starts to reduce at higher levels of output).

5. It may be difficult to use if the business sells a range of different products that cover the fixed costs in differing amounts.

6. It needs to be supported with relevant market research and economic predictions in order to be useful.

7. Fixed costs can change.

Theory into practice

Produce a break-even chart and check your workings using the break-even formula for the following car wash business.

Drip Dry Car Wash

Car wash price = £12.50 per car.
Overhead costs = £175 per week.
Labour costs per wash = £4.50 per car.
Materials and water cost = £1.00 per car.

- Make sure you label your graph in full.
- Drip Dry Car Wash during July averaged 30 cars per week – work out the margin of safety.
- How much profit would Drip Dry Car Wash make if they did 20 car washes during one week and what recommendations would you make to them about this?

Now apply these techniques to your own business – remember break-even can be used for both products and services.

Projected profit and loss accounts

The last two elements of the financial projects are the profit and loss account and balance sheet. These are often referred to as the master budget. The profit and loss account is a useful tool when forecasting your financial future as it can help to justify why the business is worth setting up. It can show the amount of profit that is predicted to be made at the end of a financial year and therefore can help a bank or other lender to decide whether or not it is worth the risk to invest in your business.

The projected profit and loss account is only as accurate as the predictions that are made by the business. You will need to be realistic about the figures that you use and be able to justify them. The projected profit and loss account consists of two halves; the income or sales half that shows all the monies flowing in to the business and the expenses half which shows all the monies flowing out of the business.

	£
Sales	0,000
Less expenses	0,000
Net profit before tax	0,000

The type of profit and loss account that you draw up will depend on whether or not your business has stock as this will need to be shown separately. An example profit and loss account without stock is shown in Figure 10.26 as Akbar's Web Design Consultancy is a service business.

Akbar's Web Design Consultancy – projected profit and loss account		
		£
Sales		19,500
Less expenses:		
Overheads	10,660	
Labour	7,020	17,680
Net profit before tax		1,820

FIGURE 10.26 *An example of a projected profit and loss account without stock*

This is a very simple version of a service-based projected profit and loss account but it does give you an idea of the level of profit that could be made and the way to set out your projected profit and loss account.

If your business has stock you will need to add extra information to your projected profit and loss account. Cost of sales is made up of direct costs such as raw materials including purchases of stock. These costs do not take into account overheads such as rent or insurance. An example of a projected profit and loss account for a fashion boutique is shown in Figure 10.27.

When you are producing your own profit and loss account you will need to consider as many expenses that are relevant to the business as possible.

Start-up balance sheets

The other part of the master budget that you will need to consider is the start-up balance sheet (Figure 10.28). Producing a start-up balance sheet is important because it gives a snap shot of the business showing assets (things a business owns), liabilities (debts a business owes) and equity (the amount invested in the business). Fixed assets are assets that are owned and expected to be retained for one year or more e.g. land, buildings, vehicles or equipment. Current assets are those that can be converted into cash more easily and are only retained for a short time. Producing a start-up balance sheet is important as it shows how the business is going to be financed, either through the investor's own money or through loans from other people known as creditors. Showing the assets of the business also allows the investor to get a snap shot of how much the business is actually worth.

Emma's High Street Fashions – projected profit and loss account for the year ended 31 March

	£	
Sales		150,000
Less cost of sales		
Opening stock	5,000	
Purchases	51,000	
Less closing stock	6,000	50,000
Gross profit		100,000
Less expenses		
Rent and business rates	15,600	
Advertising	2,000	
Wages & salaries	28,000	
Administration	1,000	
Insurance	2,000	
Interest on loans	2,100	
Telephone	600	
Accountancy fees	900	
Legal fees	1,000	
Bank charges	400	
Depreciation	500	
Repairs & maintenance	300	
Heat & light	600	
Miscellaneous	300	
		55,300
Net profit before tax		44,700

FIGURE 10.27 *An example of a projected profit and loss account with stock*

Better Books Ltd Start-Up Balance Sheet 1 April

			£
Fixed assets			
Shop premises			75,000
Fixtures and fittings			<u>5,000</u>
			80,000
Current assets			
Stock		15,000	
Bank		3,000	
Cash		<u>2,000</u>	
		20,000	
Less current liabilities			
Creditors	7,000	<u>7,000</u>	
Working capital			13,000
Total assets less current liabilities			93,000
Financed by			
Long term liabilities			
Bank loan	10,000		
Mortgage	<u>60,000</u>	70,000	
Capital and reserves			
Capital		23,000	
Capital employed			93,000

FIGURE 10.28 *An example of a start-up balance sheet*

Human resource plan

The next stage of your business plan is to outline the human resources needed by the business. The best way to do this is to produce a human resource audit in order to attract and retain the best staff possible (Figure 10.29). You will need to consider the human resource needs that the business has whilst also taking into account the supply of those people and any training issues (Figure 10.29).

Number of employees

The type of business that you choose will influence the number of employees needed. A pest control business may need few specially trained

Which kind of skills and competencies do they need to have?

Are suitably trained people to work for my business available and what is the level of demand for them?

Which are the best methods to recruit appropriate staff?

What are the training needs of these staff in the short term and longer term?

FIGURE 10.29 *Conducting a human resource audit*

employees whereas a service business may need lots of employees answering telephone calls or offering face-to-face advice.

You will also need to a look at the wage budget that you set and the projections for cash-flow and profit and loss so you can work out if you have the finance to pay your employees.

Skills and competencies

The number of employees will depend on the level of skills and competencies required. If specialist employees are needed the business may not be able to afford to employ very many as their hourly rate is likely to be high. Alternatively, if low levels of skills are needed more employees may be employed. Enough appropriately qualified staff are needed to keep the business running if someone is away due to sickness or leaves. Failing to do this can be extremely expensive if the start-up is delayed due to lack of staff. When unemployment is low, the availability of appropriately qualified specialist staff should be considered by producing a cost-benefit analysis.

> High cost of specialist staff
> vs
> Cost of employing non-specialist staff and training them

Either option may be possible but should take into account the type of work that the person is likely to do, and the level of qualifications needed for that job. It is also important to make sure that employees are suitably rewarded both before and during their training. If you opt to train staff you will need to be able to increase their salary after the training or they are likely to leave and take their specialist skills with them!

Producing a job description and person specification for your potential employees will help you to judge the skills and competencies needed.

Theory into practice

Write a job description and a person specification for your business using the examples given below to help you.

JOB DESCRIPTION	
Job title	Retail sales assistant
Responsibilities	The post holder is expected to help with general duties in the shop including cash handling and stock provision • cash handling • operating a cash register • dealing with customers • sorting out and rotating stock • housekeeping within the retail environment • financial record keeping.
Compiled by	J Burgess
Date	8th March 2006

PERSON SPECIFICATION		
Criteria	**Essential**	**Desirable**
Post title	Retail sales assistant	
Qualifications/knowledge	GCSEs in Maths and English plus 3 others at Grade C or above or equivalent.	
Work-related experience	Good customer service skills. Able to work a cash register	Experience in the retail environment
Skills/abilities & special attributes	Good organisational skills. Able to prioritise workloads. Good communications skills. Ability to work flexibly and enthusiastically	Previous experience of a retail environment.

You will need to conduct research into the availability of staff. You may find it useful to look on the Office for National Statistics website for your area (www.ons.gov.uk) to find out what unemployment is like in the area where the business is to be set up and the skills profile of people living in that area. You should also consider the provision of college and other training providers so that if you are unable to find suitably qualified people you can gain access to relevant courses in order to train them.

Alternatives to recruitment may be to outsource work to another organisation or use temporary staff to cover busy periods, for example the use of students in the summer months. If you are going to employ office staff you may wish to use an organisation providing a 'virtual PA' who answers the phone on your behalf but doesn't directly work for you.

A 'virtual PA' can be a useful resource

Recruitment methods

There are many different methods of application when looking to recruit employees (Figure 10.30).

METHOD	PURPOSE	ADVANTAGES	DISADVANTAGES
In person	Applicants go in to the organisation and apply in person. Mostly used by smaller organisations or those that recruit a lot.	Applicant and organisation can meet. Easy to do. Often advertised in the place of work. Only interested people that know the organisation already will apply.	May be difficult to plan for. May not attract the right sort of people. Difficult for the applicant to prepare. May not be able to compare candidates.
By letter	Applicants write a letter about their suitability for a job and send it in to the organisation by post or fax.	Gives the organisation the ability to compare. Allows applicants to demonstrate their suitability for the job.	Applicants are likely to only show their strengths and not weaknesses. Not in a standard format. The post may take a long time or get lost. A fax can be read by others so may not be kept confidential.
Curriculum Vitae (CV)	Applicants write all their details including education and history on a two-page sheet including referees.	The organisation can see in one go everything about an applicant.	CVs only focus on positive aspects of an applicant. May have been used to apply for lots of jobs so may not be specific to a particular role.
Telephone	Applicants call a number and notes are made about them. Sometimes tests are also done on the applicants to try to work out their personality type.	Can be used for large numbers of applicants as the information can be put into a database and can be sorted. Allows the applicant to speak to someone from the organisation and ask questions.	The telephone may be busy or engaged and good applicants never get through. They may involve using an automated service so applicants may be put off or may not operate outside office hours.
Application form	All applications are the same with standard questions and boxes to be completed.	Easy for the organisation to compare candidates. Will only ask questions and information that the organisation asks for.	Paper-based forms may take time and money to be sent out. Forms will need to be processed and put into a system to compare them. This may take a long time.

FIGURE 10.30 *Job application methods*

Follow-ups to the chosen method of job application may include interviews, selection activities (a number of activities are organised for applicants to complete and you can judge them on the basis of their performance) or a trial period of employment.

Training needs of employees

If you are employing untrained staff you will need to offer them training in order to make them effective workers in your business in both the short and longer term. When employees start work with a business whether they are experienced or not they are going to need some form of on-the-job training about the individual way your business operates.

In the longer term you may wish to send them on specialist courses to enhance or update their skills. A beauty therapist opening a new salon may wish to employ a part-time apprentice to be trained up. In the short term, training is likely to be on-the-job learning about bookings, cleaning up and generally assisting. In the long term, there will be further training and the opportunity to gain certification in beauty therapy qualifications.

A useful way to work out the training needed is to conduct a training needs analysis. To do this you will need to compare the skills and competencies employees have now compared with what you want them to have in the short or long term. The gap between now and the future is the training that is required.

Theory into practice

Produce a human resources audit for your business.

- Which skills can you offer the business?
- How many employees are needed?
- Do the employees need specialist skills?
- Are specially trained employees available to work in this business?
- How much does it cost to employ suitably trained people?
- How much do suitable training courses cost?

10.2.3 Appropriate research for a business plan

In this unit you have been made aware of the importance of collecting relevant research. The higher the quality of the information and research, the more realistic and appropriate your business plan is likely to be.

Primary research

You have already learned the importance of collecting primary research within your marketing plan, such as questionnaires, focus groups or surveys to collect information to inform your pricing or promotional strategies.

Primary research can also be used to inform other parts of your business plan. You may choose to interview business people who can help you write your business plan or competitors in similar businesses who may give you some tips or ideas such as bank managers, business advisers or fellow learners. You will need to get as much first hand feedback as you can about your business idea and the data contained within it if you are planning to work towards higher grade achievement.

Secondary research

The secondary research you collect will be used to provide you with financial data or with a comparison so you can, for example, benchmark against competitors. There are lots of sources of data available both on websites and case studies (see page 64). You have also learned a number of business tools that you can apply to your idea including Ansoff matrix, Boston matrix and product life cycle. It is important that you cover the following areas within your research to give it the breadth and depth of information that you need for higher grade achievement:

* marketing tools
* websites
* case studies
* exemplar business plans
* government statistics

* databases
* newspaper articles.

You should also remember to include statistical techniques and marketing models that you used at AS level to demonstrate your understanding within the business plan.

It is important that you identify and quote relevant sources clearly in order that your assessor can go back and check the validity of those sites. Government and academic institutions publish websites ending in gov.uk or ac.uk so it is likely that the data on these sites is going to be correct. Be critical of your sources and if some data published on a website appears to be incorrect it probably is and don't rely on it.

Key information

Your plan needs to be targeted and focused on what you want to achieve. The more specific it is to the needs of the business, the better.

You will be assessed on your analysis and interpretation of research so it is important that you demonstrate clear links, applied to all areas of the plan including financial, marketing and production information, between the data in your business plan and the research that you have collected. To get higher level achievement you need to demonstrate clear understanding and any limitations/constraints on your plan. A number of different sources of evidence and tools and highly detailed evidence should also be used.

You will also need to make in-depth judgements about the constraints on your plan by giving logical conclusions. This will require your plan to be well organised and written in a way that the reader can follow your reasoning logically. You will need to draw out and prioritise key themes from your research and then bring those together at the end in your conclusion.

Theory into practice

Ask a member of your class to read through your draft business plan and be constructive about ways it can be improved. Use the following checklist to help you.

IS THE PLAN...?	YES	NO	COMMENT
Is the plan clear with good reasoning?			
Is the plan well presented?			
Does the plan contain a wide variety of evidence?			
Does the plan contain detailed evidence?			
Is the plan clearly targeted to the new business needs?			
Is the plan clearly analysed with strengths and weaknesses or research?			
Does the plan contain clearly referenced data?			
Does the plan show understanding of relevant issues?			
Does the plan describe relevant constraints?			
Does the plan contain few, if any, errors of spelling, grammar and punctuation?			
Is the plan comprehensive with logical conclusions?			
Any other comments or improvements that could be made			

10.2.4 Business plan templates

It is important to do research into standard templates to present your plan, as the layout and template you use for your plan will ensure that your work looks as professional as possible. Lots of institutions including banks, government bodies and providers of grants for small businesses provide templates to help entrepreneurs to present their business plan. There are a number of standard business templates available from websites such as Barclays Bank (Figure 10.31), Royal Bank of Scotland (Figure 10.32) and Microsoft.

Competitor Comparison Table

	My business	Competitor A	Competitor B	Competitor C
Product/service				
Price				
Availability				
Reputation				
Delivery				

FIGURE 10.31 *Extract from Barclays Bank business plan template (www.barclays.co.uk)*

Products and services

Our products/services will be as follows:
Describe your products or services here, in greater detail than you did on page 2.

FIGURE 10.32 *Extract from Royal Bank of Scotland business plan template (www.rbs.co.uk)*

Microsoft also produce a standard range of templates that can be freely downloaded from www.office.microsoft.com by searching for business start-up plans.

When you are formatting your plan, whether you use a standardised template or not, you need to make sure you consider six key factors:

* format requirement, e.g. layout of the plan
* appropriate level of language used
* clarity of information
* accuracy of grammar and spelling
* font styles and sizes
* use of graphics.

Format

The format of the plan including the layout is the first impression of the business. Remember you will need to include information on the following areas:

* a description of the business
* its aims and objectives
* its products or services
* its marketing plan
* its financial predictions
* appendices.

If the plan does not flow, with appropriate sections, or looks muddled, investors reading the plan will think the business will be run in the same way and not have confidence in it. Make sure you include a list of sources of your information and that you appropriately reference information you have collected. This avoids any type of confusion between your work and the work of others. Using someone else's work as your own is known as plagiarism and this is definitely not allowed within your coursework.

Language

The language that you use in the plan is also critical. It is a formal document that is going to be used by investors to decide whether or not you are a good risk as an entrepreneur. This means it should be written in a business-like manner appropriate for a bank manager to read.

Clarity

Making your plan clear and easy to follow is critical with explanations of any relevant issues, analysis and logical conclusions. Remember your conclusions must be based on data that you have presented and not include new information at the last minute.

Accuracy

Grammar and spelling are critical to give the right impression. Watch out for common errors like their/there/they're and typing mistakes like 'buisness' (business) or 'comitment' (commitment). Use the spell checker carefully and check words using a dictionary if necessary. Ask members of your class or teaching staff to help you if you are not sure.

Font and graphics

You will need to choose a suitable business style font for your typed work or, if you need to write by hand, your best handwriting and written in a clear style. Graphics, tables, charts or graphs can add extra depth and understanding to your plan if done well. Make sure graphs are used with appropriate labelling and explanation. Be critical about why such information is in your plan – if you are not sure why it is there … leave it out. Appendices at the end of your plan are useful for data that you collect as part of your primary or secondary research.

Theory into practice

Research at least three different business plan templates from a range of sources.

Examine each plan and produce a list of strengths and weaknesses of each. Consider the strengths of all of the plans and the weaknesses.

Now consider whether to use a pre-prepared template for your business or whether you should use an adapted model or one constructed by you.

10.2.5 Constraints that impact on implementation

Within the marketing section of the business plan you have already considered a PEST analysis and its influence on the marketing of the product or service. It is also important to consider constraints that might affect the business as a whole and specifically the context within which the business is working. You should be able to demonstrate awareness of constraints relating to a number of different areas including:

* legal
* financial
* social
* environmental
* technological
* competitive.

Legal

Legal changes are happening on a daily basis and therefore can have a huge influence on what is happening within your business. Health and safety legislative changes may increase costs or force working practices to change. This is particularly important when considering new businesses such as those operated online.

Changes to the minimum wage paid per hour or maximum working week permitted also need to be considered. Relevant legislation should be taken into account including consumer protection law such as the Sale of Goods Act or Trade Description Act.

You will need to take into account the legal influences that are relevant for your business. What is happening within that business context from a legal point of view in terms of

* health and safety?
* employment law?
* consumer protection?
* European Union law?
* any other relevant laws?

CASE STUDY

Party Gaming

Party Gaming is a form of online gaming service including online poker that was floated on the London Stock Exchange in June 2005. As the company was listed as being worth £4.8 billion it was estimated to be the largest flotation on the London Stock Exchange in the previous five years. Party Gaming was launched at a time when online gambling was becoming more and more popular and large amounts of money could be made.

Most of Party Gaming's players at the time of the flotation were in the US (90 per cent) and there are concerns that both America and Canada may make online gaming illegal as it is difficult to regulate and takes place across US borders and even between different countries worldwide. If online gambling becomes illegal Party Gaming may have to cease trading. This is an example of an external influence that can make a profitable business go out of business because of changes in the law.

✓ 1. Describe the new legal implication for Party Gaming and the possible reasons for this change in the law.

✓✓ 2. Analyse the benefits and problems that governments may encounter if they ban online gaming.

✓✓✓ 3. To what extent has online trading made it more difficult to legally regulate businesses operating in the UK and abroad?

Financial

Financial constraints have a big influence on the likely success of your business. The ability to get access to cost-effective finance will affect the likelihood of success. You will need to consider any assets that could be used as security to finance the business, the speed of service that the financier can offer and the convenience of the investment itself – is the money accessible quickly and easily in the short term or does it involve lengthy meetings, procedures and several credit checks before the offer of finance can be made? The status of your business will affect how easily you can access money and the rate of interest at which any loan is offered. You will also need to consider any finances that you might be able to invest in the business yourself.

The failure rate for small businesses is quoted as being as high as three out of four in some industries and many of these fail because of financial constraints. Cash-flow is often a root cause of financial constraints as money is invested in provided goods or services but payment follows some time later. Profitable businesses can become insolvent if their cash-flow is not good.

Social

The business will need to consider how socially responsible it is and the effect on stakeholder groups such as consumers, the local community and staff.

You will need to consider benefits and issues surrounding your suppliers. Is it better to choose a supplier who treats their employees more ethically and uses recycled materials or are you profit-driven and do not mind how your raw materials are produced? How will such issues enhance or constrain your business? What effect might there be on your reputation?

Trends in people's lifestyles or tastes may be important. Supermarkets have moved towards providing a 'one-stop shop' service for their customers. Such changes are likely to have a negative impact on trade for high street shops and smaller businesses unless they can offer something different that will keep people coming back to them.

There may be a social impact on your business from pressure groups – does your business use ingredients that can be produced in more than one way such as battery or free range eggs? If you choose to use battery eggs it may be possible to keep prices low but risk bad publicity. If you use free range as part of your marketing strategy, is the extra cost worth the benefit?

Demographic changes may constrain your business. There are more working parents than ever before so the need for devices such as dishwashers, ironing and home cleaning services has increased. The make-up of the population is changing: the Office for National Statistics predicts (March 2005) that by 2015 there will be more people in the UK aged 65 and over than there will be children under 16. If your business' target market is young people how might this affect your business? Is there a gap in the aged 65+ market for your product or service? The number of adults termed as obese increased dramatically between 1993 and 2003 (males from 13 per cent to 23 per cent and females from 16 per cent to 23 per cent). Is your business related to the food industry and what impact might government campaigns to reduce obesity have on your business?

CASE STUDY

CO-OP FOOD RETAILER

The Co-Op food retailer calls itself 'The responsible retailer'. It is one of the largest sellers of Fair Trade products and campaigns to improve the treatment of people and animals and to reduce the amount of additives and flavourings contained in foods. The Co-Op was one of the first supermarkets to support the RSPCA's freedom food scheme whereby farmers have to meet minimum standards of care for their animals. The Co-Op is also campaigning to improve the labelling of foods to make clearer what is actually contained in foods we eat with a scheme called Honest Labelling.

For more information about the Co-Op see www.co-op.co.uk.

✓ 1. Describe the gap in the market that the Co-Op is aiming to fill with its Honest Labelling campaign.

✓✓ 2. How might pressure groups have affected the Co-Op's decision to offer a wider variety of Fair Trade and animal friendly products?

✓✓✓ 3. Judge the importance of social trends and demographic changes on a business like the Co-Op.

Environmental

Environmental constraints may also have social and legal constraints attached to them. Is your business constrained by the need to recycle its waste and what effect does production have on the environment as a whole? If you are a cleaning business, are you constrained by the need to use appropriate materials and chemicals to protect the environment and what are the consequences for others if you don't in both the short and longer term? How is your business constrained in terms of its distribution and the associated effect of pollution from cars or planes? Being environmentally sensitive should be looked at in conjunction with social impacts because what may be seen to be environmentally sensitive may seem more insensitive in terms of people. Wind-powered electricity generators provide an environmentally sensitive source of electricity for an area but have been accused of causing noise and spoiling the landscape in communities.

CASE STUDY

Phone and radio masts

There have recently been a number of campaigns against radio and phone masts being sited in areas of natural beauty or in residential areas. Phone and radio masts have also been criticised because of the possible link to cancers for people living near them. There is some debate about whether this link is proven or not and therefore phone companies are keen to press ahead with plans for expansion. With the number of people owning mobile telephones increasing and the need to support networks throughout the UK there is a need to increase the number of masts. The public want mobile phones but often want the masts outside their own area – this is known as NIMBY (not in my back yard). Phone companies like Orange have tried to minimise the impact where possible and in fact have introduced a solar and wind powered transmitter in Wales to try to be as environmentally friendly as possible.

Have a debate in your classroom on the construction of a new mobile phone mast in your area. Select one third of the class to represent local people, another third to represent the mobile telephone companies and the final third to vote at the end of the debate.

You will all need to conduct research into mobile phone masts before the debate and be able to discuss the issues in full. More information about phone masts can be obtained from www.ofcom. org.uk and www.mastaction.co.uk.

You will need to consider what is happening in terms of environmental influences now during the start-up of the business and the trends that are happening in the business context for the future by accessing information from agencies such as the Environment Agency.

Technological

Trends in technology are another influence. The World Wide Web has meant people can increasingly order goods and services without leaving their homes. You will need to consider constraints that technology may place on your new business in relation to accessing customers, distribution and meeting demand. Meeting demand may be a constraint in terms of your ability to meet fluctuating and excess demands. Amazon.co.uk were criticised for not being able to fully meet demand in December 2004 as more customers ordered products from their website than they expected. This left customers frustrated that presents were not going to be delivered in time for Christmas and Amazon received bad publicity in the newspapers as a result.

You may also be constrained technologically due to the level of finance that you have available. For example, if you are making extensive use of information technology (IT) you may be constrained by your own IT skills and the availability of web designers and software specialists.

You will need to consider how reliant you are on an employee who has written a programme for your business and what the effect of them leaving your business might be.

Protecting your ideas for software, designs, music or text relates to intellectual property and you may need to consider the constraints that protecting such ideas have on your business.

Competitive

Competitive influences have three perspectives; direct competition (same context), indirect competition and European/international competition. Tools such as market maps (see page 65) can be used to analyse competitive constraints, for example Porter's Model of Five Competitive Forces.

Indirect competition comes from ways that your customers might spend money other than with you, for example customers of a bowling alley spending their money on going to the cinema instead is a form of indirect competition.

You may also wish to consider the influence of international competition on your business and include information about influences such as the rate of the pound against other relevant currencies, interest rates and skills levels and costs of employees in different countries.

For each of these constraints on implementation you will need to discuss and make judgements about how your business is likely to be affected.

FORCE	
Entry of competitors	How easy is it for a new firm to enter your market?
	Do any barriers exist e.g. technology or expertise?
Threat of substitutes	How easy is it to get a similar product to ours?
	Are there many cheaper?
Bargaining power of buyers	How powerful are the buyers? Can they work together to buy in bulk and benefit from economies of scale?
Bargaining power of suppliers	How powerful are the sellers?
	Are there lots of suppliers or is there a virtual monopoly
Rivalry	Is there a lot of rivalry between existing businesses in this market?
	Is any one company a dominating force or is everyone equal?

FIGURE 10.33 *Porter's model of five competitive forces*

Tips for writing a business plan

When you have completed your business plan in full it is important to get a second opinion on it. Ask a friend, bank manager or your teacher to give their constructive opinion on it. The following top tips should be used as a checklist to ensure your business plan is successful:

* Make sure all your information is clearly presented and easily understood.

* Don't overestimate what your business is likely to achieve in terms of sales or profits – be as realistic as possible.

* Make sure you include suitable references to back up your analysis and evaluation – you need to show clear, justified thinking throughout.

* Get as much advice and opinion as you possibly can – someone else will always see an error that you haven't.

Knowledge check

1. Describe six reasons why a business needs to write a business plan.

2. What is the difference between aims and objectives?

3. Describe what are meant by the product life cycle and Boston matrix models.

4. What does SMART mean when referring to objectives?

5. Describe two advantages and disadvantages of using a venture capitalist to gain funding for your business.

6. In questionnaire design, what is the difference between semantic and Likert scaling?

7. What is meant by economies of scale?

8. Describe the stages of production for a made-to-order sandwich shop.

9. What are the strengths of using random sampling compared to quota sampling?

10. Describe six sources of secondary data that could help an entrepreneur set up a business and state why they are useful.

11. What is meant by diversification in business?

12. Describe the advantages and disadvantages of three potential source of finance in relation to your business.

13. What is a market map useful for and how can it be used to shape the business plan?

14. Analyse three different pricing strategies that could be used in your business plan.

15. What are the advantages of using Porter's Model of Five Competitive Forces to help shape a business plan?

16. Name three marketing tools that can be used to inform a business plan. Give a judgement about which you think is the most useful to an entrepreneur and why.

17. Describe the limitations of product life cycle theory when products involved in rapidly changing technology are used by a business e.g. personal computers.

18. 'Primary research is more important than secondary research as part of a business plan.' Discuss the extent to which you think this is true.

19. Judge the suitability of allowing a tolerance of 5 per cent for defects in a hairdressing business.

20. 'Environmental constraints are likely to be the biggest influence on businesses in the future'. Discuss the extent to which you think this is true and how environmental constraints are likely to influence business planning now and in the future.

Resources

Books

Blackwell, E (2004) *How to Prepare a Business Plan (Sunday Times Business Enterprises)*, Kogan Page

Butler, D (2000) *Business Planning: A guide to small business start-up*, Butterworth-Heinemann

Dransfield, R et al (2004) *BTEC National Business*, Heinemann

Friend, G (2004) *Guide to Business Planning*, Profile

McMullan, D (2002) *Be Your Own Boss*, Kogan Page

Proctor, T (2000) *Essentials of Marketing Research*, Prentice Hall

Journals

Business Review
Marketing
Marketing Week

Websites

Some useful websites are listed below. These addresses are current at the time of writing. However, it needs to be recognised that new sites are being launched on the Internet on a regular basis and that older sites may change or disappear.

www.allbusiness.com
Small business resource centre

www.bankofengland.co.uk
Bank of England financial data

www.bankofscotlandbusiness.co.uk
Bank of Scotland including templates

www.bgateway.com
Business Gateway start up information

www.bized.ac.uk
Bized business education site

www.biz-in-a-box.co.uk
New business start-up site

www.blackcircles.com
Site of tyre entrepreneur for useful ideas

www.bplans.org.uk
Business planning site

www.businesslink.gov.uk
Government supported business planning site

www.businessplanhelp.co.uk
Tips and ideas for business planning

www.businessplans.org
Sample plans and business planning ideas

www.chamberonline.co.uk
Chamber of Commerce Online

www.dti.gov.uk
Department of Trade and Industry

www.ehow.com
Form of search engine with links to business information

www.entrepreneur.com
Hints and tips for starting up your business

www.environment-agency.gov.uk
Environment Agency

www.ethicalexplorer.org
Ideas for social impact on stakeholders

www.glassesdirect.co.uk
Award winning business entrepreneur – glasses direct

www.hsbc.co.uk
HSBC bank

www.morebusiness.com
Entrepreneurial top tip site

www.shell-livewire.org
New business start up site aimed at 16–30 year olds

www.smallbusinessadvice.org.uk
Small business advice centre

www.smallbusinessnotes.com
Business information including sample plans

www.socialfirms.co.uk
Campaign group formed to increase corporate responsibility

www.statistics.gov.uk
Government economics and statistics

www.tso.co.uk
The Stationery Office document publishers

www.webtrends.co.uk
Provides analysis of trends in web usage

www.youngentrepreneur.com
Young entrepreneurial support

Managerial and supervisory roles

This unit contains five elements:

11.2.1 The business context within which the report will take shape

11.2.2 Planning how to gather information for the report

11.2.3 Researching into the business context and analysis of the information that is collected

11.2.4 Production of a report

11.2.5 Evaluation of the factors which can influence the environment in which a manager/supervisor performs her/his role

This optional unit requires you to write a report on the role and skills of *one manager or supervisor*. You will need to conduct research and provide detailed analysis on that role taking into account their business environment including stakeholders.

Primary and secondary research should be included such as work shadowing, interviewing (primary) or management theories and functions (secondary) to investigate the tasks that your supervisor or manager performs.

A **supervisor** is generally a more junior role of management overseeing what others are doing e.g. a supervisor in McDonalds in charge of a team in the kitchen. They tend to get paid less money and have less status and responsibility than more senior managers.

Managers can differ considerably e.g. a manager in charge of a retail shop may have only one or two staff whereas a store manager in a hypermarket may be responsible for 600 staff.

Key terms

A *manager* is someone who does the planning, organising, motivating, monitoring and directing, problem solving, training and mentoring and appraising of employees that work for them.

A *supervisor* is someone who watches over a person or activity to make sure everything is done accurately and safely.

11.2.1 The business context within which the report will take shape

To understand the role you have chosen to study, you will need to demonstrate an understanding of the common tasks and functions that are undertaken by people with this role. Managers and supervisors often have a range of tasks that are performed in different ways from organisation to organisation but there are a common set that most of them will do. These are known as common functions (Figure 11.1).

Each of these functions will be explored in detail taking into account other variables that affect them including:

* culture of the organisation
* objectives of the organisation
* structure of the organisation
* availability of resources within the organisation.

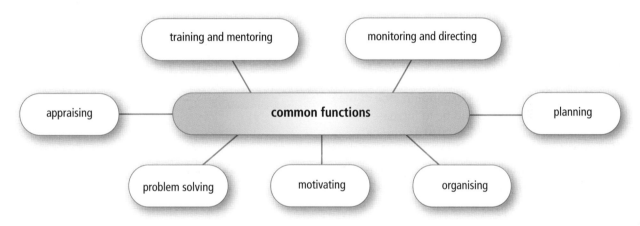

FIGURE 11.1 *Common functions of managers and supervisors*

Culture of the organisation

This means 'the way we do things around here'. Culture is the set of values that the organisation has developed over time. It might be how managers speak to each other, for example by calling each other by first names or by their title such as Mr, or it might be whether or not people are expected to stay late in the office on a Friday or go early.

Culture is about what is expected of an employee or manager by that organisation and how they should behave. Some cultures are positive where employees are encouraged to make comments, get involved and they feel valued at work. Other cultures are negative where employees feel unable to have their say or feel criticised. There

may be problems with industrial relations in such organisations with strikes or industrial action. There are four main types of culture that have been identified by researchers.

* Power culture – the culture is dominated by one or a few individuals who make decisions for the whole organisation.
* Role culture – where the culture is influenced by the roles that people are specified to do, they work to rules that they must follow.
* Task culture – where the culture is dominated by the tasks that people need to perform. Teams may develop as a result of the task so this culture can be useful for problem solving

* Person culture – when people are able to express themselves and make their own decisions.

Objectives of the organisation

The objectives of the organisation are the plans that an organisation will set out in order to achieve their overall aims.

Aims of an organisation are the very purpose or goal of why that organisation exists, for example:

* to make a profit
* to expand the organisation
* to survive as an organisation
* to promote awareness.

Objectives help to support those aims by breaking them down in to achievable plans. If an organisation has the aim of expanding, one of the management objectives could be to increase sales by 15 per cent each year until 2010 or to increase the workforce by 5 per cent each year through new recruitment until 2007. A nightclub manager might have the aim to expand the business and set the objective of spending 10 per cent more on advertising during 2007 to attract more customers. To be effective, objectives should be SMART (specific, measurable, agreed, realistic and time-constrained).

Think it over...

You will need to consider the aims and objectives of the organisation you are studying and how they have been and are being set.

Structure of the organisation

The structure of an organisation will also have a profound effect on the way that managers/supervisors operate. Structures can be categorised into three main types: flat, hierarchical and matrix (Figure 11.2). The **chain of command** and flow of messages will influence the role of a manager.

Key terms

Chain of command means the communication path that goes from the most senior manager down to the most junior employees. A long chain of command means that the message may get altered on the way down.

STRUCTURE	FEATURES
Hierarchical	• Many layers and management levels. • Resembles a pyramid – few people at top and many at the bottom. • Specialist departments. • Vertical communication. • Lengthy communication from the top down. • Long chain of command.
Flat	• Few layers. • Fewer management levels. • Fast flowing communication from the top to the bottom. • Short chain of command.
Matrix	• Links are made between different departments. • Project teams are set up to complete tasks. • May need complex management skills to manage specialist managers from a variety of areas.

FIGURE 11.2 *Structures in organisations*

The type of structure that exists in an organisation will also influence the culture of that organisation. A hierarchical organisation is likely to have a power culture as a few senior managers will make decisions for the majority of employees. A matrix structure is more likely to have a task culture as teams are brought together for specific projects.

Availability of resources within the organisation

Resources are a key issue for all organisations whether they are profit or non-profit making. The availability of resources whether they are financial, technological or human will expand or constrain the ability of a manager to do their job.

An organisation with a limited budget is likely to operate management techniques that involve cost cutting or trying to increase the productivity of workers as much as possible. An organisation that has a lot of resources available is likely to invest in new machinery and therefore need to employ additional staff or undertake training. The availability of resources will be influenced by the culture, objectives and structure within the organisation. It is important for you to make links between these and the other common functions of management that are now further explored.

Planning

Planning is an important part of a management role and takes several different forms. You will need to consider the influence of organisational culture, objectives, structure and resources on planning. The four main types of planning discussed within this chapter are:

* strategic planning
* action planning
* tactical planning
* contingency planning.

The effect of resources and culture on planning

Each type of planning works in a slightly different way but all aim to plan the future of the organisation and the best use of resources within that organisation. Resources don't just refer to machinery, building or access to finance; it is also about trying to plan for human resource needs and the management of costs.

The culture of the organisation affects planning and can be a real asset if it is forward thinking and open to new concepts such as a task culture. However, it can hold it back if managers tend to look at what has happened in the past rather than what is going to happen in the future such as a power culture.

The effect of structure on planning

The structure of the organisation may also constrain or promote planning as a very hierarchical organisation is more likely to require plans to be discussed at different levels by lots of different managers whereas a flatter structure may allow this to take place more quickly. Within your report you will need to link all of these areas together.

Think it over...

Consider the role of the manager or supervisor you are investigating. Does their organisational structure help or hinder planning? How does organisational culture affect their planning? What are the benefits of the structure in terms of planning for them? How does planning affect the availability of resources?

Strategic planning

Longer term planning is often referred to as **strategic planning.** It is where senior managers work out the direction of the organisation and how they want things to progress in the longer term. Strategic planning has four key elements to it and these form a cycle whereby plans are made and then reviewed (Figure 11.3).

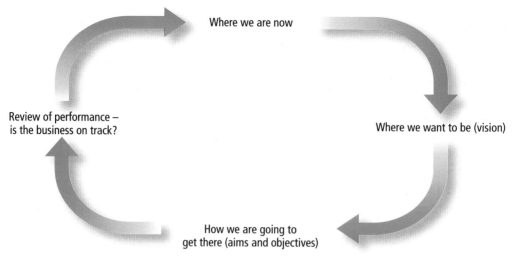

FIGURE 11.3 *The four parts of the strategic planning cycle*

Strategic planning gives more of a direction or feel for where the organisation wants to go in the future but does not in the first stages necessarily give specific data about how this is actually going to be put into place. Strategic planning gives an outline so that aims and objectives can be put into place. Once agreed, they can be cascaded down the organisation's hierarchy and be converted into specific targets and duties to be carried out. You will need to collect information about the influence of your manager or supervisor on strategic planning as well as the influence of culture, objectives, structure and resources on the organisation.

> **Key terms**
>
> *Strategic planning* is the process of working out a vision (future idea) of where the business wants to be and how it is going to get there, including reviews.

CASE STUDY

Marks and Spencer

Marks and Spencer have had a number of difficulties since the 1990s. During the 1990s there was a decline in sales which made trading much more difficult for the company. Between 2001 and 2003, Luc Vandervale was Chairman and profits grew again. However, when he left Marks and Spencer in 2004 profits declined again and in May 2005 profits (pre tax and pre exceptional items) fell from £805m in 2004 to £618.5m, a drop of 19%. Whilst many other retailers found the 2004/5 year a difficult year of trading and saw a reduction in sales, 19% was particularly unfavourable. Some of this reduction in profits was suggested to be the result of price cutting in order to shift excess stock so that Marks and Spencer could refresh their image.

One of the criticisms of Marks and Spencer in the past is that it has lacked strategic direction and neglected some of its core customers. In 2004 the Chief Executive, Stuart Rose, announced that the new strategy would give Marks and Spencer back to its customers by concentrating on the 11 million women who have traditionally shopped there.

Using information from the case study and research of your own, answer the following questions.

✓ 1. **Outline two problems for Marks and Spencer over the past 15 or so years.**
✓ 2. **What might 'lacked strategic direction' mean?**
✓✓ 3. **What are the advantages and disadvantages to Marks and Spencer of using the strategic planning cycle?**
✓✓✓ 4. **Consider Marks and Spencer's business performance today and give a judgement about the effectiveness of the new strategy.**

Action planning

Action planning is very important because it takes the aims and objectives outlined by the business and turns them into actions that will happen on a daily, weekly, monthly or annual basis. Action planning gives managers the ability to review progress and in the shorter term to see how things are going and make changes if necessary.

A manager will produce a list of actions that they want to achieve during a week and delegate them to their **subordinates** to make sure they take place. Action planning may be especially important if seasonal changes or festivals affect the business you have chosen to study. A manager of an ice cream parlour will be busier in the summer months than the winter and needs to plan for this by having larger numbers of staff in the summer or doing additional promotions in the winter to encourage people to eat ice cream all year round.

Tactical planning

Tactical planning is another form of planning that responds to what is happening in the environment around the business. It is used to respond to changes that are happening more quickly and that may not have been so well planned for. Strategic planning dictates where the company wants to go

Some companies use short-term tactics to help their long-term strategy

but tactical planning is often a reaction to what a competitor is doing, for example by offering special discounts or incentives. You may have noticed that if one petrol station in your area reduces prices, others do the same so they don't lose business. For an independent petrol station with less access to funding, tactics like this may force them out of business if they cannot compete.

Large companies sometimes use this tactic to try to reduce competition in their area by making trading more difficult and then will put up prices when their own position is more established. The success of tactical planning will depend on the culture, objectives, structure and resources that are available to the organisation.

CASE STUDY

ASDA

Asda supermarket's strategy is to become the UK's number one family shopping chain. Families, in general, like to buy low-cost products and so tactical pricing is used to try to attract them to shop at Asda.

When other supermarkets use low-cost incentives such as half-price offers, Asda often allow their customers to also benefit from these prices in their stores by price matching the goods. This tactic keeps customers shopping at Asda even though they may temporarily reduce profits.

Another tactic that Asda use is to display goods in trolleys in their entrance hall giving a price comparison with other supermarkets to show how much is saved by shopping at Asda.

As supermarket retailing is a very competitive and lucrative market it is important for Asda managers to employ as many tactics as possible and to update them in order to respond and overtake their competitors at a national and local level.

✓ 1. What other tactical planning do you think is, or could be, used in Asda stores or another supermarket retailer that you know well?

✓✓ 2. Analyse the strengths and weaknesses of using such tactical planing.

✓✓✓ 3. 'Price is the most important element of supermarket tactical planning.' Discuss this view and judge the extent to which you agree or disagree.

Contingency planning

Some managers will have the responsibility for planning what needs to happen in the event of an emergency. Producing a plan like this is known as a **contingency plan** and will provide details about

what the organisation should do in the event of a major incident like a fire or a bomb.

Most international banks have back-up systems in place in at least two separate offices worldwide or have a specified area that employees can work from if there is an emergency.

Contingency planning is about judging what should be done in an emergency situation. It is not possible to plan and manage every possible situation that might happen but trying to deal with as many scenarios as possible is important.

The extent to which contingency planning will be successful will depend on the culture within the organisation. A power culture where decisions are made centrally should support such planning as long as resources are made available to provide adequate back up.

Key terms

Contingency plans give details of the back-up plans that an organisation will follow in the event of an emergency.

Organising

Organising staff and other resources is one of the duties that a manager must undertake. Having made plans about what needs to be achieved, the next step in management is actually making sure that all the right resources are put into place so that these plans are actually achieved. Organising is about working out who is best placed to do which tasks and how the work is going to be divided out.

A good manager will make sure that the workload is spread evenly so that everyone gets their fair share. A manager will have to ensure that everyone knows what they are doing and are working together as necessary. Organising can take many different forms. It may be organising raw materials to be delivered to a factory or organising staff rotas for shift workers. A well-organised manager will be more effective and be able to help their team more. A disorganised manager will give the impression of chaos!

Badly organised managers give a poor impression to staff

Look at each of the ten statements below. Decide to what extent you agree you are like each of the statements.

STATEMENT	VERY LIKE ME	A BIT LIKE ME	NOT LIKE ME	VERY UNLIKE ME
1. I always prioritise my workload by doing the most important things first.				
2. I often write lists and accomplish all the tasks listed.				
3. I accurately work out how much time a task involves to be able to organise my day.				
4. I keep a paper or online diary to help me organise future events.				
5. I always wear a watch and arrive on time.				
6. I make use of an 'in and out tray' in my working environment so I can see the progress I am making.				
7. I often complete tasks required of me early (reports or assignments).				
8. I only ever touch a piece of paper that comes in to my working environment once, I either deal with it or bin it!				
9. If I have any spare time such as waiting for a bus I keep a notebook and jot ideas down about what I am going to do next.				
10. I reward myself for getting a job well done.				

When you have completed the table compare your results with someone else in the group. Make a note of any statements where you have answered 'not like me' or 'very unlike me' as these are areas that you should consider working on in order to become a more organised person.

If it is possible, you may wish to give this simple evaluation to the manager your are investigating to gain some idea of how they work. Any statements to which they reply 'not like me' or 'very unlike me' could be followed up for more information about their role. For example, if the manager you are studying answers 'very unlike me' to statement two (I often write lists and accomplish all the tasks listed) you may be able to ask them:

- what affects their ability to do this?
- why don't they use lists?
- how do they make sure they accomplish all the tasks they need to?

Think of any other ways that managers can be seen to be more organised and make judgements about the extent to which this is possible.

Motivating

Motivating staff is an essential part of management and there are a number of theorists who have researched how this should be done. These are:

* Taylor
* Maslow
* Mayo
* Herzberg.

Motivation means the influences on and within people that encourage and sustain them to work to the best of their ability – the 'will to work'. The extent to which the employee can feel motivated in the workplace will be influenced by the culture and techniques that managers use to improve motivation within their workforce. Improving motivation will mean that employees are happier in their jobs and this should increase **productivity**. Motivated and productive employees are more likely to make higher quality products, answer more telephone calls or give better customer satisfaction. This should lead to a better company image and, in profit-making companies increased sales, hopefully leading to bigger profits. In non-profit making organisations, having a motivated workforce should lead to a better return, e.g. improved service for the same amount of money.

Key terms

Productivity is the measurement of how much work an employee is actually doing in the time they are employed.

Taylor (scientific management)

Frederick Taylor studied motivation at the Bethlehem Steel Company in the USA in the late 1800s. He believed that there was a more efficient way for employees of the Steel Company to work. He worked out that 21.5 pounds (10 kilos) of weight was the best weight of material for an employee to lift in order to work to their best and that all employees should be given targets of material to be moved in order to earn their wages. He suggested that the role of management was to decide what a worker should do, how they should do it and when. Taylor put forward the case that workers were only motivated by money so work must be linked to payment. A manager should motivate a worker by using pay as an incentive and threaten them with less money or the sack if they did not work to the best of their ability. Using Taylorist principles, the more an employee worked the greater their pay, and the less they worked the less they got paid. This type of payment scheme is also known as **piece rate** which means that an employee is paid per piece of work that they do, for example a hairdresser getting paid per hair cut or a tailor per suit. Henry T Ford, the famous car producer, used Taylor's method of motivation to mass produce Ford cars in the early 1900s.

The positive side of motivation solely by money is that the more you produce, the better your pay but this can lead to quality issues. If you are hurrying and trying to get as much produced as possible you may make mistakes or your work may not be at a high standard which can lead to customer dissatisfaction.

Key terms

Piece rate is when someone is paid per item that they produce or service – they are paid according to how much they have actually done.

Theory into practice

Consider the following occupations and how well Taylorist principles could work for each:

* bricklayer
* toy maker
* musician
* doctor
* pilot
* teacher
* car maker.

1. Which professions would work well and not so well?
2. To what extent are Taylorist principles used within the organisation you are studying?

Mayo

Elton Mayo explored Taylor's ideas further in the 1920s and 1930s as he recognised there seemed to be more to motivation than just pay.

He did a study known as the Hawthorne Study in Chicago, USA to investigate motivation. His study found that, after a number of experiments including incentive schemes, rest periods, different hours of work and changes in lighting and heating, whatever changes were made output continued to rise. Mayo found, therefore, that rises in productivity were not only due to financial rewards but also due to management involvement, teamworking and communication. These new insights were known as the Human Relations School when considering motivation. Mayo suggested that workers should:

* be given a say in what happened to them
* have improved communication
* be organised into teams
* be given social facilities such as clubs or sports facilities.

Maslow

Abraham Maslow suggested that the needs of individuals were based on a set of needs that could be ranked into a hierarchy. The lower ranking needs were more basic such as the need for food, water and then shelter. He proposed that basic needs needed to be met first before employees could be motivated. This is known as the hierarchy of needs (Figure 11.4).

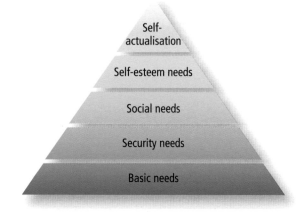

FIGURE 11.4 *Maslow's hierarchy of needs*

Basic needs are for reasonable standards of food, clothing and adequate pay.

Security needs could include job security, appropriate working conditions, clear job description.

Social needs include working in teams, social facilities, good communication.

Esteem needs are based on self-respect, for example status within the job, responsibility and recognition.

Self-actualisation is the feeling that an individual has met their potential and feels satisfied. Few people will achieve this during their lifetime.

From the diagram you can see that as the lower level needs are satisfied the employee can then be motivated to the next level of the hierarchy. Maslow's ideas can be usefully applied by managers in a number of ways and will be influenced by the structure and culture within the organisation.

* All employees have a range of needs that need to be satisfied. Any unsatisfied lower level needs will mean that employees cannot be motivated.
* Offering pay rewards or increasing salary may not motivate employees but inadequate pay will demotivate.
* Strategies such as increasing responsibility may be used to motivate workers but if basic needs such as safe working conditions are not provided, workers will remain demotivated.

Herzberg

Herzberg like Maslow believed that pay was not the only motivator and came up with his theory which had two elements to it – hygiene factors and motivators (Figure 11.5). For an employee to be motivated, all the hygiene (maintenance) factors need to be met first and then the motivators can be used to make them work harder.

HYGIENE FACTORS	MOTIVATORS
Level of supervision Too much = demotivation	Achievement
Administration Too much = demotivation	Recognition
Pay Too low = demotivation	Advancement
Working conditions Unsafe = demotivation	Responsibility

FIGURE 11.5 *Herzberg's theory of motivation*

Herzberg's theory works in a similar way to Maslow's. Figure 11.4 shows that even if recognition and advancement are offered, if the working conditions are unsafe an employee will still remain demotivated. A culture that rewards safe working and pays well is likely to have staff who are ready to be motivated.

Think it over...

Consider the workplace you are studying. Do employees tend to be motivated just by money as outlined by Taylor or are other factors taken into account such as those presented by Mayo, Maslow or Herzberg?

Increasing motivation

There are a number of practical ways that employers can seek to increase the motivation of their employees including:

* job security
* job enrichment
* job enlargement
* home and work life balance
* empowerment
* job sharing.

Job security

One of the most basic ways to make employees feel happier in their jobs is to make them feel secure. This is known as giving them **job security**. If employees feel that their job is safe they are more likely to work harder and try to progress within the business. If jobs are safe, then the motivation of employees is likely to be improved by making jobs more interesting or challenging through increased responsibility or tasks that require more effort on the employee's behalf. Complete job security is increasingly difficult to provide in business due to cost cutting, changes in technology and increasing competition from the UK and abroad but organisations should try to make employees feel as secure as possible.

Job enrichment

Making a job more interesting to employees is known as **job enrichment**. An example of job enrichment might be a junior hairdressing assistant in a salon who is usually responsible for sweeping the floors, making tea and answering telephone calls but is given the added responsibility for the reception area and bookings. Job enrichment provides the employee with additional higher level tasks that will challenge and motivate them. There are some problems with enriching jobs that need to be managed carefully. These include the need for extra training to help employees do these extra tasks and the attitude of employees towards those tasks. Enriching will only work if an employee wants the extra responsibility.

Job enlargement

Job enlargement is another method of trying to motivate employees but unlike enrichment where tasks are made more difficult and challenging, job enlargement gives the employee more tasks to do of a similar nature. This means the employee is less likely to be bored in work as they have a range of tasks to do, e.g. a customer service assistant is able to answer the telephone, word process letters, email and do some basic data entry. These tasks are all of a similar level but avoid too much repetitive work and therefore increase interest. Like job enrichment, there may be issues about motivating workers in this way as they may not want additional tasks to do and may need extra training resulting in increased costs. Once trained, they may even ask for additional pay in order to recognise the extra variety of work being done.

Key terms

Job enlargement is when employees are given additional tasks to do at the same level.

Job enrichment is when employees' jobs are redesigned to give them more difficult tasks to do such as increased responsibility.

Job security is the feeling that your job is safe.

Work and home life balance

Other ways to increase the motivation of employees in work is to make them feel more valued by giving them special working arrangements to help them balance their home and working lives. This is

Achieving work and home life balance can be a juggling act

known as the **work and home life balance**. To do this, some employees might prefer **flexible working practices**, such as flexi-time which means you work a set number of hours per week but you can choose when you actually do that work between about 6 am and 8 pm at night depending on your employer. Some employers allow employees to work additional flexi hours and claim extra days as holiday rather than paying overtime. This means that the employees feel more motivated to work as hard as they possibly can.

> **Key terms**
>
> *Flexible working practices* means the ability to make work fit in with an employee's needs, e.g. flexi-time is when employees can choose when they work as long as they do the right number of hours in a week.
>
> *Work and home life balance* means the ability to combine working and home lives so that neither dominates the other. This allows the employee to work to their best within the workplace.

Empowerment

Consulting workers about how they feel and giving them responsibility for helping with decision-making can make them feel more important. Giving such responsibility is known as **empowerment** and should also increase motivation. Sometimes empowerment can be formalised into making teams entirely responsible for their own working methods and decision-making. This is known as team **autonomy**. The benefits of having greater autonomy include higher quality products, reduced costs and greater satisfaction because employees are more interested and responsible for what they do. Empowerment can also have its limitations as it can sometimes be viewed by employees as a way to cut costs by **delayering** an organisation. This is because more responsibility is passed down the organisation to more junior employees who are paid less. Some managers may also find it difficult to pass on responsibility to more junior employees when they have to remain responsible for the work being done as they are accountable for it.

This means that the type of tasks put forward as part of empowerment may not be as challenging as they should be to fully motivate an employee.

Job sharing

Being able to balance home and work may be difficult for some employees and in order to motivate them **job sharing** might be the answer. This is when two employees share the workload of one job to make up the equivalent of one full-time person. Usually one person will work afternoons, mornings or two or three days per week and the person they are sharing with will do the opposite. This can be ideal for both parties as they feel they are doing a job with full-time responsibility but for only half the time.

CASE STUDY

St Ann's Hospice

St Ann's Hospice is based in Greater Manchester and aims to improve the quality of life for people with life-threatening illnesses as well as their families and carers. They employ 298 people, most of whom earn less than £25,000 per year and have no access to exotic trips or bonuses. Their benefits are tea, coffee, toast and vouchers. Two out of every three employees are happy with their pay and benefits.

Pay is clearly not the main motivator for working for these staff. Their motivation to work is about making a positive difference in the world. The staff respect each other and work as a team. The local community are also involved with the hospice and help with fundraising. On top of everything else they also find time to support other hospices in countries such as South Africa and Romania.

The atmosphere in work is said to be warm and friendly even though patients are suffering from serious illnesses and staff feel proud to work there. Education and skills are important at the hospice and there is regular training including job shadowing. Staff also get 27 days holiday and are able to spend time away from the job doing training.

✓ 1. What are the biggest motivators for staff at St Ann's Hospice?

✓ 2. Why is it important that pay is not the main motivator for staff?

✓ 3. Name three other types of job where pay is not the main motivator to work there.

✓✓ 4. What difference do you think a warm and friendly atmosphere would make to staff motivation?

✓✓✓ 5. Now consider the organisation you are studying and what motivates people to work there. Give a judgement as to how motivated you think staff are giving reasons to support this view.

Monitoring and directing

Monitoring and directing lead on from both organising and motivating in that monitoring is the process of actually checking back with an employee to see that they are making progress. Directing them is giving them a pointer as to where they are going wrong or what they need to do next. The methods of monitoring and direction used within an organisation will very much depend on the type of people who are employed there and the culture of that organisation.

Monitoring can be seen to take two main forms: formal monitoring whereby managers are checking or watching the employee in some way and informal monitoring whereby managers are making subtle judgements about how an employee is fitting into the workplace or noticing if that employee may have some kind of problem.

Formal monitoring

Some organisations will have very strict monitoring policies whereby staff are monitored at all times throughout their working day. Examples of these types of jobs might include customer service/call centres where employees are constantly dealing with customer enquiries. Supervisors in this case often listen in to calls to monitor customer service or have calls recorded so that they can be checked at a later date. Managers will often monitor emails that have been sent or have CCTV showing employees at the workplace. Employers have to make employees aware that monitoring is taking place.

Formal monitoring may also be necessary in order to comply with the law. For example, the Data Protection Act 1998 forces employers to ensure that personal information is protected and is only accessed if necessary. Some employers also carry out drug and health tests as part of monitoring in the workplace, for example hospitals may test their medical workers for diseases like tuberculosis so they don't pass them on to patients or employees required to use machinery may be tested for drugs.

The best way to ensure that formal monitoring is conducted properly is to have a formal monitoring policy that can be used by managers and that employees are aware of in order to make sure that everyone knows what is happening.

Think it over...

As part of your report, consider the monitoring policy(ies) used within the organisation that you are studying. Is there a formal policy and if not why not? If a policy exists what sort of information does it outline and how do managers and employees feel about it? If the organisation does not have a policy you may wish to make recommendations as to why they may benefit from having one.

Informal monitoring

Informal monitoring is a much less scientific approach to monitoring and needs extra care and attention in order to ensure that the manager does not intrude too much on an employee's privacy. All monitoring may feel uncomfortable for an employee, so it is important that employees feel happy with it and know why it is being done (Figure 11.6).

FIGURE 11.6 *Reasons for informal monitoring*

Informal monitoring may be used to help managers assist their employees in ways to improve or may be used at review times during the year.

Some kind of monitoring has always existed within the workplace but what is really important is that it is very carefully done whether formal or informal. This is because by becoming intrusive an employer may be breaching the Human Rights Act 2000 e.g. by having too much CCTV or telephone monitoring. There needs to be a careful balance between the need for employers to monitor and the rights of employees to privacy at work. Changes in technology have made monitoring seem much more menacing in some organisations where all email exchanges and Internet access are logged but what is important is for managers to make sure that employees understand when and why they are being monitored so they can feel as comfortable as possible about it.

Problem solving

Another key element of management is problem solving. Problem solving is important as it seeks to resolve or reduce difficulties that the organisation may have had or makes changes that will help them in the future. Problem solving is extremely diverse because of the very nature of the word problem itself. It literally means something that is difficult to resolve or control and will vary from one organisation to another. Something that is a problem for one manager may not be a problem for another manager so you will need to carefully analyse any relevant issues. It is the developed skills of a manager that help them to recognise how big or significant a problem actually is and what impact it will have on the business.

A problem for a small business owner might be maintaining suitable levels of cash flow in order to keep their creditors happy whilst a problem for a multinational organisation might be international trade agreements that affect their ability to import or export goods. Both will affect each organisation but the extent to which they are able to resolve or overcome those difficulties will limit the size of the problem.

CASE STUDY

The Hongwa Clothing Factory in North Shanghai

During August 2005 there was a crisis amongst clothing retailers and manufacturers as EU quota limits for clothing, which had been taken away some years before, were reintroduced. This meant that orders for clothing from China were stopped at ports and not allowed entry to the European Union if they were over the specified import limit. Clothing became stranded at UK ports whilst waiting for clearance into the UK. In order to help solve the problem the Hongwa factory, at first, switched production of garments as the quota for trousers was reached first whilst the quota for jackets and shirts was still not met. The alternative for the company was to switch clothing production to the Chinese market or to make staff redundant.

The EU quota limit was imposed to try to protect clothing manufacturers in Spain and Italy but retailers of the Chinese garments risked having their profit margins reduced as the clothing was much cheaper to buy in from China than Europe. The final solution to the crisis was to allow the imports waiting at port locations to be allowed in to the EU and to count them against the 2006 quota limits as some form of compromise.

✓ 1. How did EU quotas affect production at the Hongwa factory?
✓ 2. How did the Hongwa factory sort out their problems?
✓✓✓ 3. Using information from the case study and relevant newspaper articles (related to Chinese EU trade tariffs), to what extent do you think problems with tariffs could have been avoided for both EU retailers and Chinese manufacturers?

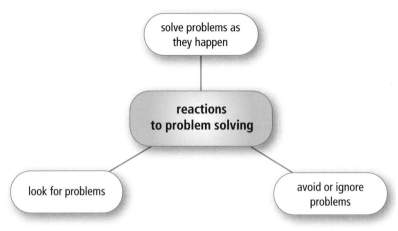

FIGURE 11.7 *Reactions to problem solving*

There are three main reactions to problem solving for managers (Figure 11.7) and the personality and management style of the person you are investigating within your report will affect which way they operate.

Looking for problems

Looking for problems is a **proactive** approach as this type of manager actually seeks out problems to solve. This means that they are constantly looking for ways to improve their business and by solving smaller issues before they become problems they hope to avoid big problems altogether. This type is likely to link their management role with the need to constantly make improvements and this known as **continuous improvement** or **kaizen**. These processes require everyone in the organisation to make improvements in some small way so that the quality of the product or service is continually being improved. The extent to which this can happen effectively will depend on the culture and resources within the organisation.

Solving problems as they happen

Other managers use the problem solving technique of dealing with problems as they arise and in order of how urgent they are. A restaurant

> ### Key terms
>
> *Continuous improvement* (Japanese version *kaizen*) means the ability across the organisation to make improvements to the way things are done including working practices and customer service. Each employee is responsible for their own small set of changes that builds up a culture of improvement.
>
> *Proactive* means when someone is seeking out problems or issues and trying to resolve them before they are actually formally presented to them.

manager may have a number of problems they need to deal with but the issue of someone ringing in that they are unwell and can't work would be dealt with first as it more important than, for example the food order for next week. If a manager has too many problems in one go and they keep having to deal with one after another this is known as 'fire fighting' as it is just like trying to put out a fire when new flames appear as quickly as the ones you have just put out. Working in an environment where fire fighting is a common management technique for problem solving can be very stressful and tiring.

Call centres

Call centres are places where large teams of people work all day answering telephone calls. You might have come across them if you have telephoned your bank, an insurance company or placed an order with a catalogue company over the telephone. There are estimated to be between 250,000 and 400,000 people working in call centres and this is due to the need for people to be able to access these services day or night. A manager or supervisor manages many of these people within a team environment.

Some call centres are extremely strict about how long employees can spend on toilet breaks and sometimes time them. Others have extreme monitoring of telephone calls including how long they are able to talk on the telephone with a customer before they move on to the next one. As employees are talking live to customers with individual queries the chance of problems arising is high which means that managers are often fire fighting throughout their shift to make sure that enough operators are answering calls and that customer queries are dealt with appropriately.

✓ 1. Describe what is meant by 'fire fighting problems' in a call centre.
✓✓ 2. Analyse the implications for customer service of employees being under pressure.
✓✓✓ 3. Give a judgement as to whether you think techniques such as continuous improvement (kaizen) could be adopted within a call centre environment.

Avoiding or ignoring problems

These kinds of managers can be described as 'putting their head in the sand' in that they choose to not see problems in front of them or if they do, to avoid them. Some problems that are not dealt with might go away by themselves anyway.

For example an unhappy or disruptive member of staff that is causing problems may choose to leave the organisation. However, this is a very dangerous strategy as what might start out as a much smaller problem can grow until it reaches enormous proportions.

Barings Bank

Nick Leeson was working for Barings Bank in the 1990s as a foreign exchange trader. He traded in the Far East for a number of years and was very successful for a time. Then his luck changed and a number of his deals went wrong and he lost the bank money. Rather than let his manager know about the problem and help to deal with it he carried on doing even more deals to try to trade himself out of the problem. Unfortunately these also went wrong. His managers avoided or ignored what was happening, partly due to the fact that Nick was doing his best to cover his problems up. This meant that what started out as a small loss soon escalated until Nick put the bank in a position where it was overtrading and then collapsed because it could not pay the debts that had been run up. Nick was sent to prison for what he had done but if the problems he had been having were noticed when they were much smaller at the start of his activities, Barings Bank might still be in existence today!

✓ 1. Name two possible consequences of managers ignoring problems in an organisation like Barings Bank.

✓✓ 2. Discuss the view that it is a manager's job to solve problems rather than an employee's.

✓✓✓ 3. To what extent was problem solving the main factor that caused the decline of Barings Bank?

Innovators and adaptors

Michael Kirton (1989) has developed a theory on the ways that managers problem solve based on the idea that there are two styles of approach:

* innovators – these are people who solve problems based on their own intuition and feelings

* adaptors – these are people who use logic and dependability to get the problem solved.

Theory into practice

Consider the type of manager you think you are or will be. Write yes or no beside each statement in the table below.

STATEMENT	YES/NO
1. I like to find problems.	
2. I like to sort out problems.	
3. I like to make things change.	
4. I like to build and support my team.	
5. I have big ideas.	
6. I am very precise.	
7. I am confident about decisions I make.	
8. I reflect on what I have done before.	
9. I like thinking more than doing.	
10. I listen to everyone's opinion.	
11. I am bossy.	
12. If I start something I must finish it.	
13. I can be difficult to work with.	
14. I work well with others.	
15. I cannot be relied upon.	
16. I am reliable.	

You may find it a useful exercise to ask the manager you are studying to do this task as well as part of your research. When you have written yes or no against each statement, count up how many odd numbers you have answered yes and how many even numbered statement you have answered yes. Work out which you have the most of.

● If you have more odd numbers you are more of an innovator.

● If you have more even numbers you are more of an adaptor.

Recognising which style is most like you can help you recognise your own strengths and act on them accordingly.

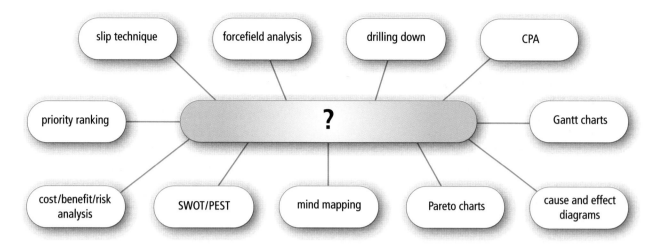

FIGURE 11.8 *Problem solving tools*

Management tools for problem solving

There are a large number of strategies that can help managers, whatever their approach, to problem solve more efficiently. You may already use some of these as part of your own study techniques. A number of them are given in Figure 11.8 but this is by no means a complete list and it is likely you will want to investigate others that you will find within your chosen organisation. A few of the techniques have been briefly outlined below.

Think it over...

SWOT and PEST are both techniques which you studied within your AS Applied Business – in small groups revise what they stand for and how they are applied.

Cost/benefit/risk analysis

This is a technique used by managers to measure the cost of doing something compared to the amount of benefit they will get as a result. It also considers the opportunity cost of taking decisions. This means the cost of the lost opportunity that a business could have taken, against what it actually did. For example, to replace a machine on a production line costs £30,000. The benefit of replacing the machine would be that it would be quicker and improve productivity. This risk is

that if the machine is not replaced it may break altogether and be totally unproductive resulting in competitors becoming more efficient and the business losing customers. However, if the £30,000 was spent, the opportunity cost is that it can't be spent elsewhere e.g. on advertising to increase sales. This is a very simplified version of what actually happens but if done in full this analysis can help a manager to problem solve.

Pareto chart

A Pareto chart is derived from the Pareto Principle that was discovered by Vilfredo Pareto. He discovered that 80 per cent of the wealth in Italy was owned by 20 per cent of the population and that 20 per cent of customers accounted for 80 per cent of sales. Examples that may relate to you could be that 80 per cent of your success comes from 20 per cent of your efforts or 80 per cent of decisions are made from 20 per cent of a meeting's time. Although 80/20 is the figure used it is really only a guide so you may find the actual figures you calculate are slightly higher or lower but the principle remains.

The Pareto Principle states that not all causes of something occur the same number of times or in the same way. This means that by working out the most frequent factors it is possible to make best use of problems to tackle resources. For example, some products might have more errors than others and by concentrating only on those a business could save money.

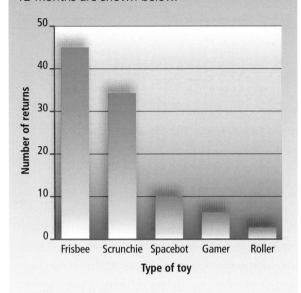
Cause and effect diagrams

Cause and effect diagrams can also be a good way to problem solve by drawing out on paper what the issues involved are before being able to come to a solution about what should happen next. Producing a cause and effect diagram is also sometimes referred to as the fishbone technique because the completed diagram looks a bit like fish bones. The purpose of using this method to problem solve is to give the manager full access to all the possible causes and their effects in order to be able to come up with a solution. A simplified version of a completed diagram is shown in Figure 11.9.

Critical path analysis and Gantt charts

Both these methods of problem solving use diagrams to help the manager to work out what to do. **Critical path analysis** requires the manager to draw out the stages that the problem needs to go through in order to solve it including the length of time for each stage (Figure 11.10). By doing this it is possible to see the minimum amount of time needed, known as the critical path. Gantt works in a similar way but rather than using a variety of shapes like critical path, each of the stages is represented by a horizontal bar again allowing the manager to work out how long a problem will take to be solved.

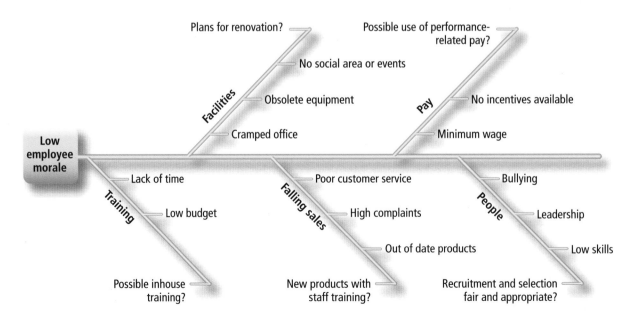

FIGURE 11.9 *Cause and effect diagram showing the possible causes of low employee morale*

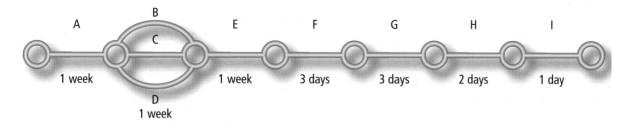

FIGURE 11.10 *A critical path analysis diagram allows a manager to work out which tasks can be completed at the same time (B, C, D) before this project goes forward*

Drilling down

Drilling down is the final technique to be explored in this unit. You are very likely to have used directories on the Internet such as Yahoo or Lycos. By using directories you are able to drill down to get the information that you need by using headings and then exploring the options within those headings. For a manager to solve a problem they can use the same technique either on computer or on paper. A very simplified example is shown in Figure 11.11.

By looking at the problem of high customer complaints shown in Figure 11.11, it is possible to see that there could be a number of reasons why customer complaints might be high and by drilling down through those reasons it is possible to work out possible causes and then to identify solutions. This diagram has only been completed in part due to space limitations but a real diagram may have many layers to drill down with lots of possible issues laid out.

The problem solving cycle

Now that you have seen the different reactions to problem solving and some of the techniques that managers may use to solve those problems, the last stage of problem solving to be aware of is the problem solving cycle (Figure 11.12). This cycle demonstrates how the whole process takes place and shows that it is an ongoing cycle that never ends as there are always new challenges and problems arriving.

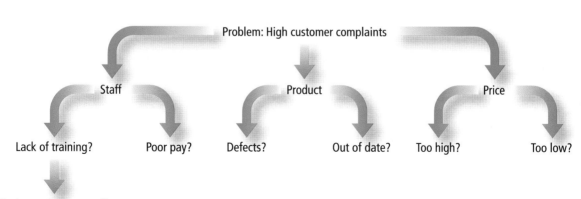

FIGURE 11.11 *Drilling down flow chart*

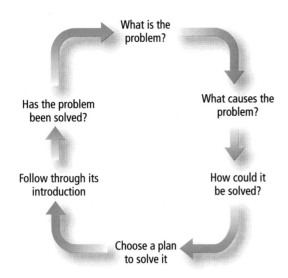

FIGURE 11.12 *Problem solving cycle*

Training and mentoring

Training and mentoring is another essential part of the management function. Training takes a number of different forms and may take place on an individual or team basis. The skill of the manager is to make sure that employees feel that training is identified to meet their own personal development but at the same time it meets future business needs. The manager will also need to make plans for how the training is going to take place and who is going to do it. Part of this process may be to train a limited number of employees externally and **cascade** that information within the business.

On-and off-the-job training

There are two main types of training in business known as **on-the-job** and **off-the-job**. On-the-job training can be organised and carried out by the management team as it involves the employee being trained whilst actually working. Off-the-job is more complicated and may involve a referral to an external agency such as a college or training provider. The Human Resource department of the organisation may need to arrange this referral. The extent to which training like this is supported depends on the culture of the organisation concerned with regard to how much they value and are prepared to pay for such training.

Budgetary constraints may also limit the amount of training that is possible so there may need to be a prioritisation of whose training needs are highest and whether or not the outcomes of training can be cascaded down to others. Some organisations have a requirement that if someone has been on a training course they must share the information with their colleagues as soon as they get back. Managers, therefore, need to organise who should go on such courses and how that information will be shared.

Requirements for training

Some types of training are not given at the manager's discretion but are required by law such as health and safety training. Managers will need to arrange for such training to take place on a regular basis and for external agencies to come in and support that training. The organisation may also wish to gain accreditation for training by opting for **Investors in People** status. This is a mark to show that the organisation invests in its staff and training. To support this status, managers would need to respond to training needs and to support their employees in the workplace.

Training for the future

Training for the future should also be considered by the manager as employees may move on to other jobs in the organisation or will need some way of improving themselves to be able to get promoted in the future. Giving training to allow employees to progress in this way is part of **succession planning**. This is when a manager gives training to more junior employees to prepare them to take over the role in the future. Good succession planning means the organisation should have a high number of well-trained, forward-looking employees.

Future training needs can also be established by completing a **skills audit,** where existing employees are audited to see if they already have skills needed to do a new role. Some employees may have the required skills but may not be using them. The organisation would use these employees instead of employing new staff.

Organisations may also do skills audits routinely to work out the skill level within the organisation. A firm of solicitors, for example, may analyse how many junior solicitors they have in training and how many are fully qualified. This is so they can plan for the future needs of the business. Sometimes organisations will use specialised software packages called Human Resource Information Systems (HRIS) to keep records of all the employees so they can work out the skill levels in the organisation automatically. This can be useful if the business does project work and needs to find people with specialist skills or qualifications very quickly. Employees may be able to do more than one job for the organisation.

Mentoring

A manager as a **mentor** is someone who is supporting and encouraging to someone else within the workplace in order that they can achieve the best performance possible. The person the manager is supporting, known as a **mentee**, may be a subordinate or someone on the same grade. The relationship is one-to-one with the mentor passing on all their knowledge, experience, behaviour and knowledge to the other person. The mentor helps to support the other person by encouraging them to break down barriers and achieve their full potential. A key benefit to someone of having a mentor is that their ideas can be discussed with the mentor and judgements made about the way forward. The mentor may also be willing to share some of their business contacts and be able to help their mentee to form new social networks.

When new employees enter a workplace they are often given a supervisor or mentor to look after and support them. This person is designed to be there to answer any questions, from where to get photocopying access to researching relevant training courses to help with career planning. A good mentor will not see the person that they are working with as a threat, but will treat the success of the mentee as a success for them as well.

E-mentoring is now another popular way for mentoring to take place as well as the face-to-face versions. By using electronic methods of communication a mentor can give encouragement to individuals in other countries or in different time zones, e.g. the BT ethnic minority network e-mentoring programme (see case study on page 130).

A *mentor* is someone who is given someone more junior to support and look after with a similar background or type of experience.

A *mentee* is the person who receives the advice from the mentor about their ideas and ways to go forward.

CASE STUDY

BT ethnic minority network e-mentoring programme

The BT ethnic minority network e-mentoring programme's purpose is to provide support and encouragement to ethnic minority people in order that they can achieve their full potential. It was designed to allow people to break through traditional 'glass ceilings' that were stopping ethnic minority workers reaching top jobs. As an e-mentoring system it can give support across the world and participants include people in Italy, USA, the Netherlands and the UK. Individuals recruited as mentors can help provide advice and guidance on cultural issues that help others to move forward and be successful. The scheme has been so successful to date that there are now over 5,000 members and pairings even though no one is paid for their services.

More information about this scheme and many others can be found at www.coachingnetwork. org.uk.

As well as the mentee, the mentor can also benefit from such a relationship as their communication skills improve and they make new contacts with people in their business field. It may also be possible for the mentor's business or situation to be improved as their mentee may have ideas for improvements that they have not heard before.

✓ 1. Explain the difference between a mentor and a mentee.
✓ 2. What is meant by a glass ceiling?
✓✓ 3. Explain the problems or limitations that e-mentors and e-mentees might face.
✓✓✓ 4. To what extent could e-mentoring benefit students in schools and colleges?

Appraising

An appraisal is a meeting between a manager and an employee that gives an opportunity for the performance of that employee to be reviewed. They can take place at differing times during a year depending on the organisation involved. Some organisations like to do mini appraisals every three months with one being identified as a more formal appraisal once a year. Other organisations carry them out six monthly and others only annually. There are a number of different measurements or scales that can be used within an appraisal system including targets or ratings.

Setting targets for an appraisal

An employee and manager will look at a set of targets or objectives that were set at the last appraisal and review them to see how much progress has been made. In an office environment, the target set could be to learn a new software package or taking part in a training day. Some employers may give an employee eight relatively simple targets whereas others may concentrate on only one or two more difficult targets that will require a high level of performance.

It is important that targets are relevant to the employee as well as the employer so that everyone is aware of what needs to be achieved and the targets are relevant to the business' needs. It is important to strike this balance as an employee may feel they would like to go on a course as part of their appraisal but if it's not a business need they may need to be persuaded to do something else instead. It is also important that unpopular targets are included within the appraisal system if needed. This requires careful management by the appraising manager to persuade the employee that such targets are in their best interest. Targets, such as cutting costs, should be cascaded down from senior managers to more junior managers so that overall business objectives are met. At the review meeting those targets will be measured against what has actually happened and then a judgement can be made about success.

STATEMENT	A	B	C	D
Knowledge of work tasks	Excellent knowledge well above expected levels	Good knowledge of work tasks	Lack of knowledge of work tasks slowing productivity	Inadequate level of knowledge of work tasks
Team working	Excellent and responsive team worker	Good team worker, well liked by colleagues	Usually works well with colleagues but occasionally has problems	Uncooperative and resists working as a team

FIGURE 11.13 *Grading an employee's role on an appraisal form*

Using rating scales

Other alternatives that can be used as part of an appraisal system include rating the performance of an employee. A set of performance criteria are outlined within the appraisal system and then the manager and employee discuss the level that they feel the employee is working at. The appraisal form will include a list of different statements made about different elements of the employee's role and there will be grades for each one (see Figure 11.13).

By having no 'middle' point score a manager is forced to acknowledge good or weaker performance from every employee.

Another version of this type of scaling is to have a set of statements and then to have a set of responses to all expectations such as:

A Exceeded expectations
B Achieved expectations
C Fell below expectations
D Unacceptable performance

Linking appraisals to pay

Appraisals are used by many different organisations to get some kind of measurement of individual employee performance and may also be used to motivate and identify gaps where training needs to take place. Some appraisal systems are linked to pay whereby that individual is rewarded with a cash bonus if their performance is at the right level or higher than expected. The pay element of the review is commonly only awarded once a year in order that costs do not increase too much. This can limit the amount of motivation that an appraisal system can provide but does attempt to control costs.

Linking appraisals to career development and training

Appraisals may also be used to encourage employees to take on more responsibility and to help them plan opportunities to improve themselves as part of career development. Appraisals can identify an objective that needs to be met and the employee and manager can agree additional training that may be required in order to achieve this. A copy of the appraisal is sent to the Human Resources or Personnel department so that money can be set aside from the training budget to pay for the training that is needed. Appraisals are a useful enhancement to career development because by identifying what training is needed for the future, employees can plan what they want to do next in their career and not feel stuck in their current position. By linking training to the appraisal system it ensures that training is targeted in the right places and is not undertaken ad hoc.

Self-appraisal

The most useful appraisal systems used by managers tend to have some element of self-appraisal by the employee. This means that the employee can consider targets for themselves in order to improve performance and by 'owning' these targets is more likely to work harder and therefore be more productive. The key to success when using self-assessment is to make sure that targets are linked to the best interests of the employee and the business, for example by linking attendance with bonuses. This means if the employee has very good attendance in work they will receive a bonus but at the same by being in work more they will be more productive and therefore earn more money for the company. Both the employee and company will benefit!

Appraisee report

A further method of appraisal is also used in some large organisations and that is where the appraiser and appraisee give a report on each other so communication is from the manager to the employee and vice versa when giving judgements about performance. Using such a method can help employees to feel empowered as their opinions are taken into account more when judging management performance.

Issues involved in appraisal systems

Most organisations have some kind of appraisal system in place whether formal or informal but this does not mean that appraisals are always used successfully and usefully within business. Sometimes a badly done appraisal can be worse than not having done one at all because it may seem unfair and actually demotivate an employee. Time must be allocated correctly for an appraisal so that the manager and employee are both well prepared. If a manager does not spend the right amount of time considering the employee's performance they may give the impression that they don't care. Appraisals may also cause problems when there is a personality clash between a manager and employee. Some of the key advantages and disadvantages of appraisals are given in Figure 11.14.

APPRAISAL SYSTEMS	
Advantages	Disadvantages
Allows an employer and employee to discuss and work together on improving performance leading to better use of resources or more profits.	Need tight control so that all appraisers set the same level of target to ensure they are fair. Managers and employees need training to know what is expected of each of them.
Is a formal system for monitoring and measuring satisfactory and unsatisfactory performance.	Needs to have achievable targets but at the same time not too easy as this is likely to take away their worth and costs may go up if performance is exceeded.
Can be linked to payment so rewards are given for good performance, e.g. pay rises, prizes or time off in lieu.	Targets need careful control to ensure that they are not too difficult to meet as this may cause employees to feel demotivated.
Allows whole business objectives to be filtered down and 'owned' by all employees and therefore are more likely to be achieved by being integrated into both the hierarchy of the organisation and the culture.	Will only be useful if both the employer and employee believe in it and see it is valuable. If it is just 'added' to the organisation it may cause damage as employees and managers will not believe in it.
May give the employee and the employer a chance to get to know each other better and therefore improve their working relationship.	May not be given enough time and therefore doing an appraisal interview badly is worse than not doing one at all. May not work if there is a personality clash between the manager and employee.
Allows the business to plan training and development so that future work force needs can be met, for example planning for people to take over when someone is going to retire.	Budgetary constraints may mean there is a limited amount of money available for training and therefore needs identified within the appraisal system may not be able to be met.

FIGURE 11.14 *Advantages and disadvantages of appraisal systems*

11.2.2 Planning how to gather information for the report

Like any business you will also need to consider the aims and objectives of your own research and the individual objectives that will support that aim. What do you hope to achieve overall and which objectives can you set yourself in order to measure your progress?

In planning your report you will also need to consider the following areas.

* The sources of information that you are going to be able to access and the time limits restricting your access including technological resources.

* Whether it is possible to access the manager's or supervisor's stakeholders (anyone that is affected by them, e.g. subordinates, employees, more senior managers and the manager themselves).

* Preparing a questionnaire or set of interview questions in advance of meeting or writing to the person you are studying may provide you with required information.

* You may also find it useful to work shadow your respondent (the person you are studying) to observe them at work.

You will also need to be able to relate the management theories and information that were presented in Section 11.2.1 (The business context within which the report will take shape) to the person you are studying.

The type of research methods that you plan to use will be critical to the success of your report. If you ask the wrong questions, you will get the wrong answers/information and it always takes a lot more time to collect relevant data than you expect.

You will need to devise some kind of action plan to help you sort out what to do first and to measure your success in manageable sections. Use your objectives to help you plan for this. You may find it useful to use an action planning list like the one in Figure 11.15.

You may also find it useful to make use of the management tools that you have learned about so far such as SWOT or Gantt charts to help to plan what you need to do and the amount of time you have available. Remember to allow enough time to ask for permission from both the organisation and the individual manager/supervisor before you start to collect your data. More information about the appropriate research methods to choose is shown in the next section.

OBJECTIVE AND ACTIONS	RESOURCES	WHEN I PLAN TO DO THIS	ACHIEVEMENT DATE
To collect statistics of employees working for the manager as at 10 February including starting dates and length of service.	Company Statistics Manager. Human Resources department.	10 February Meeting with Human Resource manager 10.00 am.	Produce a graph in Excel based on the statistics to use in my report 11 February.

FIGURE 11.15 *An example of an action planning list*

11.2.3 Researching into the business context and analysis of the information that is collected

Your report will be a very individualised piece of research so it is important that you choose the right research methods and make sure that your research is focused and targeted appropriately. To achieve higher grades you will need to make sure you target your report to the specific requirements of the chosen business context so you must take this into account when planning the methods you use. You must also make sure that you use both primary and secondary research within your report. You already have knowledge of both of these from your AS level studies but as part of your revision they are outlined for you in the context of your report.

Primary research methods

Your report is a new and unique piece of research so it is important that you produce good quality primary research. Primary research has not been collected before and will give you an insight into how the manager or supervisor at your organisation actually manages. There are a number of ways that primary research can be collected including questionnaires, discussion, visits and interviews.

Questionnaires

Questionnaires can be a useful tool when collecting research information as they can help to gather a lot of information about your manager or supervisor in one go. They are also very useful as they can be referred to at a later date so you can ask a number of questions and then spend time considering the responses. Remember that questionnaires should not be so long that they put off the manager / supervisor from answering them – two pages is the normal maximum length for a questionnaire. Also consider what information you think is relevant and what is not relevant for the purposes of the report. You are producing a

report demonstrating the role of the management function in order to relate it to management theory, so you will need to ask as many questions about management as possible. Don't waste questions asking irrelevant questions that are not needed within your report such as:

* the age of your manager / supervisor (they may find this impolite and not want to help you)
* where they live
* their gender (hopefully you should know this)
* their job title.

Make sure your questionnaire is put into appropriate sections including relevant questions on each section and uses space to make your page look clear and easy to read. You may find it helpful to label the sections using the subheadings from this chapter including:

* planning
* organising
* motivating
* monitoring and directing
* problem solving
* training and mentoring
* appraising.

Remember you will need to use a number of primary research methods if possible, so it may be more useful to use a questionnaire for only one or two areas of research and then use another method to collect data for another part of the report.

Theory into practice

Choosing one or two of the subheadings listed above, in small groups mind map a number of possible questions that you could ask your manager/supervisor. Remember to try to ask targeted questions that include a mixture of open and closed questions. It is also useful to consider the type of response that you are after – do you want it to be qualitative i.e. a judgement or opinion or are you after something more quantitative such as how many times a week the manager conducts appraisals or how long they last for?

Face-to-face discussion

Face-to-face discussion is a good way to gain information from your supervisor/manager and has the added benefit that you can ask extra questions as they come up, unlike a questionnaire that may restrict answers or may be completed without you being present. The other benefit of face-to-face discussion when gathering information is that you can pick up extra clues from the manager about how they feel about their job and judge their reactions. It can be useful, if the manager will allow it, to tape record the discussion so that you can listen to it later and pick up extra information. *You must ask the manager in advance if you would like to do this and respect their wishes if they do not wish the conversation to be recorded.*

If you are going to do a face-to-face discussion you will need to be very well prepared and have a number of areas and questions that you want to explore. Managers/supervisors are very busy people and they will expect you to be organised and knowledgeable about what you actually want to know. One way of doing this is to have a set of prepared questions. You will also need to be able to make notes so make sure you have a pen and paper or laptop available.

Visit

A visit can be a very useful way of collecting data about your manager at first hand. It allows you to see how the manager fits into the workplace and how the other workers behave towards the manager. If you are permitted to, a useful and very valuable idea is to interview or survey relevant stakeholders of the manager being studied such as subordinates, co-managers, senior managers, owners, suppliers or even customers! By doing this it is possible to gain information about how management is perceived within that organisation from a number of different viewpoints that should eventually lead to a more reliable conclusion about the management. Particular management techniques can be discussed including strengths and weaknesses or possible ideas for improvements.

Face-to-face discussion is an important source of information

Interview with the manager at your centre

If you are unable to get in to the organisation, perhaps because of security clearance or for health and safety reasons, the next best thing is to get the manager to visit you at your centre. This will still give you the opportunity to question them about their role. You will need to have a set of prepared questions and ensure you make notes and ask extra questions as they come up. If you are going to meet the manager as a group, you will need to mind map a set of shared questions and organise who is going to ask the questions and lead the session. Try to ask for resources from the organisation, if possible, so that you can gain extra insight into how management works in context. Useful resources may include staff development policies, management training programmes, general company information, induction videos and so on. All of these sources may include relevant information for your report.

Information on individual qualities of the manager

Using face-to-face discussion, whether it is in the organisation or at your centre, is a really useful way to gain information about key strengths that you manager has including:

* *The type of skills and competencies they possess.* This may include information such as qualifications they have, training courses they have attended, years of work experience they have and any specialist knowledge related to their sector.

* *The type of personality they have.* Are they outgoing, confident, shy, organised? You will need to consider different personality types and how they help/hinder their management roles.

* *What motivates them as an individual.* You may wish to refer back to some of the motivational theorists you have learned about – are they motivated by money, status, recognition, family; what makes them do what they do?

* *How they approach the different management roles (planning, training, appraising etc).* Which aspects of their role do they enjoy the most

and what do they like least, which are they good at/find easy and which are more of a struggle? What makes them think that they find particular areas more difficult or easier?

* *How they deal with different situations and scenarios within their role.* You may be able to get information from the manager on what has been their greatest management challenge or their worst moment. Alternatively, you could write some relevant scenarios and then ask the manager how they would deal with that scenario to get an idea of their attitude and style of management.

Theory into practice

You have already used the SWOT analysis tool to look at the strengths and weaknesses of whole organisations. Now apply it to the individual supervisor or manager that you are studying. Ideally you should be using the framework as a discussion tool to identify their strengths, weaknesses, opportunities and threats.

Think it over...

Thinking back to your primary research data consider the following.

* What type of primary data will you need to collect?
* Which research methods will you use to collect that data?
* Justify why these are the best methods to use.

Secondary research methods

Secondary research methods are also important to show within your report. You will need to include some kind of bibliography within your report, perhaps as an appendix, giving detailed and relevant information about management and the business including the sector that the manager operates within.

There are lots of relevant journals, books and websites containing information that could be included within your report. If you use a piece of text from a source, you must make sure it is referenced correctly to acknowledge it has been written by someone else by using quotation marks followed by the surname of the author and the year of publication and page number. The full reference to the book or article should be included in your bibliography at the end of your work e.g. Richards, C (2005) *GCE A2 level Business for OCR*, Heinemann. This will make it easier for your reader to look up your reference if they would like to follow it up. For example:

> 'Using appropriate referencing makes your report look more professional and avoids copying other people's material' (Richards 2005 p22).

You will need to show understanding of a number of different managerial/supervisory styles, gained from textbooks and other sources, including:

* democratic
* consultative
* autocratic
* supportive
* collaborative
* passive
* directive.

Each one is outlined below but it is crucial that you gain more information from additional sources as well, such as journals, so that you produce a well-researched and balanced report. Keep considering the style of management adopted by your manager/supervisor taking into account the culture, structure, objectives and resources of the organisation. Remember the wider the **span of control** of the manager, the less likely it is they will feel able to consult all of their subordinates and the more likely it is they will adopt a more autocratic style of management.

When looking at each of the managerial styles, consider the extent to which a manager may operate using more than one management style. For example a manager may be a supportive democratic manager or a supportive directive manager. These are hybrids of the different management styles.

Theory into practice

Produce a bar chart or pie graph to demonstrate the extent to which the manager you are studying falls into the individual management categories outlined within this chapter. Ask the manager to comment on your findings to try to measure the accuracy of your thinking and remember to be sensitive to their responses. They may appear to operate in a more autocratic or democratic style than they realise!

Democratic

This kind of management style is used by someone who leads their subordinates by listening to opinions and allows them to have influence over their working lives. Majority decisions are important in that whatever most people want will usually be the way that the manager leads their employees. This type of manager is also highly likely to delegate to their subordinates to share out the workload. There is a lot of two-way communication with this type of manager so views are listened to at a more senior and junior level. Voting may be used in order to formalise decision-making but generally more informal discussion is used.

The positive side of this type of management is that it is useful if complex decisions need to be made as lots of different view points are taken into account. The more negative side of this style of management, though, is that decision-making may take a long time and in real terms cost the business money. The success of democratic management is also highly dependent on the number of employees involved – a wide span of control may make decision-making difficult to manage.

Consultative

Like the democratic manager, the consultative manager actually asks employees their views and opinions when making decisions. This process may take place on an individual basis with a single employee, a group, a team or even involve **unions** in order to work out the best way forward. This means that they are likely to be able to build team-based organisations. The type of consultation that takes place will very much depend on the level of the manager involved and how senior they are. The difference between the democratic and consultative management styles is that whilst the democratic manager listens to views and goes with the majority decision, the consultative manager will listen to all view points but finally go with their own decision.

One of the key elements of consultative management is the diagnosis of the problem they need to resolve and the definition of it. Once this has been done and the facts obtained there can be an action plan and evaluation of different ways in which to solve that problem.

The consultative manager is also one that delegates tasks to others within the team-building framework as part of solving the problem. This manager may make use of tools such as newsletters or team briefings in order to consult with employees and gain additional ideas and understanding.

> ### Key terms
> *Unions* are groups of workers who join together to negotiate pay and working conditions, for example the National Union of Teachers.

Autocratic

The autocratic manager is someone who believes that they know what is best and will not listen to the view points of employees. They will direct and tell employees what to do and not listen or ask for any feedback at all. This type of manager has very little confidence in their subordinates and will have a system of threats in place if an employee does not do as they are told – this is known as punitive feedback. Autocratic management is particularly useful during crisis management. This is when an urgent decision needs to be made and therefore someone needs to take charge. An autocratic manager will make the decision and get things moving forward.

This type of management style is commonly found in more low-skilled professions where the managers have little confidence in the opinions and judgements of their subordinates, believing their methods to be the best. Low-skilled factory working may be an example of such a type of employment. Autocratic management may not work well in all institutions as lack of decision-making in more skilled professions may lead to demotivation as employees feel they are not being listened to. There is also likely to be a lot of confidence and trust in that manager so in the event that they leave or are away for any reason, their absence may cause real problems.

Supportive

A supportive management style is one that allows employees to grow and develop within their working environment. This type of management style should allow employees to consider promotion opportunities as a supportive manager doesn't feel afraid or threatened by progress but welcomes the improvement of employees as something positive. A supportive management style is also very useful if an employee is having personal difficulties that may be affecting their ability to do their job. A supportive manager is likely to try to help them to make arrangements and get themselves back on track, for example helping with childcare arrangements or providing support for someone going through a difficult time with a personal relationship.

In a very creative or forward-thinking culture such as education, IT or nursing, a supportive manager may give an employee time to explore different ideas that they may not have been able to do otherwise. Being a supportive manager can allow employees to be empowered and therefore bring new and exciting ideas to the organisation. Increasing the amount of support that employees feel they are getting from their manager means that staff become more motivated and as a result are more productive at work and less likely to leave. This in turn will save the organisation money in terms of recruitment and training.

Collaborative

A collaborative manager is someone who works as part of the team and takes part in activities as well as manages. This is particularly important in creative environments such as a web design company if a number of different opinions are required in order to allow new ideas and concepts to be explored. The collaborative manager needs to have excellent people management skills as they are managing the team and working with it and need to be able to:

* define what needs to be done
* resolve conflicts between team members
* delegate tasks
* prepare regular reports
* evaluate individual and team progress.

The collaborative manager also needs to be able to work with people at differing levels within and outside the organisation. It may be important to involve experts for some management projects and work with a small group of permanent employees on another. Skills to operate at these different levels and from different perspectives are essential. It is important that a collaborative manager has very good listening and multi-tasking skills as they will need to be able to listen to what is going on and participate in a project as well as suggest improvements to performance.

Theory into practice

In pairs, practise being a collaborative manager. Ask one of your class members to tell you about something they did at the weekend for about five minutes at the same time as you are typing or writing up an assignment. At the end of the five minutes try to repeat what they told you back to them. Speak for five minutes without allowing your class member to speak or correct you. This will give you an idea of how difficult it can be to both work and listen to what is happening around you.

Passive

The passive manager is someone who lets everything happen around them and doesn't make any decisions themselves. They allow decisions to be made by subordinates and watch the whole thing pass by them. This can be a very challenging and liberating experience for some employees as they feel they have a complete say and free reign to get on with their work. This style of management is also known as 'laissez-faire' as it allows the subordinates to do as they wish.

The disadvantages of allowing employees to do as they wish are numerous, for example it relies on the staff being able and qualified to be able to make the right decisions and it expects that employees are team workers and self motivated. There may also be a lack of coordination present as everyone is doing their own thing which can lead to problems of direction as everyone is moving their own way. The passive manager abdicates responsibility to their team and in doing so becomes a provider of materials rather than a manager leading everyone forward together.

Directive

This is probably one of the most common management styles as it uses a 'top down' approach. This means that an instruction is given by a very senior member of staff and then it is cascaded down the organisation by the next most junior person being told what to do. This style of management can be particularly useful in times of emergency when direction is needed in order to get things done quickly e.g. evacuating a building.

However, directive management is one-way communication and may create stress for both the manager and employee as the employee may feel they have no influence on their working environment as they are told what to do and the manager may find it difficult to coordinate what is going on. Like the autocratic manager, the directive manager may inhibit creativity as they dictate how and when a job is completed.

File Edit View Favorites Tools Help

Back · · Search Favorites

Address http:// Go Links »

AstraZeneca

AstraZeneca are one of the largest pharmaceutical companies in the world producing medicines to fight diseases such as cancer and respiratory problems. They constantly look to improve people's health by conducting research into new medicines and treatments. They also try to improve their current product range by making adjustments so that patients get the most from their medicines. Their products are sold in over 100 countries throughout the world and they employ 64,000 people.

With such a large business operation, AstraZeneca are always looking to employ the best managers possible and in doing so they have devised a set of key capabilities that they believe their managers should have and should be offered within their training programmes. These key capabilities are:

- provides clarity about the direction that the business is heading — strategically
- ensures commitment
- builds relationships
- develops people
- shows personal conviction
- builds self awareness.

For more information on AstraZeneca go to the website www.astrazeneca.co.uk.

http:// Internet

✓ **1. Looking at each of the capabilities required by AstraZeneca, rank them in order of importance and explain why you have chosen your order.**

✓✓ **2. Using a local newspaper or a website, consider the type of capabilities that most other companies are looking for in their managers. Are there common themes or does each company have its own set of required capabilities?**

✓✓✓ **3. Produce a list of the key capabilities that you think a manager would need to demonstrate in an organisation near to you. Justify the choices you make.**

Theoretical approaches to management

The theoretical approaches to management of Taylor, Mayo, Maslow and Herzberg have been outlined earlier in this unit (see pages 115–7). Further important management theories that you should be aware of include:

✱ the systems approach

✱ contingency and 'what if' modelling – Fiedler

✱ trait theory – Handy.

The systems approach

The systems approach to management requires a manager to look at their section of the organisation and how it interrelates with other sections in the organisation. This means that managers need to look at the organisation as a whole and in turn as part of an external environment. A production manager may want to keep costs low through economies of scale by producing lots of similar goods on a large scale, whereas a marketing manager may want to respond to customer demands by updating products regularly or offering individual service. Each style of management relates to their own area but a systems approach to management looks at the work of both the marketing and production areas in order to come up with a solution. The systems approach manager sees both sections as interrelating to each other and makes decisions based on information from both areas. By approaching the organisation as a system, it is argued that managers are more likely to find solutions to problems using scientific analysis and as a result these solutions will be more effective when carried out.

Defining the organisation as a system means it needs to interact with its external environment. This is known as an open system and consists of:

* inputs – materials or human resources are input into the system

* transformation – these inputs are then transformed by manufacturing or management

* outputs – finished goods are put back out into the environment either as products or services

* feedback is given from the environment.

Within the system there are often subsystems that operate to achieve company goals. These may be departments such as production or finance that attempt to work together in order to achieve organisational goals that could not be accomplished by one single subsystem. This shows that by working together, more can be achieved than if each subsystem works independently and shows how the system can develop **synergy**.

> **Key terms**
>
> *Synergy* is the measurement of power that is gained by group working which is higher than the same number of individuals working together.

Contingency and 'what if' modelling

Fred E. Fiedler developed the contingency theory that personality is fixed and suggests that a major factor that influences how leaders operate is based on the personality of the leader involved.

The leader is asked to rate a person they have worked really well with and also someone they have not liked working with (least preferred co-worker) using scales from 1–8 (Figure 11.16). The results of the ratings give an indicator of people's emotional reaction to people they cannot work well with. The more likely they are

Unfriendly	Guarded
1	1
2	2
3	3
4	4
5	5
6	6
7	7
8	8
Friendly	**Open**

FIGURE 11.16 *The lower the points on the scales, the more likely the leader is task-motivated*

to become emotional with a person they cannot work well with, the less favourably they are likely to react in a situation.

Leaders that describe the least preferred co-worker in fairly good terms tend to be relationship-motivated which means they are considerate of the feelings of others.

Leaders that describe a co-worker in an unfavourable way tend to be task-motivated which means that they will be much more task-controlling and less concerned with the human side of the business.

The type of leader that someone is can have a powerful influence on the way they manage their department. By allowing leaders to understand their own particular style, a leader is able to understand which situations match their style and an organisation can match leaders to situations as needed. This will make the leaders more effective.

Some leaders will be effective in one situation but not others. It has been suggested that task-motivated leaders are best used in extreme circumstances such as natural disasters, e.g. flood or fire. This is because the task-motivated leader will only focus on the job to be completed and gain satisfaction from completing the task. The relationship-motivated leader is likely to waste time in such a situation taking other factors into consideration which could lead to loss of life.

Pret A Manger

Sinclair Beecham and Julian Metcalfe have combined good direction and day-to-day activity to lead their business, Pret A Manger, to become part of one of the world's biggest corporations, McDonalds. Their desire for high-quality standards and the ability to make others follow has led them to win awards including being rated by *Fortune* magazine as one of the Top 10 Companies to work for in Europe. Starting out as a small sandwich business in the 1990s with a £17,000 bank loan, these two business leaders invested in high-quality sandwiches, cakes and drinks that were made from the finest ingredients. This ethos and good leadership has helped them to expand and become so interesting that for £25 million McDonalds bought a share in them! Since then they have continued to expand and in 2005 had 150 shops and in that same year turned over £150 million in the UK alone.

More information about Pret A Manger can be found at their website www.pret.com.

✓ 1. Describe the skills that are needed for strong leadership.

✓✓ 2. Analyse each of these skills in relation to Pret A Manger.

✓✓✓ 3. To what extent do you think strong leadership helped Pret to expand?

It is very important for organisations to match the right leadership motivation to the right task. If a leader is placed within an environment where there are lots of manual workers who enjoy being told what to do, a manager with task-motivation is likely to be more able to lead.

Fiedler's work does provide a basis for thought in terms of leadership but like other theorists has received criticism from some areas. One of the key areas of criticism is training. It has been suggested that through training, a management style can be adapted or even amended which affects the way a leader behaves and should be taken into account when recruiting leaders. Redesigning the job may make a manager more effective so they can work using the motivational style that they prefer. There has also been some debate in terms of differences of gender when considering this approach to leadership – women are more often (due to their caring nature) seen to be relationship-motivated and men more task-motivated.

The 'what if' aspect of leadership asks the leader to face different situations and take into account predicted and **opportunity costs** in order to try to make plans. This type of modelling was developed in the 1960s and 1970s to encourage leaders to consider what they would do in various scenarios and through doing this would strengthen their ability to think clearly and strategically about what they could do in the future. By taking the leader out of the day-to-day business to consider different ideas, they are also likely to be able to suggest improvements to their own leadership and the way that the business is run.

Key terms

Opportunity cost means the cost of investing money in one area of a business and then not being able to spend that money somewhere else.

Trait theory

Trait theory suggests that there are a number of key traits that a manager should have in order to be a good leader or manager. These are said to be common to successful leaders and managers. It is suggested that intelligence, character, physique and social category are important traits but Charles Handy suggests that the following four categories contain the essential traits:

* intelligence

* use of initiative

* self-assurance

* able to take an overview of a situation.

Theory into practice

Using the information provided and research of your own describe the relevance of these management theories (or others that you are aware of) in relation to the manager and organisation you are studying.

11.2.4 Production of a report

So far within this chapter you have learned about the way to research and collect data that is relevant to your report. The next stage is to actually get the information and produce a suitable report that provides enough analysis and evaluation to allow you to get the highest possible grade. Through your work at AS level you have already written a number of reports so this section will be a reminder of things that you should already know and may include some ideas to help you write even more effective reports.

Report writing is a skill in itself and can be done in a number of different ways. You will need to be able to demonstrate that you are able to collect and present information in order to achieve an A2 level. Producing a formal report can be a good way of organising your ideas and making sure that you cover all the elements of the mark bands. An example of a part-finished formal report (with a limited number of headings) is shown in Figure 11.17.

REPORT ON THE MANAGERIAL FUNCTION OF KENNETH BERMAN AT CRAZY CRISPS LTD

TERMS OF REFERENCE

To investigate, analyse and evaluate the managerial style operated by Kenneth Berman as part of OCR A2 Applied Business Studies Unit 11 and to present information that clearly demonstrates both integrated and strategic thinking.

PROCEDURE

An interview with Kenneth Berman on 15 March 2006.
A questionnaire given to Crazy Crisp employees on 31 March 2006.
Secondary research collected using both online and text book resources.

FINDINGS

1 BACKGROUND TO CRAZY CRISPS
- 1.1 Aims and objectives
- 1.2 Structure of the organisation
- 1.3 Availability of resources within the organisation

2 MANAGEMENT FUNCTIONS AT CRAZY CRISPS
- 2.1 Planning
- 2.2 Organising
- 2.3 Motivating

3 MANAGEMENT STYLES
- 3.1 Democratic
- 3.2 Consultative

CONCLUSIONS
APPENDICES

FIGURE 11.17 *Example of the layout of a formal report*

As shown in Figure 11.17, terms of reference and procedure give background information as to why you are doing the report and identify your methods of collecting information. Your findings should be organised under appropriate headings and be presented in such a way that a reader can easily follow what is being presented. Your conclusions should be logical and based on the information that you have already presented within the report – do not add completely new information here. Conclusions are a chance to evaluate what you have already shown in your findings. A simple checklist is shown in Figure 11.18 to help you improve your report.

Your report will also be more effective if you include any relevant information as appendices, such as your bibliography including books, journals and websites, a copy of your questionnaire or your interview notes.

Under each of the headings shown in Figure 11.17 you must provide as much information and analysis as possible. In order to achieve success at the higher levels you will need to make sure you include both breadth (a sufficient variety and amount of different information) and depth (enough detail to support your report).

Your report should be written to the specific requirements of your chosen business so try to avoid putting in general information analysing any business sectors that are not related to your chosen organisation. It is important that you really target your research and analysis into the development of your report and keep it specific to the business that you are investigating.

Remember, analysis means looking at the advantages and disadvantages of your findings. To show that you can operate at A2 level you will also need to be able to make judgements about what you find and consider these findings in the broader context of the organisation and the future for that organisation in its sector. Synthesising information is also required for high grade achievement at A2 level, which requires you to extract the data that is relevant and be constructively critical of it. More information on evaluating relevant factors is also contained in Section 11.2.5.

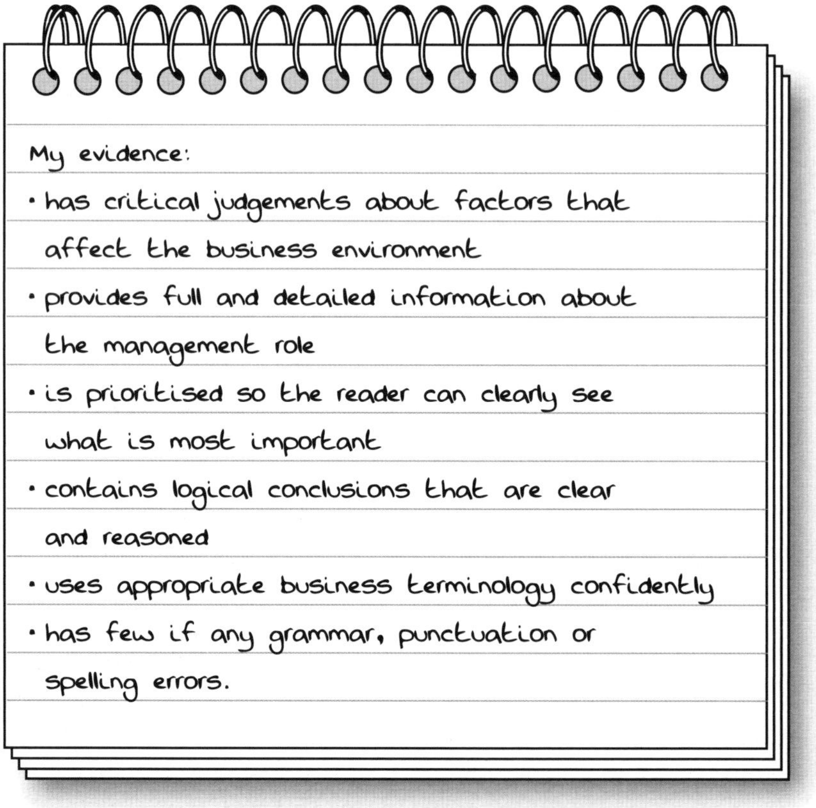

My evidence:
- has critical judgements about factors that affect the business environment
- provides full and detailed information about the management role
- is prioritised so the reader can clearly see what is most important
- contains logical conclusions that are clear and reasoned
- uses appropriate business terminology confidently
- has few if any grammar, punctuation or spelling errors.

FIGURE 11.18 *Checklist of points for your report*

You have been given guidance about the type of information and the way that you need to write your business report to try to achieve the highest grades possible at A2. Some more general advice and tips on report writing are given below. When you have finished a first draft of your report, ask a friend in your group to read your report and check that you have followed all the points of advice.

1. The report is factual, objective and well presented.
2. Headings and subheadings are used.
3. The spacing between headings is the same throughout the report.
4. Numbered points make it easy to follow.
5. The information is accurate.
6. The information has good reasoning behind it.
7. The report is written in the third person for example instead of 'Kenneth Berman said' or 'I asked Kenneth Berman', it reads 'it was found that Kenneth Berman preferred a democratic management style'.
8. Appendices are used to add relevant information including examples of resources, questionnaires and interview notes.
9. Relevant quotes are highlighted and acknowledged in the bibliography.
10. It is free of grammar, spelling and punctuation errors.

11.2.5 Evaluation of the factors which can influence the environment in which a manager/supervisor performs his/her role

In this unit you have already been reminded of the importance of analysis and evaluation skills and how demonstration of these within your report is likely to lead to higher grades.

You need to evaluate the factors which can influence the environment in which a manager performs his/her role by considering the four main issues outlined below:

* whether one particular management or supervisory style is more likely to generate results and foster good employee–employer relations than using alternative management/supervisory styles

* how a management/supervisory role can be affected by changes to the business's aims and objectives or a change in the culture/structure of an organisation

* whether a certain management style is more likely to foster better employee–employer relations than another

* whether management/supervisory functions will change depending on the nature of the business.

Good employee–employer relations

You need to evaluate how much the manager's style affects the motivation and productivity levels of employees compared to the effect there would be if other management styles were used. You will need to analyse the management style that is being used by the manager and consider whether their style helps or hinders employees where they work. A creative organisation such as a design company may have very highly motivated employees that need very little supervision and operate best with a laissez-faire attitude to management. Alternatively, a factory production line might operate best with an autocratic manager. You should consider the type of results that are important – service, sales, value for money?

You will need to analyse the strengths and weaknesses of the style used in relation to the organisation you are studying. To fully evaluate your answer you will also need to make judgements that take into account the style and relate it to the whole business context, for example you may wish to consider the influence of competitors or the way that employees expect to be treated within the environment they are working (norms and values).

Changing aims and objectives

In your report, you will have described the culture and structure of the organisation. You must also consider what is happening within the business and its sector that may force changes to take place, for example the impact of a merger or takeover that has happened or could happen to the organisation. You may also wish to consider the impact of other changes, such as delayering as part of a cost-reduction exercise and the effect on the structure including spans of control and change in culture.

What is critical within the evaluation is to consider the impact and the positive and negative aspects of that impact followed by a judgement about the final effect overall. You should consider the strengths and weaknesses of the planning within the organisation – do they help to drive things forward or does planning take such a long time to organise that opportunities are lost. Is the organisation proactive or reactive? Remember the more constructively critical you are in your report the higher your final grade is likely to be.

The effect of management styles

You have considered employee–employer relations within the unit and the type of management styles that prompt different reactions from employees. You have also gained information about the effect of motivation. Taking both of these areas into account you should consider the advantages and disadvantages of the management style used within your organisation and its effect on employees and consider whether or not it is the most effective style for this organisation. You may find it useful to add data from other organisations or make comparisons with competitors from the same industry sector. You should also consider employee relations from the point of industrial relations by considering whether or not the organisation's employees are members of a union, how they negotiate across the organisation and the strengths and weaknesses of that process.

CASE STUDY

Morrison Group

In March 2004 Morrison completed the takeover of rival supermarket retailer Safeway. The newly combined companies now represent around 15% of the grocery market and the fourth biggest supermarket group in the UK. Employing 150,000 staff in factories, head office, stores and distribution allows Morrison to support 10 million shoppers each week. Whilst Morrison and Safeway now openly trade as one retailer this has not been without complication in terms of the structure and culture of the two supermarket retailers being brought together. During the transition there were a number of reduced profit warnings and rumours that Safeway employees were not keen to swap 'French cheeses for pork pies'.

Morrison were said to be imposing their culture on Safeway employees which was not what they wanted and this was causing difficulties between the different managers. In September 2005 there were further problems for the fully integrated company when 8,000 workers at eight Morrison distribution centres were balloted for strike action.

For more information see www.morrisons.co.uk.

✓ 1. Using the information from the case study and relevant newspaper articles and websites, produce a display detailing some of the issues that were faced by Morrison when they took over Safeway.

✓✓ 2. Analyse which issues they could have predicted or planned for and which were unforeseen?

✓✓✓ 3. Give a judgement overall about how the Morrison management team performed over this time using financial and results information to back up your thinking.

Looking in newspapers and on the Internet, investigate industrial relations including industrial action (strikes and work to rule). Examples you could use include fire fighters or underground workers. Describe the main management skills that are needed to manage such situations.

Some useful sources of information include:

- ACAS – the Advisory, Conciliation and Arbitration Service – tries to help avoid industrial conflict and action by finding ways of settling disputes between employees and employees (www.acas.org.uk)

- Department of Trade and Industry (www.dti. gov.uk) is a government department set up to give advice to businesses, employees and consumers

- The Confederation of British Industry (www. cbi.org.uk) gives support and information to UK businesses.

* Does the business offer a service?

* How skilled are the employees?

* How much management control is needed?

* What are motivational levels like?

* Do different sections of the business have different ways of operating within the organisation?

* Is there a common style of management for everyone?

* How are management decisions communicated?

* Is there open communication or does a **grapevine** operate?

A *grapevine* is the informal communication channel often found in organisations and usually based on gossip and hearsay.

Changing nature of the business

Finally you will also need to make judgements about how management is affected by the business type and how one management style may work well in one type of business but fail miserably in another. You should consider the nature of the work:

Again, at this point you may wish to make useful comparisons with other businesses in the same sector to try to ascertain how their management style works. Are they a larger or more successful company? What do they do that makes them better or worse than your organisation and what evidence is there to support this view?

1. What is meant by culture within an organisation?

2. Describe each of the four main types of culture.

3. What is the difference between aims and objectives?

4. What are the advantages and disadvantages of hierarchical and flat structures within business?

5. What does subordinate mean?

6. How is tactical planning used by supermarket retailers in your area?

7. 'Contingency planning represents a huge opportunity cost to a business.' Discuss this view.

8. Compare and contrast the motivational theories of Taylor and Maslow.

9. Describe the advantages of introducing job enlargement into the workplace – what might the limitations also be?

10. Outline the differences between formal and informal monitoring at work.

11. What are the disadvantages of 'fire fighting' problems in the workplace.

12. What is meant by an opportunity cost?

13. How useful is the Pareto Principle for business planning?

14. 'On-the-job training is more beneficial to business.' Discuss this view.

15. What is the purpose of a skills audit and how useful is it to an organisation?

16. Outline three limitations of the appraisal process.

17. What is meant by an autocratic manager?

18. What is meant by synergy when working together?

19. What is meant by trait theory in relation to management?

20. What are the benefits of having good employer–employee relations in the workplace?

Resources

Books

Alred, G, Garvey, B and Smith, R *The Mentoring Pocket Book*, Management Pocket Books

Bartol, DC and Martin, KM (2002) *Management*, McGraw-Hill Education

Chaffey, D (2002) *E-Commerce and E-Business Management*, Pearson Education Limited

Dooley, D, Guy, P, Goymer, J, Richards, C, Richards, N (2006), *BTEC National Business Book 2*, Harcourt Education

Gillespie, A (2002) *Business in Action*, Hodder & Stoughton

Harvey-Jones, J (2003) *Making It Happen: Reflections on Leadership*, Profile Business

Kirton, M (Ed) (1989) *Adaptors and Innovators: Styles of Creativity and Problem-Solving*, Routledge

Martin, M and Jackson, T (2002) *Personnel Practice (People and Organisations)*, Chartered Institute of Personnel and Development (CIPD)

Parsloe, E and Wray, M (2000) *Coaching and Mentoring*, Kogan Page

Journals

Business Review
Personnel Management

Websites

www.acas.org.uk
The Advisory, Conciliation and Arbitration Service

www.adviceguide.org.uk
Citizens Advice Bureau with guides to the workplace

www.businesslink.gov.uk
Business Link Advice for businesses

www.cbi.org.uk
Confederation of British Industry

www.cipd.co.uk
Chartered Institute of Personnel and Development

www.coachingnetwork.org.uk
Useful tips

www.dti.gov.uk
Department of Trade and Industry on coaching and mentoring

www.investorsinpeople.co.uk
Investors in People website

www.managementqualifications.co.uk
Management Qualifications website giving advice

www.mindtools.com
Tools that can be used to help managers

www.mybusiness.co.uk
My Business provides information on management issues for small businesses including resources

www.personneltoday.co.uk
Personnel Today human resource information provider (UK)

www.statistics.gov.uk
National statistics published by the government

Promotion in action

This unit contains six elements:

13.2.1　Devising a strategy

13.2.2　The environment within which the strategy will take shape

13.2.3　Planning the strategy

13.2.4　Researching of the strategy and analysis of the information that is collected

13.2.5　Producing a plan of action

13.2.6　Internal and external influences on promotional activity

Unit 13 Introduction

This unit requires you to produce a **promotional strategy** including the use of *at least two* different types of **media** for promoting *a new product or service* that currently undertakes some form of promotional activity. It is recommended that it is a *medium- to large-sized business*.

You will need to investigate what is meant by **promotion** and the different methods and strategies that are used by organisations. Some of the methods you may already know from your own experience of promotion including advertising on television, telesales or emails that you have received from organisations telling you about their latest discount or offer.

You have also gained some knowledge at AS level when you completed Unit 1 (Marketing Proposal), Unit 4 (The Impact of Customer Service) and A2 Unit 10 (A Business Plan for the Entrepreneur).

You need to investigate your strategy by considering the concept of promotional activity, research into the relevant business environment and influences on your promotional activity linked to your findings and analysis.

You should pick a business to study that has a varied portfolio of products or services, e.g. Nokia, Nike or NTL to consider the different types of promotions they use before coming up with a promotional strategy for a new product or service of your own!

Key terms

Media is the term used for different forms of promotional channels such as television, newspapers and radio.

Promotion is the term used for making customers aware of the products and services that a business offers including any special deals.

Promotional strategy is the goal or purpose of any activity that you take to increase awareness or sales of a product or service.

13.2.1 Devising a strategy

Before you are able to take practical steps to outline your campaign it is important to consider the planning of your strategy from a longer-term perspective. This is known as strategic planning and you may have come across this idea in other units of your course.

Strategic planning has four key elements to it and these form a cycle whereby plans are made and then reviewed.

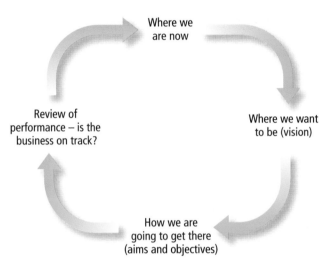

FIGURE 13.1 *The strategic planning cycle*

Strategic planning gives more of a direction or feel for where the organisation wants to go in the future with a promotional idea but does not in the first stages necessarily give specific data about how this is actually going to be put into place.

Strategic planning gives an outline of what is needed to channel ideas and the influences on those ideas. As part of your strategic planning you will need to go through a number of steps:

* understand the business environment within which your strategy will take shape

* plan the strategy

* research the business environment to inform strategy development

* analyse and gather data to inform the development of the strategy

* produce a plan of action based on research and analysis

* monitor and evaluate various aspects of the strategy with a view to recommending improvements and future updates to the strategy.

This unit will guide you through the process and remind you of the importance of collecting research data to help you decide on an appropriate form of promotional activity for your chosen business.

Understanding the business environment within which your strategy will take shape

Understanding the business environment within which the strategy takes place helps fulfil the first stage of the strategic planning cycle – where are we now? It is important at this stage to consider:

* the size and resources of the business

* competitors of the business

* current product portfolio and stages of the product life cycle for the products or services

* current promotional campaigns

* background to the organisation.

The size and resources of the business

The business and its promotional activity will be influenced by the size of the business and the resources that it has. Your strategy needs to be realistic for the size of business that you are working with. Companies like Cadbury, BT, Heinz or Virgin spend millions of pounds on promotional activity each year and you will need to make your plan as realistic as possible for the size of the organisation you have chosen. The overall turnover of the business should help you to make judgements about the size of the budget available for your campaign so you may wish to get a set of the business' published accounts if possible. The size of the business will also affect the number of people able to be allocated to the promotional project and how much time they can spend implementing the campaign.

Competitors of the business and their promotional campaigns

Using a market map helps identify gaps by seeing where competitors are placed. A market map uses two scales and you can choose different measurements in order to compare businesses within the same market. The two measurements used for comparison in the market map shown in Figure 13.2 are frequency of usage and price for the chocolate bar market. The market map contains a variety of chocolate bars placed in different areas of the map. This is a snap shot of the market.

By producing a market map you will be able to establish who the competitors are for your business, how competitive that market is and any areas of the market that may be available to be filled by your new product or service and promotional strategy. Remember, you are going to be rewarded for your creativity in this unit so market mapping may be able to give you some useful ideas.

Theory into practice

Produce a market map. To do this, you will need to make a list of potential competitors and their products or services. You will then need to apply your own set of scales in order to plot your map, for example low/high price, low/high quality or high/low use of technology.

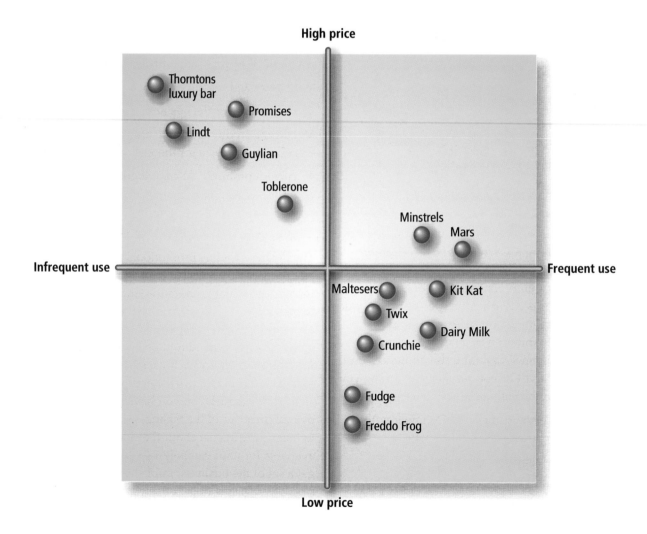

FIGURE 13.2 *An example of a market map for the chocolate bar market*

Using either commercial breaks between television programmes, newspapers, magazines or the Internet, think of as many different types of promotional activity, e.g. adverts or offers that your competitors use. Think about what makes those activities successful or not so successful.

Current product portfolio and stages of the product life cycle for the product or service

It is important to consider the product portfolio of your chosen business. This means the variety of products that they offer and the stage of the product life cycle they are in. Remember, the concept of product can be applied to both a physical product and a service. By gauging which stage of the product life cycle each product or service is in, you will be able to see how balanced the organisation's portfolio is by using the Boston matrix and you may be able to identify areas or gaps that exist to give you ideas. It is also useful to apply the Ansoff matrix to consider any gaps there are for a new product or service by considering whether or not the product or service should be a new product or service offered within an existing market or a new product or service in a new market. More information about the product life cycle, Boston matrix and Ansoff matrix are contained in Unit 10 of this book (see pages 69–73).

Detailing the role of branding within the business and what makes its other products or services unique (its unique selling point or USP) is useful. Your new product and its promotional strategy will need to complement the existing portfolio and add to the range so you will need to analyse how important you think brand image is and what the organisation does to maintain and improve its image.

Current promotional campaigns

Using your Boston matrix and Section 13.2.5 (Production of a plan of action) on page 169 to help you, you will need to consider the current promotional activities that are used by your chosen organisation giving details about the different methods of communication and types of media that are used when sending a message to their customers such as:

* advertising
* online
* newspaper and specialist journal
* sponsorship
* PR
* merchandising
* sales promotions
* direct mailing.

Background to the organisation

You should also conduct some research into the background to the business and its culture. For example how long it has been established and the use of relevant company colours (turquoise for Heinz or purple for Cadbury) can provide data that will help you to make links between current promotion activity and your promotional strategy. You may find it useful to add some of this data to the back of your promotional strategy portfolio as appendices.

Making links between your strategy and data

At every stage of your planning and data collection you will need to consider relevant theoretical concepts and apply them to your chosen business context. You will need to demonstrate that you have understanding of the different forms of promotional activity that are already being used by the business or could be used, before detailing your strategy including promotional activity for at least two different types of media.

To achieve higher marks, you will need to demonstrate clear and comprehensive understanding of promotional activity and the influences that help or hinder those activities.

You will also need to make clear links between the results of your detailed research analysis into the business and the choices that you have made for your promotional campaign.

13.2.2 The environment within which the strategy will take shape

You have already considered the business environment within Section 13.2.1 including factors such as culture, resources and product portfolio that affect how promotional activity is carried out. Promotion is a vital way that businesses can stay ahead of their rivals and is becoming increasingly competitive. The best way for businesses to stay ahead of their competitors is for them to work to:

✴ understand the needs of their customers

✴ satisfy the wants and needs of customers for new products and services

✴ produce relevant and appropriate forms of promotional activity targeted to specific customer needs.

Understanding the needs of customers

By understanding the needs of customers, a business is able to work out what it must do to make sure it retains high sales and the share of the markets that it operates in (market share). Businesses will spend large amounts of money researching their customers to try to find out their changing needs. Primary and secondary research is used (see Section 13.2.3) to consider trends affecting those customers such as their incomes, ages, tastes and preferences. These are all used to build up a picture of their customer. You will need to carry out such research so that you can demonstrate understanding of the customers your promotional activity is aimed at. Understanding the needs of customers can also help the business to anticipate what the customer might want next, how they behave, where their advertising should be targeted and so on.

Satisfying the wants and needs of customers for new products and services

Promotion attempts to satisfy the wants and needs of customers by introducing new products or services and persuading customers that they want to buy them. This process includes market-led and product-led new product development.

✴ Market-led new product or service development comes from views (wants and needs) of customers that are collected from the relevant market place. Tomato ketchup was produced in a squeezy plastic bottle as a response to customers wanting to be able to get all of their ketchup out of the bottle.

✴ Product-led new product or service development is when a product can be changed or updated as manufacturers seek to update and improve their technology or type of service. Mobile phones have seen huge transformations from a basic telephone service to being able to offer MP3, videophone,

Products can be updated to improve their technology

television, text messaging and camera facilities. Manufacturers seek to improve the product and then *persuade* consumers that they want or need them.

Producing relevant and appropriate forms of promotional activity targeted to specific customer needs

The success of any promotional campaign depends on how relevant it is to the targeted customers in terms of their wants and needs. If a promotion does not appear relevant to a particular audience they will not listen to its message and take action. If the message becomes changed in some way or there are difficulties in understanding it the group targeted will not see it as relevant to them. Ensuring the message is clear and for the right groups of people is extremely important. To be relevant, a business will also need to carefully chose which method of media it uses to transmit the message, e.g. email, television or radio. Choosing the right type of media is critical to make the promotional activity relevant as it needs to be received by the right audience at the right time in order to make the decision to buy the product or service. More information is available in Section 13.2.5 on pages 169–185.

Think it over...

Think of any promotional campaigns that you have heard of that have been unsuccessful. A historical one that you may wish to research is the Sinclair C5. Think about what was wrong with the campaign or product so it was not relevant to consumers and share your ideas with other students in your class.

The appropriateness of a type of promotional activity is central to its success. In some cases there are legal restrictions that constrain promotional activity due to the type of product, e.g. cigarettes, alcohol or medicines.

CASE STUDY

Alcohol in Russia

Whilst advertising for smoking has been significantly reduced and packets distributed with health warnings, there has been no such ban on the advertising of alcohol within the UK in spite of increasing numbers of people both drinking alcohol and becoming addicted to it.

Parliament in Russia strictly restricted television advertising of beer and alcoholic drinks containing more than 0.5 per cent alcohol in 2005. The first stage of the restrictions was to:

- ban the advertising of such products between the hours of 7 am and 10 pm
- ban beer advertisements in the form of a cartoon
- prohibit these products being associated with certain organisations, for example sports or children's organisations
- forbid the portrayal of animals or people within the advertisements.

This was in a response to an increase in drinking amongst young people and children as beer prices in 2004 were as low as 40p for a bottle. Beer itself was viewed as a soft drink much like lemonade and it was not uncommon to see children drinking it after school as there were few restrictions on its sale to under 18s. Reducing the advertising of alcohol was seen as one way to try to restrict its use.

Organise a debate about the possibility of banning the advertising of alcoholic drinks in the UK. Divide your class into two. One half of the class can represent beer manufacturers who wish to maintain alcohol advertising on television and one half can represent pressure groups who wish to ban it. Some useful websites to help with your discussion are:

www.drinkaware.co.uk
www.alcoholconcern.org.uk
www.lifebytes.gov.uk.

There are also some decisions to be made about the ethical or moral appropriateness of promotional activity, for example the exclusive advertising of snack foods during children's television programmes may be seen to be unethical but are certainly not illegal. A business would have to choose its own ethical position in relation to this and decide what it felt to be appropriate.

Using all of the business tools that you have learned in 13.2.1 when considering the business environment and taking into account the information contained in planning the strategy and collecting the research, you will need to investigate how your business operates in terms of promotional activity.

13.2.3 Planning the strategy

Having identified the type of promotional activity already taking place, you will need to make links to why this activity takes place in the first place and what is contained within existing promotional strategies. You will need to understand that when businesses conduct strategic planning they need to make sure they:

* set aims and objectives

* target potential customers

* select appropriate types of research.

Setting of aims and objectives

Aims and objectives are central to most aspects of business as they are the driving force behind what happens with the business. The aims are the overall purpose or goals and the objectives are the list of plans that help those aims to be achieved. Marketing aims and objectives work in exactly the same way as any other objectives in that they should be SMART (specific, measurable, agreed, realistic and time-constrained).

You will need to consider the aims of promotional strategy(ies) that are being used within the business already and the objectives that support them.

Theory into practice

A New York Style Delicatessen is going to open in London and wants to establish good sales through promotional activity. The New York Style Deli offers the opportunity to experience an authentic New York eating experience in London complete with pancakes with syrup, serve-yourself hotplates and a small seating area.

The owner and manager have set out the following aims and objectives for a promotional strategy which provides them with a clear starting point to get organised and start producing a leaflet with a money-off coupon, organise printing and delivery. Identifying such a starting point allows the manager to produce an action plan with steps that must be taken in order for both the objectives and aim to be a success.

Aim: To increase customer awareness of the New York Style Deli.

Objectives: To send out a direct mail shot to all households within a five mile area within the next two months including a money-off voucher.

To invite a famous celebrity chef for breakfast to review the menu and provide a press release within one month.

1. Using your own ideas and help from Section 13.2.5, what are the advantages of each of these promotional activities.
2. How SMART are the objectives?
3. How could success be measured?
4. Which other promotional activities would you recommend?

Targeting potential customers

Market segmentation explains how a market should be divided up and potential customers identified as target segments. Choosing to launch a promotional activity to a specific group of people should mean that the business gets value for money. This is because those customers are most likely to take part in the service or buy the product. Market research companies spend a lot of time and money collecting data on the needs, wants and desires of different groups of people so that specific groups or segments of people can be targeted during promotional activity. These companies include:

Mintel	(www.mintel.com)
Dun and Bradstreet	(www.dnb.com/uk/)
Mori	(www.mori.com)
CIM	(www.cim.co.uk).

Selecting appropriate types of research

Selecting the most appropriate types of research in order to collect data to inform promotional strategy is as important as an outline of the strategy in the first place. This is because the business will only collect the right data if it uses the right methods to collect it. There are two main types of research: primary and secondary research. You have already become aware of these in Unit 1 of your AS studies.

Primary research (also known as field research) is research that is collected by the business themselves through the use of activities such as:

* questionnaires

* focus groups

* surveys.

Data is collected for the first time and can specifically attempt to answer questions relating to a product or service. As the data needs to be collected and then analysed it can be very expensive and time-consuming.

Secondary research (also known as desk research) is research collected by someone else and includes a variety of sources such as market research companies, government statistics, competitor data, journals and magazines. Secondary research is much quicker to collect and less expensive but may not be specific enough to answer all of the research needs for a particular strategy.

You will need to include a mixture of both secondary and primary research within your promotional strategy to make sure it is balanced and contains all the necessary detail. More information about research collection and analysis is available in Section 13.2.4 on page 160.

Promotional objectives

You have already considered the setting of business aims and objectives for existing promotional strategies both current and historical. You are now required to set aim(s) for your own promotional strategy and a set of supporting objectives to include the following:

* making customers aware of the product/service and allowing them to recognise its existence

* convincing the public of the purpose and benefits of the product/service

* persuading customers that the product/service can benefit them

* leading customers to act, e.g. make the decision to buy

* changing customers' attitudes

* creating desires in customers

* giving reassurance to customers

* reminding customers that the product exists.

You will need to take into account the use of your aims and objectives when considering promotional activity as a whole.

As you are promoting a new product or service there are a number of different internal and external influences on them that you should also take into consideration (see Section 13.2.6 on pages 185–191).

Making customers aware of the product/service and allowing them to recognise its existence

You will need to consider the best methods of making customers aware of the new product or service and what the organisation already does to make this happen, e.g. advertising or public relations. You will need to measure customer recognition using SMART objectives. The promotional method chosen will depend on the type of organisation you are studying and the audience that you are aiming to attract, e.g. younger audiences listen to Radio 1 whereas older listeners tend to listen to Radio 2. Your audience would influence where you chose to promote.

Convincing the public of the purpose and benefits of the product/service

Trying to convince the public that they need a product and it will benefit them is likely to need to be approached in a variety of forms, for example a demonstration of its use with some kind of discount voucher may convince your audience to get involved and purchase the product. You may have seen such demonstrations in department stores or supermarkets with the opportunity to try before you buy.

Persuading customers that the product/service can benefit them

Choosing a target audience to work with for your promotional strategy means that you need to persuade a specific group of people that there is something unique or improved that can benefit them specifically. This may involve practical steps through advertising or public relations to convince customers that their lives will improve as a result of receiving a particular product or service. You may have seen advertisements for legal services that promise to try to collect compensation for consumers who have been involved in accidents at work or in public places. These often give details of the likely amount they may receive and how it could be put to good use.

Leading customers to act

Often customers will be aware of a service or product on offer but promotion is also about giving them the incentive to go out and actually make the decision to buy. They will need to move on from being aware of the product and thinking about the product to actually going forward and taking action. As part of your campaign you will need to include promotional activities that lead the customer to buy such as money-off vouchers

Product demonstrations may persuade potential buyers

or promotional material at the point of sale to encourage interest.

Changing customers' attitudes

Some promotional objectives will include the desire to change how people think about a product or service to entice them to buy more. Successful campaigns that have been able to do this include a promotional campaign by the RSPCA to persuade customers to buy free range eggs rather than those laid by battery hens. As a result of the campaign, a significant number of free range eggs are now being sold.

Creating desires in customers

Creating a desire in a customer means creating a product or service that they would ideally like to have but may not always need. The desire may come from wanting to be perceived by others in a certain way due to the image of a product, for example a specific fashion designer, watch or handbag. There are lots of different types of chocolate bars in existence but chocolate companies will still aim to create desire for a new one.

Giving reassurance to customers

A promotional objective may also seek to reassure customers that a product or service is still working well, particularly if there has been some bad publicity. A manufacturer's defect or problem with supply may put customers off buying the product or problems with availability may affect the desirability. In these cases, the purpose of the promotional objective would be to maintain levels of demand and reassure customers about the product or service.

CASE STUDY

iPod Nano

During 2005, Apple received some publicity that the iPod Nano was suffering from problems of screen scratching. It was rumoured that such scratches could severely restrict the ability of users to be able to view photos and album art. Due to the strength of the brand and desire of customers to continue to buy iPods there was little effect on demand for these items. Apple did, however, issue a press release as part of their public relations promotional activity reassuring customers about their products and suggesting that very few Nanos were affected. Their press release suggested that 'less than one-tenth of one per cent' were affected.

Many customers took comfort from this and continued to be satisfied with their purchases until November 2005 when several buyers from the US, UK and Mexico joined together to file a legal claim against Apple in the US. This led to Apple issuing all their new Nanos with soft fabric cases and care instructions being given on the Apple website.

For more information about Apple iPod products see www.apple.com.

✓ 1. **What is meant by the strength of the brand?**
✓✓ 2. **Why might a press release be used to reassure customers and what are the advantages and disadvantages of communicating to customers in this way?**
✓✓✓ 3. **Judge how effective Apple have been in reassuring their customers. Were there any improvements they could have made to their promotional activity?**

Reminding customers that the product exists

The more loyal customers are to a brand, the more likely they are to keep buying it. To keep the image of a brand and maintain interest in the product, customers may need reminding that it exists through promotional activity such as sponsorship deals or public relations exercises. One example of the way that customers are reminded of Vodaphone's services is by sponsoring the shirts of football players. By doing this, customers are reminded of Vodaphone during every football game.

Writing your own objectives

As part of your promotional strategy you will need to clearly outline your own promotional objectives. You will need to choose these objectives carefully and link them to results of primary and secondary research data that you have collected. Remember to make your objectives SMART.

13.2.4 Researching of the strategy and analysis of the information that is collected

Effective research that is clearly targeted and focused is essential. It should contain details of what is happening now and inform the promotional strategy for the new product or service

You will need to carry out primary *and* secondary research. It is recommended that you do secondary research before primary so you can get an idea of the promotional activity in the market as a whole to give you ideas.

Secondary research

Secondary research is information that has been collected and published by someone else. It is useful to a business because it exists already and can provide information about what is happening in a market. Businesses can make use of two sorts of secondary data: data available within the business such as sales records, invoice payments and loyalty cards or data available outside the business such as marketing reports, newspapers or websites. More information about secondary research and possible sources of information is available in Unit 10 on pages 63–5.

As part of your collection of secondary data you will need to make sure you have lots of examples of promotional activity that other businesses use to promote a similar range of products or services. Whilst you are comparing the activity you should try to examine as wide a range of media (such as television, newspapers and so on) that are being used as possible. Remember your promotional strategy must include the use of at least two different types of media.

Primary research

Primary data is very important because it gives you first hand information for two main purposes: to find out more general information about what is happening in a market and to focus on the likelihood of success for your new product or service including the best way to promote it. Your primary research will be useful in three main ways:

* to work out whether or not there is a place for a new product or service in a market using, for example, a questionnaire or survey

* to collect information on what kind of promotional features attract customers in the business you are studying

* to collect information on the way that marketing works in your chosen business at first hand.

Gathering information on customer tastes and needs for a new product or service

Primary research is often the best way of gathering information on whether or not a customer will want to buy a product or service. You will need to collect data from new and existing customers in order to fully explore

Collect the names of businesses that operate in the same or similar market to your business. Thinking about the new product or service that you are going to promote, consider promotional activity that is currently being undertaken in this area by completing the following table. The table has been completed for a new fruit flavoured soft cheese product. You may find it useful to turn to page 153 for more details on the different types of media that can be used if you are unsure.

BUSINESS NAME	PRODUCT DETAILS	PROMOTIONAL ACTIVITY	MEDIUM USED
The Dairy	Strawberries and cream soft cheese	A money-off coupon was used to encourage customers to buy this new product. The offer was for 50p off per pot of cheese and the retail price of the product is at full cost £1.20.	Information leaflet including sales promotion delivered to areas of customers via direct mailing.

By completing this table you will get an idea of the type of media commonly used for products or services similar to the one that you are going to promote so that you can either choose a similar method as part of your strategy or try to identify any gaps or different types of promotional activity that you can use.

all possibilities. Primary research can identify potential tastes for a product or service and the extent to which customers are likely to need it. Primary research, therefore, can be used to identify if there is a demand for a new product or service including any relevant information such as preferred customer taste or desirable shape or look. Remember you will need to analyse your own data as its quality will influence your ability to analyse your own results.

There are a number of different primary research methods that you could use to collect data about the market within which you are choosing to work or a specific product or service including a survey, questionnaire, observation focus group or test panel. Your choice of method will influence the type of data that you will be able to collect and there is a cost implication associated with each in terms of both time and money to set up your method. A popular and relatively easy method of collecting data is to use a questionnaire to collect your data. It may be possible to use the questionnaire with potential

customers and/or to use it to gather information from the competitors of your business or even from the business itself.

Questionnaire

A full examination of questionnaire design and sampling techniques is available for you to use in Unit 10 on pages 62–3 but the key elements that you need to remember are given in Figure 13.3 to remind you.

USING QUESTIONNAIRES	
Quantitative or qualitative questions	**Quantitative research** is much more concerned with facts and figures that can provide statistical judgements, e.g. 'Do you eat chocolate?' where the answer is either 'yes' or 'no'.
	Qualitative research collects information about why people act in the way that they do, including their motivation, judgements and opinions e.g. What is your opinion of ginger flavoured chocolate?
Different questioning techniques	**Likert scaling** uses statements which are agreed or disagreed by using scales such as:
	Strongly agree, Agree, Have no opinion, Disagree or Strongly disagree
	Semantic scaling uses scales e.g. 1 to 8 with 1 being a customer would definitely try a new product and 8 being a customer would definitely not buy it.
	Ranking 1 to 5 using a number of key words to judge what is most important to a potential new customer, e.g. price, taste or brand name.
	Open or closed questions where the answer is either closed (Yes or No) or open for any answer so that your respondents can add extra detail about their decisions.
Sampling	**Random** where every person has an equal chance of being picked.
	Stratified where particular groups are identified, for example based on where they live or economic status.
	Quota where a quota is decided by you as to how many people you want to ask and the type of respondents you are looking for, e.g. 50 men aged 16 to 20.
	Judgement where you choose a deliberate sample of people to specifically answer your questions (subject to bias).
	Convenience where you choose to collect data from the most convenient place, e.g. a specific road or outside a shop.

FIGURE 13.3 *Key factors of using questionnaires*

You will need to collect information on your new product or service to be used to give you ideas for your promotional activity. Remember you will be expected to analyse the effectiveness of your promotional strategy and your conclusions should be supported by the collection of appropriate and relevant data. If your questionnaire is flawed then it is likely that your results will also be flawed so checking your questionnaire is working effectively is time well spent.

Part of the process of checking your questionnaire is also to test it on a smaller number of respondents in the sample group that you are aiming to use. For example, if you expect to ask 30 women aged 18 to 20 about their views on a new car hire service to be offered by a national chain then you would expect to test that questionnaire on at least two potential respondents before you gave it out to the 30 people who are actually going to take part.

Look at this questionnaire given out to a quota sample of 20 students aged 16 to 21 to gain information about their needs, wants and desires for the launch of a new cheese and pickle flavoured doughnut to be offered by a national bakery business.

CHEESE AND PICKLE DOUGHNUTS
What is your name?
How old are you? 16–20 20–24 24–28 28–32
How often do you eat doughnuts? Every day   A couple of times a week   Occasionally   Sometimes   Never
How much would you pay for a doughnut? 50p 60p 80p 90p
What is most important to you when buying a doughnut?
Where do you buy doughnuts from?
Which is your favourite flavour of doughnut?
Answer the following statement by circling the point on the scale that most accurately gives your opinion with 1 being strongly agree and 8 being strongly disagree: I like cheese and pickle   1   2   3   4   5   6   7   8
Would you eat a cheese and pickle doughnut?
Which of the following is most likely to persuade you to buy a cheese and pickle doughnut? Rank them 1 to 5 Sales coupon TV advert Internet pop up Free trial
What gender are you? Please circle Male or Female
What makes you buy a doughnut?
How many doughnuts do you buy at one time?
How many times a week do you access the following Radio   _____ per week Television   _____ per week Newspapers   _____ per week Internet   _____ per week Email   _____ per week

Answer the questionnaire yourself to test it! What are the problems with it? What improvements could you make to it in terms of its layout, the questions used and the information gathered?

Discussion with individuals in your chosen business

It may be possible, even in the medium or large sized business that you have chosen, to interview or have a discussion with a representative from the business about what they feel attracts customers to their current products and/or services. If this is not possible face to face you may be able to contact them via telephone or online (remember to check this with your teacher first). You will need to carefully plan how the discussion should take place as they are likely to be very busy and therefore may not have a lot of time to spare.

You will also need to have a set of ideas for open ended questions that will help guide the discussion. You could discuss existing promotional activity that they feel has been successful or you might be able to ask their opinion about the ideas you are currently working on to test if they think it would be a good idea. By looking at the results from your questionnaire you could also ask them to comment on the data that you have collected so far.

Visits to your chosen business

A visit to your chosen business can also be a really useful way of collecting primary research material especially if you are able to carry out a survey within the marketing department. If it is possible, you may wish to try using a questionnaire by post or over the telephone but remember to ask permission from your teacher first. Many large businesses have visitor centres or education officers who may be able to answer any questions that you have. Again, like the questionnaire or discussion, make sure you are prepared and know exactly what information you are looking for and why.

Advertising agencies

If your business is an especially large one it is likely that it may use an advertising agency to conduct promotional activity on its behalf. You may find it useful to carry out research into how advertising agencies conduct promotional activity, for example Saatchi and Saatchi, Cheeze and Leo Burnett.

Analysing your collected information

When analysing your collected information you need to understand some of the techniques that can be employed. As well as statistical techniques, you also need to analyse promotional activity that businesses are using against a common set of criteria:

* aesthetics
* message
* fitness for purpose
* originality
* communication.

Aesthetics

Marketing aesthetics is centred around the notion of satisfying customer needs by making their experiences more pleasurable or aesthetically pleasing. Aesthetics seeks to respond to the sensory needs of potential customers including the way promotion activities look, sound, taste, touch and smell. You will need to make such judgements about your promotional activity. Aesthetics is a powerful tool in marketing as it can be used to make one product stand out from another and therefore give it **added value** and a better perceived brand image.

Products and service that can be distinguished easily from others as they relate more effectively to these sensory needs are likely to be more differentiated and therefore successful. As you have already learned, aesthetics can take a number of forms and some of these principles are shown in Figure 13.4.

Look	The promotional activity should appeal to its audience through the use of good design principles relating to: • colour • design • font • background • logos • use of celebrities to enforce image • use of beautiful men and women to sell products • icons and images associated with different cultures.
Sound	The use of different types of noises to support promotional activity: • styles of music e.g. pop or classical music • use of different language e.g. French or German within the advertisement such as Stella Artois • human accents such as those from the US • animal noises e.g. birds tweeting • noises from nature e.g. waves crashing • catch phrases e.g. Va Va Voom or Every little helps.
Taste, smell and touch	Appeals made to the audience's taste buds using words that they will associate with their own tastes such as smooth, dry, rich, creamy and so on. Use of actors in campaigns showing them tasting the product and their reaction e.g. Joanna Lumley eating Müller Yoghurts. Allowing the target audience to try before they buy allows them to taste, smell and touch the product so they can make their own associations. Likening the touch or smell of a product to something else so the target audience associate it with that e.g. shampoo with silk or wild flowers. Making associations between the product and a type of lifestyle or place so by buying the product they are buying the lifestyle e.g. Spa bath products being associated with going to a luxurious spa resort.

FIGURE 13.4 *Principles of marketing using aesthetics*

Key terms

Added value is when something is made better within a product or service, for example the use of the best possible people and ingredients or the use of branding to add perceived value to the product.

The Lynx and Radox effects

Personal hygiene products such as those produced and marketed under the brand name Lynx have made extensive use of aesthetics. Each advertising campaign features good looking men and women laughing and having fun, with the women being attracted to the men as a result of their wonderful smell. By showing young and attractive women dressed in sexy clothing, the viewer is given the message that if you wear Lynx you too will attract young women and therefore will be more desirable. Advertising campaigns aimed at young men will often feature such hidden messages that a certain product or service will add to their sex appeal and as a result they will be more successful with women.

Advertising campaigns aimed at women tend not to feature such obvious references to sexual attraction. They centre more on the idea of fantasy situations. Radox produced a campaign slogan 'Radox – where will your bath take you?' that shows a women escaping through her bathroom into a tropical paradise as a result of using Radox products. It shows her in pleasant surroundings with soothing music, all of these appealing to her senses.

For more information see www.leverfaberge.co.uk and www.saralee.com.

✓ 1. How do Lynx and Radox use look, taste, smell and touch to enhance the promotional activity associated with their products?

✓ 2. What are the main differences between advertising to men and women as suggested in the case study?

✓✓✓ 3. 'Image is more important than the product itself.' Give your reasons for and against this statement and, using examples you are familiar with, judge the extent to which you think this is true.

✓✓✓ 4. 'Write a list of the last 10 advertisements that you have seen in any form of media. How did they make use of aesthetic principles? Make judgements about their effectiveness and recommendations for improvements.

Message

The message of a promotional activity is what you are actually trying to get across to your target audience so it is linked closely with your promotional objectives. The message is what is actually communicated by the business to the target audience and may be weakened depending on the amount of interference, known as noise (you will learn more about this in the section on communication). There are lots of different issues that you should take into account when preparing your message including:

* identifying a problem
* catching attention
* explanation
* action
* targeting the right audience
* translation.

Identifying a problem

Sending a message to your target audience is most successful when that message attempts to identify a problem or want and then shows that the solution can be provided by the product or service that is being offered. Many washing powder messages include images of children covered with dirt, communicate that XYZ Powder is the solution to this problem and then show a child in a 'sparkling white' outfit at the end.

Messages giving information to potential dieters empathise with those overweight by making suggestions like 'I used to be overweight and miserable but after starting this new diet programme I am now much happier and losing weight.' If your audience can feel emotionally attached to what is being portrayed in the message, they are more likely to respond to it.

CASE STUDY

WERTHER'S ORIGINALS

Werther's Originals are old fashioned boiled sweets that have long been associated with an advertisement featuring a silver haired grandfather sharing sweets with his adoring grandson. The purpose of this campaign is to emphasise that it is possible to share Werther's across generations and that it is still ok to eat sweets in adulthood. Werther's have been made by the German manufacturer Storck for over 100 years and represented something from 'the good old days'. This emotional attachment that has been linked to generations sharing moments together has kept this brand doing well during all those years.

More information about Storck brands is available at www.storck.com.

✓ 1. Think back to your early childhood and consider the brands and products that you have grown up with. What emotional attachments do these manufacturers or service providers make between you and situations that happen in your life?

✓✓ 2. How much empathy do you remember from their advertising campaigns and what are the advantages and disadvantages of using such techniques in a campaign?

✓✓✓ 3. 'It is impossible to feel true empathy within advertising as everyone is individual.' To what extent do you think this might be true?

Catching attention

A message needs to have impact and catch your audience's attention straight away. It needs to convey information in a clear and concise way rather than being over wordy and boring. A jingle or tune that may be added as part of the message may help to keep reinforcing the message. McDonald's have had a very successful campaign message that states 'I'm lovin it' and this has been adopted into many every day sayings as it provides a very clear message. Make sure your message is not too short or too long to convey the right amount of information.

Explanation

The message needs to explain what makes the product or service special. It needs to communicate how it will benefit the consumer and what is new and exciting about the product or service. The unique selling point (USP) should be outlined. This is when the message explains why this product or service is so much better than the competition. It gives the audience a reason to believe in the product or service and how their lives will be improved after they have purchased it. Giving very clear benefit explanations gives the target audience a reason to believe in the product and its positive effects.

Action

The message should also appear to start a 'conversation'. This means that there starts to be two-way communication between the business and the audience. The message needs to create impact and awareness but then it requires the audience to actually take action to go and purchase the product or service.

The action should be communicated clearly to potential customers and include contact details such as a telephone number, address, website or email address. A potential customer may be interested in a product or service but if it is too difficult to remember the details of a website or address they may not bother to move from awareness to purchase. If you plan to use a promotional website to help your activity make sure it is simple and easy to remember! You will need to keep reinforcing the message over a number of weeks or even months so you will need to plan to keep this happening in a variety of ways but still conveying the same consistent message. If something is missing or not working within the message, it should be refined to make sure that the right message is being sent.

Targeting the right audience

When portraying a message it is important that it is being conveyed to the right audience. This means that the message may sometimes be sent to a third party who then communicates their wants and needs to the final purchaser of the product or service. This is particularly relevant for products aimed at children. The message may be sent directly to the child and they then use 'pester power' to actually receive the product or service that they want. Conversely the same can be true if the message is sent to a parent as the parent will receive the communication of the message but will purchase the product or service on behalf of the child. Other such audiences may include the elderly, relatives or even pets. It is important to consider:

* who is going to receive the message?
* where are they going to receive the message?
* when are they going to receive the message?

Translation

When you are considering your message it is also useful to think about differences in language that make a translation from one language to another completely break down the message. Some translations work well but for others the meaning associated with the words is completely different. The German manufacturer Schwarzkopf is a leading brand of shampoo in the UK but the literal translation into English is 'black head'. Blackheads in English are associated with facial spots so the message about good quality hair products may be lost if translated. There may also be differences between the meaning of words in the UK compared to those of other English speaking countries such as Australia or the United States.

Fitness for purpose

The promotional activity should also be fit for the purpose for which it is being used. If an activity is designed to make a particular group of people aware of a specialist product or service's existence, a specific targeted advertisement in a specialist magazine would be more suitable than a national television campaign. The activity needs to satisfy the promotional objectives. Promotional activity is also restricted by legal and ethic issues as they influence the type of promotional activity that is permitted. Advertising of services, such as online gambling, need to be targeted at audiences of people over 18 and conducted accordingly. There may be restrictions on the advertising of medicines that have to include information such as the requirement to consult a doctor before they are taken.

The promotional activity should also be fit for purpose in that it should not be used to make claims or imply things that are not true. Misleading advertising is investigated by the Advertising Standards Agency (www.asa.org.uk) who monitor and control advertising to make sure false claims are not being made. More information about these types of influences is found in Section 13.2.6 on page 185.

Originality

Originality is really important when considering promotional activity. Businesses will always be looking for new and interesting ways to promote their products or services so they stand out from their competitors. The first business to come up with a new innovative way of promoting their product will get the edge over its rivals as they may start to copy the activity and it will lose its originality.

Communication

Communication with customers is very important in terms of promotional activity because by choosing the right method of communication including the appropriate media (see section 13.2.5 on page 169), messages will be received by potential customers. If the communication is successful and the customer understands what is expected of them (the message) then they will go out and buy the product or service.

When businesses communicate with potential customers there is always the possibility that the message will not be received as there may be some kind of interference in the communication (noise). Noise refers to any barrier that could get in the way of the message being passed from the business to the potential customer such as:

* problems with language – people may not understand what is actually being communicated

* cultural differences – different perceptions of the communication may result in the communication being interpreted differently

* competition – the actions of competitors will influence how well it is received, for example if competitors are bombarding the potential customer with information it may get lost amongst other communications.

* conclusions – the receiver of the communication may read it as they expect it to read rather than what is actually says

* interest – the communication needs to attract the interest of the customer or they will not take any notice of it

* appropriate media – communication will only be successful if the right form of media has been chosen so that it can reach the target audience.

Businesses also need to make sure that their communication is consistent in that it must keep strengthening the same message over and over again. If the emphasis of a new product or service is on its quality, this should be reinforced over again.

13.2.5 Producing a plan of action

Promotion sets out to capture the imagination of your customers and show the added value of the new product or service that you are bringing to the market. This means that you will be seeking to demonstrate that your product or service is of a higher quality or that it includes additional features or benefits such as brand image that make it better than its rivals. To do this you may need to use a variety of techniques including imagery.

You may also find this section useful as a reference point when trying to analyse the promotional activity that is already being carried out by the business you are studying. The plan of action will, therefore, seek to look at two areas; the promotional activities themselves including an explanation of different types *and* an understanding of how and in what ways promotion can be used to create repeat business or encourage customers to keep stockpiles of your product.

The range of promotional activities

The main types of promotional activity are outlined in this unit and include:

* advertising using mass media such as TV, radio and cinema

* Internet

* mobile media

* newspapers, magazines and specialist journals

* sponsorship

* public relations

* merchandising

* sales promotions

* direct mailing.

When you are considering which methods of promotional activity are currently used by your business and which you may like to consider as part of your own promotional campaign, it is useful to consider the AIDA and DAGMAR decision-making tools to help you judge the likely effectiveness and suitability of the promotional activity for your new product or service.

AIDA

AIDA is a tool that tries to outline what needs to be contained within advertising to make it effective. AIDA stands for:

Awareness	it should raise awareness that the product or service exists
Interest	it should create interest in the product or service
Desire	it should stimulate desire for the customer to want to obtain the product/service
Action	it should promote action for example where the customer can find out more information or actually go to buy the product or service.

By applying AIDA to your promotional activity, whether it uses advertising or another method of promotion, you will be able to gauge how effective you think it will be.

1	Unawareness	This is the stage before the customer is aware of the product or service.
2	Awareness	They then move into becoming aware of it as a result of some kind of promotional activity .
3	Comprehension	This is the stage when the customer develops understanding and knowledge about the product including its potential benefits.
4	Preference	As a result of the knowledge and understanding the customer then develops a preference for the product or service over similar ones.
5	Conviction	This is the final stage just before purchase when the customer has the final commitment and belief in the product or service to go out and buy it.

FIGURE 13.5 *The stages of DAGMAR*

DAGMAR

DAGMAR is another model that attempts to define the stages that customers move through in the purchasing of a product or service (Figure 13.5). It shows the psychological state of mind of customers at each stage of the process. DAGMAR itself stands for Defining Advertising Goals for Measured Advertising Results. Promotional activities should be designed to move customers through each stage and state of mind until they finally purchase the product or service rather than the competitors'.

If customers are led through each of these stages it is likely that they will go on to purchase the product or service. Different types of promotional activity may be used at the different stages to enhance them or because they are more suitable for the desired outcome. Direct mail, for example, clearly outlining the details and benefits of the product or service is useful to aid comprehension in a clear and detailed way. A sales promotion such as a cash bonus or free sample may help to secure the final conviction to go out and buy it.

Choosing the right form of advertising media

A wide range of media is available for any business to use as part of its promotional activity and within your promotional strategy you will need to include at least two different promotional media. You will learn more about the influences on the promotional strategy in Section 13.2.6 but some initial influences that may help you choose are outlined below. Remember, you will need to make clear links between the research data you

have collected and your promotional strategy including the need to outline the influences on the promotional activity that you have chosen. Your choice of media will be influenced by the following:

* *The product* – how complicated is it to explain and would it be better to convey the message in a written form such as a magazine or email rather than verbally over the radio?

* *The target audience* – the number of people that you are trying to get your message to will influence the choice and the characteristics of that audience for example their income or gender.

* *Impact* – the effect that you want the message to have and how much sound and vision that are needed to create it.

* *Time* – the amount of time that you want the advertisement to last for, e.g. a day, a moment, a week etc. Do you want your customer to be able to go back and refer to it such as in a magazine or would you like it to create an immediate awareness and then be over?

* *Cost* – there are always costs associated with any advertising campaign and therefore you will need to consider the cost of your activity in relation to the number of people you are targeting and the type of product that you are promoting in relation to the amount of money involved.

You will need to take into account AIDA, DAGMAR and these influences in order to choose and build the right promotional strategy for your new product or service. Each type of promotional activity is outlined in this unit including any advantages or disadvantages associated with that method of promotion. This should give you an understanding of how and why promotional activity is used and enable you to analyse some of the issues that are involved and how they relate to your chosen business.

Advertising using mass media

Television, radio and cinema represent three different types of advertising media that can be used to promote a product or service and you may choose to use them in your promotional campaign, particularly if you are studying a medium- to large-sized organisation. They are higher cost promotional forms of media but they have access to large audiences with high coverage.

Television

With over 350 television channels available in the UK in 2005 via satellite and cable and with this number increasing all the time, television is a very powerful medium through which advertising can take place. Units of advertising on television are known as advertising spots and are calculated in lengths of time such as 15, 30 or 60 seconds and businesses pay for the length of spot that they wish to buy. The cost and availability of the spot will depend on the type of television programme that it is linked to, for example, a 30-second spot during the break in *Coronation Street* on ITV 1 is very expensive due to the high number of potential viewers. Some very large businesses such as Cadbury may sponsor television programmes so that they receive an advertising spot for a number of weeks as part of the start of the programme.

The main advantages of television are:

* high audience numbers and potential to access a large number of people

* relative low cost per viewing compared to the number of people that are watching

* high impact using vision and sound to create a

Television advertising has the potential to be exposed to national audiences

feeling or demonstration of how the product or service may be used

* through the increasing number of channels, advertising can be targeted to specific groups such as advertisements for CDs and mobile phones associated with younger people on VH1 UK.

There is also a trend amongst mobile phone manufacturers to increase the capability of their phones and it is likely that televisions will become a common feature of mobile phones in the future. This will provide yet another opportunity for advertising using mobile television as a medium.

There are also a number of disadvantages to television and these include:

* it is expensive to use and may not be accessible to even medium-sized businesses unless they have a large budget available

* there is limited space to show all the advertisements that could be shown and this can lead to a form of auction amongst businesses paying the highest price to have theirs shown at peak times

* to look professional the businesses need to spend a lot of money or employ an advertising agency to create the right look and image so it can be expensive to produce an advertisement

* with an ever increasing number of channels there are likely to be fewer viewers watching a single channel which leads to the advertising having to be done in a number of spots on a number of channels thus leading to greater costs

* many viewers consider advertising annoying and as an opportunity to make a cup of tea or do something else so they don't even watch them – on some channels in the United States advertising spots arrive around every 10 minutes and this often interrupts the viewing and is distracting.

Cinema

Cinema like television has large audiences and high impact through the use of visual and audio imagery so many of the advantages that relate to television also relate to cinema. The key difference between them, though, is the ability to specifically target an audience in a particular area of the UK or of a particular age.

As the Board of Film Censors classifies each film by age category, advertising can be very closely linked to that age range so a film with a U classification will need advertising suitable for all and one with an 18 rating will only be seen by people aged 18 or over. By having such specific audiences the advertising can also be very specific.

The amount of time available for an advertisement is also sold in spots like television. The disadvantages of cinema are similar to television in that the advertising may be missed or the message may be seen for a short amount of time and therefore forgotten or even only seen once. Unlike television audiences, it is possible that viewers may not return to the cinema again for a month or two so there may be no opportunity to reinforce the message.

Radio

Radio in recent years, like television, has benefited from technological change. In 2004, Ofcom announced there were over 210 digital radio channels and over 350 channels available offering a huge variety of information and potential for promotion. Whilst traditional channels such as BBC radio may not be able to officially use advertising within their radio programmes sometimes products are used and linked with the business as part of public relations work such as giving a free product or service as part of a competition.

Advertising on the radio is sold in the same way as television and the number of available spots and coverage will depend on the area where the radio station is broadcast. Most radio channels are targeted to a specific location, often local geographical areas and to a specific age group or type of person. This can help advertising to be more specifically linked to the right radio channel to get to the right audience. Some of the advantages and disadvantages of radio are outlined in Figure 13.6.

ADVANTAGES	DISADVANTAGES
It can be used in a variety of places including the car, train and through mobile phones so it is able to move with the audience.	National advertising may be limited due to the number of channels involved.
It is relatively cheap particularly if it is broadcast on specific local commercial radio stations.	There is no visual impact with radio, just sound and therefore it is targeted at only one sense. Listeners may also be distracted by other activities whilst they are listening to the radio such as driving their cars.
It can be used to target specific groups of people including by: • status • gender • age • ethnicity • area of residence.	Radio advertisements are often short and may have the capacity to be forgotten easily unless there is a follow up to them.

FIGURE 13.6 *Advantages and disadvantages of advertising on the radio*

CASE STUDY

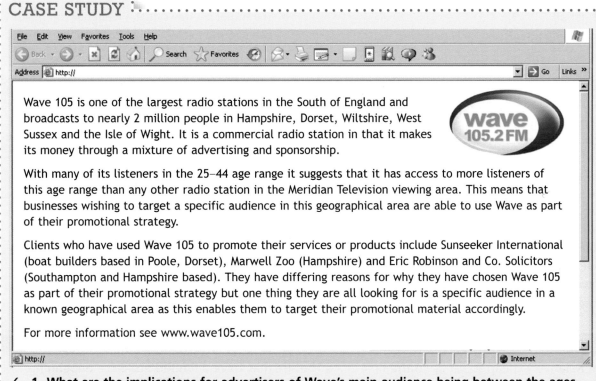

Wave 105 is one of the largest radio stations in the South of England and broadcasts to nearly 2 million people in Hampshire, Dorset, Wiltshire, West Sussex and the Isle of Wight. It is a commercial radio station in that it makes its money through a mixture of advertising and sponsorship.

With many of its listeners in the 25–44 age range it suggests that it has access to more listeners of this age range than any other radio station in the Meridian Television viewing area. This means that businesses wishing to target a specific audience in this geographical area are able to use Wave as part of their promotional strategy.

Clients who have used Wave 105 to promote their services or products include Sunseeker International (boat builders based in Poole, Dorset), Marwell Zoo (Hampshire) and Eric Robinson and Co. Solicitors (Southampton and Hampshire based). They have differing reasons for why they have chosen Wave 105 as part of their promotional strategy but one thing they are all looking for is a specific audience in a known geographical area as this enables them to target their promotional material accordingly.

For more information see www.wave105.com.

✓ 1. What are the implications for advertisers of Wave's main audience being between the ages of 25 and 44?

✓ 2. When might it be more appropriate to use a local radio station rather than a national one?

✓✓ 3. What are the disadvantages of using a medium such as radio?

✓✓✓ 4. Judge the effectiveness of radio advertising in your area amongst the 16–25 age group by collecting the opinions of class members as a sample group and making judgements about how reliable that data might be.

Make a list of all the commercial radio stations that are available in your area and complete the following table.

NAME OF RADIO STATION	PURPOSE	TARGET AUDIENCE AND LISTENER PROFILE	POTENTIAL FOR PROMOTION
Wave 105	South Coast radio station aiming to offer 'The South's Best Variety of Hits' taken from the 70s to today	84% of listeners aged 25+ 52% men 48% women	Sponsorship Events Competition Advertising

Internet

The Internet via the World Wide Web is becoming an increasingly important tool as part of promotion due its capacity to reach a world wide audience and the fact that it is relatively cheap. The main different types of promotional activity that are possible through the Internet are:

* company website
* email
* banner advertising and pop ups
* search engine or directory listing.

Company website

A company website is an extremely powerful way of promoting a company as it provides a resource that is available 24 hours a day for customers to both access information and potentially make orders. As the time between the customer becoming aware of the product to actually buying can be very short it encourages prompt action. It can also be a very powerful way of capturing information about any problems or ideas for future products or promotional campaigns by allowing the customer to interact directly with the business through the use of email links, chat rooms or comment boxes.

Most medium- to large-sized businesses have a company website so it is important to make sure that the website is professional, eye-catching and encourages customers to return for the latest news about products or services that are available. Other promotional methods may be used to encourage this to happen.

The website will incur costs in three main ways:

* the initial set up so that a designer can make the website in the first place

* web hosting as an Internet Service Provider (ISP) will charge for actually allowing the website to be given space on their network

* maintenance fees for web designers and technicians to keep updating and securing the site. Internet security is becoming increasingly important, particularly for businesses that choose to both promote and trade online.

Websites may either be kept 'in-house', which means that the company will employ their own designers and maintenance team to look after the site, or be contracted out to another company so they can look after the website on behalf of the company.

ADVANTAGES	DISADVANTAGES
• Relatively cheap to set up in the first place. • Easy to update – designers and technicians can be working on amendments and changes and introduce them quickly.	• The site may have a limited audience depending on the level of accessibility amongst the target audience. If few people within the target audience have Internet access, this may not be helpful. • Awareness of the site is also crucial. The target audience needs to be aware of the site in order to go to it. It may be necessary to use other promotional activity to support the site itself.

continued ▶

ADVANTAGES (contd)	DISADVANTAGES (contd)
• The number of 'hits' (visits) can be monitored so that the company can judge the effectiveness of the website. • Orders can be made online in a variety of methods such as credit card or Paypal. • The company can interact with customers with email links, chat rooms or comment boxes.	• Technical problems can restrict the ability of a website to promote effectively. This is because any time the website is 'down' (unavailable) a customer is unable to access information and may get a bad impression of the business. • Spelling, name and information issues may also be a problem, e.g. if information is posted on a website incorrectly or if a website has a similar name to another one and receives 'hits' in error, Some sites often use similar names to famous ones in order to benefit from typing errors, e.g. www.yahoo.com and www.yaho.com.

FIGURE 13.7 *Advantages and disadvantages of Internet promotional activities*

CASE STUDY

eBay

eBay has been one of the most successful website launches of the last decade. It has gone from strength to strength across countries and even continents. Every day there are literally millions of products and services both new and old that are available to be traded.

Such success might make you think that eBay could become complacent and believe itself to be unstoppable but eBay still makes use of other promotional techniques in order to strengthen customer loyalty and to increase the number of eBay users that are attracted to its services.

In October 2005, eBay launched its campaign 'You can get 'it' on eBay' which featured the use of the word 'it' and the availability of any items including 'it' on eBay. Part of the 'it' campaign also included the website www.whatis-it.com which features a direct link to www.ebay.com.

In the UK, television advertising was conducted between November and December 2005 to expand the amount of traffic and number of users accessing www.ebay.co.uk.

One of the reasons for eBay using such a wide variety of promotional media is that it is important to promote products and services in different ways in order to capture the largest target audience possible.

✓ 1. Which type of promotional activity did eBay use for its launch?
✓ 2. Why should a business never become complacent about its promotional activity?
✓✓✓ 3. Which new form of promotional activity is now being used? Discuss the likely effectiveness of its use.

Email

Email is a powerful promotional tool as it can be used to make customers aware of the latest information about a product or service. Combined with a link to the website, a customer can be taken directly from their email account to the company website for additional information.

Email is also a useful medium for promotional activity as it gives the opportunity for the company to promote in a visual and auditory way. Photographs of hotels and swimming pools can be used to promote a service offered by a holiday business. Video clips could also be added or sound files so that the target audience can get a realistic idea about the product or service on offer.

Email can also be used to give incentives to customers in a relatively short amount of time, e.g. if you respond to this email within 48 hours you can benefit from a discount or others include the opportunity to print out a voucher that can be used, e.g. for money off in a supermarket.

ADVANTAGES	DISADVANTAGES
• Quick and easy to send out to a wide variety of customers.	• Spam (unsolicited email) is not permitted to be sent as part of the the Privacy and Electronic Communications (EC Directive) Regulations 2003.
• Potential for access to a high number of people.	• The target audience may find it annoying and get the wrong impression of the company.
• Ability to use sound, vision and video clips within the email.	
• The business is able to monitor the success of email and links from the email directly to the website.	• The target audience may not read it and delete it without receiving the promotional material.
• Customers can communicate directly with the business to let them know about any thoughts on their products or services.	• The business will need to produce some kind of database in order to know who to send information to in the first place and this may be costly to avoid spamming.

FIGURE 13.8 *Advantages and disadvantages of using emails for promotional activity*

In the UK, legislation prevents 'spam' emails from being sent out to consumers so bear this in mind when you are constructing your promotional activity if you choose to use email.

It is interesting, however, that according to the Information Commissioner who regulates the Privacy and Electronic Communications (EC Directive) Regulations 2003, only 2 per cent of junk email is sent by rogue companies based in the UK and that the other 98 per cent is sent by businesses (mostly US) that are not governed by UK law!

Banner advertising and pop ups

Banner advertising is a form of online advertising. Banners are placed on websites for a certain length of time. They can be placed within any part of a web page with the agreement of the business that owns the site. Banners can include images, sound or video. They commonly link to the relevant website that is being advertised. Many websites feature banner advertising and are automatically linked to pop up windows.

A pop up is a window that opens by accessing the website. It will open during the time you are accessing the web page often in two ways: either as a small window that covers part of the website you are accessing or behind the page you are advertising so as you close the site you are on you see the pop up in full. Pop up advertising can be useful if it is closely linked to the website host's business such as computer servicing pop ups being linked to websites offering sales of computers.

The payment to use a banner or pop up on a website is often linked to the number of visitors to the site so the business is charged according to how many people actually click on the banner or pop up.

FIGURE 13.9 *www.msn.co.uk as shown above has a banner advertisement using a video clip*

video clip

ADVANTAGES	DISADVANTAGES
• Available to a large audience. • May be linked to a relevant website. • Paid for by clicks so directly linked to the number of visits.	• May be annoying. • May not produce quality leads if customers click on banners by mistake or only click on pop ups to close them.

FIGURE 13.10 *Advantages and disadvantages of pop up website advertising*

Search engine or directory listing

With a huge variety of possible websites available it is important that a business can use techniques to make it easier for their site to be found from the vast quantity of material available online. Having an easily remembered web address may help to achieve this or search engines or directories can be used to help potential customers find the company and become aware of products or services that are available. Traditional paper-based directories have also been adapted in many cases so that they are also available online such as Yellow Pages being used as a tool for promotion online as www.yell.com.

Search engines and directories can be used in two main ways for promotion. Banners or pop ups may be linked to them so that as a search takes place on any subject, the pop up gives details or information about the product or service. They can also be used to actually promote the product or service being offered by the business paying the search engine, e.g Google, or directory provider so that their product or service appears nearer to the top of the search list results.

A search engine works by the user keying in relevant words or phrases to a search box and then it produces a set of possible websites that are related to those words as links. Directories may have a search function but they usually work by the user 'drilling down' through subject titles such as travel or finance.

It is no coincidence that larger company websites are found more commonly on searches rather than smaller ones. This is because they have paid to promote their business nearer the top of the search list. Using search engines as a method of promotion can increase web traffic to the company website but this may prove costly if the business wants to be included in the top

20 and most valuable results lists. It may also be difficult to monitor the amount of increased business that is directly linked to the search engine in terms of actual sales.

Ezine sponsorship

An ezine is a form of electronic magazine that can be sent via email. Sponsoring an ezine means that the business can promote itself through a form of electronic sponsorship. The business receives advertising and promotion space as part of the sponsorship deal and receives regular opportunities to keep promoting their product or service. This may be in the form of some kind of banner or a few lines giving details about the product or service as text, photographs or video clips within the ezine.

The advantage of using ezines via email is that they can be closely linked to the target audience that is appropriate to the product or service. A mobile phone company may choose to sponsor an ezine that promotes new innovations to business people. This would allow them the opportunity to promote their latest models within the publication and gain additional publicity and hopefully sales.

The disadvantage to such a service is that the business relies on distribution being made by the ezine itself and therefore if the ezine is successful, the promotion will be successful but if it is not, the promotion will not be either. Medium- or large-sized businesses need to be sure that the ezine reflects their company image and targets the appropriate group of customers they are looking for.

Mobile phone technology

Mobile phones have become an increasingly important part of everyday life and as such can be a real asset in terms of promotion. Many large businesses are already using text messages to promote their products or services. Competitions such as those offered by Walker's Crisps require customers to send in a number or word as a text message to confirm whether or not they have won a competition prize. When used in this way, companies automatically receive details of mobile phone numbers that can be used to send information about the latest range of products or services on offer.

Newspapers, magazines and specialist journals

Newspapers, magazines and specialist journals are all still very popular methods of promotion. Figure 13.12 compares their use.

ADVANTAGES	DISADVANTAGES
• Quick and easy to send. • Wide potential audience. • Can instigate immediate response via delivery confirmation or reply needed. • May include multimedia such as sound and video to enhance material.	• Message may not be received. • Difficult to judge direct impact on sales. • May be annoying to customers. • Takes time and effort to build an appropriate database.

FIGURE 13.11 *Advantages and disadvantages of using mobile phones for promotional activities*

	NEWSPAPERS	SPECIALIST JOURNALS AND MAGAZINES
Explanation	May be produced on a daily, weekly, morning, evening, national or local basis. Advertising takes place directly and is costed based on the size of advertisement in terms of number of columns or cm space. It can also take place as part of public relations promotion through the use of articles to launch a product or service.	Specialise in more specific target audiences, e.g. women, health, fishing and in a more glossy format. Available weekly, monthly and quarterly. Advertising is costed per page, number of columns, cm space or public relations articles.
Advantages	Widely read. Can be linked to a specific type of audience through the choice of paper. The reader can read it again and again. It is quite quick to produce an advert to appear in a newspaper. The newspapers are published regularly.	Can be directly linked to the publication's specialism. Can be used to give away free samples or money-off vouchers.
Disadvantages	May be ignored and not read. Need to keep being changed to create impact and therefore don't last long. May be of poor quality due to printing problems. May be competing against lots of other advertisements and be missed.	Can be expensive, e.g. in best sellers such as *Cosmopolitan*. Has limited impact using colour – no sound or movement as paper-based. For glossy advertising it may take time to produce the advertisement.

FIGURE 13.12 *Advantages and disadvantages of using newspapers and journals for promotional activities*

Sponsorship

Sponsorship is when the business decides to invest in something that will be seen on a regular basis that is not directly linked to the business. Common sponsorships include football teams, new buildings, charity events and other sporting occasions such as the Global Challenge for yacht racing. Some large organisations also sponsor television programmes, such as *Coronation Street* which is sponsored by Cadbury. This guarantees that Cadbury products will be promoted at least five times per week and associated with a very successful television programme. However, it is extremely expensive and only available to very large businesses.

Celebrity endorsements are also used to encourage the use of a product or service. Gary Lineker can be seen on television advertising Walkers Crisps and Jamie Oliver can be seen cooking with Sainsbury's products or shopping there. This encourages customers to take notice of the business' promotional activity and associate it with the relevant celebrity.

Like ezines, though, sponsorship or endorsement is only as good as the team or event

Sponsorship deals are often linked to successful sports such as rugby or football

you are sponsoring or person you associate with your product. If a football team is doing well there is likely to be a lot of opportunity for promotion but if they are not doing so well it may reduce the size of the potential audience and may damage the image of the business. When Kate Moss (supermodel) was having personal difficulties in 2005, some of the businesses that use her to endorse their products had to immediately disassociate themselves from her in case it damaged their image or reputation too. It can also be difficult to make a direct link between sponsorship or endorsement and promotional success because its direct influence on sales figures may be difficult to judge. Either method will often be used alongside other methods of promotional activity.

Public relations

Public relations means managing the relationship between the business and its stakeholders including customers. A stakeholder is anyone who is affected by the business so this may include employees, shareholders, government, local community or pressure groups. Managing public relations is about trying to improve the image, reputation and awareness of the business so that sales are increased.

A business may consider using campaigns such as increased recycling or ethical production to improve its image. Public relations can take a variety of forms including giving a press release to newspapers, television and radio to make them aware of the latest service or product that is on offer or a press conference where interested parties are invited to discuss a new launch with company representatives and ask questions. It may include a trade fair, free trial or exhibition of services so that it can be reported on in order to increase the number of people that are aware of the business. Public relations also works by trying to increase the amount that a business is talked about by the media or target audience so there is more interest in what is going on.

Celebrity endorsements and sponsorship may be included as part of public relations. Some organisations will also give large donations of money to events such as Children in Need or Comic Relief as part of public relations. Morrison

Good public relations seeks to improve image and awareness

supermarkets, for example gave £552,000 to Marie Curie Cancer Care in 2003 as part of their charitable donations.

Another method of increasing public relations coverage is to ask newspapers, magazines or television companies to trial or review a product or service and report back on it. However, this could be associated with the risk of negative publicity if it is not well received.

It is argued that 'there is no such thing as bad publicity' so many companies are prepared to take the risk. Companies such as Easyjet with their role in Airline television programmes have grown and grown but still show some of the problems that they encounter with difficult passengers.

Other businesses in the past though have suffered due to the impact of public relations. Gerald Ratner was the Chairman of Ratners the Jewellers and famously suggested at a conference that his jewellery was of a low quality. This was a public relations disaster that ultimately led to the collapse of the business.

Merchandising

Merchandising is when a business promotes its products or services close to where potential customers are likely to see them. It is often undertaken by other companies on behalf of the business such as supermarkets merchandising new foods on behalf of manufacturers.

DISPLAY	PRESENTATION	SPACE
This relates to the way that products or services are presented to customers and may involve the use of special signs, displays, taste testing etc to encourage customers to buy the product or use the service.	This relates to the way that the goods are presented themselves. Large manufacturers will ask for their products to be presented in the best possible places such as at eye level and in the most walked through areas.	Facings are the number of products that a retailer displays on a shelf. Food manufacturers will want as many as possible to be on shelves in order for them to take up the most space possible rather than their competitors.

FIGURE 13.13 *Methods of merchandising*

Merchandising for both products and services may take place at the checkout when customers are paying for goods and queuing in line. This gives them time to make 'impulse purchases', for example sweets or drinks and to get information about services such as credit cards or insurance.

Demonstrations and trials within retail environments are also part of merchandising. Wine tasting in supermarkets is a common form and allows customers to try a product before they buy it. Demonstrations of products such as kitchen equipment may take place in-store so customers can see how they can be used, sometimes with a taste element such as smoothie makers being used and then sample drinks being given away.

A blood pressure or heart monitoring service may be offered to promote the services of a gym in a supermarket foyer. Offers of services within a store as part of merchandising are often offered in do-it-yourself (DIY) stores such as B & Q or Homebase. Software may be used to provide free kitchen or bathroom planning and this also demonstrates how products sold by the store can be used. Demonstrations may also be used as part of 'how to' events that help novices learn about techniques and provide the opportunity to ask questions.

Loyalty cards can lead to higher sales

or later action such as a loyalty card that can be used to get additional free gifts later.

Sales promotions

Sales promotions are used to provide a short-term incentive for customers to use a service or buy a product and by doing so will increase sales. It can be used in a number of ways by medium to large businesses including sales promotions directly to customers or even to intermediaries such as wholesalers or retailers. They can also be used with employees working for the company such as the sales representatives who are given bonuses or incentives if they sell more by a certain date. The idea of a sales promotion is that something will be given either in the form of money off or an incentive such as free products or additional services in exchange for higher sales.

Sales promotions can be used in two main ways to increase sales: immediate action such as buy one get one free (known as BOGOF) or a free gift, such as a free head massage with a hair cut,

Direct mailing

You have already explored the use of email in this unit on page 176 and this is one form of direct mail using the Internet. Using direct mail either by hand, post or newspapers can mean that a large target audience can receive the promotional material. There are lots of examples of different types of direct mail and it arrives in two main forms:

* a mail shot where specific addresses are targeted for use by the business

* a mail drop where promotional material is given out unaddressed, e.g. with your postal delivery or newspaper.

The mail itself can take a variety of forms including letter, newsletter, poster, catalogue, brochure, leaflet, sample, voucher, form of questionnaire or booklet.

ADVANTAGES	DISADVANTAGES
• May be personalised (name, address etc).	• Can be expensive due to production and postage costs.
• Can give a good impression through glossiness and use of colour.	• May be seen as 'junk' and therefore ignored or put into the bin without reading.
• Can be measured by checking receipt as follow up or by vouchers with barcodes that can be read when presented.	• Paper-based material has reduced impact as not linked to sound or vision.
• Can be re-read or kept for use at a later date	• Can be expensive to buy an existing mailing list or takes time to produce a new one.
• Can be targeted to specific groups using personal information.	• The business needs to avoid sending unsolicited mail to customers or they will contravene the Privacy and Electronic Communications (EC Directive) Regulations 2003.
• With samples the customer can actually try the product in their own home or book the service directly from the promotion, e.g. free gym trial.	
• May be used to include visual or auditory material such as a promotional DVD to make use of multimedia, e.g. holiday promotions such as Centre Parcs or Disney.	

FIGURE 13.14 *Advantages and disadvantages of promotion using direct mail*

Understanding how and in what ways promotion can be used

Promotions can be used to influence the levels of stock that customers are buying and holding of a product and the likelihood of them trying a new product or service. This can be very useful to a business as it can help them to manage their sales at different times of year. You have probably seen sales in retail shops in months like January when stock is sold off more cheaply to make room for new stock to brought in for the spring. This is an example of using promotion to reduce the amount of old stock. Promotions can be used in a number of ways including:

* bringing forward a decision to buy

* encouraging repeat purchases

* encouraging stockpiling

* encouraging long-term loyalty

* encouraging consumers to try a new product.

Bringing forward a decision to buy

Bringing forward a decision to buy is a very useful way to try to spread out the purchasing of a product or offering of a service during the year. Some customers are likely to bring forward the date when they would like some work done in order to benefit from additional savings whilst others will only want the work done at the usual time of year.

A business installing central heating boilers will be extremely busy in October and November when customers' replace their faulty boilers as the weather gets colder. By offering free servicing for a year with the fitting of a new boiler in July and August (traditionally quieter months), a customer may decide to bring their purchase forward and have their boiler fitted earlier so they can get the extra support free. This benefits both the customer and the business because the customer has a working boiler as the weather gets colder and the business is busier at traditionally quieter times.

Some double glazing companies also use offers such as if you buy five windows you will get a sixth free if you buy by a certain date or a free door if you buy four windows by a certain date.

Holiday companies often offer free travel insurance if a holiday is purchased by a certain date, whilst others provide free activities and products for children for booking early.

Clothing catalogue companies may send free items if an order is placed by a certain date such as a free handbag, suitcase or item of clothing such as a nightdress or dressing gown.

Think it over...

Consider the market your business is in and the promotional activity that happens there. Are there opportunities for any free products or services to be offered to customers buying earlier? What effect do these have on levels of service or stockpiling? What might happen if such offers were not made?

Encouraging repeat purchases

Some businesses will use promotion to build up customer loyalty by offering a discount for cash or early payment in order to encourage the customer to keep coming back. Special promotional codes are often sent to existing customers allowing them to benefit from a reduction in price or an additional service such as free entry to a club at a holiday park or free delivery on a product to the home. This method is often used by Amazon.co.uk to encourage customers to continue purchasing items from their website.

Encouraging stockpiling

Many promotions also encourage customers to buy in bulk by offering extra products for the same price. This encourages customers to spend more and therefore increases sales. Common forms of this promotion include businesses such as Boots who offer 3 for 2 on gifts during the time leading up to Christmas when customers are likely to want to make a number of purchases. Bookshops, such as Waterstones and WHSmith also tend to make such offers at festive times and at the start of the summer holidays when customers are likely to want several books to read.

Encouraging long-term loyalty

Using promotional activity to build up long-term loyalty may be accomplished in a number of ways. For example, bonus points are given to customers throughout the year which can be exchanged at more quieter times. Successful schemes that operate include a loyalty card scheme offered by Morrisons supermarket known as Morrisons Miles which rewards customers with points for petrol purchases that can be converted into a £5 voucher for use in their stores. Tesco use a similar card known as a Clubcard that rewards

Encouraging bulk buying is a useful way to increase sales

customers with money-off vouchers and the opportunity to buy products or services using points to make part-payment.

Encouraging consumers to try a new product

Of course promotion is also used in order to try to persuade customers to buy a new product or service and this is one of the most important areas that you will need to consider when you are planning your own promotional activity. Promotional activity to persuade customers to buy a new product or try a new service can be communicated in a number of ways as you have already learned. You will need to consider what is most appropriate and likely to be taken up by your target audience. A furniture company offering a sales promotion on a new bed may use a voucher for £99 off to create interest in that new product. A trial pack that can be given out in a shopping centre or via a website may create interest in a new shampoo but is not suitable for a retailer selling pets or a manufacturer of cars.

Remember you will need to include at least two types of promotional activity as part of your promotional strategy.

13.2.6 Internal and external influences on promotional activity

Businesses need to take into account influences that may impact on the scope and type of promotional activity that they can undertake. You will need to understand the two key types of influence that impacts on the activity and those can be categorised as internal and external.

Internal influences

These are influences that come from within the business itself. They will have an impact on the scope and type of promotional activity that can be undertaken. You will need to understand

and apply these influences to your promotional activity, describing their impact on your promotional campaign. Internal influences can include:

* the aims and objectives of the business as a whole
* the aims and objectives of the planned campaign
* market research
* the message to be communicated and the targeted audience
* the promotional budget
* the timescale involved.

The aims and objectives of the business as a whole

The business' overall aims and objectives will influence your promotional activity as they will outline the vision and way in which the whole organisation is moving forward and therefore your promotional activity must fit within this. If the aim of the business is to expand and two of the objectives to go with this are to increase sales by 10 per cent each year until 2010 and to increase public awareness by 10 per cent by 2015, the promotional strategy will need to support this and have its own aims and objectives to make sure that it is working to make this happen. There may be implications for the promotional strategy if the business is seeking to reduce in size, e.g. budget or cost cuts. If your business is seeking to become a world leader or international supplier of its products or services your promotional strategy may need to be linked more closely to **mass market** audiences, for example through television or radio rather than at merchandising level to create awareness.

> **Key terms**
>
> *Mass market* is a market that has a wide audience, and products or services which have become everyday items.

As part of your promotional strategy you will need to consider the future path of the business and what kind of image your business is seeking to portray. You will need to collect details of the overall aims and objectives of the organisation and then make your promotional strategy be part of those.

The aims and objectives of the planned campaign

Having become aware of what the business needs to achieve overall, it is important to give aims and objectives that relate specifically to your promotional strategy for the new product or service. Your aim is going to be to introduce the new product or service that you have chosen and your objectives will relate to specific promotional media.

Salt and vinegar flavour chocolate is a new product that a famous chocolate company has decided to launch.

The aim of the promotional strategy is: 'To establish Salt and Vinegar Choc as a new product in the chocolate market.'

The objectives of the promotional strategy are:

- to make at least 20% of the target audience aware of Salt and Vinegar Choc within six months
- to differentiate the product from other chocolate bars as a new savoury alternative at lunchtimes
- to provide 5 million trial tasting opportunities within 12 months.

To achieve these promotional objectives there will be two main types of promotional activity:

1. a television advertising campaign
2. a demonstration in retail stores as part of merchandising linked with a sales promotional voucher for money off with purchase of the chocolate.

Consider your own product or service and the promotional strategy that you are going to use. What is your overall promotional strategy and what are the objectives that are linked to that strategy?

Market research

You have already learned about collecting market research in this unit and also in Unit 10 on pages 60–5. Market research is an important source of information that can be used to influence and inform your promotional strategy. This is because it will give you information about what is currently happening with your business and what your competitors are doing.

Market research will attempt to identify the gaps in the market that your new product or service should be aiming to fill. The level and amount of money that is available to your chosen business will affect the ability of the business to collect data. The larger the organisation, the more likely it is that market research can be done on a bigger scale. The accuracy of market research can also lead to successful products being produced and then successfully sold or a costly withdrawal of an unsuccessful product.

The message to be communicated and the targeted audience

The message to be communicated by the business to the target audience will heavily influence the promotional activity and its scope as it may form part of an existing image that needs to be supported and continued to be portrayed or it might be a new message about an alternative type of product or service that is now being offered. Tesco, for example, when first launching car insurance still made use of the 'Every little helps' catchphrase and therefore whilst promoting the new service reminded the target audience of existing services offered by Tesco.

The target market that the business has decided to aim for will also influence the promotional activity. This means that one type of promotional activity such as using mobile phone text messages may be more suitable for one target market, e.g. teenagers, than another.

The promotional budget

The promotional budget will have a huge impact on the promotional activity that can be undertaken. Some forms of promotion such as television, celebrity endorsement or sponsorship can be very expensive so you will need to consider the size of the promotional budget that is going to be available to launch your new product or service. You should collect research information from the business you have chosen to help you judge the size of the budget that you will have available and be able to justify the figures that you have chosen within your promotional strategy.

The timescale involved

The timescale involved is a critical influence on promotional activity because it will very much depend on the type of market that your business is operating in. If your competitors frequently bring out new products or new promotional campaigns it will be necessary to speed up the time period from idea to launch. If there are fewer competitors or it's a strong brand name you may be able to take more time to plan and then implement the strategy. As a general rule, businesses will always try to work to shorter timescales rather than longer as they risk a competitor bringing out a similar idea and then establishing market share before they can.

External influences

These relate to influences that are external to the business but will still have an impact on the scope and type of promotional activity that can be undertaken. The influences are categorised into six main areas and you will need to examine each of these areas to decide the extent to which each affects individual promotional activity and the promotional strategy as a whole:

✱ social, cultural and economic

✱ ethical and environmental

✱ legislative and regulatory

✱ pressure groups

✱ competitors

✱ technology.

Social, cultural and economic

The influence of what is happening from a social, cultural and economic basis relates to people and as people are your target audience, what is influencing them is going to influence your promotional activity. Social trends over the past decade have led to an increase in the number of single-parent families and promotional activity should reflect this by showing higher numbers of single parents within advertising on television or posters so that people can feel that the business is in touch with what is happening. Smoking, for example, was a habit for 50 per cent of the adult population in the 1950s but now only represents 25 per cent which is a huge shift.

The European Union has expanded rapidly as well, providing an opportunity for culturally diverse communities to be brought together and to share ideas and values. There may be the opportunity to promote a new product or service in a new EU member country. Tesco has been particularly successful at moving into Poland, Hungary and Slovakia for example. Cultural differences influence the way that target audiences operate and therefore influences promotional activity. Issues within the world such as natural disasters and acts of terrorism may also affect the way that your promotional activity is presented with reassurances made about safety or security. Such influences may even help to influence the shaping of your original idea.

Economic influences also play a great part in influencing your strategy. When unemployment and interest rates are low, more people are in work and are paying less in monthly payments. This means they are more likely to have more money to spend on luxuries. However, if unemployment and interest rates are high then the reverse is likely to happen. This has an implication for your promotional activity because it may be that in more difficult economic conditions your business may attempt to cut costs as sales reduce which may influence the size of the budget available to spend and where promotional activity takes place.

Ethical and environmental

An ethical business is one that seeks to make money but without compromising and exploiting others in order to do this. It is about the business' moral code and this leads to possible differences of opinion as what one person thinks is acceptable, another will think is unethical.

This may also be from an environmental point

of view, such as recycling or reducing emissions as part of production or paying people a fair rate for work they have produced. In terms of promotional activity it is about making sure that the business promotes to the right audience in the right way, not necessarily as a result of legal constraints, but because they believe they are doing the right thing. There has been some criticism of television advertising aimed at children whereby high fat foods, sweets or toys are promoted during times or on channels that are exclusively watched by children. This is likely to encourage them to adopt an unhealthy lifestyle or pester their parents for gifts. You would need to consider whether your business would want to promote in such a way and the potential damage to its reputation or image.

Competitions with prizes that appear to be too good to be true often are! A scratch card promoting a company with a free gift or service may be unethical if the customer needs to ring a premium rate telephone number to claim it. It may cost £9 to make a call for which a customer receives a ball point pen worth 20p.

Reality television has given the opportunity for businesses to sponsor shows that may show everyday people or celebrities in distress due to homesickness or particular tasks. A business will need to make a conscious decision about whether or not they want to be associated with such television or promotional activity.

From an environmental point of view, you should also consider the impact of your activity on the environment. Flyers, leaflets and direct mail which is not targeted may commonly end up thrown away without being read so it is important to consider the number of resources needed for your activity and what will happen to them both during and after the activity. Promoting further travel by plane etc may encourage environmental damage through the increased use of airline fuel and so the impact of the promotional activity will need to be taken into account.

Legislative and regulatory

Legislative and regulatory changes happen frequently as a result of a change in UK and EU law or as a result of recommendations from industry-led regulators who ask businesses to sign up to voluntary codes of practice. The effect of such changes on promotional activity can be far reaching so you will need to research and acknowledge the influence of any such changes on your promotional activity.

Legislation

Changes in the law can take a variety of forms, for example changes in taxation may have an affect on the pricing of your product or service and therefore influence your promotional activity. A legal lifestyle change may also influence where and when promotion takes place, for example banning smoking in public places.

Theory into practice

Making use of your own ethical code, in small groups within your class consider advertising that you have seen recently in any form of media from an ethical point of view.

Is it ethical for charitable organisations to produce advertising material that shows shocking scenes or deprivation or distress?

Is it ethical for loan companies to advertise consolidation loans that encourage people to move all their debts into one place and then potentially go out and spend more money to get into further debt?

It is ethical for mobile phone ring tone, wallpaper and games companies to advertise products during family viewing times that appeal to younger children but that should only be purchased by people aged 16 or over?

Smoking ban

Smoking has already been banned in all enclosed public spaces in the Republic of Ireland, Norway, Sweden, New Zealand and Bhutan. This means that smoking is now not permitted in restaurants, pubs, bars and nightclubs. In Scotland, there has been a total ban since 26 March 2006, and in England, Northern Ireland and Wales it is due to come into force in 2007. The effect of the smoking ban may influence the way that pubs promote their services by emphasising the new smoke-free environment. It may also be an opportunity for medium- to large-sized businesses to consider promoting products or services within bars or restaurants to help people give up smoking or may even be an opportunity for beer producers to sponsor ashtrays or smoking areas outside of these places to promote their products.

✓ 1. **What impact is there likely to be on the promotional activity of manufacturers and sellers of tobacco products as a result of this ban?**

✓✓ 2. **What potential promotional activity might increase as a result of the change in the law and what are the advantages and disadvantages of this increase?**

✓✓✓ 3. **Judge how important you think advertising might be for manufacturers and retailers of tobacco products.**

Consumers are protected by law from being sold products that are unsafe as businesses must sell safe products and services as part of their 'duty of care'. These laws also influence the way that data is stored for promotional purposes and the way that it is presented to customers. Businesses must not lie about or make false claims about what their product or service actually provides. There is more information about all aspects of legislation in Unit 17 of this book, including the key elements of legislation such as:

* Sale of Goods Act 1979
* Trade Descriptions Act 1968
* Consumer Credit Act 1974.

It is also important to consider the legislative framework during the collection and distribution of the promotional activity itself. The Data Protection Act restricts access to, and use of personal information that may be used for mail shots or credit checks so this needs to conform to data protection principles.

The Telephone Preference Service that came into force as a result of the Privacy and Electronic Communications (EC Directive) Regulations 2003 makes it illegal to phone people in order to promote new products or services if they have registered with this service. If a large percentage of your target audience has signed up to the service, a telephone-based promotional campaign is not likely to work well and different methods will need to be used.

Regulators and voluntary codes of practice

Within the world of marketing and in particular promotional activity there are a number of different national organisations who are likely to have an influence on your promotional activity. The three main ones are:

* Ofcom
* Advertising Standards Agency
* Direct Marketing Association.

Ofcom

Ofcom is the industry regulator that licenses commercial television and radio. It seeks to protect viewer and listener interests by making sure that broadcasters operate according to published guidelines. As well as covering what is contained within programmes, it also looks at advertising and sponsorship. Ofcom seeks to make sure that viewers and listeners are not offended or encouraged to take part in harmful practices, it ensures the number of breaks during programmes is limited and that all advertising is checked for suitability before it is transmitted.

Ofcom has the power to issue penalties if businesses do not comply with their code of practice.

Advertising Standards Association (ASA)

The ASA is an organisation that publishes a voluntary code of practice and guidelines. Organisations agree to abide by these and by agreeing to do so they are able to display symbols to show that they are part of the scheme. The ASA promotes best practice and in doing so aims to help consumers by making sure that advertising is:

* legal, decent, honest and truthful

* responsible

* fairly competitive.

The ASA can ask for advertising to be changed or withdrawn but cannot legally enforce this. It is likely that a business would comply, though, as they would not wish to receive any bad publicity as a result.

Direct Marketing Association (DMA)

The DMA also promotes best practice through a code of conduct and aims to protect consumers from unethical or inappropriate material. It has a number of different elements to its code of conduct including coverage of areas such as direct mail, telephone- and Internet-based methods such as email or text messaging. The DMA administers preference services like the Telephone Preference Service to help consumers control the amount of unsolicited (not asked for) promotional material that they receive.

Pressure groups

There is a huge variety and number of pressure groups in the UK aiming to affect the way that businesses operate from a number of different perspectives. A pressure group aims to influence the way that a business operates and in doing so will try to influence the type and level of promotional activity that takes place. A public relations activity may be to have a trade fair or event that promotes sales of a product or service.

Pressure groups aim to influence the way businesses operate

A pressure group may enhance or destroy the success of that activity by demonstrating outside.

There are a number of different types of pressure group that may influence your promotional activity. A pressure group may be set up as a result of a specific issue such as those that were set up in response to the concerns of local residents about a new mobile phone mast (see the case study on page 101 of Unit 10). Others are set up to fight a range of issues related to the same subject such as Compassion in World Farming aiming to improve the lives of all farm animals worldwide. Human rights groups such as Amnesty International may also have an influence on promotional activity.

Competitors

Competitors can have a huge influence on promotional activity as they are seeking to make sure their own sales are as high as possible and won't want to lose custom as a result of your activity. They may seek to copy successful promotional activity and it will be up to you as part of your strategy to come up with a new and interesting idea. The more unique your strategy is, the greater the likely impact.

Competitors can also influence your promotional activity when you consider the number of them and the regularity of their own promotional activity. If they promote their products and services regularly then it may be necessary for your business to do the same to retain market share. The type of product or service will affect the ability of new competitors to start trading in the market and the type of promotional activity that they are going to use.

The ability to substitute your product or service with another competitor's product will also affect promotional strategy as it will be important to make it very clear to consumers why your product or service is best and what makes it better and different (added value and **differentiation**).

Technology has an impact on promotional activity

Technology

Technological influences can have a huge impact on promotional activity in that the channels that can be used for promotion are changing and updating all the time in terms of the number of them, their capability and impact. Mobile phone technology has moved forward so video phoning is possible and televisions are also a feature so television advertising can now be accessed by television and telephone. Televisions with DVD players can now be fitted to cars to provide a further opportunity for television promotion.

Electronic billboards can provide moving images and be changed more frequently to add impact. Taxi companies can use digital display boards to promote messages around cities from their rooftops. Technological change is having a huge impact on the way that people work and are exposed to promotional material and this has a big impact on the way that promotional activity needs to be carried out, particularly with younger generations who tend to adopt new technology more quickly.

Key terms

Differentiation means making your product appear different from your competitors.

Some top tips for writing your promotional strategy

* You will need to explain, analyse and make judgements about the various forms of promotional activity that can take place and how internal and external influences impact on those. The higher the level of detail and breadth within your work, the higher the likely grade you should achieve.

* Your promotional strategy needs to contain appropriate aims and objectives through which your strategy is written. You should use background information on the various types of promotional activity that are currently in place within the business to help you decide on an appropriate strategy.

* You must promote a *new product or service* for a medium- to large-sized business that already has a varied product portfolio.

* You must use *at least two different forms of media* as part of your promotional activity.

* You will need to include your two finished concepts, e.g. a poster, advertisement, details of an ezine to be used or story board for an advertisement, with clear detailed evidence of how you made your choices.

* You will need to include appropriate research material of a *primary and secondary* nature including references – you may find it helpful to include some of this material as appendices at the back of your portfolio.

* You will need to evaluate by drawing conclusions and making judgements about the likely effectiveness of your campaign by giving clear arguments based on the research and analysis that you have collected.

* You will be assessed on your grammar, punctuation and spelling so ask a friend to proof-read your work for any typing errors.

Knowledge check

1. Name the four elements of the strategic planning cycle.
2. What is the purpose of a market map?
3. Name two products or services that you know well and describe the USP for each.
4. Name two colours that are associated with specific products or services.
5. Describe two reasons why a business carries out promotional activity.
6. What is the purpose of a market research company and why might businesses use them?
7. What is meant by creating desire in customers?
8. What is the purpose of an advertising agency?
9. What is meant by the promotional message?
10. Give two examples of how promotional activity is used in your area to persuade customers to bring forward their purchasing decisions.
11. What are the advantages of using promotional activity to encourage repeat purchases and are there any limitations?
12. Name three aesthetic principles that a manufacturer may take into account when producing a new shampoo.
13. Name three different aesthetic principles that a manufacturer may take into account when producing a new type of chocolate drink.
14. What is meant by stockpiling?
15. What is the difference between market-led and product-led product or service development and what are the advantages and disadvantages of each?
16. Outline and describe one problem that may be associated with using demonstration as a method of promotional activity.
17. 'Primary research is always more useful than secondary research to a business.' Discuss this view and make judgements about it using real business examples as much as possible.
18. To what extent can promotional activity be used to change people's attitudes? Use real life examples where possible.
19. How can legislation change the way that promotional activity is carried out?
20. 'Promotional activity may be seen to be unethical as it seeks to encourage people to buy more than they need.' Discuss this view and give a judgement of the extent to which you think this is true.

Resources

Books

Ali, M (2001) *Marketing Effectively*, Dorling Kindersley

Blundell, R (2001) *Effective Business Communication*, Financial Times/Prentice Hall

Bunting, H S (1996) *Advertising*, Hodder & Stoughton

Chaffey, Dave (2002) *E-Commerce and E-Business Management*, Pearson Education Limited

Gillespie, A (2002) *Business in Action*, Hodder & Stoughton

Hackley, C (2005) *Advertising and Promotion: Communicating Brands*, Sage Publications Ltd

Marcouse, I, Gillespie, A, Martin, B, Surridge, M, Wall, N, Brewer, M, Hammond, A, Ruscoe, C, Swift, I and Watson, N (2003) *Business Studies*, Hodder & Stoughton

Pricken, M (2004) *Creative Advertising: Ideas and Techniques from the World's Best Campaigns*, Thames and Hudson Ltd

Journals

Business Review
European Journal of Marketing
Innovative Marketing
International Marketing Review
Marketing Today
Marketing Week

Websites

www.businesslink.gov.uk
Business Link advice for businesses

www.cbi.org.uk
Confederation of British Industry

www.mindtools.com
Tools that can be used to help managers

www.marketingtoday.com
Useful website with lots of marketing information and resources including articles

www.mybusiness.co.uk
My Business provides information on management issues for small businesses including resources

www.statistics.gov.uk
National statistics published by the government

www.e-zinez.com
The handbook of ezine publishing

www.adassoc.org.uk
Advertising Association

www.asa.org.uk
Advertising Standards Agency

www.the-dma.org
Direct Marketing Association

www.ofcom.org.uk
Ofcom website with regulatory information

www.tpsonline.org.uk
Telephone Preference Service registration site

www.dti.gov.uk
Department for Trade and Industry

www.oft.gov.uk
Office of Fair Trading

www.ipa.co.uk
Institute of Advertising Practitioners

www.isba.org.uk
Incorporated Society of British Advertisers

www.cim.co.uk
Chartered Institute of Marketing

www.mintel.com
Mintel International produce secondary research

www.dnb.com/uk/
Dun and Bradstreet market research company

www.mori.com
Mori market research company

www.informationcommissioner.gov.uk
The information commissioner's office who work to oversee acts like the Data Protection Act 1998 to protect the public's personal information

www.emailuniverse.com
Lots of useful and relevant information about using email and ezines as part of promotion

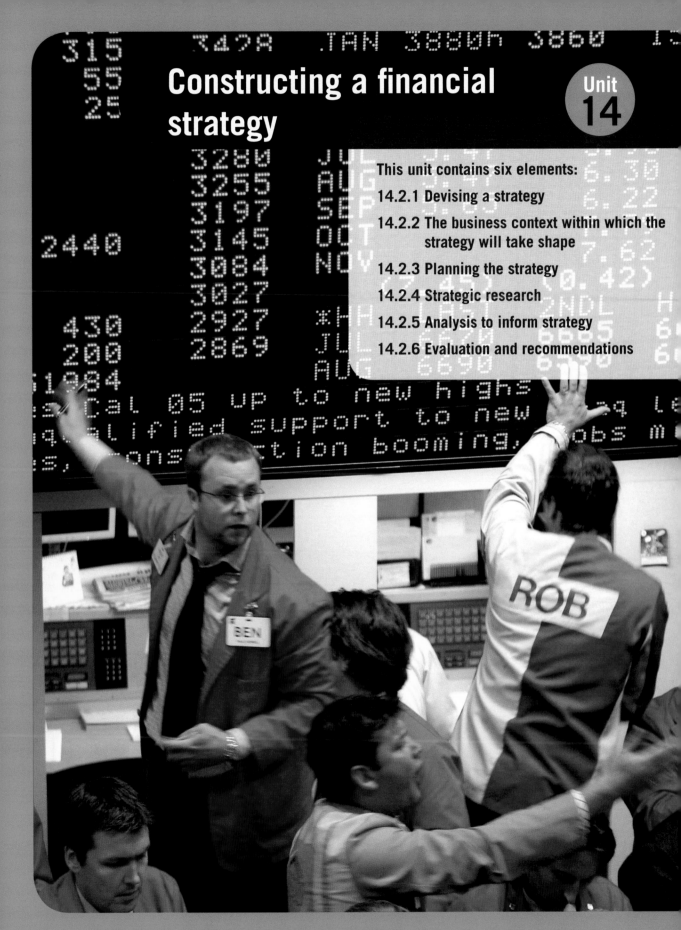

Constructing a financial strategy

Unit 14

This unit contains six elements:

14.2.1 Devising a strategy

14.2.2 The business context within which the strategy will take shape

14.2.3 Planning the strategy

14.2.4 Strategic research

14.2.5 Analysis to inform strategy

14.2.6 Evaluation and recommendations

This unit requires you to use a case study supplied by OCR to construct a financial strategy within a given business context. Within the case study you will be provided with a series of financial data which will inform your subsequent investigation. You will then be required to apply this knowledge and understanding to given data to produce your own set of final accounts suitable for the business context. You will need to use a variety of financial ratios to comment on the financial position of the business before finally evaluating critically how the business, in the given context, should plan its financial activities in the future.

Your financial strategy needs to show that you understand the reasons behind keeping financial records, the consequences of not producing accurate records and the processes involved in creating a series of final accounts that would be fit for publication.

14.2.1 Devising a strategy

In order to complete this unit you will need to devise a financial strategy using a case study which will focus on a particular business. You will therefore have to consider the following in the light of the supplied business context:

* understanding the business context within which the strategy will take shape
* planning the strategy
* researching the business environment to inform the strategy
* analysing the gathered data to inform the development of the strategy
* producing a plan of action based on research and analysis
* monitoring and evaluating various aspects of your strategy with a view to recommending improvements and future updates to your strategy.

The case study will be broken down into manageable tasks.

Understanding the business context within which the strategy will take shape

In order to complete the first part of the strategic planning cycle read the case study supplied by OCR and make notes on:

* what kind of business it is
* within what kind of market it is trading
* what its competition is
* what problems/ideas are being highlighted within the case study.

Having answered these questions you are now in a position to proceed with the second stage of the strategic planning cycle.

Researching the business environment to inform strategy development

Having gained an insight into the business you will now need to undertake some research on similar businesses. This background information will help you make judgements concerning the strengths and weaknesses of the business within the case study.

Analysing the gathered data to inform the development of the strategy

Having undertaken some secondary research into similar businesses and used the financial data supplied within the case study you will then be required to analyse your information. One of the tools you use for this unit is ratio analysis (see page 239). This will help you analyse the financial information supplied. In order to produce a detailed analysis you need to make reference to the case study and any secondary research that you have conducted into similar businesses, similar products or recent trends, such as healthy eating, population trends or economic trends.

Producing a plan of action based on research and analysis

This will be the set of accounts that you produce using the financial information supplied with the case study. The accounts will have to be produced in a format suitable for the type of business being investigated.

Monitoring and evaluating various aspects of your strategy with a view to recommending improvements and future updates to your strategy

The final stage of the strategic cycle will lead you to make judgements. You will need to consider your research and analysis and make recommendations on how the business could plan its financial activities in the future. Remember to refer back to the case study. What were the first problems/ideas you flagged up? Evaluate how your ideas will help solve these problems.

14.2.2 The business context within which the strategy will take shape

The OCR case study will set the business context within which you will need to formulate your strategy. It will set the scene outlining the current financial needs of the business and what the business would like to be able to achieve in the future. You will be required to develop a strategy that will enable the business to achieve its financial aims and objectives. In order to complete the set tasks you will need to understand how to:

* calculate accurately profit and loss accounts
* meet legal requirements
* show the assets and liabilities of the business
* compare the business' financial position to previous years
* prepare accurate budgets/forecasts for future years
* obtain additional finance
* plan any further expansion.

Why keep financial records?

The main reason people go into business is to make money. How is a business going to know if it is making any money if it does not keep accurate records of the money flowing into and out of the business?

To monitor performance

All businesses need to know how they are performing throughout the year. If sales suddenly start to fall this trend needs to be quickly identified and remedial action taken. Businesses will also need to track how much they are spending on running the business. If these costs are steadily rising it is likely that profits will start to fall.

To formulate strategic plans

By looking at past financial facts and figures it is possible for a business to identify trends, whether good or bad, and make plans to improve, or build upon them. For example if a particular product line has been selling well it might be worth increasing production, backed up with a new marketing campaign to try to improve an already developing existing market. This may be at the expense of a less popular product

To comply with legislation

Public limited companies are regulated by the Companies Acts 1985 and 1989 concerning the preparation and publication of financial statements. Companies are required to submit a copy of their accounts annually to Companies House. Companies with a turnover greater than £1 million are also required to have their accounts independently audited. The auditors are appointed each year at the annual general meeting. The auditors complete their report after examining the books and accounts, and report on the accuracy of the accounts in terms of whether they give a true and fair picture of the financial health of the business. The report and financial statements are given to the shareholders at the annual general meeting.

Think it over...

Do you know how much money:

* you currently have available to spend
* you are likely to receive within the next four weeks
* you are likely to spend over the same period
* you received last month
* you spent last month?

These questions would be quite difficult for you to answer if you have not kept a record of your recent income and expenditure. As an individual with few commitments this is not too much of a problem. But consider how a business would cope if it did not record the money it had coming in and going out. How long do you think it would stay in business?

The Inland Revenue is very keen to receive a final set of accounts so it can calculate how much corporation tax is due to be paid. Customs and Excise require figures from the final accounts to be submitted every three months to calculate the VAT liability of the business.

Consequences of not keeping financial records

You will also be required to understand the negative consequences to a business if financial information is found to be inaccurate. These include:

* criminal action
* cash flow problems from a high tax bill or criminal action
* shareholders losing confidence and investing elsewhere
* bad public image
* change to management structure.

Criminal action

Failure to submit figures to the Inland Revenue will result in the Inland Revenue chasing the company for its accounts. If this fails it will be fined for failure to submit its accounts and finally it could be prosecuted for non-compliance.

If a business knowingly submits accounts that are incorrect it would be committing a fraud. When this comes to light the business could be fined, and may also be prosecuted. However, if a business simply makes an innocent mistake it is likely to receive a fine for late payment and be charged interest on the outstanding tax liability. Legal proceedings would only be instigated if it can be proved that the business knowingly tried to defraud the Inland Revenue through the submission of incorrect information.

Cash flow problems

If a business fails to keep correct records it may only have a vague idea of the amount of money it has available to spend at any one time. It may spend money that it does not have. It may also be unaware how many **debtors** and **creditors** that it has. If a business has insufficient money coming in to meet its outgoing payments it will very quickly suffer **liquidity** problems.

If a business has failed to declare the correct profit and loss it might also suddenly find itself facing a very large tax bill. This would impact on the business' immediate cash flow. It may find itself with insufficient cash to meet the debt.

Look at the example in Figure 14.1. Sunny Days Beach Company sell products for use at the seaside, such as buckets, spades, balls or inflatables. The business' main season is May through to late September. However, the weather has been really bad throughout August and September and sales have fallen to an all-time low. It has just received a letter from the bank informing the business it is seriously overdrawn. The business did not keep accurate records and had failed to realise that its income and expenditure were as outlined in Figure 14.1.

The business is now facing an overdraft of £9,300. If it had kept accurate records it could have taken the following measures:

* reduced the amount of stock purchased – the extra stock is unlikely to be sold now that the season is nearly over

	August £	September £
Sales	12,000	8,000
Total income (a)	12,000	8,000
Expenditure		
Stock	7,000	8,000
Rent	4,000	4,000
Wages	5,000	5,000
General expenses	500	500
Total expenditure (b)	16,500	17,500
Opening balance	4,700	200
Cash inflow/outflow (a–b)	(4,500)	(9,500)
Closing balance	200	(9,300)

FIGURE 14.1 *Sunny Days Beach Company*

* reduced the wages – cut back on staff as the business has ceased to require its current staffing level.

Both of these measures would have eased the businesses cash flow problems.

Shareholders losing confidence and investing elsewhere

Shareholders are people who invest in a business in order to receive a yearly **dividend**.

Should it become apparent that a business does not keep accurate financial records and therefore is unable to plan an effective strategy to take the business forward shareholders are likely to lose confidence in the business. They will then have two options:

* vote in a new board of directors at the annual general meeting

* sell their shares in the business.

Bad public image

The only way the general public will become aware that a business is failing to record its activities is when it hits the media headlines. The information supplied to the public will often be sensational with the sole result of creating a bad image of the business concerned. This situation could have the consequence of shareholders selling their shares as they no longer wish to be associated with the business and customers voting with their feet and withdrawing their custom from the business. It could also have staffing issues, as staff become concerned about future job prospects.

Change to management structure

A limited company is run by a board of directors on behalf of the shareholders. When things start to go wrong the shareholders can vote in a new board of directors in order to get the business back on track. However, in very large businesses when the shares are owned by thousands of different people it might be difficult to get sufficient people to vote in order for changes to take place.

14.2.3 Planning the strategy

In order to plan an effective financial strategy using the OCR case study you will need to construct a set of final accounts allowing you to gain a snapshot of the current financial condition of the business. Before you can tackle this task you will first of all need to understand the different types of income and expenditure which are often included in a set of final accounts.

In order to illustrate the following generic financial terms, we are going to base the examples on Joe's Home Decorating Service.

Making decisions and agreements are crucial to planning a business strategy

Joe's Home Decorating

Joe has just been made redundant from his job. Joe is a qualified painter and decorator and has therefore decided to start up his own business. In order to get started he is going to invest £500 into a bank account and donate his computer to the business – worth £240. After his first year of trading Joe has made a net profit of £23,000. He has taken £21,000 out of the business as wages. Within sole trader accounts this is known as drawings.

Capital

Opening capital is the amount of money or value of items that a person uses to start up a business. This could include the initial investment into the bank account, a computer they already own or tools and equipment of their trade.

Let us now calculate Joe's opening capital for the first year of business:

Bank	£500
Computer	£240
Opening capital	£740

Closing capital is the net worth of the business after it has been trading for a year. Below is the calculation of Joe's closing capital. The closing capital of year one becomes the opening capital of year two.

Opening capital	£740
Add net profit	£23,000
Less drawing	£21,000
Closing capital	£2,740

The capital of a limited company is the number of shares multiplied by the value of the shares that have been issued. It will also include any reserves that the business has decided to create from retained profit. How the figures are laid out in the financial accounts will be dealt with in greater depth when we consider the completion of final accounts for limited companies.

CASE STUDY

Joe's Home Decorating turns into a private limited company

Time has moved on and Joe's decorating business has now been running successfully for five years and he has decided to expand the business. Joe is about to turn his business into a limited company – J e P Decorating Ltd. His friend Paul is going to join him in the business. They have decided to invest £20,000 each into the business. This will take the format of 40,000 ordinary shares with a face value of £1 each.

This is how Joe would record his capital in the balance sheet.

Capital and Reserves	£
40,000 ordinary shares at £1 each	40,000

Bank loans

Often businesses will need to borrow money from external sources in order to help them start up or expand their business. One way to raise this external finance is to organise a loan through a bank. Money borrowed from a bank will have a set repayment date and carry an agreed interest rate. The interest charged on the loan will either be fixed or variable. If a fixed interest rate is selected the interest rate charged will be slightly higher than the current base rate when the loan is taken out but will not be subjected to interest fluctuations. If a business opts for a variable rate of interest it could find the repayments increasing if interest rates rise, or reap the benefit of reduced payments should interest rates fall.

Fixed assets

Fixed assets are those items that a business needs in order to run the business efficiently. They will usually have a life expectancy of greater than one year. They include:

* premises
* vehicles
* machinery
* office equipment including computers.

As you can see from the above list, these are very often expensive items which a business may not be able to purchase outright. A business may take on a loan in order to acquire them. The loan would usually be taken out over a period of time, for example five years, and would therefore be classified as a long-term liability within the accounts of the business.

Theory into practice

Consider an expensive item that you would like to purchase in the near future. How would this expenditure be classified? How are you planning to finance your selected purchase?

Expenses

Expenses are those items that a business needs to pay for in order to run. These would include such items as wages of employees, rent of premises, electricity and heating costs, telephone expenses and motor expenses.

Purchases, services and credit

Some businesses sell goods and others sell services. If a business sells goods in order to make a profit it will need to buy certain items, this could be the raw materials to manufacture its products or even finished goods in order to sell on.

Trade credit is a facility which is offered to businesses that trade business to business. This means that a business can receive goods or services on credit with a promise to pay later. Trade credit is normally allowed for a period of 30 days. This enables the purchasing business to sell goods on to its customers before it has made payment for them. Consider the following example.

Quick Snacks buys £200 of crisps from Unique Crisps on 1 February 2006. Quick Snacks' invoice states that the payment of £200 must be made before 1 March 2006.

Throughout February Quick Snacks has sold £175 of the stock it purchased on 1 February 2006. On the 28 February 2006 Quick Snacks pays Unique Crisps £200.

In this example Quick Snacks has managed to sell 87.5 per cent of the stock prior to the repayment date.

This same scenario can also work for businesses that purchase the services of another business. For example, Quick Snacks may purchase the services of an accountant to prepare accounts for the Inland Revenue. Once the accountant has finished the accounts he would send Quick Snacks an invoice with a request for payment in 30 days.

Sales and credit

A sale occurs when a business has formed a contract with a third party who will pay an agreed price for the product or service. As outlined above it is common for a business to sell its goods on credit to other businesses or selected individuals. This means that the customer will be able to take benefit of the product or service prior to payment. Payment will be due, usually within a 30-day period.

Using documents

You now need to gain an understanding of the documents that businesses use when buying and selling items. It is these documents that start the double-entry process of bookkeeping.

Below is a flow diagram to illustrate the different documents used between Quick Snacks and Unique Crisps.

Purchase order
Quick Snacks want to order 50 boxes of mixed crisps from Unique Crisps.

Delivery note
Unique Crisps packages up the crisps and sends the package to Quick Snacks. Included in the package is the delivery note which states the contents of the package.

Goods received note
Quick Snacks receives the parcel. The person who signs for the package will check its contents and complete the goods received note. This will then be passed onto the accounts department. The goods received note records that one of the boxes of crisps is damaged. This will be returned to Unique Crisps.

Invoice
Unique Crisps sends Quick Snacks an invoice. This will outline the goods sent and the amount owed. It will set out the terms of payment. For example, if the terms are 30 days, this means the invoice must be paid within 30 days of receipt of the invoice.

Credit note
Unique Crisps send Quick Snacks a credit note for the damaged box of crisps. This reduces the amount owed on the invoice.

Statement of account
When a business makes multiple purchases from another business over a period of a month it will be sent a statement of account. This totals all the invoices and deducts any credit notes and payments made. The final balance is the amount owed at the end of that month. Payment is due within 30 days.

Remittance advice slips
It is usual for a business to add a remittance advice slip at the end of the statement of account or invoice. This is a tear-off strip which gives the account number of the customer and the amount owed. It enables the customer to make payment quickly and easily. When Unique Crisps receives payment from Quick Snacks the remittance advice slip will tell them who the money is from.

Cheque
Quick Snacks will send a cheque to Unique Crisps as payment for the goods received.

FIGURE 14.2 *Documents used by businesses when buying and selling*

Double-entry accounting

In order to complete this unit you will need to have the knowledge, understanding and skills necessary to practise double-entry accounting.

Double-entry accounting is based on one simple idea. This is that every transaction has an impact on two accounts – each transaction will increase the value of one account and, at the same time, the value of another account will decrease.

While studying double-entry accounting you always need to consider the following:

* Debit the account which receives goods, services or money.

* Credit the account which gives goods, services or money.

In order to help clarify the theory, two businesses will be used as examples throughout the first section. The first we met earlier – Joe's Home Decorating (prior to it becoming a limited company). The second business upon which example questions are set is Quick Snacks. Both of these businesses are sole traders.

The division of ledgers

Throughout this section we have been identifying how a business functions. You should now be familiar with a range of new business terminology.

It is now time to think about how and where we record all these different actions. These include the following:

* sales of goods or services to customers

* debtors – customers who owe the business money for goods or services received on credit

* purchases – goods or services bought with the sole idea of resale

* creditors – people or businesses that the business has purchased goods from on credit

* purchase of fixed assets – items that help the business to become more efficient

* expenses – items that need to be bought in order for the business to function.

In order to record all of the above financial transactions a business will break its account books into four sections:

* The sales ledger contains the personal accounts of all the debtors (customers) who have received goods or services and have yet to pay for them.

* The purchase ledger contains the personal accounts of all the creditors – people the business has bought goods from and whom they will pay at a later date.

* The general ledger keeps a record of the monetary value of sales, purchases, sales returns and purchase returns. It contains the accounts which record the amount of money that has been spent on the expenses of the business. The other main account that is held within the general ledger is the cash book. This is the account that records all the money that has come in and gone out of the business.

* The journal records extraordinary items such as the start-up capital of a business and the purchase of fixed assets. These are then posted to the general ledger in their own accounts. It is also used to record the correction of errors made in the double-entry accounting.

Dr	Bank account		Cr
2007			
1 Feb Capital	500		

Dr	Computer account		Cr
2007			
1 Feb Capital	240		

This shows that the bank and computer account have received this from the capital account. The accounts have received the goods and money – *debit the receiver*.

In order to practise the above you should make the initial entries for Quick Snacks. Use 1 August 2006 as the start date. This business started up with opening capital consisting of:

- £2,500 cash placed in a business bank account
- a van worth £4,000.

Theory into practice

A business buys a new van paying with a cheque for £7,500.

- Which account has received the fixed asset?
- Would this be a debit or credit entry in the accounts?
- Which account gave the money to purchase the fixed asset?
- Would this be a debit or credit entry in the accounts?

In order to record transactions, T-line accounts are drawn up following the layout below:

Dr	Name of account		Cr
Date Description Amount		Date Description Amount	
This is the debit side of the account and is illustrated by the Dr.		This is the credit side of the account and is illustrated by the Cr.	

How to record opening capital

We will use Joe's Home Decorating as an example, and use a starting date of 1 February 2007:

Bank	£500
Computer	£240
Opening capital	£740

We will now begin Joe's accounts and complete the double entry on the general ledger:

General ledger

Dr	Capital account		Cr
		2007	
		1 Feb Bank	500
		1 Feb Computer	240

This shows that Joe gave the business these items and therefore this is a debt to Joe. If you find that a difficult concept, consider that the capital account has given these items to the bank and computer account as illustrated below. Therefore credit the giver.

You will note that the description within the account always states where the other half of the double entry will be found.

How to record purchases for cash and on credit

Joe is just about to start trading and needs to get some materials so that he can complete his first job. He makes the following transactions throughout his first month of trading:

✱ 3 February – Wickes, paint, £45, paid by cheque.

✱ 10 February – Paints & Wallpaper Ltd, £132 on credit.

✱ 16 February – Tiles UK, 500 tiles, £287 on credit.

We now need to record these transactions in the books of account. Note we do not keep on drawing up new accounts. Every account must convey the full history of all the transactions that have taken place.

General ledger

Dr	Bank account		Cr
2007		2007	
1 Feb Capital	500	3 Feb Wickes	45

This entry shows us that we have made a purchase from Wickes paying by cheque – we have paid out this amount out therefore it is a credit entry.

Dr	Purchase account		Cr
2007			
3 Feb Bank*	45		
10 Feb Paints &			
Wallpaper	132		
16 Feb Tiles UK	287		

These entries show that we have received goods to the value of the amounts stated. The entry Bank* shows that we have paid for these goods. The other two entries are named accounts. Joe has received these goods on credit with a promise to pay later. These are all debit entries as we have actually received the goods.

Purchase ledger

Dr	Paints and Wallpaper Ltd		Cr
2007			
10 Feb Purchase			132

Dr	Tiles UK		Cr
2007			
16 Feb Purchase			287

These entries illustrate that these businesses have given Joe goods on credit. When a supplier sends goods to the business on credit it is always a credit entry as they have given the business goods – remember *credit the giver*.

Theory into practice

Continue the accounts that you have already created for Quick Snacks as follows:

- 3 August – purchased £400 of crisps from Unique Crisps on credit

- 12 August – purchased ten trays of soft drinks from Pops Ltd for £324 paying by cheque

- 25 August – purchased some more stock from Unique Crisps on credit for £219.

How to record sales for cash and on credit

Joe has now come to the end of his first month in business. He has completed three jobs. Two of these have been small contracts for which he has been paid in cash. The last one lasted for over two weeks and was for a housing association. He has sent them an invoice and they will pay within 30 days. The details are outlined below:

1. 12 February – Mrs Peters, paid £250 by cheque.
2. 24 February – Mr Brown, paid £153 by cheque.
3. 27 February – Westside Housing Association, sent an invoice for £1,560.

Theory into practice

Complete the table below using 1–3 above.

NUMBER	AMOUNT TO BE DEBITED	ACCOUNT TO BE CREDITED
	Which account receives goods or money?	Which account gives goods or money?
1.		
2.		
3.		

Now, using this information, complete the double entry:

General ledger

Dr		Bank account		Cr
2007			2007	
1 Feb Capital	500		3 Feb Wickes	45
12 Feb Sales	250			
24 Feb Sales	153			

The bank has received money for Joe's services and therefore both entries must be debit entries The description is sales as this is how the money has been earned. The personal name is only used when the goods have been sold on credit. Remember the description represents where the other half of the double entry is.

Dr	Sales account		Cr
	2007		
	12 Feb	Bank	250
	24 Feb	Bank	153
	27 Feb	Westside Housing Association	1,560

All entries represent sales. The sales account has given the money to the bank account or to the receiver of Joe's services.

Sales ledger

Dr	Westside Housing Association		Cr
2007			
27 Feb Sales	1,560		

This account shows that the Westside Housing Association owe Joe £1,560 for the service that they have received from Joe. Westside Housing Association are therefore a debtor to Joe's business.

How to record expenses occurred within the business

So far we have only recorded transactions which involve purchases or sales. Businesses will also have to meet other types of expenditure in order to survive.

Let us now consider possible expenses that Joe might occur in his business. These might include:

* the expenses of running his van – petrol, repairs, taxation, insurance, stationery
* mobile telephone calls.

When Joe pays for his petrol and other expenses he must ask for a receipt. These receipts are the financial documents that are used to record money spent on the expenses of the business.

Throughout February Joe has paid out for the following expenses. He has paid for everything using his debit card. The money has been taken straight out of his business bank account:

* 5 February – petrol, £37
* 15 February – Staples, £16 for stationery
* 21 February – petrol, £42.

General ledger

Dr	Bank account				Cr
2007			2007		
1 Feb	Capital	500	3 Feb	Wickes	45
12 Feb	Sales	250	5 Feb	Motor expenses	37
24 Feb	Sales	153	15 Feb	Stationery	16
			21 Feb	Motor expenses	42

The three new transactions were all paid at the point of purchase. The bank therefore has given money for these goods – *credit the giver*.

Dr	Motor expenses account		Cr
2007			
5 Feb	Bank	37	
21 Feb	Bank	42	

The bank has given money for the petrol. Therefore the motor expenses account has received the value of this – *debit the receiver*.

Dr	Stationery account		Cr
2007			
15 Feb	Bank	16	

The bank has given money for the stationery. Therefore the stationery account has received the value of this – *debit the receiver*.

How to record the wages of the owner

Joe has just completed his first month of trading and now needs to draw some money out of the business in order to live.

If a business has been set up as a sole trader the term used for the money taken out of the business by the owner in order to live is known as drawings.

Joe has decided that he can afford to pay himself £400 this month. This is recorded as follows:

General ledger

Dr		Bank account		Cr
2007		2007		
1 Feb	Capital	500	3 Feb Wickes	45
12 Feb	Sales	250	5 Feb Motor expenses	37
24 Feb	Sales	153	15 Feb Stationery	16
			21 Feb Motor expenses	42
			28 Feb Drawings	400

Dr	Drawings account		Cr
2007			
28 Feb Bank	400		

The bank has given Joe £400 – *credit the giver*. This money has been received by Joe and it therefore appears as a debit entry in this account.

Balancing the accounts

At the end of each trading month a business will balance its accounts to see what its current financial position is. Joe will balance his accounts at the end of February in order to monitor the businesses performance and to find out:

* the value of the month's sales

* how much money was spent on purchases

* how much the business spent on expenses

* how much money is owed to creditors

* how much money is owed by debtors.

The method used to balance the accounts is always the same and can be applied to all the different accounts that you compile. Just follow the steps outlined below:

* *Stage one* – identify the side which holds the greatest value.

* *Stage two* – write the word 'balance' on the smaller side under the last entry in the account.

* *Stage three* – add up the side which holds the greatest value.

* *Stage four* – deduct each individual transaction on the smaller side of the account.

* *Stage five* – the remaining balance is the amount you put under the £ sign with the description of balance. Each side should now balance.

* *Stage six* – the balance is now brought down to the opposite side for the start of the next trading month.

Now look at this worked example. Each stage is annotated with the corresponding stage number above.

General ledger

Dr		Bank account		Cr
2007		2007		
1 Feb	Capital	500	3 Feb Wickes	45
12 Feb Sales		250	5 Feb Motor expenses	37
24 Feb Sales		153	15 Feb Stationery	16
			21 Feb Motor expenses	42
			28 Feb Drawings	400
			28 Feb Balance c/fwd	363
		903		903
1 Mar Balance b/dn		363		

* *Stage one* – we can see that the side which holds the greatest value is the debit side.

* *Stage two* – the word 'balance' is placed after the last entry on the credit side.

* *Stage three* – add up the debit side and place the total of £903 as above.

* *Stage four* – deducted 45, 37, 16, 42 and 400 from the total of £903. The balance of £363 is inserted alongside the word balance on the credit side.

* *Stage five* – both sides now have the same totals and this can be inserted.

* *Stage six* – Bring down the balance for the start of the next trading month. This shows that Joe currently has £363 available to spend in his bank account.

The trial balance

Joe's decorating business has not processed many financial transactions during his first month of trading. However, during the course of a normal working day a business may make many thousands of transactions. It is therefore necessary to have a method which can check the accuracy of the double-entry accounting. The method used is known as the trial balance. It is often completed monthly but will definitely be completed at the end of a business' financial year. Although time-consuming, there are advantages in drawing up a trial balance.

* A business is able to assess the accuracy of the double-entry accounting.

* If both sides of the trial balance agree it indicates the business' financial transactions have been entered into the double-entry system correctly.

* It can save time when drawing up the final accounts of the business.

* It can bring to the attention of the management the number of outstanding debtors and creditors.

* It can be used as a check against fraud if different people work on different sections of the business' ledgers

How to draw up a trial balance

The hard work is involved in completing all the bookkeeping and balancing the accounts at the end of the financial year. The trial balance is simply a matter of collecting all the brought-down balances and placing them in a table. Hopefully, if you have completed the bookkeeping correctly both sides of the trial balance will balance. Let us put together Joe's trial balance for the month ended 28 February 2007.

The first thing you must remember is that the trial balance is an 'as at' statement. This means that it is only correct on the date it is completed. If we complete Joe's trial balance for the 28 February it will only be correct for that one day. As soon as trading resumes on the 1 March the balances in the accounts will change and therefore the trial balance will no longer be accurate. Remember to use the brought-down balances.

	Debit £	Credit £
Capital		740
Bank	363	
Computer	240	
Purchases	464	
Sales		1,963
Motor expenses	79	
Stationery	16	
Drawings	400	
Paints and Wallpaper		132
Tiles UK		287
Westside Housing Association	1,560	
	3,122	3,122

FIGURE 14.3 *Joe's Home Decorating trial balance as at 28 February 2007*

It is possible that the trial balance will still agree even if there are errors in accounts. Therefore a trial balance that does agree will only be *prima facie* correct – at first glance it appears there are no errors in the bookkeeping system, but this does not prove that there are no errors. We will be covering this section of theory later in this unit.

Theory into practice

Complete the trial balance for Quick Snacks as at 31 August 2007.

More complex accounting entries

So far in this unit we have looked at the very basic entries of capital, fixed assets, purchases, sales, expense and drawings. We now need to consider how the following financial transactions would affect the accounting entries.

Sales returns

Sometimes goods are sold to customers and are then returned for a wide variety of reasons, e.g. the seller may have sent the wrong items, they may have arrived damaged or they might even be the wrong colour! Once these items are returned the seller sends the customer a credit note which has the effect of reducing the amount the customer owes on their invoice – it reduces their debt to the business.

In order to expand his business Joe has been selling customers tiles and blinds. Mrs Gough ordered two sets of blinds worth £350 for her front room. Joe delivered the goods on the 2 May 2007. On the 4 May 2007 Mrs Gough returned one set of blinds worth £220 to Joe as they were damaged. Joe gave Mrs Gough a credit note and took the damaged blinds back.

The bookkeeping entries would be as follows:

General ledger

Dr	Sales account		Cr
	2007		
	4 May Mrs Gough	350	

Dr	Sales returns account		Cr
2007			
4 May Mrs Gough	220		

Sales ledger

Dr	Mrs Gough's account		Cr
2007		2007	
4 May Sales	350	4 May Sales returns	220

Step one is to record the sales in the sales account and Mrs Gough's account. You must then take the goods out of Mrs Gough's account – she is giving them back, so *credit the giver*. By returning the goods she has reduced her debt to Joe and now only owes him £130. The entry for the returned goods is then placed in the sales returns account. Sales returns always go in their own account and not on the debit side of the sales account. This is so that the business can monitor the value of sales returned. This may highlight a potential problem.

Theory into practice

Record the following transactions in the books of Quick Snacks. Continue in the accounts that you have already created and balanced:

- 4 September – sold £480 of crisps and soft drinks to QP Petrol station

- 9 September – QP Petrol Station returned £120 of the goods as they were damaged on arrival.

Purchase returns

Businesses will also buy some stock and then return it for the same reasons that customers may have returned goods to them. The same theory applies when recording purchase returns as with

Many business purchases are stored for future use

sales returns. The returned item goes into its own account and *does not* appear as a credit entry in the purchase account.

On 7 May Joe purchased £870 of tiles from Tiles UK. When he started using them he discovered that the tiles in one of the boxes were damaged. He contacted Tiles UK and they agreed to send him a credit note for £89 as way of compensation for the damaged tiles and inconvenience. This was agreed on the 19 May.

General ledger

Dr		Purchase account		Cr
2007			£	
7 May	Tiles UK		870	

Dr		Purchase returns account		
		2007		£
		19 May Tiles UK		89

Purchase ledger

Dr		Tiles UK account		Cr
2007		£	2007	£
19 May Purchase returns	89		7 May Purchases	870

The first entries show the item being purchased from Tiles UK. The second set of entries show the value of the goods being then taken out of the Tiles UK account and placed in the purchase returns account. Joe now owes Tiles UK £781 for the tiles that he has been able to use.

Discounts allowed and discounts received

One of the reasons that a lot of businesses fail is not due to lack of profitability but problems with liquidity. Liquidity is the amount of money that the business has available to pay its immediate debts. One of the reasons for poor liquidity is because customers have received goods or services on credit and have then failed to pay on time.

One method to encourage customers to pay early is to offer a cash discount. This allows the customer to deduct an agreed percentage from the invoice if they pay within the stipulated time period.

In his first month of trading Joe's Home Decorating was owed £1,560 from Westside Housing Association. If this business were to take three months to pay, this could leave Joe with serious cash flow problems. To avoid this situation he could offer them a cash discount of 3% if they pay within 30 days. They would therefore pay £1,513.20 (£1,560.00 less 3% of the invoiced cost, £46.80).

Although this means that Joe has received less money it does mean that he will have sufficient money in the bank to continue buying supplies in order to continue working.

We must now consider how these entries would be recorded in the books of account. So far within this chapter we have only used a simple bank account. We are now going to combine this with the cash account and create the three-column cash book.

The three-column cash book

The three-column cash book behaves the same as any other account. The debit side of the account records all the money coming into the business. The credit side is a record of the money that has been spent. This account also holds the cash account. This part of the cash book records the cash that business actually keeps. Due to security reasons, businesses these days keep very little cash and often it is only sufficient to meet the immediate needs of the business.

You will also notice that the account holds two memorandum columns. The first is the **discount allowed** column. This column records the discounts that have been taken up by customers. The second memorandum column is the **discount received** column. This is a record of the discounts the business has made use of by paying its bills early. These columns are not balanced off against each other but totalled at the end of each month. This is illustrated in the example in Figure 14.4, using the three-column cash book for a fictional business, The Highland Co. An easy way to remember how to post the discount columns to their own accounts is that they always go on the same side as the corresponding entry.

✳ Discounts allowed go with payment received therefore it is a debit entry.

✳ Discounts received go with payments being made therefore it is a credit entry.

Three-column cash book

Date	Details	Discount Allowed £	Cash £	Bank £	Date	Details	Discount Received £	Cash £	Bank £
(a) 1 Feb	Capital		50	3,000	(b) 8 Feb	Couch & Co.	16		800
(d) 16 Feb	M. Frank	3		300	(c) 12 Feb	Motor expenses			1,500
(e) 19 Feb	Sales		75		(g) 28 Feb	T. Ball	8		130
(f) 24 Feb	T. Vale	5		180	(h) 28 Feb	Rent		50	
					(i) 28 Feb	Drawings			400
					(j) 28 Feb	Balance		75	650
(k)		8	125	3,480			24	125	3,480

FIGURE 14.4 *Three-column cash book for The Highland Co.*

Explanation of entries

(a) The Highland Co. started up with an opening capital of £3,050 – £3,000 in the bank and £50 cash being held in the business.

(b) The business has paid Couch & Co. £800 having deducted £16 from the original invoice for early payment.

(c) The business has paid out £1,500 motor expenses paying by cheque.

(d) M. Frank has paid £300 for goods received. He has deducted a cash discount of £3 for prompt payment.

(e) The business has made cash sales of £75.

(f) T. Vale has paid the business £180 for goods received. He has deduced £5 for early payment.

(g) The business has paid T. Ball £130 having deducted the cash discount of £8.

(h) The business has paid its rent in cash – £50.

(i) The owner has taken £400 out of the business for personal use.

(j) This is the balance of money left at the end of the month.

(k) These are the totals of the memorandum columns, bank and cash. The cash and bank accounts are balanced in exactly the same way as the other accounts. You add up the largest side, and then deduct each item from the smaller side.

We now need to consider how we enter discount received and discount allowed into the double-entry accounting system. The example will be based on some of the entries in the cash book above.

On 15 January The Highland Co. purchased goods from Couch & Co. to the value of £816. The invoice stated that if payment was made before the 15 February a cash discount of £8 could be taken. The Highland Co. took advantage of this discount paying Couch £800 on 8 February. The bookkeeping entries are as follows:

General ledger

Dr	Purchase account		Cr
2007			
15 Jan Couch & Co. 816			

The entries to show payment are as recorded above in the cash book.

Dr	Discounts received account		Cr
	2007		
	15 Jan Couch & Co.	16	

Purchase ledger

Dr	Couch & Co. account		Cr
2007		2007	
8 Feb Bank	800	15 Jan Purchases	816
8 Feb Discount			
allowed	16		

Carriage in and carriage out

When a business buys purchases to sell on they may be charged for postage and packing or delivery. These charges are classified as carriage in. The impact of these charges is to increase the cost of the actual purchase.

Carriage out is the cost of dispatching sales to customers and is therefore classified as an expense.

Trading profit and loss account and balance sheet

Having entered the business transactions into the accounts and drawn up a trial balance it is now time to draw up the final accounts of the business. These consist of the trading profit and loss account and the balance sheet.

The final accounts of a business can be drawn up at any time in order to establish the financial position of the business but it is generally done on a yearly basis. Some businesses may choose to draw one up on a more regular basis in order to monitor the profitability of the business throughout its financial year.

The trading profit and loss account is drawn up in order to calculate two types of profit – **gross profit** and **net profit**.

> **Key terms**
>
> *Gross profit* is calculated within the trading account and is the amount by which the selling price of the purchases in which the business deals exceeds the purchase price.
>
> *Net profit* is the gross profit less the cost of running the business. This includes all the different expenses the business has to meet in order to continue to trade.

> **Theory into practice**
>
> You are required to make the following entries in the accounts of another fictional company Zaine & Co. Ltd. You will need to create a three-column cash book. Remember, each entry will have to be posted into two accounts. When you complete all the double-entry accounts, balance the accounts and draw up a trial balance.
>
> - 1 April – Started business with £2,500 in the bank and £200 cash.
> - 2 April – Purchased £600 of stock on credit from Frederick Ltd.
> - 6 April – Sold £850 of goods to Buddies & Co. on credit.
> - 9 April – Paid rent £400 by cheque.
> - 18 April – Purchased £692 of stock on credit from Frederick Ltd.
> - 20 April – Returned £52 worth of goods to Frederick Ltd as they were damaged.
> - 26 April – Cash sales £580.
> - 29 April – Paid Frederick Ltd for the goods purchased on 6 April, taking advantage of 2% cash discount.
> - 30 April – Received a cheque for £833 from Buddies & Co. as full payment for goods received on 6 April.

In order to calculate gross profit a business has to consider opening and closing stock. Stock is the value of goods that a business has at any moment in time. One of the best ways to illustrate this is through the use of a simple example, as the case study below shows.

Fixed and current assets

The balance sheet is drawn up to illustrate the financial position of the business. This final account contains all the assets and liabilities of a business. Business assets will consist of fixed assets and current assets.

Fixed assets are those items which the business has purchased in order to function efficiently. They have not been purchased for resale. Fixed assets consist of:

* premises, buildings and land
* machinery
* equipment
* fixtures and fittings
* computer equipment.

Current assets are items that are owned by the business but can be turned quickly into cash. They form the working capital cycle of the business. Current assets consist of:

* stock
* debtors
* bank
* cash.

Current assets are recorded in order of liquidity. Stock is considered to be the least liquid of all the current assets as a buyer has to be found first, they may then turn into a debtor before the business actually receives the cash.

Liabilities

The liabilities of a business refer to its own debts. These are the people that the business owes money to for goods or services received on credit. Liabilities can be further broken down into current liabilities and long-term liabilities.

Current liabilities are debts that are owed to other people for goods and services received on credit and are due for repayment within one year. Current liabilities include a business' creditors, and bank overdrafts, proposed dividends and corporation tax.

Long-term liabilities are debts that are owed to other people which will be paid over a period of time longer than one year. A long-term liability is often a bank loan.

How to construct the trading profit and loss account and balance sheet

It is usual for the trading profit and loss account and balance sheet to be compiled from the trial balance, which is extracted at the end of the financial year. Let us work through the following example.

It is the end of the financial year and Joe has completed all his double-entry accounting, balanced off his accounts and extracted the following balances:

	£ Debit	£ Credit
Capital		740
Sales		30,000
Purchases	8,000	
Computer	240	
Van	6,000	
Bank loan		6,000
Motor expenses	1,800	
Creditors		750
Debtors	2,600	
Drawings	17,000	
Bank	1,020	
Electricity	120	
Purchase returns		250
Sales returns	110	
Discounts allowed	10	
Discounts received		40
General expenses	600	
Carriage out	20	
Advertising	60	
Telephone and stationery	200	
Totals	37,780	37,780

FIGURE 14.5 *Joe's Home Decorating trial balance as at 31 January 2007. Closing stock was valued at £120*

	£	£	£
Sales (a)			30,000
Less sales returns (b)			(110)
			29,890
Less cost of sales (c)			
Opening stock (d)		0	
Purchases (e)	8,000		
Less purchase returns (f)	(250)		
Plus carriage in (f)	0		
		7,750	
Less closing stock (g)		(120)	
Cost of goods sold (h)			7,630
Gross profit (i)			**22,260**
Add discounts received (j)			40
			22,300
Less expenses (k)			
Electricity		120	
Motor expenses		1,800	
General expenses		600	
Carriage out		20	
Advertising		60	
Telephone and stationery		200	
Discount allowed (l)		10	2,810
Net profit (m)			19,490

FIGURE 14.6 *Joe's Home Decorating trading, profit and loss account for the financial year ended 31 January 2007*

Explanation of trading, profit and loss account

(a) *Sales* is the total value of the sales a business has made throughout its stated financial period. In this case it is a financial year from 1 February to 31 January. The sales figure recorded represents those items which have been invoiced. The goods may not necessarily have been paid for. This figure is posted from the sales account at the end of the financial period.

(b) *Sales returns* is the total value of the goods returned to the business. The figure is posted from the sales returns account at the end of the financial period.

(c) *Less cost of sales* is a heading which represents the section which calculates the value of the purchases that were sold.

(d) *Opening stock* is the value of stock that a business has at the beginning of its financial year. This figure is usually obtained through a stock check. In this case Joe's Decorating has only just started and therefore he has no opening stock.

(e) *Purchases* represent the total value of all the goods bought with a view to resale. This figure is calculated on the value of the invoices received regardless of whether or not the items have been paid for. This figure is posted from the purchase account at the end of the financial year.

(f) *Purchase returns* is the total value of the goods returned by the business. The figure is posted from the purchase returns account at the end of the financial period. Joe has not had to pay for any delivery charges of postage and packing. But if he had, carriage would be added here within the trading account.

(g) *Closing stock* represents the value of the stock that has not been sold at the end of the financial period. The figure is often obtained through a physical stock check. The closing stock of one year becomes the opening stock of the following year. In the example the closing stock figure of £120 will become Joe's opening stock figure for the next financial year.

(h) *Cost of goods* represents the true value of the purchases sold after the consideration of returns, carriage in and adjustments for opening and closing stock.

(i) *Gross profit* is the amount of profit made from the sale of goods.

(j) *Discounts received* represent the cash discounts that the business has taken advantage of. By taking advantage of cash discounts the business has managed to obtain purchases at a lower price and therefore increased gross profit.

(k) The *less expenses* section of the profit and loss account is where all the costs of running the business are recorded.

(l) *Discount allowed* represents the cash discounts that customers have taken advantage of. It is recorded as an expense because it means that customers have been able to secure the goods for a lower value. This has the impact of reducing net profit.

(m) *Net profit* represents the final profit of the business after all expenses have been taken into consideration.

	£	£	£
Fixed assets (a)			
Motor van			6,000
Computer			240
			6,240
Current assets (b)			
Stock (c)		120	
Debtors (d)		2,600	
Bank (e)		1,020	
Cash (f)		0,000	
		3,740	
Current liabilities (g)			
Creditors		(750)	
Working capital (h)			2,990
Net assets (i)			9,230
Long-term liabilities (j)			
Bank loan			(6,000)
			3,230
Financed by (k)			
Opening capital (l)			740
Add net profit (m)			19,490
			20,230
Less drawings (n)			(17,000)
Closing capital (o)			3,230

FIGURE 14.7 *Joe's Home Decorating balance sheet as at 31 January 2007*

Explanation of entries in balance sheet

The balance sheet is an 'as at' financial statement. This means that it is true only on the day it was completed. This is because the financial situation of a business moves on rapidly. For example, a debtor may settle their account on the next day and therefore the value of debtors falls while the value of the bank account increases.

(a) *Fixed assets* are those items that will be used within the business and have a life expectancy of more than one year.

(b) *Current assets* can be turned quickly into cash and are considered to be the 'life blood' of a business.

(c) The *stock* figure shown in the balance sheet is always the closing stock figure. This figure is normally located outside of the trial balance.

(d) The *debtors* figure represents the value of the debts currently outstanding for goods sold to customers on credit.

(e) *Bank* represents the money a business currently has in its bank account. If the bank has an overdraft this would be recorded under current liabilities.

(f) *Cash* represents the value of money the business actually holds on its premises.

(g) *Current liabilities* is the debts of the business which must be repaid within one year. These usually consist of creditors – suppliers that have sold goods or services to the business on credit.

(h) *Working capital* is calculated by taking current liabilities away from current assets. It represents the amount of money that a business has available to spend after meeting all its immediate debts. A negative figure here could indicate that the business may be facing liquidity problems.

(i) *Net assets* are the total value of the assets less current liabilities.

(j) *Long-term liabilities* consist of the business' debts which will be paid over a period of longer than one year. They will include bank loans which have been taken out over a number of years.

(k) The *financed by* section of the balance sheet represents the value of the money that has been committed to the running of the business.

(l) *Opening capital* is the value of the business at the start of the financial year. Because this is Joe's first year of trading it also represents the value of the money and goods that were invested in the business at its conception.

(m) *Net profit* is added to the opening capital.

(n) *Drawings* are taken away from the value of opening capital and net profit. Drawings represent the amount of money the owner of the business has taken for their personal use.

(o) *Closing capital* represents the value of money that has been left in the business after net profit has been added and drawing deducted. The closing capital of one year becomes the opening capital of the next year.

Theory into practice

Using the trial balance in Figure 14.8 Tiles for Everyone has asked you to complete their final accounts for the year ended 31 December 2007. You need to draw up a:

- trading, profit and loss account
- balance sheet.

Having now acquired the skills to produce basic trading profit and loss accounts and balance sheets you need to consider more complex situations and bookkeeping entries. These are fully explained below.

Bad debts

You have already learned within this chapter that most business trade on credit.

A business will buy and sell goods with the expectation of receiving and making payment at a later date. However, it is becoming increasingly common for a business to come to the end of its financial year and accept that a proportion of its debts are never going to be repaid. These debts become known as bad debts. Such debts must be written off so as not to overstate profits. The process for writing off a bad debt is illustrated in the following example concerning Couch & Co.

	£ **Debit**	£ **Credit**
Capital		68,274
Sales		129,000
Purchases	51,600	
Discounts allowed	2,200	
Sales returns	5,160	
Purchase returns		2,580
Discounts received		890
Opening stock	4,000	
Debtors	12,384	
Creditors		5,950
Premises	90,000	
Vehicles	16,500	
Motor expenses	2,500	
Wages	24,000	
General expenses	5,700	
Electricity	3,000	
Advertising	900	
Drawings	32,000	
Cash	400	
Bank	6,350	
Bank loan		50,000
Totals	256,694	256,694

FIGURE 14.8 *Tiles for Everyone trial balance as at 31 December 2007. Closing stock valued at £3,600*

Couch & Co. sold goods to the value of £300 on credit to F. Randall on 23 January 2007. By the end of the year Couch & Co. has decided it is unlikely to receive this money and will therefore write the debt off. The ledger entries are as follows:

Sales ledger

Dr		F. Randall account		Cr
2007		2007		
23 Jan Sales	300	31 Dec Bad debts account	300	

General ledger

Dr		Sales account		Cr
		2007		
		23 Jan F. Randall	300	

Dr		Bad debts account		Cr
2007		2007		
31 Dec F. Randall	300	31 Dec Profit and loss account	300	

	£	£
Gross profit		54,000
Less expenses		
Bad Debt		300

FIGURE 14.9 *Extract from Couch & Co.'s profit and loss account. For year ended 31 December 2007*

Let us consider a further example. On 23 June 2007 Couch & Co. sold £203 of goods to A. Jones. On the 23 December 2007 Couch & Co. heard that he had been declared bankrupt, and therefore the business wrote the debt off at the year end. Out of the blue on 4 March 2008 Couch and Co. received a cheque for £203 from A. Jones apologising for the length of time it had taken him to pay his debt. This is known as a bad debt recovered.

Look a the relevant bookkeeping entries below:

Sales ledger

Dr		A. Jones account		Cr
2007	£	2007		£
23 Jun Sales	203	31 Dec Bad debts account		300
2008		2008		203
4 Mar Bad debt recovered	203	4 Mar Bank		203

Sales ledger

Dr		Sales account		Cr
2007	£	2007		£
		23 Jun A. Jones		203

Dr		Bad debts account		Cr
2007	£	2007		£
31 Dec F. Randall	300	31 Dec Profit and loss account		503
31 Dec A. Jones	203			

Dr	Bad debts recovered account		Cr
2008	£	2008	£
31 Dec Profit and loss	203	4 Mar A. Jones	203

Below are extracts from the profit and loss accounts to show how these two situations impact on gross profit.

	£	£
Gross profit		54,000
Less expenses		
Bad debt	503	

FIGURE 14.10 *Extract from Couch & Co.'s profit and loss account for year ended 31 December 2007*

	£	£
Gross profit		64,000
Plus bad debt recovered		203

FIGURE 14.11 *Extract from Couch & Co.'s profit and loss account for year ended 31 December 2008*

Bad debts recovered are added to gross profit as the money has now been received and has therefore added to the overall profit of the business.

Provision for bad debts

As bad debts are becoming increasingly common businesses now open up an account which is known as the provision for bad debts account. This account allows the business to estimate the value of the debts they think will become 'bad' over the next twelve months. This follows the accounting concept of prudence which states that a business must not overstate its assets. Debtors are a current asset and therefore allowing a business to construct a provision for bad debts account means that this asset will not be overstated. The adjusted debtors value will reflect the amount that the company expects to receive within the financial year.

Points to remember when constructing a provision for bad debts account are:

* the first entry to the profit and loss account always appears on the credit side of the account and takes the full amount

* the profit and loss account only takes the full amount in the first year; in subsequent years the entry is the difference

* the whole provision is always deducted from the debtors figure in the balance sheet.

Couch & Co. has had the following debtors for the past three years:

* Year One – £32,000

* Year Two – £37,000

* Year Three – £38,000.

Couch & Co. are experiencing an increasing number of bad debts and have therefore decided to create a provision for bad debts of 3% of the total debtors.

The calculations would be as follows:

Year	Debtors	3% of debtors	Profit and loss	Balance sheet
One	32,000	960	960	960
Two	37,000	1,110	150*	1,110
Three	38,000	1,140	30	1,140

*As per point two above, only the difference is charged against gross profit after the provision has been established.

The ledger entries would be as follows:

Dr	Provision for bad debts account		Cr
Year One	£	*Year One*	£
Balance	960	Profit and loss account	960
Year Two		*Year Two*	
Balance	1,110	Balance	960
		Profit and loss account	150
	1,110		1,110
Year Three		*Year Three*	
Balance	1,140	Balance	1,140
		Profit and loss account	30
	1,140		1,140
		Year Four	
		Balance	1,140

	£	£
Year One		
Gross profit		34,000
Less expenses		
Provision fo bad debts	960	
Year Two		
Gross profit		36,000
Less expenses		
Provision for bad debts	150	
Year Three		
Gross profit		
Less expenses		
Provision for bad debts	30	

FIGURE 14.12 *Extracts from Couch & Co's profit and loss account for the three years*

	£	£	£
Year One			
Current assets			
Debtors	32,000		
Less provision for bad debts	960	31,040	
Year Two			
Current assets			
Debtors	37,000		
Less provision for bad debts	1,110	35,890	
Year Three			
Current assets			
Debtors	38,000		
Less provision for bad debts	1,140	36,860	

FIGURE 14.13 *Extracts from Couch & Co.'s balance sheet for three years*

Calculate the amount to be charged to the profit and loss account and balance sheet for Quick Snacks if their debtors were as follows. 2004 is the first year the business has felt the need to use a provision for bad debts account which is going to be based on 2.5% of the value of debtors at the year end.

Use the table below for your initial calculations.

Year	Debtors	2.5% of debtors	Profit and Loss	Balance Sheet
2004	21,000			
2005	25,000			
2006	26,000			

Now post the entries to the provision for bad debts account.

Finally, show the profit and loss and balance sheet accounts.

Depreciation

As we have already seen fixed assets are items that are purchased by the business for a specific purpose and not for resale.

Can you name four fixed assets?

Due to their high initial costs, fixed assets cannot be charged directly to the profit and loss account in the year they were purchased. If this were to happen the net profit figure would be dramatically reduced and not reflect a 'true and fair' picture of the financial position of the business.

It is recognised that fixed assets will deteriorate through wear and tear and reduce in value from year to year. You are probably aware that as soon as you purchase a new car it begins to reduce in value.

In accounts, fixed assets are depreciated. Every year an amount is deducted from a fixed asset's value as a representation of its loss in value. Depreciation is deducted from gross profit the same as other expenses in the profit and loss

I cost £5,999 but what am I worth now?

account. The adjusted value of the fixed asset is shown in the balance sheet and is referred to as net book value. The deduction for depreciation ensures that fixed assets are valued correctly with relevant wear and tear and age having been taken into consideration. By charging depreciation against net profit each year it has the effect of spreading the cost of the fixed asset over the number of years that the business uses the asset.

Within the balance sheet fixed assets are shown as having three values:

* *cost* – what the fixed asset actually cost to purchase

* *aggregate depreciation* – the total of all the depreciation charged against the fixed asset

* *net book value (NBV)* – cost less aggregate depreciation. The net book value of the fixed asset represents the value left for the businesses to use.

There are two methods by which fixed assets can be depreciated.

Method one – straight line or at cost

Using this method two things have to be considered:

* How long will the business use the asset?

* What will be the fixed asset's **residual value** when the business no longer needs it?

The straight line formula is:

$$\frac{\text{Cost of fixed asset} - \text{residual value}}{\text{No. of years to be used in business}} = \text{Amount to be depreciated each year}$$

For example, a business buys a new lorry for £120,000. Its estimated life in the business is ten years. After ten years it will be sold for £15,000:

$$\frac{120,000 - 15,000}{10 \text{ years}} = £10,500$$

Over the next ten years £10,500 will be charged against the profit of this business each year. After three years the depreciation would be £31,500.

We now need to consider how this is recorded in the books of account, the profit and loss account and balance sheet:

Dr	Lorry account	Cr
Year One	£	
Bank	120,000	

Dr	Provision for depreciation account		Cr
Year One	£	Year One	£
Balance	10,500	Profit and loss account	10,500
Year Two		Year Two	
Balance	21,000	Balance	10,500
		Profit and loss account	10,500
	21,000		21,000
Year Three		Year Three	
Balance	31,500	Balance	21,000
		Profit and loss account	10,500
	31,500		31,500
		Year Four	
		Balance	31,500

Explanation of entries

All fixed assets are recorded in named accounts at cost. Depreciation is never recorded within these accounts.

The provision for depreciation account is just a collection of all the depreciation charged against the fixed asset. Each type of fixed asset will have its own provision for depreciation account. The account clearly shows how much will be charged to the profit and loss account. The balance figure is the aggregate depreciation figure that will be used within the balance sheet.

	£	£
Year One		
Gross profit		64,000
Less expenses	10,500	
Year Two		
Gross profit		66,000
Less expenses	10,500	
Year Three		
Gross profit		62,000
Less expenses	10,500	

FIGURE 14.14 *Extracts from the profit and loss account for three years*

	Cost £	Aggregate depreciation £	Net book value £
Year One			
Fixed assets	120,000	10,500	109,500
Year Two			
Fixed assets	120,000	21,000	99,000
Year Three			
Fixed assets	120,000	31,500	88,500

FIGURE 14.15 *Extracts from the balance sheet for three years*

Method two – reducing balance (or written-down method)

Using this method the fixed asset is depreciated by a set percentage each year. The percentage is calculated on the reducing value of the fixed asset as illustrated below, i.e. the cost less depreciation to date.

The following example uses the purchase of a new lorry for £120,000 to be depreciated by 20% per annum using the reducing balance method.

Purchase price	£120,000
Year 1 Depreciation	£24,000 (20% of £120,000)
	£96,000 NBV after 1 year
Year 2 depreciation	£19,200 (20% of £96,000)
	£76,800 NBV after 2 years
Year 3 depreciation	£15,360 (20% of £76,800)
	£61,440 NBV after 3 years

FIGURE 14.16 *Total depreciation after 3 years is £58,560*

As you can see, a greater amount of depreciation has been charged using the reducing balance method than from the first method. But if the calculations were to continue, the depreciation charged to the profit and loss account would gradually become more using the straight line method as the percentage for reducing balance is calculated on the decreasing value of the asset.

The value shown for the fixed asset on the balance sheet is its net book value. If the fixed asset were to be sold at any time this is the price the business hopes they would receive. It reflects what is left of the asset's useful economic life.

We now need to consider how this is recorded in the book of accounts, the profit and loss account and the balance sheet.

Dr		Lorry account		Cr
Year One	£			
Bank	120,000			

Dr		Provision of depreciation account		Cr
Year One	£	Year One	£	
Balance	24,000	Profit and loss account	24,000	
Year Two		Year Two		
Balance	43,200	Balance	24,000	
		Profit and loss account	19,200	
	43,200		43,200	
Year Three		Year Three		
Balance	58,560	Balance	43,200	
		Profit and loss account	15,360	
	58,560		58,560	
		Year Four		
		Balance	58,560	

Below are extracts to illustrate how depreciation is dealt with in the profit and loss account and balance sheet.

	£	£
Year One		
Gross profit		64,000
Less expenses	24,000	
Year Two		
Gross profit		66,000
Less expenses	19,200	
Year Three		
Gross profit		62,000
Less expenses	15,360	

FIGURE 14.17 *Extracts from the profit and loss account for three years*

	Cost £	Aggregate depreciation £	Net book value £
Year One			
Fixed assets	120,000	24,000	96,000
Year Two			
Fixed assets	120,000	43,200	76,800
Year Three			
Fixed assets	120,000	58,560	61,440

FIGURE 14.18 *Extracts from the balance sheet for three years*

Adjustments for final accounts – accruals and prepayments

The figures used with the trading profit and loss account must represent all the expenditure and income relevant to the financial period being accounted for.

Accruals

There are two types of accruals:

* expenses owed by the firm

* revenue owed to the firm.

It is important that all expenses which have incurred during the financial year are transferred to the trading profit and loss account regardless of payment timing. It is also important that any income owed to the firm is included within the sales figures of the business.

Let us consider the following example of accrued expenses. Couch & Co.'s financial year runs from 1 January to 31 December. At the end of the financial year, the business had spent £890 on electricity but had an outstanding bill for £200 which was paid on the 3 January.

This would be entered into the accounts as follows:

Dr		Electricity account		Cr
31 Dec Balance (a)	890	31 Dec Profit and loss (c)		1,090
31 Dec Accrued (b)	200			
	1,090			1,090
3 Jan Bank (e)	200	1 Jan Accrued (d)		200

Explanation of entries

(a) This is the balance on the account and represents the total amount of money spent on electricity throughout the financial year.

(b) This is the amount that is owed. It is placed on the debit side of the account as it increases the amount that has been consumed in electricity for the financial year in question.

(c) This is the amount of electricity that has been consumed within the year and is therefore the total amount posted to the profit and loss account.

(d) The accrued amount is brought forward to the credit side of the account. This is the amount owed to the electricity company and is therefore a current liability.

(e) This shows the payment made on 3 January. It means that the business no longer owes any money for its electricity.

Let us now look at an example for revenue owed to the business. This will usually occur within rent receivable, or commission accounts. Couch & Co. rent part of their premises to a small haulage business – Here and There. The agreed rent is £400 per month. The balance on the rent received account at 31 December was £4,400.

If the rent is £400 per month then 12 months' rent is £4,800. This indicates that Here and There owe Couch & Co. £400 for outstanding rent. This would be entered in the accounts as follows:

Dr		Rent received account		Cr
31 Dec Profit and loss (c)	4,800	31 Dec Balance (a)		4,400
		31 Dec Accrued (b)		400
	4,800			4,800
1 Jan Accrued (d)	400			

Explanation of entries

(a) This is the total of all payments received from Here and There for rent.

(b) £400 accrued represents the amount Here and There owe Couch & Co.

(c) This is the total amount to be posted to the profit and loss account.

(d) The accrued amount is brought down to the debit side of the account to show that this amount is owed to the business.

Prepayments

These are payments made in advance by the firm for goods or services that it will consume in the future. One of the most common forms of prepayment is insurance. Businesses often pay for their car insurance on a yearly basis. This means that the business may not have consumed all of the insurance by the end of its financial year. It can also represent payments made to the business in advance for products or services it will receive in the future.

Let us first consider payments made in advance by the business. We will use the example of Couch & Co. again. Remember this business' financial year runs from 1 January to 31 December. The business runs a fleet of vehicles which it insures on a yearly basis. The insurance falls due on

1 April each year. The premium for the year 1 April to 31 March was £3,840.

You now need to consider how many months' insurance Couch & Co. have consumed. 1 April to 31 December is nine months:

$$\frac{£3,840}{12 \text{ months}} \times 9 \text{ months} = £2,880.$$

This is the amount that must be charged to the profit and loss account. Couch & Co. have made a prepayment of three months which equates to £960.

This is illustrated in the accounts as follows:

Dr		Insurance account		Cr
	£			£
31 Dec Balance	3,840	31 Dec Prepaid		960
		31 Dec Profit and loss		2,880
	3,840			3,840
1 Jan Prepaid	960 ↓			

Prepayments can come in the form of income. The most common occurrence of this would be rent paid in advance from a subtenant. Let us now consider the following example.

You should remember that Couch & Co. rent part of their premises to a small haulage business. The agreed rent in £400 per month. On 31 December the balance in the rent received is £5,200. This means that Here and There have actually paid in advance by £400.

This would appear in the accounts as follows:

Dr		Rent received account		Cr
	£			£
31 Dec Prepaid (b)	400	31 Dec Balance		5,200
31 Dec Profit and	4,800			
loss (c)				
	5,200			5,200
		↓ 1 Jan Prepaid		400

Explanation of the account

(a) This is the balance of the account. It is a credit balance as it represents an income. Remember your double entry. The money would have gone into the bank – debit entry. The account has been balanced and this is the total amount that has been received from Here and There.

(b) This shows the proportion of the £5,200 that has been paid in advance. It is placed on the

debit side of the account as it has the effect of reducing the amount to be transferred to the profit and loss account.

(c) This is the amount that will be added to the gross profit. Remember it is income.

(d) The prepayment is carried forward into the next year to show that Here and There have already paid their January rent.

The impact of prepayments and accruals on the profit and loss account

When dealing with accruals and prepayments it is the adjusted figure that is posted to the profit and loss account. If the adjustment has been applied to expenses this will have the impact of either increasing or decreasing the amount that has to be deducted from gross profit.

If the adjustment has been applied to an income, for example rent received, this will increase or decrease the amount that has to be added to gross profit.

The impact of prepayments and accruals on the balance sheet

The amount that an item has been prepaid or accrued has to be itemised within the balance sheet. Prepaid expenses would appear under the current assets. Accrued expenses and prepaid income would appear under current liabilities.

Let us now consider how this might appear in a task within the OCR model assignment.

	£ Debit	£ Credit
General expenses	7,450	
Insurance	6,000	
Rent receivable		3,900
Wages	4,800	
Commission received		1,200
Bank	2,800	
Debtors	7,000	
Creditors		3,600

FIGURE 14.19 *Extract from a trial balance for the Get it Done Company for the year ended 31 December 2007*

Notes to accounts

* Closing stock £2,800

* General expenses owing £300

* Insurance has been prepaid £100

* Rent receivable has been paid one month in advance

* Owed £400 in wages

* The business was owed £500 in commission

Tip – unless instructed to do so you may not need to make all the adjustments within the actual ledger accounts. However, you will need to calculate the correct amounts to be charged to the profit and loss account.

Workings

* General expenses £7,450 + accrued £300 = £7,750

* Insurance £6,000 – prepaid £100 = £5,900

* Rent receivable = £3,900 divided by 13 = £300 per month x 12 = £3,600

* Wages £4,800 + accrued £400 = £5,200

* Commission received £1,200 plus accrued £500 = £1,700

See Figures 14.20 and 14.21.

	£	£
Gross profit		67,000
Add rent receivable		3,600
Add commission		1,700
Less expenses		
General expenses	7,750	
Insurance	5,900	
Wages	5,200	

FIGURE 14.20 *Extract from profit and loss account for year ended 31 December 2007*

	£	£	£
Current assets			
Stock		2,800	
Debtors		7,000	
Bank		2,800	
Accrued commission		500	
Prepaid insurance		100	
Total		13,200	
Current liabilities			
Creditors	3,600		
Accrued general expenses	300		
Accrued wages	400		
Prepaid rent receivable	300	4,600	
Working capital			8,600

FIGURE 14.21 *Extract from balance sheet as at 31 December 2007*

Errors that do not show up in the trial balance

Earlier on in the unit you learned that a trial balance only proves the arithmetical accuracy of the double-entry accounting. There are six kinds of errors that can still be in the accounts although the trial balance still balances. These are all outlined below.

Original errors

These are errors that are made with the initial entry into the accounts. For example, on the 6 March 2007 Couch & Co. received a purchase invoice for goods purchased from Brown Ltd. The invoice was for £340. This has been recorded in the purchase ledger and Brown Account as £430. The trial balance will still balance as the same figures have been used in both the credit and debit entries. The error was noticed on 30 March 2007.

To correct this error, decrease both the purchase account by £90 and decrease the debtor's account by £90.

The bookkeeping entries would be as follows (the entries to correct the error are in italics):

Journal

		Dr £	Cr £
30 Mar	Brown account	90	
	Purchase account		90

Original purchase invoice recorded in books as £430 instead of £340.

Dr	Purchase account			Cr
		£		£
6 Mar	Brown account	430	*30 Mar Error*	*90*

Dr	Brown account			Cr
		£		£
30 Mar	*Error*	*90*	6 Mar Purchases	430

Errors of omission

This error occurs when the whole of the entry has never been made. For example, Couch & Co. had lost a copy of a sales invoice sent to R. Green for £600 on 10 March 2007. The error was found on 30 March 2007.

This is easily resolved as all you need to do is enter the invoice into the normal accounts.

The bookkeeping entries would be as follows:

Journal

		Dr £	Cr £
30 Mar	R. Green account	600	
	Sales account		600

Sales invoice never entered into the accounts.

Dr	Sales account		Cr
			£
		30 Mar R. Green account	*600*

Dr	R. Green account		Cr
		£	£
30 Mar	*Sales account*	*600*	

Errors of commission

This kind of error means that a posting has not been carried out correctly. The debit and credit entries have both been made on the correct side of the account, but the wrong account has been used. The most common mistake is to post the entry into the wrong personal account.

For example, on 15 March Couch & Co. sold £350 worth of goods to G. Grey. The entry was made correctly in the sales account. However, the debit entry was made in G. Gray's account in error. The error came to light on 30 March 2007.

The entry is corrected by cancelling the entry in the G. Gray account and placing it correctly in the G. Grey account. The bookkeeping entries would be as follows:

Journal

		Dr £	Cr £
30 Mar	G. Grey account	350	
	G. Gray account		350

Sale of goods to G. Grey recorded in error in the G. Gray account.

Dr	G. Grey account		Cr
		£	£
30 Mar	*G. Gray account 350 (error)*		

Dr	G. Gray account		Cr
		£	£
15 Mar	Sales account		350
30 Mar	*G. Grey account 350 (error)*		

Error of principle

This is caused by a mistake being made in the principles of bookkeeping. The entry is made into the wrong class of account. The purchase of a fixed asset might have been recorded into an expense account rather than the debit side of the fixed asset account.

For example, Couch & Co. purchased an office table for £235 on 21 March paying by cheque. The entry has been credited to the bank account but the debit entry was recorded in the office expenses account. The error was located on 30 March 2007.

The entry is corrected by crediting the office expenses account and debiting the office furniture account.

The bookkeeping entries would be as follows:

Journal

		Dr £	Cr £
30 Mar	Office furniture account	235	
	Office expenses account		235

The purchase of fixed assets recorded in the office expense account.

Dr	Office expenses account				Cr
		£			£
21 Mar	Bank	235	30 Mar	Office furniture account (error)	235

Dr	G. Gray account			Cr
		£		£
30 Mar	Office expenses account (error)	235		

Compensating errors

As the name suggest these errors cancel each other out and this is why the trial balance still balances. These errors occur when two separate errors of the same amount occur in the ledgers. There will be one error that affects the debit side of the account and a second error which affects another account by the same amount.

For example, during March Couch & Co. had entered a sales invoice correctly in the debtors account but had not posted the entry into the sales account. The sales account was therefore undercast by £100. A cheque received from Brown Ltd for £100 had been recorded in the debtors account but not in the cash book.

In order to correct this error the cash book needs to be debited and the sales account credited with the missing entries. The bookkeeping entries would be as follows:

Journal

		Dr £	Cr £
30 Mar	Cash book	100	
	Sales account		100

Receipt of £100 from Brown Ltd had not been recorded in the cash book. The sales account had also been undercast by £100.

Dr	Sales account			Cr
		£		£
			30 Mar Error	100

Dr	Cash book			Cr
		£		£
30 Mar	Brown Ltd	100		

Complete reversal of entries

These errors occur when the entries have been made on the wrong side of the accounts. The debit entry has been made as a credit entry and vice versa.

For example, a cheque for £120 received from Wanderlust Ltd, a supplier, on 27 March has been made on the credit side of the bank account and the debit side of the customer account. The error was discovered on 30 March 2007.

When dealing with reversal of entries you need to first eradicate the original entry and then record it correctly. This often means the value is doubled. The bookkeeping entries would be as follows:

Journal

		Dr £	Cr £
30 Mar	Bank account	240	
	Wanderlust Ltd		240

Cheque for £120 received from Wanderlust Ltd had been recorded on the credit side of the cash book and the debit side of Wanderlust account.

Dr	Bank account			Cr
		£		£
30 Mar Error		120	27 Mar Wanderlust Ltd	120
30 Mar Wanderlust Ltd		120		

The credit entry on 27 March states that Couch & Co. have paid Wanderlust £120 when in fact they received it. The first debit entry of 30 March eliminated the error. The second entry shows the bank account receiving the money from Wanderlust.

Dr	Bank account			Cr
		£		£
1 Mar	Balance	120	30 Mar Error	120
27 Mar	Bank	120	30 Mar Bank	120

The 1 March balance is the amount Wanderlust owed Couch & Co. on 1 March. They made payment on 27 March but the original entry was made on the debit side. This has had the effect of doubling their debt instead of clearing it. The first credit entry on 30 March clears the mistake and the second credit entry shows Wanderlust Ltd making the payment and clearing their initial debt.

Suspense accounts and the correction of errors

Sometimes when the trial balance is completed it does not balance. This is because there is an error or errors within the accounts. When this situation occurs the business will calculate the difference between the debit and credit balances and place the difference in a suspense account on the side which had the lowest value. The trial balance will now balance. The business will then investigate the accounts to try to locate the error.

Let us look at the following example, showing an extract from a trial balance:

	Dr	Cr
Totals	26,900	26,400

The difference is £500 and a suspense account is drawn up.

Dr	Suspense account		Cr
	£		£
		Balance	500

Upon further investigation the following errors were discovered:

* The sales account had been undercast by £400.

* A cheque for £200 sent to R. Frederick had been entered in the personal account but not the cash book.

* Sales returns from Smitherson for £100 had been entered in the Smitherson account but not the sales returns account.

The first stage is to consider how to correct each error and record it in the journal and then post the entries to the relevant accounts. Let us take each error in turn.

1. Sales undercast by £400. All previous errors implicated an error in two accounts. This error impacts just on the sales account. Therefore the other half of the double entry will be posted to the suspense account:

Journal

	Dr £	Cr £
Suspense account	400	
Sales account		400

Sales account undercast by £400.

2. Cheque sent to R. Frederick for £200 which had not been entered into the cash book but had been correctly entered in the R. Frederick account. Again just one error has been made. We need to credit the bank account and debit the suspense account:

Journal

	Dr £	Cr £
Suspense account	200	
Bank account		200

Cheque sent to R. Frederick not entered in the Bank account. However, correctly entered in the creditors' account.

3. Sales returns from Smitherson for £100 entered correctly in the personal account but not in the sales returns account. Again just one account involved. The sales returns account needs a debit entry and the suspense account needs a credit entry.

Journal

	Dr £	Cr £
Sales returns account	100	
Suspense account		100

Sales returns from Smitherson recorded correctly in debtors' account but omitted from the sales returns account.

Having entered all the corrections in the Journal they then need be posted to the accounts.

Dr	Suspense account			Cr
Sales account	400	Balance	500	
Bank account	200	Sales returns account	100	

The balance on the suspense account has now been cleared.

The errors which impact on the suspense account

If two accounts are identified within the description of the error the correction will not impact on the suspense account. If only one account is identified within the description of the error the other half of the correction will affect the suspense account.

The extended trial balance

You are already aware that the trial balance is a list of all the balances in the ledger accounts, made up prior to the preparation of the profit and loss account and balance sheet with a view to checking the accuracy of the double entry booking. So far, when year-end adjustments are required we have been working them out separately. However in order to keep track of such adjustments and to set out all the required figures neatly an extended trial balance could be used.

Format of the extended trial balance

The best way to see how the extended trial balance works is to work through the example below. The example supplied is similar to a task that you might encounter within the case study supplied by OCR.

Useful Signs Ltd extracted the balances shown in Figure 14.22 from its accounts on 31 December 2006.

Notes to accounts

1. Closing stock is valued at £1,480.
2. All fixed assets are to be depreciated at 25% using the reducing balance method.
3. The provision for doubtful debts has been carried forward from last year. It is felt that debtors of £30 should be written off and the provision increased to 5% of debtors.
4. Included in the Selling and Distribution expenses are £20 of payments which should have been classified as purchases.
5. In Establishment expenses rent and rates has been prepaid by £50.

6. Also in Establishment expenses are amounts paid for electricity – electricity was accrued by £28 on 31 December 2006.
7. The cash book did not reconcile with the bank statement because bank charges and interest had been omitted from the cash book – total value £38.

	Dr £	Cr £
Capital		14,201
Purchases and sales	17,430	26,795
Cash at bank		1,240
Cash	50	
Plan and machinery at cost	12,750	
Provision for depreciation		1,360
Motor vehicles	2,400	
Provision for depreciation		600
Fixtures & fittings at cost	840	
Provision for depreciation		510
Stock at 1 January 2006	1,090	
Debtors and creditors	1,750	1,184
Provision for bad debts		50
Selling and distribution expenses	330	
Establishment and administration expenses	740	
Financial expenses	60	
Loan		6,500
Drawings	15,000	
Totals	52,440	52,440

FIGURE 14.22 *Useful Signs Ltd trial balance as at 31 December 2006*

The first step is to draw up a trial balance from the list of balances above and insert them into the first two columns of the extended trial balance.

The next step is to make all the various adjustments. Remember that each adjustment has to be entered into the accounts twice, in accordance with the rules of double-entry accounting. The adjustments will fall into three categories:

West Flight Engineering has just drawn up its trial balance to discover the total of the debit side is £29,100 against £29,900 on the credit side. Upon further investigation the following errors were discovered. Remember some errors may affect the suspense account and some may not. Read each one carefully – are two accounts named within the error? If so the error will not affect the suspense account.

You are required to:

- draw up the suspense account
- enter each error into the journal
- post the relevant entries to the suspense account.

1. A sales invoice dated 10 October for £2,690 had been posted to the Downs & Co. account instead of the Downs Ltd account.

2. On the 16 October a cheque for £300 received from a debtor had been posted correctly to the debtors account but had not been posted to the cash book.

3. On the 19 October it was discovered that the purchase account was undercast by £200.

4. On the 24 October a sales invoice to Hamsworth Engineering for £600 had been completely omitted from the accounts.

---

* accruals and prepayments
* adjustments to stock figure
* other adjustments.

In order to make the explanation easier to follow, we will look at each type of adjustment individually. We will start with other adjustments.

Other adjustments

These adjustments are recorded in the 'Adjustments' column. In this example there are seven such adjustments:

1. Plant and machinery depreciation
2. Motor vehicles depreciation
3. Fixtures & fittings depreciation
4. Write off bad debt of £30
5. Increase the provision for bad debts to 5% of debtors
6. Included in selling and distribution expenses are £20 of payments which should have been classified as purchases
7. Bank statement and cash book not reconciled. Bank charges and interest not charged to the cash book.

Adjustments to stock figure

The adjustments required to the stock figure is not quite the same as those described above. You bring in the closing stock figure from the stock account, which is drawn up specifically for the preparation of financial statements.

The closing stock figure of £1,480 is entered into the extended trial balance as follows:

* Debit: Stock (balance sheet)

* Credit: Stock (profit and loss account).

These entries will then be posted to the debit of the balance sheet column and the credit column of the profit and loss.

Accruals and prepayments

In establishment expenses rent and rates have been prepaid by £50 and electricity is accrued by £28. Enter these amounts in the prepaid column under establishment and administration expenses.

Completing the profit and loss account and balance sheet

1. Add up the accruals figures and the prepayments to their respective expense balance and transfer the new total to the relevant column of the profit and loss columns. The accruals and prepayments then need to be transferred to the balance sheet columns.

2. Add up adjustments column, just to make sure that debits and credits are equal. If they don't balance go back – you have not completed all the adjustments correctly.

3. Add up the remaining figures across the extended trial balance. For example, fixtures and fittings is £840 and is a balance sheet figure. Provision for depreciation is £510 + £83 = £593 and is also a balance sheet figure.

4. The final stage is to use the figures in the last two columns of the extended balance to complete the profit and loss account and balance sheet.

All these figures have been typed in italics to aid identification in Figure 14.23.

Ledger Account	Trial balance Dr	Trial balance Cr	Adjustments Dr	Adjustments Cr	Accruals	Pre-payments	Profit and loss Dr	Profit and loss Cr	Balance sheet Dr	Balance sheet Cr
Balances b/fwd										
Capital		14,201								14,201
Cash at bank		1,240		38						1,278
Cash	50								50	
Plant & machinery at cost	12,750								12,750	
Provision for depreciation		1,360		2,848						4,208
Motor vehicles	2,400								2,400	
Provision for depreciation		600		450						1,050
Fixtures & fittings at cost	840								840	
Provision for depreciation		510		83						593
Stock at 1.1.2006	1,090						1,090			
Debtors	1,750			30					1,720	
Provision for bad debts		50		86			36			86
Creditors		1,184								1,184
Purchases	17,430		20				17,450			
Sales		26,795						26,795		
Selling & distribution	330			20			310			
Establishment & administration	740				28	50	718			
Financial expenses	60		38				98			
Loan		6,500								6,500
Drawings	15,000								15,000	
Depreciation – plant and machinery			2,848					2,848		
Depreciation – motor vehicles			450				450			
Depreciation – fixtures & fittings			83				83			
Bad debts			30				30			
			86						86	
Stock (balance sheet)									1,480	
Stock (profit and loss)								1,480		

FIGURE 14.23 *Useful Signs Ltd extended trial balance for the year ended 31 December 2006*

From the extended trial balance, the final accounts can then be drafted.

	£	£	£
Sales			26,795
Less cost of sales			
Opening stock		1,090	
Purchases		17,450	
		18,540	
Less closing stock		1,480	
Cost of sales			17,060
Gross profit			9,735
Less expenses			
Selling and distribution		310	
Establishment and administration		718	
Finance		98	
Depreciation – plant and machinery		2,848	
Depreciation – vehicles		450	
Depreciation – fixtures and fittings		83	
Bad debts		30	
Provision for depreciation		36	4,573
Net profit			5,162

FIGURE 14.24 *Profit and loss account for the year ended 31 December 2006*

	At cost	Total depreciation	Net book value
Fixed assets	£	£	£
Plant and machinery	12,750	4,208	8,542
Motor vehicles	2,400	1,050	1,350
Fixtures and fittings	840	593	247
			10,139
Current assets			
Stock		1,480	
Debtors	1,720		

continued ▶

	At Cost	Total depreciation	Net Book Value
	£	£	£
Less provision for bad debts	<u>86</u>	1,634	
Cash		50	
Prepayments		<u>50</u>	
		3,214	
Less current liabilities			
Creditors	1,1,84		
Bank overdraft	1,278		
Accrued	28	2,490	
Working capital			<u>724</u>
Net assets			10,863
Long-term liabilities			
Loan			<u>6,500</u>
			4,363
Financed by:			
Capital			14,201
Add net profit			<u>5,162</u>
			19,363
Less drawings			15,000
			4,363

FIGURE 14.25 *Balance sheet as at 31 December 2006*

Did you know that Virgin is a private limited company?

Limited company accounts

When you receive the OCR case study you may be required to complete the accounts of a limited company. So far within this unit we have only looked at how to complete the accounts of sole traders. We now need to consider the differences and similarities between the two different layouts.

Before we do this we need to consider the actually differences between limited companies and sole traders. Can you remember the work you completed for your Unit 3 examination?

See if you can answer the following questions. If you cannot, look back at your past notes or undertake some research.

- What does limited liability mean?
- What are shareholders?
- What does divorce of ownership from control mean?

There are three main differences between sole trader and limited company profit and loss accounts:

* Cost of sales is calculated outside of the main accounts and found within the notes section of the accounts.

* The expenses are grouped together under collective headings. For example, financial charges could include accountancy fees, bank charges or interest payments. As a rule use the headings that are supplied within the case study.

* A limited company will have multiple owners and therefore the profits have to be shared out. These payouts are known as dividends.

In order to complete and understand limited company accounts you need to become familiar with the terms in Figure 14.26.

TERM	DEFINITION
Authorised share capital	When a limited company is formed it has to complete two documents, the Memorandum of Association and Articles of Association. These are submitted to Companies House and outline the activities of the business. These documents also outline the total number of shares that the business will be able to issue.
Issued share capital	This is the number of shares that the business has currently issued. Often the issued share capital is less than the authorised share capital.
Ordinary shares	These are the most popular form of shares. They entitle the owner to have one vote per share at the annual general meeting. The shareholders will be entitled to a share of the profits. However, if the business does not make any profits the shareholders do not have to receive a dividend.
Preference shares	These shares carry a fixed interest rate but no voting rights. These shareholders are paid before the ordinary shareholders. They are considered to be a lower risk of investment.
Dividends	These are the payments made to the shareholders as a reward for investing in the business. Some businesses choose to pay out dividends part-way through the year and these are known as interim dividends. Final dividends are those paid out at the end of the financial year.
Board of directors	A limited company is not always run by its owners. The shareholders vote at the annual general meeting to decide who they want on the board of directors to run the business on their behalf. This is known as divorce of ownership from control. A private limited company may actually be run by its owners. As a reward for working within the business they will receive a salary, the same as other employees, and this will be deducted from net profit. This is a significant difference to sole traders – their drawings are deducted from net profit in the balance sheet. The reason being all the profit earned belongs to the sole trader.
Par/face value of a share	All shares will have face/par value. This is the amount that they are considered to be worth. However, they may be floated onto the market at a higher price.

continued ▶

TERM	DEFINITION
Revenue reserves	A limited company may decide not to share all its profits with its shareholders but move some into reserves. These can then be used for expansion in future or even paid to shareholders at a later date as dividends. The type of revenue reserves that you are likely to meet are the general reserve and the fixed asset replacement reserve.
Profit and loss account	When the profit of a limited company is shared out some may be left over. This is known as retained profit and goes in the profit and loss account. When compiling the appropriate account of a limited company always check the trial balance to see if there is already a profit and loss account that needs to be included.

FIGURE 14.26 *Terms associated with limited company accounts*

The profit and loss account

The main differences between the two profit and loss accounts have been outlined above – some figures are given as totals in the profit and loss accounts for limited companies.

The appropriation account

So far within this unit you have calculated net profit and then stopped. However, you now need to take this a little further. Having calculated net profit the next stage is to create the appropriation account.

	£	£
Operating profit (a)		43,200
Less corporation tax (b)		8,640
Net profit after taxation (c)		34,560
Less Transfer to General reserve (d)		10,000
		24,560
Less proposed dividends (e)		
8% Preference shares (f)	6,000	
Ordinary shares (g)	10,000	16,000
Retained profit (h)		8,560
Profit and loss account b/d (i)		2,000
Retained profit c/fwd (j)		10,560

FIGURE 14.27 *Healthside Ltd appropriation account for year ended 31 March 2006*

Explanation of entries

(a) This is the net profit after interest but before taxation.

(b) This is amount of corporation tax that is expected to be due on the profits earned. This amount has yet to be paid and will therefore also appear in the balance sheet under liabilities due in under one year.

(c) This is the net profit after corporation tax has been deducted. This is the amount of profit that is available for dividends.

(d) £10,000 of the profit has been transferred to the general reserve. This could be used for further expansion or to pay dividends in later years.

(e) This is a heading. 'Proposed' means that these dividends have yet to be paid and must therefore appear under liabilities due less than one year in the balance sheet.

(f) This is the dividend that will be paid to the preference shareholders.

(g) This is the proposed dividend to be paid to the ordinary shareholders.

(h) Retained profit is the amount of profit that has not been distributed in previous years.

(i) The profit and loss account contains the retained profit from previous years.

(j) Retained profit c/fwd is the total amount of profit that has not been distributed.

The limited company balance sheet

There are a few differences in the top half of the balance sheet that you need to be aware of and these are outlined below.

✳ Fixed assets and current assets remain the same.

✳ Current liabilities are known as liabilities due in less than one year and will now include the extra items of corporation tax, and proposed dividends.

✳ Long-term liabilities are known as liabilities due in more than one year

The financed by section of the balance sheet is where the major changes occur.

It is now known as shares and reserves and follows the layout in Figure 14.28.

Shares and reserves	£	
Operating profit (a)	43,200	
Authorised share capital (a)		
50,000 7% Preference shares @ £1 each	50,000	
100,000 Ordinary shares @ £1 each	100,000	
	150,000	
Issued share capital (b)		
20,000 7% Preference shares @ £1 each	20,000	
50,000 Ordinary shares @ £1 each	50,000	
	70,000	
General Reserve (c)	12,000	
Retained profit	8,000	20,000
	90,000	

FIGURE 14.28 *Example of how a limited company balance sheet records shares and reserves*

Don't panic – always remember to double check your sums!

Explanation of entries

(a) This is the total number and value of shares that the business could issue. This figure is not used in the calculation but just as an indication to show the percentage of shares that have actually been issued.

(b) This section represents the number of shares the business has issued.

(c) These two entries represent the revenue reserves the business currently has.

Fully-worked example of limited company accounts

In section 14.2.5 you will use two sets of limited company accounts, for Breakthrough Ltd and Headway Ltd. These will give you a good idea of how to lay out company accounts suitable for publication. Investigating the different layouts for limited company accounts should also form part of your research.

14.2.4 Strategic research

The main focus of your research for this unit will be the OCR case study. Focus your primary and secondary research on the following themes.

1. Similar types of business as the one stated in the case study.

   * Can you find out the industry average for gross profit and net profit ratios? What type of assets and liabilities does the business own? What percentage gearing do these types of business have?

   * What have been the recent trends for these businesses? Are they expanding or diversifying their portfolio of products?

2. What is the trend within the market the business working in?

   * Is it in growth?

   * Is it in decline?

3. Has this type of business been in the news recently?

The other information that you might need to research is:

* legal requirements when preparing limited company accounts

* different layouts that are acceptable

* different types of published accounts.

14.2.5 Analysis to inform strategy

In order to formulate a strategy you will be required to undertake some analysis of the figures that are contained within the OCR case study. This section focuses on the interpretation of accounting ratios.

Without the use of ratios it is very difficult to compare one business with another or even compare two different years of the same business. You may be able to see that sales have increased, but by applying some ratios it will be easy to see if gross and net profit have moved by the same percentages.

Ratio analysis only works effectively if you compare 'like with like'. If you tried to compare Asda with Ford your results would be very different and not comparable, as they operate within different sectors.

Limitations to ratio analysis

Although an extremely useful tool when analysing the financial health of a business it must be remembered the results do have limitations, and therefore must not be considered in isolation from other factors. Some of the possible limitations are outlined below:

* they only illustrate what has happened in the past – based on historic accounts

* impossible to compare two businesses that are very different

* they do not disclose the future plans of the business

* how skilled the workforce is

* how well located the business is

* whether the business has an excellent customer base

* how old/obsolete are the fixed assets – will they need to be replaced in the near future

* the businesses relationship with their suppliers.

The ratios that we will be looking at fall into three categories:

* profitability

* liquidity

* efficiency.

You will practise calculating these ratios comparing two different businesses: Breakthrough Ltd and Headway Ltd.

	Breakthrough Ltd £	Headway Ltd £
Sales	240,000	360,000
Less cost of sales	144,000	252,000
Gross profit	**96,000**	**108,000**
Less expenses		
Financial	31,608	31,488
Administration	7,142	12,512
General	6,000	10,000
Total expenss	44,750	54,000
Net profit	51,250	54,000
Less interest (2)	3,250	0
Net profit after interest	**48,000**	**54,000**
Less corporation tax	10,560	11,800
Net profit after tax	37,440	42,200
Net profit and loss accounts b/fwd	21,000	34,000
Less proposed dividends	20,000	42,000
Net profit and loss accounts c/fwd	38,440	34,200
Balance sheet as at 31 December 2006		
Fixed assets (3)	**281,432**	**425,952**
Current assets		
Stock	52,000	60,000
Debtors	72,000	72,000
Bank	34,000	12,000
	158,000	144,000
Creditors - amounts falling due within one year (4)	80,160	130,600
Total assets less current liabilities	**359,272**	**439,352**
Creditors falling due more than one year	50,000	
Total assets less total liabilities	**309,272**	
Capital and reserves		
Authorised share capital		
500,000 Ordinary shares at £1 each	500,000	600,000
Issued share capital		
250,000 Ordinary shares at £1 each	250,000	400,000
Profit and loss account	38,440	34,200
General reserve	20,832	5,152
Shareholders funds	**309,272**	**439,352**

FIGURE 14.29 *Profit and loss accounts for Breakthrough Ltd and Headway Ltd for year ended 31 December 2006*

Notes to the accounts

(1)

	Breakthrough Ltd £	Headway Ltd £
Opening stock	72,000	40,000
Purchases	124,000	128,000
Less closing stock	52,000	60,000
Cost of goods sold	144,000	252,000

(2) Breakthrough Ltd: loan taken out this year
   – £50,000 over 10 years, interest rate 6.5%

(3) Fixed assets schedules:

	Cost	Depreciation to date	Net book value
	£	£	£
Breakthrough Ltd			
Factory			175,000
Equipment	125,000	37,000	88,000
Vehicles	36,000	17,568	18,432
			281,432
Headway Ltd			
Factory			300,000
Equipment	220,000	129,888	90,112
Vehicles	52,000	16,160	35,840
			425,952

(4) Creditors – amounts falling due within one
year:

	Breakthrough Ltd £	Headway Ltd £
Creditors	49,600	76,800
Corporation tax	10,560	11,800
Proposed dividends	20,000	42,000
144,000	80,160	130,600

Profitability ratios

Profitability ratios help assess whether a business has met its objectives. It enables managers and owners to compare the profitability of the business over a period of time.

Return on Capital Employed

Commonly referred to as ROCE, this ratio is often considered to be the most important of the profitability ratios. It looks at the relationship between the capital and the net profit earned. Investors in a business will expect this ratio to be higher than a percentage rate they could earn from placing their money in a savings accounts.

$$\frac{\text{Net profit after interest}}{\text{Shareholder funds (capital)}} \times 100 = X\% \text{ ROCE}$$

Theory into practice

Making reference to the accounts of Breakthrough Ltd and Headway Ltd, answer the following questions.

- What is the ROCE for Breakthrough Ltd?
- What is the ROCE for Headway Ltd?
- Compare the two results. Which business is performing well? Justify your answer.

Gross profit margin

This ratio illustrates the relationship between the amount earned through sales and the cost of sales. It represents the amount of gross profit earned for every £100 worth of sales. A high gross profit margin indicates that the business control over the cost of its purchases, and if it increases so that cost of purchases has been reduced. This could be due to a change in supplier, or being able to secure discounts for bulk orders.

$$\frac{\text{Gross profit}}{\text{Sales}} \times 100 = X\% \text{ Gross profit margin}$$

Theory into practice

Making reference to the accounts of Breakthrough Ltd and Headway Ltd, answer the following questions.

- What is the gross profit margin for Breakthrough Ltd?
- What is the gross profit margin for Headway Ltd?
- Compare the two results. Which business has the most control over their purchases? Justify your answer.

Net profit margin

This ratio illustrates the relationship between the amount earned through sales and the total expenses of the business. It represents the amount of net profit earned for every £100 worth of sales. A high net profit margin indicates that the business control over the cost of its expenses, and if it increases so that cost of expenses has been reduced.

$$\frac{\text{Net profit}}{\text{Sales}} \times 100 = X\% \text{ Net profit margin}$$

Theory into practice

Making reference to the accounts of Breakthrough Ltd and Headway Ltd, answer the following questions.

- What is the net profit margin for Breakthrough Ltd?
- What is the net profit margin for Headway Ltd?
- Compare the two results. Which business has the most control over their expenses? Justify your answer.

Liquidity ratios

Liquidity ratios look at a business' ability to pay its immediate debts. Does the business have sufficient funds to pay its creditors, expenses, loans at the due time?

Current ratio

This ratio compares the current assets against the current liabilities and indicates whether the business has sufficient short-term funds to meet its short-term liabilities. If a business has a low current ratio it may mean that the business could experience liquidity problems in the future as it has a higher level of short-term debt than funds.

$$\frac{\text{Current assets}}{\text{Current liabilities}} = x :1$$

It has been the practice in the past to state that the 'best' current ratio for a business should be 2:1. However, it is now widely accepted that there is no 'best' current ratio. When analysing the current ratio of a business you need to establish the 'normal' current ratio for that type of industry. If the business under investigation has a lower current ratio this may in fact indicate the possibility of liquidity problems in the future.

Theory into practice

Making reference to the accounts of Breakthrough Ltd and Headway Ltd, answer the following questions.

- What is the current ratio for Breakthrough Ltd?
- What is the current ratio for Headway Ltd?
- Will either business suffer from liquidity problems in the future?

Acid test ratio

This ratio deducts stock from the current assets, as it is the least liquid. The ratio's purpose is to see if a business has sufficient liquid funds to pay its immediate debts. Once again this may indicate that a business may find it difficult to pay its current liabilities on time.

$$\frac{\text{Current assets} - \text{stock}}{\text{Current liabilities}} x :1$$

It must be remembered no matter how profitable a business is, unless it has adequate liquid funds it may fail.

Theory into practice

Making reference to the accounts of Breakthrough Ltd and Headway Ltd, answer the following questions.

- What does the acid test ratio for Breakthrough Ltd show?
- What does the acid test ratio for Headway Ltd show?
- Compare the two results. Which business is the least likely to suffer liquidity problems? Justify your answer.

Efficiency ratios

These ratios are used to assess how efficiently a business has used its resources. Has it made the best possible use of them or could things be improved in the future in order to improve the overall profitability of the business?

Stock turn

This ratio looks at how often a business turns its stock around. It enables managers to analyse how effective their stock control system is. A reduction in stock turn could represent a slowing down of trade. Stocks are not being sold and therefore piling up in the warehouse.

$$\frac{\text{Cost of sales}}{\text{Average stock}} = x \text{ times}$$

Average stock is calculated by adding opening stock and closing stock together and dividing by two.

Theory into practice

Making reference to the accounts of Breakthrough Ltd and Headway Ltd, answer the following questions.

- Calculate the stock turn ratio for Breakthrough Ltd.
- Calculate the stock turn ratio for Headway Ltd.
- Compare the two results. Which business has most control over their stock? Justify your answer.

Debtor collection period

This ratio looks at the relationship between credit sales and level of debtors. It calculates how many days on average it takes the business to collect its debts. The shorter the duration, the better – a very short duration may indicate an effective system of credit control and a good system for chasing late payments.

$$\frac{\text{Debtors}}{\text{Credit sales}} \times 365 \text{ days} = \text{total number of days} \atop \text{it takes debtors to pay}$$

Often within accounts it is impossible to distinguish between credit and cash sales. If this is the case you will need to use the total sales figure.

Theory into practice

Making reference to the accounts of Breakthrough Ltd and Headway Ltd, answer the following questions.

- Calculate the debtor collection period for Breakthrough Ltd.
- Calculate the debtor collection period for Headway Ltd.
- Compare the two results. Which business has most control over their debtors? Justify your answer.
- How can a business reduce its debtors collection period?

Creditor collection period

Creditors are people that the business owes money to in the immediate future. This ratio shows the relationship between credit purchases and the value of creditors at a set moment in time.

$$\frac{\text{Creditors}}{\text{Credit purchases}} \times 365 \text{ days} = \text{total number} \atop \text{of days it takes debtors to pay}$$

Often within accounts it is impossible to distinguish between credit and cash purchases. If this is the case you will need to use the total purchase figure. If the figure increases it means a business it taking longer to pay creditors. The

business may receive a bad credit rating, with suppliers refusing to supply it with goods and services on credit. The business is also not able to make benefit of discounts offered for prompt payment.

Theory into practice

Making reference to the accounts of Breakthrough Ltd and Headway Ltd answer the following questions.

- Calculate the creditor collection period for Breakthrough Ltd.
- Calculate the creditor collection period for Headway Ltd.
- Compare the two results. Which business has most control over their creditors? Justify your answer.
- What could be the consequences of a business having a very long creditor collection period?

Calculating a range of ratios

In order to achieve this part of the assignment you will be required to calculate a range of ratios and interpret their meaning. You then will need to put together a conclusion based on your analysis, linking your ideas to the strategy indicated within the case study.

Theory into practice

Put together all the results so far for Breakthrough Ltd and Headway Ltd.

Compile an analysis and evaluation of their current financial health. If you were offered the chance to invest in one of these businesses which one would you choose? Justify your answer.

14.2.6 Evaluation and recommendations

Having completed all the tasks outlined in the case study your final task will require you to focus on a final conclusion based on the business' financial health and then make recommendations of how the business should develop in the future.

The given scenario will provide you with a number of options available to the business in terms of financial planning for the future and you need to evaluate critically which option or combination of options would be most suitable for the business to follow.

In order to complete the final task of the assignment you are advised to consider the following sections. All of the sections below relate to the business' working capital. As you are already aware this is the relationship the business has between its current liabilities and current assets. You should now be familiar with how to calculate the current and acid test ratios. You have also started to consider the implications of a business having insufficient current assets to meet its immediate debts. We now need to consolidate some of this under the following headings to enable you to produce a sound evaluation and recommendations.

Costs of the business holding too much cash, including loss of interest and opportunity costs

It is possible for a business to have too much cash. Cash sitting in a business' bank account may earn token interest, but will it not match the amount that could be earned if it were invested in a longer-term account. Money invested in a long-term account is still easily accessible by the business should it suddenly experience liquidity problems. However, the business may lose some interest as a penalty if it has to withdraw the money without notice.

If a business is holding too much cash it also has to consider the opportunity cost of this situation. Opportunity cost is based on the fact that you can only spend money once and therefore reflects what else could be done with the money. For example, rather than having too much cash would the business be better to update its fixed assets in order to improve the efficiency of the business? How else could the money be invested to improve the profitability of the business? The danger of investing the surplus cash is that once it has been turned into stock or fixed assets these

would have to be sold, probably at a loss if the money were suddenly required to support the working capital of the business.

Costs of the business holding too little cash, such as inability to meet creditors' demands and need to borrow at expensive rates

If a business is unable to meet its immediate debts it might need to arrange a bank overdraft. This is an agreement between the bank and a business which allows it to spend the bank's money up to an agreed limit. Bank overdrafts can be a flexible method of borrowing cash on a short-term basis. The down side is that they can often be expensive.

If a business continues to make late payments to creditors it may end up with no suppliers. A business might also get a reputation of being a late payer, making it difficult to negotiate credit terms with other businesses. As you have seen earlier in the unit if a business makes payments early it is often able to benefit from cash discounts which in turn improves overall profitability.

Methods of improving cash flow

It is essential that a business monitors its cash flow regularly so that it is aware of times that it may need to arrange a bank overdraft. It will also be able to identify how its money is being spent. This information will help a business budget effectively and avoid overspending.

Another way a business can improve its cash flow is to put into place a system whereby debtors are continuously monitored and chased if they fail to pay within the specified timescale. In a large business this could be a specific job, but in a smaller organisation it is one well worth allocating to an individual as part of their job description. The longer a debtor takes to pay the greater the chance the debt will never be paid. Debtors that fail to pay can be written off against expenses as a bad debt.

As we have already discussed another way to encourage early payment by debtors is to offer them a cash discount if they pay prior to the specified timescale.

Cash versus profit

Some people find it difficult to understand that a business can be highly profitable but ceases to trade due to liquidity problems. However, there are a number of differences between the cash flowing in and out of a business and the how net profit is calculated. These differences are considered below.

Cash is the asset that allows a business to operate. Without cash, the business will cease to trade for the following reasons.

* Without cash the business will be unable to pay its employees.

* Suppliers will cease to provide materials, products or services.

* Banks will call in loans.

* Shareholders will withdraw their investment if the business is unable to pay dividends due to lack of available cash.

* Landlords will evict a business from its premises if it is unable to pay its rent.

* Gas, electricity and water supplies will be cut off if the business fails to pay its bills.

Profit is the amount of money that a business makes after it has taken away all its expenditure. Profit is different from cash as it will be calculated by taking into consideration 'non monetary' items which are not taken out of the cash flow. Profit is also calculated on the total sales and purchase regardless of payment.

Think it over...

Consider the above statement. Can you think of all the non-monetary items that you have dealt with so far in this unit? You should have thought of depreciation and provision for bad debts as two non-monetary items.

These items reduce the profit of a business but do not have any impact on the actual money flowing into and out of the business.

For example, Couch & Co. buy a car for £6,000 paying by cheque. The business has decided that it will write off £1,200 in depreciation in the first year. This is then charged against the profit and loss for that year. You instantly have the first difference between the cash flow and profit. The cash flow lost a total of £6,000 but the profit was only reduced by £1,200.

Now consider provision for bad debts. This concept allows the business to charge a percentage of the debtors against its net profit. This is another difference between profit and cash flow. The percentage being charged has been taken off net profit but no cash has been taken out of the cash flow.

Think it over...

Can you think of another reason why cash flow and profit of a business could be very different? You should consider the relationship of debtors and creditors.

As explained earlier in the unit when a business calculates its turnover it must add up all the invoices raised for that financial year regardless of whether they have been paid or not. If the invoice has not been paid the amount will have appeared in the profit and loss account as turnover but the actual cash would not yet have been received and therefore the cash figure will be lower.

The same applies for purchases made by the business. The business may have included purchases in the trading account which will have the effect of lowering the gross profit but these have not been paid for.

The business changing its aim, due to such things as expansion, diversification, downsizing, and its impact on financial planning

Within the case study you will be supplied with a scenario which may identify what the business is planning to do in the future. This could be possible expansion, diversification or even downsizing. You will need to consider the financial statements you have prepared and ratio analysis undertaken to consider whether this is a feasible possibility.

If expansion is a possibility consider the following factors.

* How much is turnover likely to increase?

* How much are the expenses going to increase?

* What are the predicted ratios likely to be? Are they an improvement on the current ratios?

* What is the likely cost of this expansion? How quickly will this cost be recovered?

* What would happen if the expansion does not take place?

* What are the competitors doing?

* How sound is the research that these figures and ideas have been based on?

If diversification is a possibility all of the above points should be considered as well as:

* What impact would diversification have on the other products/services the business currently offers?

* Why is diversification such a good idea?

* Does the business have the capacity, knowledge skills and understanding to diversify?

If downsizing is a possibility consider all the above factors but in terms of decrease and also:

* What is the reason to downsize?

* What will be the impact on current customers if this were to take place?

* Would all the customers move to an alternative business?

* Would it be better to sell the business as a going concern?

Knowledge check

1. Describe **two** reasons why businesses keep financial records.

2. Define the term 'opening capital'. Use examples to illustrate you answer.

3. Explain the term 'statement of account'.

4. Enter the following transactions into the books of account for Sally's Cleaning business:

    * 20 March – started business with £2,000 in a business bank account

    * 21 March –purchased a vacuum cleaner for £130, paying by cheque

    * 21 March – purchased general cleaning materials for £67, paying by cheque

    * 23 March – received a cheque for £75 from Mrs Harrison, and £125 from Mrs Bloom.

5. Identify **four** reasons why a business would draw up a trial balance.

6. Suggest **two** methods a business could adopt to improve the time it takes their customers to pay for goods received.

7. Design a pro forma for a trading profit and loss account for a sole trader business.

8. Design a pro forma for a balance sheet for a sole trader business.

9. Explain what constitutes a bad debt. Why do businesses create a provision for doubtful debts?

10. Explain what is meant by the term 'depreciation'.

11. Describe **two** different types of error that could still be within a trial balance although it balances.

12. Outline the main limitations of ratio analysis.

13. Identify the formulae used to calculate the following ratios:

    a. net profit margin

    b. gross profit margin

    c. acid test

    d. stock turn

    e. debtor collection period.

Resources

Cox, D., Fardon, M. and Robinson, S. (2004) *Business Accounts*, 3rd edition, Osborne Books

Dyson, J.R. (2003) *Accounting for Non-Accounting Students*, 6th edition, FT Prentice Hall

Harrison, I. (2004) *Introducing Accounting for AS*, Hodder Arnold

Nicholson, M. (1989) *Accounting Skills*, Palgrave Macmillan

Wood, F. and Sangster, A. (2005) *Business Accounting 1*, 10th edition, FT Prentice Hall

Launching a new product or service in Europe

This unit contains six elements:

15.2.1 Devising a strategy

15.2.2 The business context within which the strategy will take shape

15.2.3 Planning the strategy

15.2.4 Research of the strategy and analysis of the information that is collected

15.2.5 Production of a plan of action

15.2.6 Evaluation of the strategy

This unit requires you investigate, understand and consider various issues that must be taken into account as a business consultant giving support and guidance to a medium-to-large-sized UK business who is planning to expand and operate in another European Union (EU) member state. To do this you will need to demonstrate understanding of the characteristics of the European market and its potential impact on UK businesses. It is important that you choose an appropriate business that you have links with as you will need to access information on many aspects of the business. **Suggesting that a business sets up an online operation from a UK base to operate in Europe is not a suitable approach to gain enough evidence for this unit.**

You will need to make sure that the product or service you choose is to be launched for the first time in Europe even if it has been marketed in the UK already. You may wish to do this by considering the changes that would need to be made to the product or service if it were to be launched in Europe, such as language, culture or different promotional methods. You will need to make sure you include a written summary showing how your business will deal with the many issues you need to consider as part of the launch. This unit will give you an overview of how the EU business environment affects different aspects of business activity and decision-making from a wider, more strategic perspective.

15.2.1 Devising a strategy

Before you are able to take practical steps to implement your activities, it is important to consider the planning of your strategy from a longer-term perspective. This is known as strategic planning and you have already learned about this in Unit 13 on pages 156–60. The key elements of strategic planning are:

* where we are now
* where we want to be (vision)
* how we are going to get there (aims and objectives)
* review of performance to see if the business is on track.

As part of your strategic planning for this unit you will need to go through a number of steps that involve:

* understanding the business environment within which the strategy will take shape
* planning the strategy
* researching the business environment to inform strategy development
* analysing the gathered data to inform the development of the strategy
* producing a plan of action based on research and analysis
* monitoring and evaluating various aspects of the strategy with a view to recommending improvements and future updates to the strategy.

By concentrating on understanding the business environment within which the strategy will take place, you will be conducting the first stage of the strategic planning cycle – where are we now. There are two approaches that you may wish to consider when launching the product into another EU member state and these are:

* launching an existing product from the UK into a new EU member state market so that it is a new product or service in that market (market development)
* launching a new product into a new EU member state market (diversification).

By using an Ansoff matrix, you can help your business plan for growth by matching strategies for existing and new products to existing and new markets. More information about Ansoff is available in Unit 10 of this book on page 69. You should remember that producing a brand new product or service to be launched into a new EU market is likely to be the most risky option due to the amount of research and development involved before the product can actually be placed within the EU market.

Characteristics of Europe and theoretical concepts

At every stage of your planning and data collection you will also need to consider relevant theoretical concepts and apply them to your chosen business context. You will also need to demonstrate that you have understanding of the impact of characteristics of the European market and its potential impact on UK businesses.

To achieve success at the higher banding levels, you will need to demonstrate clear and comprehensive understanding of the characteristics of the European market. You will also need to make clear links between the results of your detailed research analysis into the business environment and the choices that you have made for your European strategy, including how the business will deal with the many issues it needs to consider when launching this new product or service.

Produce a list of different medium- or large-sized businesses that operate in your area. Do you have links with any of them in your school or college via a part-time job or someone you know who works there? Carry out research and draw up a table (see below) to help you choose an appropriate business to study. The first row has been filled in as an example.

BUSINESS	BACKGROUND IN UK	LINKS TO GATHER INFORMATION	TRADING IN EU
Medium-sized chain of Garages Ltd	Commercial vehicle repair service based in Southern England	Friend working there in the Head Office	Not at the moment, possibility of setting up repair service in EU

Remember you will need to get permission from the organisation before you can conduct detailed research into its activities. Discuss possible suitable business options with your teacher.

15.2.2 The business context within which the strategy will take shape

You may have already learned a great deal about the competitive nature of business and the implications of different promotional activities and campaigns in Unit 13 (see pages 152–3). Investigating the environment that the business works in now will help to shape the possible options that are open to the business for expansion into Europe.

You will be seeking to launch a new product or service in Europe and therefore will need to understand the existing products or services that are offered by the business and the types of promotional activity that take place and also the characteristics of the European market chosen. In Section 15.2.4 (Research of the strategy and analysing the information that is collected) you will conduct research into the current situation in your organisation. As part of this section you will investigate the characteristics of the EU as a whole and the implications for the business

trading in this way. Whilst collecting this data, you will need to make decisions about whether or not you choose an existing product or service in a new market or a new product or service in a new market.

As part of your assignment you will need to consider a number of key characteristics that define the EU and its individual member states including:

* demographic profile
* main imports and exports
* income level
* labour skills and employment rates.

Demographic profile

The European Union began in the 1950s as the European Economic Community and since then has increased over the years until in 2005 there were 25 member states (Figure 15.1) with two additional member states waiting to join in 2007 and other potential entrants wanting to join.

Figure 15.2 gives you a brief idea of the significant changes that have happened over this time.

FIGURE 15.1 *Map of Europe showing all the EU states (EU-25)*

PERIOD	SIGNIFICANCE	NUMBER OF MEMBER STATES
1950s	Members joined together, known as European Economic Community (EEC): West Germany, France, Belgium, Italy, the Netherlands and Luxembourg.	6
1973	3 new member states joined: Denmark, UK and Ireland.	9
1981	1 new member joined: Greece.	10
1986	2 new members joined: Spain and Portugal.	12
1990	East Germany and West Germany were reunified so Eastern Germans became part of the EEC.	12
1992	New powers were given to the community, now known as the European Union (EU), to work together and increase cooperation.	12
1995	3 new member states joined: Austria, Finland and Sweden	15 These countries are known as the EU-15.
2004	10 new member states joined: Cyprus, Czech Republic, Estonia, Hungary, Latvia, Lithuania, Malta, Poland, Slovenia and Slovakia.	25 These countries are known as the EU-25.
2007	Bulgaria and Romania are expected to join and Turkey is also being considered for entry.	Possible 27 or 28 member states.

FIGURE 15.2 *Changes in the EU*

Over more than 50 years the concept of a European Union has expanded from a small number of countries to a massive undertaking. As the number of member states has increased so too has the number of languages and variety of cultures and beliefs.

To gain a real understanding of the EU market that your business is seeking to operate in it is necessary to get a basic understanding of the demographic profile of the EU as a whole including its population and average age. You will need to collect specific information as well on the individual member state where the UK business expects to launch.

Population

In 2004 there were almost 457 million people living in the 25 EU member states, with Germany having the largest share of that population (18 per cent) and France, Italy and the UK having around 13 per cent each. These four countries contained 57 per cent of the total EU population in 2004 (Source: Europe in Figures Eurostat Yearbook 2005). There is even a wide variation in the population of the different countries as Germany, being the largest, has 82.5 million inhabitants compared with Malta that has just under 0.4 million inhabitants.

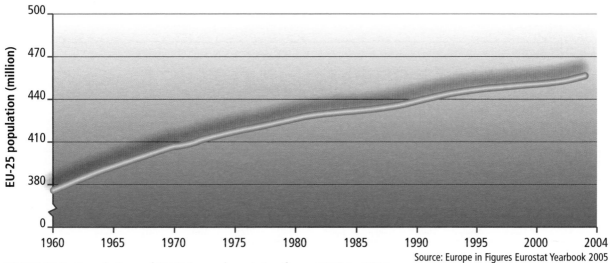

FIGURE 15.3 *Population of 25 EU member states from 1960 to 2004*

Source: Europe in Figures Eurostat Yearbook 2005

Figure 15.3 shows the increasing population of the EU since 1960 and this trend is likely to continue in the future especially as new member states are expected to join.

The world's population in 2004 was 6.3 billion people according to the Population Reference Bureau, so although the EU appears to be very large it still only represents just over 7 per cent of the world's population and a small percentage in comparison (Figure 15.4).

Average age

Like many other areas of the world, the average number of young people within the EU has gone down as a percentage of the overall population. This reduction in young people is a result of fewer children being born within the EU in more recent years and people living longer, so older people represent a larger percentage of the overall population. Figure 15.5 shows the number of

EU
457 million
(7%)

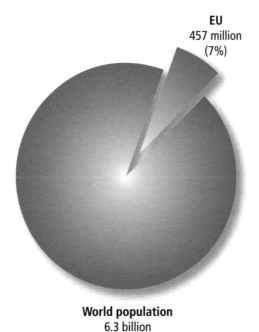

World population
6.3 billion

FIGURE 15.4 *Pie chart showing the population of EU as a percentage of the world's population in 2004*

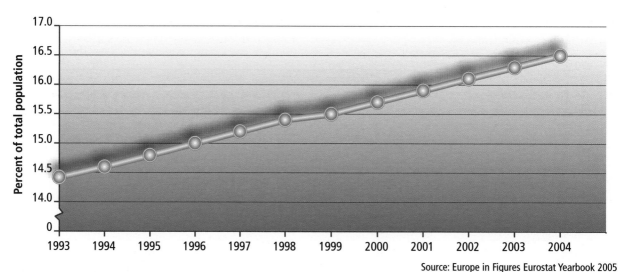

Source: Europe in Figures Eurostat Yearbook 2005

FIGURE 15.5 *The percentage of the population over 65 is steadily growing within the EU*

people aged over 65 as a percentage of the EU population. Having fewer younger people and a higher percentage of those over 65 may have implications for the launch of a product or service in the EU as it will depend on the target audience that the business has chosen to use. It may also affect the availability of employees that can work for EU businesses in the future. Some analysts predict that the EU will need over 20 million additional workers in the future from outside of its borders to fill all the job vacancies that will become available.

Population density

Population density is the measurement of how many people are living in a particular area of the EU per km². There are wide variations throughout the EU market as some countries have much higher population densities than others. In 2002 the highest densely populated countries were the Netherlands, Belgium, the UK and Germany (Source: Europe in Figures Eurostat Yearbook 2005). This has implications for the launch of any new product or service as highly populated

countries may be more popular with businesses offering a new product or service as they offer a large potential audience. This may also mean these countries have more competing businesses trading within them so they will need to balance the potential of an attractive new market against the threat of fierce competition.

Main imports and exports

Within the EU goods are freely traded between the member counties and you will learn more about this as you progress through this unit. A measurement is also made of the imports and exports that the EU as a whole makes with, and to, the rest of the world. In 2003, €880,400 million worth of goods were exported from the EU and €936,300 million worth of goods were imported into the EU from other countries in the world (Source: Europe in Figures Eurostat Yearbook 2005).

Figure 15.6 shows that there are more goods imported into the EU than the EU exports. These goods include any physical product that is moved

IMPORTED INTO THE EU	DIFFERENCE	EXPORTED FROM THE EU
936,300 million	55,900 million	880,400 million

FIGURE 15.6 *Import and export of goods from the EU in 2003*

Source: Europe in Figures Eurostat Yearbook 2005

in or out of the EU including animals, materials, chemicals and equipment.

The EU also trades services which, although you can't physically see them being exchanged, are traded in the same way. Services that are imported and exported to and from the EU are shown in Figure 15.7 below, such as transport, travel and tourism and financial services. In fact, Europe is the major tourist area in the world. You will need to consider the implications of EU imports and exports for the EU member state in which your product or service is to be launched.

Theory into practice

Using the graph below which shows the imports and exports of services, you will notice that the EU exports more services than it imports. You have already learned that the opposite is true for goods. Thinking about the different business sectors that you have already learned as part of your course (primary, secondary and tertiary), why do you think this might be?

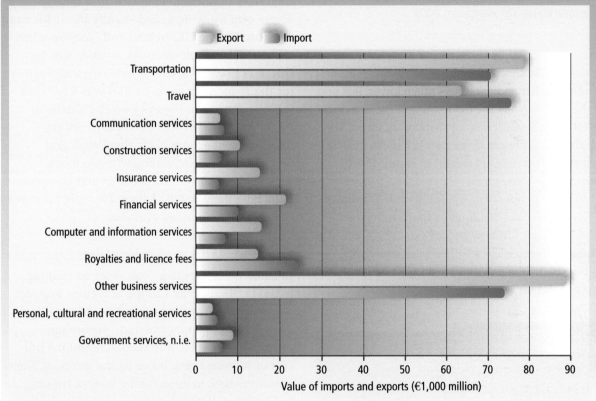

FIGURE 15.7 *EU-25 International trade in services in 2003 by main items*

Source: Europe in Figures
Eurostat Yearbook

Income level

In the EU as a whole there is a wide difference in income levels between individual member states This is a result of differences in the amount that individuals are paid for work between the EU member states. In 2002, the average gross annual earnings (earnings before tax/other payments are taken directly from pay) in industry and services was €29,540.08 averaged across the EU as a whole which is £19,693.39 (based on an exchange rate of £1 = €1.50) for the 25 member states.

COUNTRY	ANNUAL GROSS AVERAGE EARNINGS PER PERSON FOR BUSINESSES EMPLOYING 10 OR MORE PEOPLE IN 2002 IN EUROS
Denmark	€43,577.17
United Kingdom	€40,533.02
Germany	€39,440.00
Poland	€7,172.43
Hungary	€5,870.66
Slovakia	€4,582.29

Source: Europe in Figures Eurostat Yearbook 2005

FIGURE 15.8 *The top and bottom three EU member states for earnings, 2002*

In some individual states their own average figure is much higher and for others much lower. It is one of the challenges of the EU to try and make income levels more equal across all 25 member states. The top three and bottom three member states in 2002 that published data are shown in Figure 15.8 to illustrate the differences.

In 2002, people working full time in Denmark received just over 9½ times as much money as those working full time in Slovakia which is a huge difference These differences over time should reduce as pay and working conditions become similar across the 25 member states.

Theory into practice

The income and pay levels in countries throughout the EU are changing all the time, Figure 15.8 is just a snapshot of how things looked in 2002. Look up the latest data on pay levels between the EU member states by using resources such as www.europa.eu.int to get the latest research and statistics that you can use to develop your strategy.

Labour skills and employment rates

Employment rates and labour skills differ widely between EU member states and so targets have been set to improve skills levels and rates for individual countries and for the EU as a whole.

Employment rates

Making sure that people are skilled and employed is a priority for the EU to make it more competitive against other international businesses. In 2000, at the Lisbon summit a target of 70 per cent for the total employment rate across the EU was set and planned to be achieved by 2010. Full employment means that nearly all the people eligible to work are in work rather than claiming state benefits, for example Job Seeker's Allowance in the UK. There is a huge difference in employment rates between the EU countries.

For example, Poland and Slovakia both had high rates of unemployment in 2004 (nearly 20 per cent for women and slightly lower for men) compared to the UK, Ireland and Norway when the rate of unemployment for women was less than 4 per cent. The overall rate of unemployment for the 25 member states in 2004 was 9 per cent (Source: Europe in Figures Eurostat Yearbook 2005). These differences in employment rates mean it may be more likely that Polish and Slovak nationals are willing to move to another EU member state to find work or that businesses launching there will find there are higher numbers of potential employees available.

Training, skills and education

In 2003, €25,842 million was spent on training in the **EU-15** (Source: Europe in Figures Eurostat Yearbook 2005) and a further €12,915.7 million given as employer incentives to encourage unemployed people into work without the full cost of training being taken by the business. Such initiatives seek to improve the level of training and number of people employed within the EU.

As with the training and employer incentive, the EU member states are also seeking to increase the level of education achieved by people living within them. In 2003, just under 16.9 million students were receiving tertiary education in the EU. Throughout the EU it is apparent that the higher the level of education that has been achieved by an individual, the less likely it is that they will be unemployed, particularly if they have completed higher education. This notion has remained consistent in the EU over the last five years so it is in the interest of the EU as a whole to increase the number of individuals going on to higher education.

Economic impact

You have already learned a bit about the background to the EU and some of the differences between the member states. When business are trading within the EU they need to take into account two main areas:

* the Single Market
* European Monetary Union.

The Single Market

The idea of having a Single Market was largely created by the end of 1992 and is one of the fundamental reasons that the EU was set up in the first place all those years ago. It is the notion that goods, services, people and capital can be moved throughout the EU freely. As a result of its creation, it means that there is no need to pay any customs or excise charges to other member states. It also means that goods could be brought in to the EU from countries, such as the US and China as a whole and then be broken up and distributed to a number of countries, again without having to pay extra costs to the individual states involved. This has meant that costs have decreased for countries trading within the EU and for countries outside the EU trading with it.

Creating a single market involved passing more than 1,000 pieces of legislation as part of preparations for integration. It also meant that EU countries had to start developing ways for their businesses to deal with company law, business rules and accounting principles in a similar way so they were able to trade more efficiently across the EU.

Removing barriers to trade meant that it became easier for businesses to trade and set up right across the EU, whilst giving protection to customers everywhere with the same EU laws regardless of which countries they are living in and which businesses they are working with.

Another benefit of the Single Market has been the lowering of costs between member states making them more competitive as money is allowed to be invested or used more wisely throughout Europe. It is estimated between 1992 and 2002 the Single Market was responsible for:

* €900 million in extra prosperity (extra wealth for EU citizens)
* 2.5 million extra jobs
* 30 per cent increase in trade
* increased investment from outside the EU into the EU
* increased competitiveness by the EU with the rest of the world.

Having a Single Market also means that Europeans are able to move throughout Europe as they wish. It means that European citizens are able to work, study, shop and retire in any EU country of their choice and as legislation is updated all the time, could benefit from more legal rights on an ongoing basis. Goods and services can be purchased by European citizens from other member states where they can be produced and priced more cheaply. This has meant that competition between businesses operating throughout the EU has been increased and has led, like the airline industry, to lower prices for everyone. All the EU member states have to operate within these Single Market rules and if a country is found not to be participating correctly action is taken against them by the European Commission.

Airline travel

British Airways has benefited from the Single Market

easyJet and British Airways (BA) have been two of the main beneficiaries of the Single Market as demand for their services has significantly increased. Cheap airlines, such as easyJet or Ryanair would never have been able to fly freely wherever they wanted and without national restrictions until it came into force. This was a result of EU directives that supported the free movement and transport of people and goods/services throughout the member states. Restrictions on flight routes had to be lifted as part of this.

British Airways, as a direct result, have now been able to become the second largest domestic airline in France. This would not have been possible without the Single Market. An increasing number of potential customers have also been attracted to easyJet and BA as a direct result of the Single Market and changing technology. A high percentage of EU citizens, some suggestions say as high as 50 per cent, are able to access the Internet so a combination of free trade and greater access to a number of different airlines has meant greater choice and more competitive prices. A number of business people believe that the rapid growth of the cheaper airlines could not have happened without the Single Market being in place.

✓ 1. How did EU directives help the airline industry?

✓✓ 2. What part did IT play in the expansion of these airline companies including the advantages and disadvantages of using IT?

✓✓✓ 3. There are now a huge number of airlines making use of online booking within Europe including www.flybe.com, www.jet2.com, www.wizzair.com, www.skyeurope.com. Write a report analysing the benefits and problems associated with the change of EU directives and increasing competition. Make recommendations for British Airways or easyJet on strategies they could use to remain competitive.

French businesses working in the UK

In 2005, work began on the £500 million contract to rebuild and resurface the city of Portsmouth's whole road network by Colas Limited, part of the French-owned contractor Colas SA. Without the ability to trade freely and competitively throughout Europe, such a 25-year contract could never have been given. As a result of increasing competition, the people of Portsmouth should benefit from a higher quality service at a more competitive price making better use of their council tax money. This was a huge contract and a major change in the history of contracting in Portsmouth.

Yellow Buses based in Bournemouth were sold to Transdev (a French public transport company) in 2005. The Single Market has made it easier for many French companies to compete in the UK and in September 2005 it has been suggested that there were over 1,700 French owned and subsidiary companies operating in the UK. UK companies have of course been able to trade in France as well and in 1999 there were over 1,500 UK companies trading in France with this number being likely to increase.

✓ 1. What benefit is there for Portsmouth residents of increased competition?
✓ 2. How has the Single Market helped Colas SA to fulfil contracts in the UK?
✓✓ 3. Why might it be popular for UK and French businesses to trade in each other's national member states and what are the advantages and disadvantages of doing this?

Economic and Monetary Union

All 25 member states of the EU are linked into the Economic and Monetary Union (EMU) either by being within it or are affected by it. Eleven member states fixed their currency to the euro in January 1999 with Greece joining in January 2001. In January 2002, euro notes and coins were introduced as national currencies, such as the drachma and franc, were gradually withdrawn. The countries trading in euros are known as the **eurozone**.

COUNTRY	CURRENCY BEFORE 2002
France	Franc
Germany	Deutschmark
Spain	Peseta
Italy	Lira
Ireland	Punt
Greece	Drachma
Belgium	Belgian franc
Luxembourg	Franc
The Netherlands	Guilder
Austria	Schilling
Portugal	Escudo
Finland	Markka

FIGURE 15.9 *Eurozone countries and their currencies before 2002*

Key terms

Eurozone is the area of the EU where the euro is the currency used.

All the 25 member states are required to adopt the euro in the future as soon as their economies are ready to join, with the exception of the United Kingdom, Sweden and Denmark who have opted not to join at the moment.

By adopting the euro, businesses and people can benefit from saving money as they don't need to change their currency when they travel or trade across borders. The euro is also a recognised international currency so it can be traded worldwide. Another benefit for businesses of using the euro is that it makes it easier to compare prices between countries as they are in the same currency. Some economists think being part of the eurozone may limit the individual member states' ability to control their own money and that these benefits to changing money would be lost.

CASE STUDY

Should the UK join the eurozone?

There has been much debate about whether or not the UK should join the eurozone. In 2005, the UK was still deciding whether or not to join and this is to be reviewed regularly. So what are the arguments for and against changing over to the euro in the UK?

Arguments for

- Risk of currency changes either in favour or against UK businesses would be gone.

- Interest rates in the UK would be exactly the same as those in the rest of the eurozone. (Remember at one stage the rate was 2 per cent in the eurozone and 4.75 per cent in the UK.)

- Many businesses are already trading in euros and there is an indication that many more will start to do so in order to take payments from customers and suppliers, so whether or not the UK officially adopts the euro it is likely to become commonplace anyway.

- It would be easier to compare prices between the UK and other EU member states and prices will be lower as additional costs are avoided.

- Britain needs to trade within the eurozone and be part of it if it is going to be an effective member of the EU.

- Taking holidays and moving round Europe will become much easier including buying products online from differing member states both to and from the UK.

Arguments against

- Interest rates and other economic conditions such as levels of taxation and public spending will be dictated from the ECB and therefore may not be right for the UK.

- The UK will lose the benefit of exchange rate fluctuations to make additional profits.

- The UK has a history of using the pound and should not give it away.

- It may weaken links with business partners in the US and the rest of the world if the exchange rate in euros is not as good as the rate in pounds.

- If the euro is introduced, prices will become higher (this was noted in several EU member states as retailers and other suppliers rounded up their prices upon introduction).

- The UK is doing well in the EU already and does not need to join the euro, so why bother?

You have been presented with some of the arguments both for and against the UK joining the euro. Have a debate in your class. You may be able to think of more ideas of your own.

Split the class into three groups. Make one group those in favour of the UK joining the euro, one group in favour of not joining the euro and the third group to remain neutral. Ask the neutral group to vote at the end of the debate as to whether or not your class thinks the UK should join.

When a business needs to exchange currency it can make savings or increase costs as a result of the transfer. Akbar Miah is trading between the UK and Portugal. He exports English mustard and then sells it to restaurants all over Portugal. The table below shows the impact of changes in the euro/pound currency exchange rate. It costs Akbar £9,000 per month to produce the mustard to be exported.

MONTH	EURO VALUE	EXCHANGE RATE	£ VALUE
September	€16,800	1.50	£11,200
October	€16,800	1.65	£10,182
November	€16,800	1.55	£10,839

If he sells his mustard to the restaurants each month for €16,800 the effect of the change in exchange rates on his profits is shown in the table using the exchange rates above.

MONTH	EURO VALUE SHOWN IN £ USING EXCHANGE RATE ABOVE	COST OF PRODUCTION	PROFIT
September	£11,200	£9000	£2,200
October	£10,182	£9000	£1,182
November	£10,839	£9000	£1,839

These profit fluctuations have changed only as a result of the euro to pound rate changing and are totally outside Akbar's control.

If the pound becomes stronger (more £ to the €), exports from the UK to the EU eurozone will become more expensive. This means that Akbar will make smaller profits.

If the pound becomes weaker (fewer £ to the €), exports to the eurozone become cheaper and this increases Akbar's profits.

By working only within the eurozone businesses avoid these possible fluctuations but don't get the opportunity to benefit or be disadvantaged by such changes.

1. Using the example to help you, now work out what would happen if Akbar was selling £13,000 of goods to restaurants in Europe if the same changes in the euro exchange rate took place.

2. Which is best for Akbar when he is exporting – a strong pound or a weak one?

Since January 1999, the European Central Bank (ECB) of the European Union has been responsible for setting the official short-term interest rate of countries using the euro. Their target is to keep **inflation** and **interest rates** low across the eurozone so that these countries could benefit from prices and wages increasing more slowly to keep their businesses competitive The downside to having interest rates set by one central bank is that what might be good for one country may not necessarily be good for another, for example Italy and Spain both traditionally had problems with inflation whereas Germany has always had low-inflation.

In March 2005 it was announced that interest rates in the eurozone were to remain at 2 per cent whilst in the UK they were 4.75 per cent. This was a problem for France and Spain as property prices quickly increased as people felt able to borrow money at such a low rate, leading to an increase in demand for houses. To respond to this, both France and Spain would have liked an increase in interest rates. Italy and Germany at this time, however, were in the opposite position as they both needed a drop in interest rates to encourage people to spend more. This would have been likely to increase the number of people working (both had rising unemployment) through higher demands for goods and services. The longer that the eurozone is in operation the more likely it is that such variations will become smaller and therefore what is good for one country should be good for the others as well.

There have also been problems with limits for individual member states in terms of how much of a budget deficit they are allowed to have whilst operating in the eurozone. A budget deficit means the amount of money that a member state can borrow in order to carry out its activities. Member states are only allowed a deficit that represents a maximum of 3 per cent of their **GDP** (Gross Domestic Product – the amount of output in goods or services that a country produces). Countries exceeding this amount are liable for heavy fines by the **European Commission** but many of the countries operating in the eurozone have exceeded this limit including Portugal who had a deficit of 6.8 per cent in May 2005 with Greece, Germany, Italy and France all having exceeded that limit as well. Having a deficit that is greater than 3 per cent means that these individual countries are borrowing more than they should be and this could lead to them having to make large interest payments and their economies becoming unstable. This is because like any business or person, a member state needs to be able to pay back its debts eventually.

Legislation

Member states of the EU have their own set of laws created by the parliament of that state known as national legislation. Every EU member state has developed its legal framework in a slightly different way, for example UK legislation is based on statute, case and common/custom laws that have been passed over a number of years. The French legal system is completely different and is based on codified law where the French Parliament sets out the laws of the country under a set of five codes: civil code, commercial code, law on subcontracting, penal code and criminal procedure code. This type of codified law sets out rules that are equal for all and must be followed by everyone, whereas UK legislation changes as new cases are brought to court.

When the UK and France joined the EU, as well as creating economic integration they also created legal integration. This means that the 25 member states not only have their own national legislation but they also adopt legislation set down by the EU as a whole. The **European Parliament** is responsible for passing legislation that affects all the member states of the EU. In 2005 alone, over 5,000 pieces of legislation were voted on by Members of the European Parliament (MEPs). The European Commission advises the European Parliament on changes to policy and directives that should take place before they are voted on in the European Parliament.

European Commission is the group of people made up from all EU states that advises the European Parliament.

European Parliament is the group of members of parliament from all the EU member states who pass legislation that affects all member states.

Members of the European Parliament (MEPs) are voted in during European Elections every five years. The last elections were in June 2004. There are 78 MEPs that represent the UK and they are drawn from all the political parties that are represented in the UK including Labour, Conservative, Liberal Democrat and independent parties.

Look up information about the MEP for your area by accessing the website www.europarl. org.uk and going on to the UK MEPs section of the page.

1. Where are they based and what do they do? (Look for speeches and how they have voted.)

2. What are the interests of your local MEP and do they match your own EU interests?

The different elements of EU law are brought together and are known as the European Constitution. This Constitution is being ratified (agreed) by individual member states over the next few years. In 2005, 13 countries had ratified the European Constitution including Luxembourg, Spain, Germany, Cyprus, Greece, Hungary, Italy, Latvia, Lithuania, Malta, Slovenia and Slovakia. Two member states had voted no to the European Constitution and these were France and the Netherlands. The other member states had either postponed their decision or were in the process of ratification.

The purpose behind the European Constitution is to bring together all the countries so that they all abide by a set of legal principles and that citizens within member states are citizens of their individual country but also of the EU as a whole. The key impacts of the European Constitution for UK businesses trading in the EU from a legal point of view are the regulations, directives and Social Charter which affect both employers and employees.

European directives

The European Parliament meets in two places in the EU: in Strasbourg and Brussels.

European directives come directly from the European Parliament but are only applicable to member states of the EU when the objectives they contain have been added as part of national law, unless the individual state has announced a reason for an opt-out. Directives must be incorporated into existing or new member state legislation within the time set out by the Council of Ministers (usually two to three years unless opted-out). Over time the EU will seek to reduce the number of possible opt-outs so that all citizens across the EU will work within the same set of guidelines. A brief summary of some of the directives that relate to employers and employees are shown in Figure 15.10 on page 267.

Figure 15.10 shows just a small number of the directives that currently are or need to be implemented by the UK's Department of Trade and Industry (DTI). When a directive is given by the EC, individual member states must comply as soon as possible. In December 2005, there were 20 directives that the DTI needed to consider. For 15 out of those 20 directives, legislation had been passed for implementation, five were still to be done. The UK is not alone in taking its time to implement some directives. Many of the other EU member states are also taking time to get their own legislation changed to comply so this is a lengthy process that needs time to be followed and checked.

Many of the EU employment directives seek to protect employees and promote equality at work. Five of the main directives that affect all UK businesses trading in Europe are:

The European Parliament in Strasbourg

* **Equal Treatment Directives (75/207 and 2000/73)**

This sets out that there should be no discrimination either directly or indirectly on the grounds of sex, marital or family status in employment, training or working conditions. Sexual harassment was added by directive 2000/73 and gave details about what could be defined as 'sexual harassment' to avoid unwarranted comments or other attention being given to employees in the workplace of a sexual nature.

* **Equal Pay Directive (75/117)**

This directive requires that all discrimination on the grounds of sex in relation to pay should be stopped.

* **EU Employment Directive (2000/78)**

This directive requires all employers to stop any discrimination on the grounds of sexual orientation or religion and that discrimination should be outlawed on the basis of age or disability. In the UK, legislation on age discrimination comes into force in 2006 and disability discrimination was made unlawful in 1996.

DIRECTIVE	UK LAW PASSED BEFORE THE END OF 2005	DATE FOR IMPLEMENTATION AND WHETHER IMPLEMENTED IN 12/05
2002/73/EC directive on equal treatment of men and women in employment and vocational education		2005 No
97/80/EC directive on the burden of proof in cases of discrimination based on sex	Sex Discrimination (Indirect Discrimination and Burden of Proof) Regulations 2001	2001 Yes
2002/14/EC establishing a general framework for informing and consulting employees in the EC	Information and Consultation of Employees Regulations 2004	2005 No
2000/78/EC establishing a general framework for equal treatment in employment and occupation		2003 and 2006 No
2001/86/EC supplementing the Statute for a European company with regard to the involvement of employees	European Public Limited-Liability Company Regulations 2004	2004 No
98/23/EC extension of directive 97/81/EC agreement of part-time work concluded by UNICE, CEEP and the ETUC to the United Kingdom of Great Britain and Northern Ireland	Part-time Workers (Prevention of Less Favourable Treatment) Regulations 2000	2000 Yes

FIGURE 15.10 *Some of the EU directives that relate to employers and employees*

Source: www.dti.gov.uk/er/
europe/directives.htm

* **EU Race Directive**

This is the principle that people should be treated equally regardless of their racial or ethnic origin and sets out minimum standards of protection for all member states.

* **Directive on the burden of proof in cases of discrimination based on sex 97/80/EC**

This directive puts the responsibility with employers to prove they have not discriminated against an employee because of their sex rather than the employee having to prove that their employer discriminated against them.

Think it over...

There are hundreds of directives that have been implemented by the EU and you will need to consider the relevant directives for your business. The main ones have been covered for you but there are many others that might relate to your business depending on what it sells in terms of services or goods. These can be as different as the price set for imports of butter and cheese to the units of measurement used to weigh produce.

CASE STUDY

EU Metrication Directive

The EU Metrication Directive 1979 (implemented by all member states by the end of December 1999) required all EU member states to use metric measurements (grams and kilograms) rather than imperial measurements (pounds and ounces) on the roads, for shopping, homes and workplaces. This was a huge change for the UK where sellers and buyers of fruit, vegetables and delicatessen items had always preferred to use imperial measurements. From 1 January 2000, all market traders were told to **only** display their prices in grams and kilograms. This led to some traders going against the rules as a protest and in July 2000 the late Steve Thorburn was prosecuted by trading standards officers and fined for selling a pound of bananas from his stall in Southwick Market rather than selling it as approximately half a kilogram. Most traders and the public have got used to being moved over to grams and kilograms and in the future it will be completely usual to trade in this way

There are some exceptions to metrication for the UK as part of this directive, for example beer, cider and milk can all still be sold in pints (imperial) but this could obviously change in the future.

✓ 1. **Why do you think traders felt annoyed when they needed to change over from pounds and ounces to grams and kilograms?**

✓✓ 2. **What is the benefit to EU citizens of travelling throughout Europe of having the same system of measurement?**

✓✓ 3. **Outline problems that might have been in place for businesses trading in Europe before the change and any possible issues after the change.**

European regulations

Member states are also obliged to comply with all the elements of EU regulations as well as directives. Regulations give more detail about what employers and employees must do in order to comply. As regulations have a direct effect, individual member states do not need to pass their own law to bring them into effect and any laws of member states are automatically overruled by regulations when they come into force. Individuals can rely on regulations in any court cases in their own country and throughout the EU. Like the directives, there is an ever increasing number of regulations and they are being updated all the time.

Working time regulations

An example of such regulations are the Working Time (Amendment) Regulations 2002 (2002/3 128). The EU Working Time Directive (93/104/EC) sets out a number of minimum standards and treatments for employees including:

* a limit of 48 hours per week which a worker can be required to work (they can choose to work more)

* a limit of 8 hours work in 24 which night workers can be required to work

* a right for night workers to receive free health assessments before commencing night work and at regular intervals thereafter

* a right to uninterrupted rest periods of 11 hours daily in each 24 hours and of 24 hours in each 7 day period.

* adequate additional rest breaks for workers whose pattern of work puts their health and safety at risk

* a right to a rest break of at least 20 minutes after 6 hours consecutive work

* a right to a minimum of four weeks paid leave with workers having a right to paid annual leave from the first day of employment.

In 2005 there were still negotiations with the European Commission to consult on the way that the working time was calculated, particularly in relation to doctors on call and so individual member states do have the power to clarify any points raised within the regulations.

Food labelling regulations (2003/89/EC)

Food labelling regulations came into force in November 2005. They require the clear labelling of 12 major allergens (ingredients that people are commonly allergic to) in food including gluten, hazelnuts, peanuts, almonds, soya, egg, milk (and derivatives), sesame and histamine. UK businesses working both within the UK and the rest of the EU must comply with these regulations. This did cause some problems in establishments such as schools or college where homemade cakes being brought in to school did not seem clearly covered by the regulations and as a result some schools decided to stop them being brought in for fetes and events whilst others continued as usual. It also caused problems for national chains and manufacturers as they applied the new regulations. In December 2005 alone, Iceland had to recall a batch of cottage pies, Sainsbury's supermarkets had to recall packs of sunflower seeds and Marks and Spencer recalled packs of own brand duck spring rolls, all because their packs were labelled incorrectly. The food was perfectly acceptable to eat but did not give information for people with allergies such as nuts or shellfish.

Social Charter

The European Social Charter supplements the European Convention on Human Rights by protecting the social, economic and cultural rights of individuals and was adopted in 1961 and then revised in 1996. The charter was drawn up out of a wish to prevent the loss of rights that Europeans had seen during World War Two. The Charter gives rights and guarantees to workers including housing, health, education, employment, social protection, free movement of individuals and non-discrimination. The European Committee of Social Rights checks whether countries are doing what they should do as part of the Charter and takes action if necessary. Workers rights and guarantees as a result of the charter include:

* the right to work

* the right to just conditions of work

* the right to safe and healthy working conditions

* the right to a fair remuneration (pay and other benefits)

* the right to organise

* the right to bargain collectively

* the right of children and young persons to protection

* the right of employed women to protection

* the right to vocational training

* the right to protection of health

* the right to social security

* the right to social and medical assistance

* the right to benefit from social welfare services

* the right of physically or mentally disabled persons to vocational training, rehabilitation and social resettlement

* the right of the family to social, legal and economic protection

* the right of mothers and children to social and economic protection

* the right to engage in a gainful occupation in the territory of other Contracting Parties

* the right of migrant workers and their families to protection and assistance.

Some of the directives and regulations that you have learned about came into force as a result of changes to EU legislation as part of the Social Charter, e.g. maximum working week and equal opportunity laws. More recently, throughout Europe there have been changes in the rights of parents to maternity leave and paternity leave and in October 2006 age discrimination is enforceable whereby an employer cannot discriminate on the grounds of age. As the laws of the EU say that all persons are equal, EU states in December 2005 gave equality to same sex couples who wanted to get married via the Civil Partnership Act. This gave these couples the same rights as heterosexual couples including pension payments and workplace benefits.

Another change that took place as a result of the Social Charter was the implementation of the National Minimum Wage. In 2004, 18 out of the 25 countries of the EU had a minimum wage and the others were in the process of introducing one in order to comply with the Social Charter. The introduction of the National Minimum Wage Act 1998 led to an increase in pay for workers paid at the lowest levels. In October 2005, the main rate for workers aged 22 and over was raised to £5.05 in the UK and from October 2006 it will be £5.35. Having a minimum wage in member states of the EU helps citizens to receive fair remuneration.

Theory into practice

Using websites and articles that you can find in the newspapers, find out information about the latest pieces of legislation, directives and regulations that have been passed within the EU and the effect that they have on UK business trading in the UK and member states.

Customs

Whilst being part of the EU and legal and monetary integration have helped to make the pay and living conditions of citizens similar across the whole of the 25 member states there are other differences that UK businesses need to take into account such as:

* business practices

* banking systems

* working hours

* national holidays

* languages

* social customs and lifestyles.

Business practices

Business practices take two forms: directives that must be applied by businesses and European business etiquette.

Directives

Even within the area of business practice, EU directives are being brought in to help make all businesses conform in the same way. Directive 2005/29/EC on Unfair Commercial Practices prohibits pressure selling, misleading marketing and unfair advertising conditions including rules about advertising to children. The European Parliament passed this directive in May 2005 and member states have two and a half years to implement it as part of their national legislation. The idea behind implementing such a directive is that it will give all businesses a set of guidelines for what is permitted across all EU countries. At the moment, unfair practices can vary between member states. By having a set of common rules businesses will be able to save money on legal costs and be able to market their products on a Europe-wide basis.

Fraud as a result of unfair practices

Before the Unfair Commercial Practices directive was brought into force it was much more difficult for individuals and businesses to seek legal redress in countries that they were not living in. Fraud can, of course, happen in any country including the UK but this directive seeks to make the treatment of fraud the same whether you are working in your own EU member state or another one within the EU. Examples of such unfair practices include UK citizens receiving letters from Spain saying they have won money but it then costs them more than £1,000 to claim it, free holidays in Malta given out on scratch cards that end up costing £3,000 to take the 'free' holiday and a Dutch communications company giving the misleading impression that a prize was being held for UK citizens when they had won no such prize.

✓ 1. Using your local newspapers or going online and using the www.euroconsumer.org.uk website, look up the latest scams and problems for businesses and individuals trading with the UK and Europe.

✓✓ 2. Produce a wall display warning other students of the dangers of the latest scams and give recommendations for what to look out for when answering competitions.

✓✓ 3. Outline the advantages and disadvantages to legitimate businesses of running competitions for free holidays and offers in the light of such fraudulent activity.

✓✓✓ 4. To what extent do you think this new legislation will reduce fraud across the EU and enable EU citizens to claim legal redress in other EU countries.

Business etiquette

When dealing with businesses in other member states there are also differences in business etiquette.

In Slovakia, for example, it is not the custom to use a person's first name at a business meeting and they should be addressed as Doctor, Engineer and so on. It is also usual to start meetings with a local alcoholic drink and a toast.

In Estonia it is common practice after shaking hands with business associates to give them your business card. Some Estonians have a fairly sarcastic sense of humour and do not like jokes made about their culture.

If you take a gift to a business meeting in Italy make sure it is not wrapped in yellow or black as these colours are the colours used for funerals and purple signifies bad luck. Gifts should also not carry the logo of the business.

These differences are significant but represent only three countries out of the possible 24 that a UK business can trade with so careful attention needs to be given to the business practices of the European markets that your business will be launching in.

Banking systems

One of the targets of Economic Monetary Union is to have financial systems that are linked together. Member states operating within the eurozone are already closely linked by the European Central Bank, but different member states have different banking regulations compared to others and this will need to be worked on in the coming years in order to make sure that member states can work together. Different regulations have made it more difficult for European Banks to move across borders and start trading in other countries. Charges between the counties have also been different with charges in Greece being higher than many other European states.

There is also a difference in the level of technology between states. By the end of 2005,

Chip and pin helps to avoid fraud

all bank cards issued should have been Europay, Mastercard and Visa (EMV) chipped so that a pin number and chip is used to help to avoid fraud across the EU. However, ten European countries were only issuing pilot schemes during 2005 including Italy, Spain and Poland leading to inevitable differences in payment methods and fraud prevention that businesses need to be aware of.

Working hours

Bringing 25 member states, that have developed independently, together means that working hours and patterns of work are very different across the EU member states. All 25 member states are responding to the EU directive that states that a maximum 48 hour week should be worked but even within that time limit there are differences between countries as shown in Figure 15.11.

In Lithuania, a full-time working week is less than 40 hours but in Austria it is 45 hours. These differences mean that workers moving between countries will need to expect to do more or less hours than when they were in their home member state. Some workers in European states are described as doing around 41 hours for a full-time week but, for example in Hungary it is commonplace to do as many hours as is necessary to get the job done.

As well as differences in the number of hours there is also a difference in the hours of a working day. For example, in Spain it is usual to have a siesta during the day when Spanish employees get two or three hours off in the afternoon but have to go back to work in the evening. In Finland, employees are required to work a maximum of eight hours per day and 40 hours per week unless they wish to do overtime and then they must be paid at the stipulated minimum overtime rate.

It is possible to limit the hours of work as a whole across the EU but there are always likely to be differences in the actually working day as some countries are affected by different climates and member states' governments are able to add their own influence as well. The French government, for example, in 1998 voted to introduce a 35-hour working week which meant that traditional long lunches in France were reduced. In 2005 it was announced that the government was now reviewing this decision and may lengthen the hours again despite protests from workers and unions in France.

National holidays

Across the EU there are 109 public holidays! This is a high number and if as part of integration every country took holidays in honour of its fellow member states there would be a lot less time in the year left to work. Some holidays are common to member states such as Christmas Day (25 December) and 1 May (Labour Day or May Day) whereas others are only taken by individual countries. For example, Greek Cypriot National Day is celebrated on 1 April and 9 May is known as Europe Day throughout the EU.

UK workers have fewer public holidays than any other EU country. The average number of days across the EU is 10.8 days but the UK only has a basic eight days (extra days are given if Christmas Day, Boxing Day or New Year's Day fall on a weekend) compared to Ireland with ten, Slovakia with 15, Spain with 16 and Estonia with 18. As national holidays fall on different days of

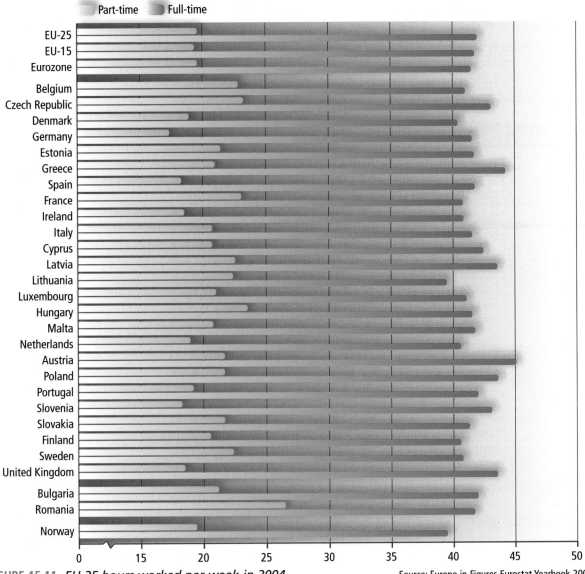

Part-time ▢ Full-time ▢

EU-25
EU-15
Eurozone
Belgium
Czech Republic
Denmark
Germany
Estonia
Greece
Spain
France
Ireland
Italy
Cyprus
Latvia
Lithuania
Luxembourg
Hungary
Malta
Netherlands
Austria
Poland
Portugal
Slovenia
Slovakia
Finland
Sweden
United Kingdom
Bulgaria
Romania
Norway

0   15   20   25   30   35   40   45   50

FIGURE 15.11 *EU-25 hours worked per week in 2004*

Source: Europe in Figures Eurostat Yearbook 2005

the year in member states, businesses need to be aware of them as they may not be able to arrange deliveries or meetings on those days.

Languages

The EU has more than 20 main languages spoken by the 25 member states so this can lead to problems for businesses who wish to trade in other countries. Whilst English is one of the most popular languages spoken there are some areas where it is important for UK businesses to get help with translation services.

As well as the official languages there are also a number of regional languages that exist in EU member states that are starting to be recognised.

In Spain, Catalan is spoken by more people in the EU than Finnish or Danish and Spain also has speakers of Galician and Basque within its territory. In June 2005, the EU took the decision to support regional languages by publishing documents in many additional languages than the basic 20 official ones of the EU.

LANGUAGE	DETAILS
Welsh	Spoken in Wales by 20.5% of the Welsh population of 3 million people (2001).
Cornish	Seeing a revival in the 1990s and classes in Cornish are now being held in Cornwall.
Breton	Spoken in Brittany in northern France although is not officially recognised by the French government.
Irish	Spoken in the Republic of Ireland. 1.43 million people aged three and over in 1996 said that they were Irish speakers
Frisian	Spoken in Germany and the Netherlands by an estimated 603,000 inhabitants of whom half say it is their first language.
Sardu (Sardinian)	Spoken by an estimated 1.3 million people living in Italy.

FIGURE 15.12 *Some of the minority languages spoken in the EU*

Figure 15.12 shows just some of the main minority languages spoken in the EU. UK businesses launching products and services in EU member states need to be aware of these differences but should take comfort from the fact that more and more of us are learning and speaking other languages. In 2000, research was carried out into languages spoken by the EU-15 member states and it was found that 53 per cent of Europeans can speak at least one European language in addition to their mother tongue (Eurobarometer Report 54). English was found to be known by 41 per cent of the European population surveyed so this is useful for UK businesses trading abroad. English was also found to be the first language for 32.6 per cent of Europeans with their second language being most commonly French.

Social customs and lifestyles

Again with social customs and lifestyles there is a huge variety across the EU member states. This is because each of the cultures (the set of expected rules on ways to behave) of member states are different and have evolved over hundreds of years.

* Bull fighting, for example, is seen as very much part of life in Spain whereas other Europeans think that it is cruel.

* Germany has traditionally closed down many of their factories and businesses in the summer months as part of national holidays.

* In France it is perfectly acceptable to eat frogs' legs and snails.

* The UK is known for its endless queuing and obsession with the weather.

* In Malta most shops open between 9 am and 7 pm with a three hour lunch break and are closed on Sundays and public holidays.

* In Slovakia it is common to have live fish swimming in tanks in supermarkets ready to be killed to order ensuring they are fresh.

There are also religious differences between the different member states so this needs to be taken into account when promoting products and services in order to not offend members of a country or religion. Differences in the climates of the member states and whether or not they have coastal shores all make a difference to the lifestyle and customs of those member states. As Slovakia is land-locked some older Slovaks have never seen the sea and take their holidays in mountains or by lakes. A UK business selling products that are associated with the sea in the UK would need to promote their product or service differently there.

Trade

There are two main ways that trade takes place within the EU; between the member states (intra trade) and with countries outside of the EU (extra trade). Figure 15.13 gives you an idea of the trade that went on between the EU and other countries of the world in 2003.

The EU imported more goods in 2003 than it exported and the same was true for the United States. China, Japan and Canada, by contrast, all exported more than they imported.

The way services are exported and imported within the EU also shows that, in some areas, the EU exports more services than it imports but in others the opposite is true. Look back at Figure 15.7 on page 257. The EU exported more transportation, construction and financial services to international countries than they did import. For travel, royalties and communication services it imported more.

These graphs give an idea of the type of trade that is going on inside the EU and with the EU and there are key differences between member states and trading outside the EU. There are some significant differences that have been presented to you already in this chapter between trading inside the EU and trading with countries outside the EU.

Trading within the EU

Within the EU there should be free movement of goods, services, people and capital so there are no tariffs or additional payments that need to be met by businesses trading with fellow member states. This reduces costs and has led to an increase in the demand for services and goods between the member states.

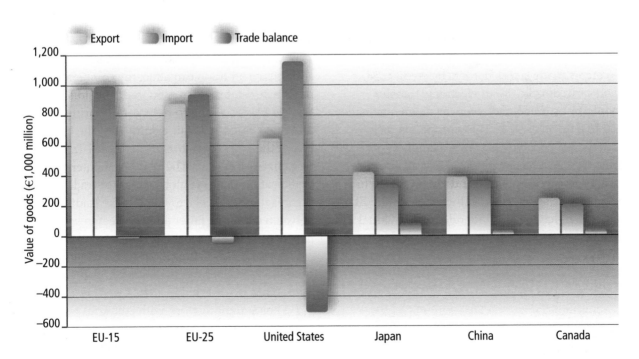

FIGURE 15.13 *International trade in goods in 2003*

Source: Europe in Figures Eurostat Yearbook 2005

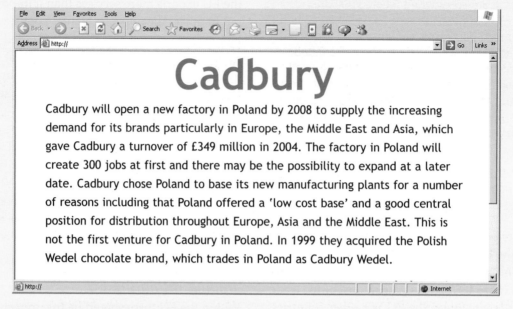

Cadbury

Cadbury will open a new factory in Poland by 2008 to supply the increasing demand for its brands particularly in Europe, the Middle East and Asia, which gave Cadbury a turnover of £349 million in 2004. The factory in Poland will create 300 jobs at first and there may be the possibility to expand at a later date. Cadbury chose Poland to base its new manufacturing plants for a number of reasons including that Poland offered a 'low cost base' and a good central position for distribution throughout Europe, Asia and the Middle East. This is not the first venture for Cadbury in Poland. In 1999 they acquired the Polish Wedel chocolate brand, which trades in Poland as Cadbury Wedel.

1. **What do you think is meant by a 'low cost base'?**
2. **What advantage might Cadbury have by being centrally located in Europe?**
3. **How might Cadbury acquiring the Wedel chocolate brand in Poland have helped them to expand there?**

There is still work to be done to make trade easier between member states and the EU is always updating proposals. In December 2005 the European Commission put forward proposals to make the EU a 'Single Payments Area' so that payments made across borders by credit card, debit card, direct debit or electronic transfer should be as cheap and secure as payments made within a member state. These proposals seek to save the EU economy €50 to €100 billion per year! There were also proposals for all audio-visual services (TV, broadband, mobiles etc.) to be given one set of rules for the whole of the EU rather than having separate rules of individual member states to give Europeans more choice.

Theory into practice

Look up the latest press releases given by the European Commission on proposals for trade in the future using websites such as www.europa.eu.int making particular note of any changes or proposals that are likely to relate to your UK business trading in Europe.

Trading outside the EU

Trading with countries outside the EU is more complicated than within the EU as there are tariff and non-tariff barriers to the goods and services that can be offered by the EU. Subsidies and restrictions on trade can affect the competitiveness of member states when they trade outside Europe but the EU is seeking to reduce such tariffs and make trading as fair as possible. The EU is one of the key negotiators in the World Trade Organization (WTO). The WTO is an international organisation that sets global rules for trade within organisations. It seeks to try to make trading between countries fairer and has been responsible for negotiations between the countries.

The WTO was set up in 1995 and developed from GATT (General Agreement on Tariffs and Trade) that was started in 1948. Over these years WTO has sought to work with countries to resolve trade problems and to make trade much easier but this can be difficult to do if the people and governments of those countries feel that they are treated unfairly. There have been various tariffs and quota limits imposed by and on the EU

US tariffs on EU products

In 1999 the US imposed 100 per cent duties on some French, German, Danish and Italian products including Roquefort cheese, mustard, truffles, foie gras, tomatoes and pork, costing France alone $28 million. This was allegedly in direct response to the EU refusing to accept beef from cows that had been treated with growth hormones. The US decided that the UK products were exempt. Imposing duties on these products has meant that some of them have had to be dramatically increased in price. French Roquefort, for example has now become a highly priced premium product to take into account these additional costs. Such changes to the cost of producing and importing a product mean that a business could find the demand for its product being reduced and therefore may not be able to continue selling it.

Consider the products and services that your business offers.

✓ 1. Are they any trade agreements that may affect their distribution in an EU member state?

✓ 2. Are there any products or services they offer that may be affected by EU tariffs or bans imposed on other countries such as the US or China?

✓✓ 3. What are the implications for your product or service of such EU tariffs or bans – advantages or disadvantages?

✓✓✓ 4. Using your analysis from Question 3, make recommendations for your business on how to cope with such restrictions and any strategies they could use to remain competitive if a ban or tariff was introduced.

including as recently as December 2005 when the EU sought to impose an import tariff on bananas coming from countries with 'Favoured Nation Status' mainly in Latin America. This tariff was rejected by the WTO at the time and was still being discussed through into January 2006. Tariffs on bananas has become a long running dispute known as the 'banana wars'.

European assistance to businesses

The EU offers assistance to business throughout the 25 member states in different forms. There are three main forms:

1. Financial assistance
2. Advice and representation
3. Information.

Financial assistance

Some of the financial assistance is given in the form of a grant or loan to help UK businesses to strengthen in the UK or become established in other areas of the EU. Grants may or may not be payable back to the EU but loans always are so it will depend on the type of business that is being run which is the most suitable and possible for them.

The size of loans available from the EU will depend on the area and the type of business being set up or expanded. A business loan during 2005 of up to £30,000 was available for people living and starting up businesses in Devon, Dorset or Somerset. A grant of up to £100,000 was available for businesses in the Yorkshire area from the Viking Fund. This money was only available for businesses setting up in this area. In Caerphilly County Borough there was up to £15,000 available for people wanting to create community enterprises to provide services to the community and generate employment.

Grants are also available in Europe so that businesses can get funding to relocate or expand into other European countries. Grant-Guide was set up by the EU to give advice and funding to businesses setting up in countries other than their own and hopes to be a very comprehensive source of information in the next few years. In December 2005, grants were available for up to €13,800 to finance investment and create new jobs in Poland.

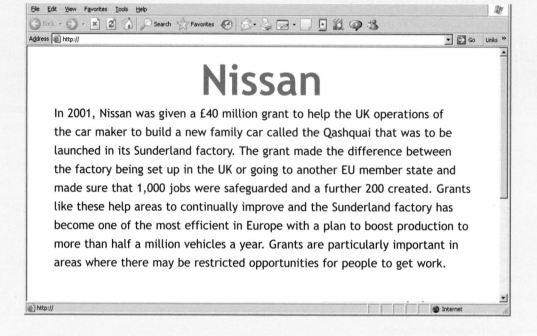

Nissan

In 2001, Nissan was given a £40 million grant to help the UK operations of the car maker to build a new family car called the Qashquai that was to be launched in its Sunderland factory. The grant made the difference between the factory being set up in the UK or going to another EU member state and made sure that 1,000 jobs were safeguarded and a further 200 created. Grants like these help areas to continually improve and the Sunderland factory has become one of the most efficient in Europe with a plan to boost production to more than half a million vehicles a year. Grants are particularly important in areas where there may be restricted opportunities for people to get work.

✓ 1. What difference did getting an EU grant make to Nissan investing in Sunderland?

√√ 2. Why would the UK government be pleased with an EU grant and what effect would the new factory have on the local area including the benefits and possible disadvantages?

Theory into practice

Using the Grant-Guide website, www.grant-guide.com, search for grants that are available in the member states that your business might like to launch their product or service to. What kind of assistance is available and what can it be used for?

Advice, representation and information available

As part of the WTO negotiations, discussions and proposals put forward by the European Commission and votes held in the European Parliament, EU businesses both in the UK and other member states are represented by officials from their own national member state. They are also given advice from three further sources:

* Association of European Chambers of Commerce

* UK Trade and Investment Team

* Link2exports website.

Association of European Chambers of Commerce

The Association of European Chambers of Commerce (www.eurochambres.be) provides advice and papers for businesses trading throughout the EU as part of a network of 2,000 regional and local chambers of commerce. The Association also campaigns for extra support to be given to member state small- and medium-sized enterprises to help them to trade across Europe on an equal basis.

UK Trade and Investment Team

UK Trade and Investment Teams (www.uktradeinvest.gov.uk) are based up and down the UK providing advice and guidance for UK businesses seeking to expand into Europe. The service is available in local areas by researching International Trade Advisors and entering the business' postcode. The South East Trade UK Trade and Investment Team, for example, planned visits to Poland in February 2006 as more than £272 million of exports had been sent to Poland in 2004/5 from this area. They also provide other assistance such as workshops including 'EU Bidding Effectively'. All these initiatives are designed to help UK businesses be as effective as possible within the EU.

Link2exports

The Link2exports (www.link2exports.co.uk) gives advice to UK businesses wishing to trade in EU member states including facts and figures on individual member states, detailing the size of the populations there and amount of trade that takes place between that member state and the rest of the EU. This can help UK businesses learn more about where they are likely to get strong competition and areas where there may be more opportunity for them to fill a niche.

15.2.3 Planning the strategy

Having identified the type of business activity taking place already you will need to make links between this activity and the launch of the product or service into the EU market. You will need to understand that when businesses conduct strategic planning they need to make sure they:

* set aims and objectives

* select appropriate types of research to generate the required information

* gain sources of information that are useful for European expansion.

You may find it useful to read through section 15.2.4 to give you ideas to be used to plan your strategy.

Setting of aims and objectives

Aims and objectives are central to most aspects of business, as they are the driving force and outline what happens with the business. The aims are the overall purpose or goal and then the objectives are the list of plans that help those aims to be achieved. Product or service launch objectives work in exactly the same way as any other objectives in that they should be SMART (Specific, Measurable, Agreed, Realistic and Time-constrained).

You will need to consider the aim of the product or service launch before you will be able to build the associated objectives to go with it. For more information on how to do this see Unit 13, pages 185–7.

Types of research and sources of information

Selecting the most appropriate types of research and sources of information in order to collect data for a possible promotional strategy is as important as an outline of the strategy in the first place. This is because the business will only collect the right data if it uses the right methods to collect it. You will need to consider all the possible sources outlined so far within this unit and in Section 15.2.4 that follows. Make sure you make good use of the list of resources at the end of this unit. Produce an action plan that you can use to help you plan your research.

ISSUE TO BE INVESTIGATED	SOURCES OF HELP	TIMESCALE FOR COLLECTION	DATE COMPLETED
Current advertising methods	Business Marketing Department www.asa.owrg.uk	by 15 December	14 December

FIGURE 15.14 *An example action plan*

15.2.4 Research of the strategy and analysis of the information that is collected

You will need to conduct effective research that is clearly targeted and focused on both what is happening in the business now in the UK or other markets and on the new product or service that you are seeking to launch so that an effective strategy can start to emerge from the data.

You will need to carry out primary *and* secondary research. It is recommended that you do secondary research before primary so you can get an idea of the promotional activity in the market as a whole to give you ideas.

Secondary research

Secondary research is information that has been collected and published by someone else. It is useful to a business because it exists already and can provide information about what is happening in a market. Businesses can make use of two sorts of secondary data: data available within the business such as sales records, invoice payments and loyalty cards or data available outside the business such as marketing reports, newspapers or websites. More information about secondary research and some possible sources of information is available in Unit 10, page 64, but there are also additional sources of information that are important when studying business expansion into the EU.

Competitors

As part of your collection of secondary data you will need to make sure you have background information and comparative data on the EU market in which you are intending to launch your product or service.

Theory into practice

Collect the names of businesses that operate in the same of similar market to your business in the UK and in the EU. Where are these businesses based? Which countries do they export to and how are their products or service similar or different to those that you are going to be offering?

Draw up a table as shown below. By completing your table you will get an idea of the products or services offered by similar UK businesses in EU member states and be able to work out any gaps in which the business you are studying could expand.

BUSINESS NAME	PRODUCT OR SERVICE DETAILS	BUSINESS HEAD OFFICE	PRODUCT OR SERVICE OFFERED IN OTHER EU MEMBER STATES THAN UK?
Tesco	Retail super/ hypermarkets	UK	In 2001 there were the following Tesco stores open in: Poland (42), Hungary (44), Czech Republic (12), Slovakia (10).
Carrefour	Super/ hypermarkets Cash and carry Discount stores Convenience stores	France	In 2005 Carrefour had various types of store open in: Spain (3,029), Portugal (388), Italy (1,460), Poland (102), Belgium (512), Greece and Cyprus (650), Czech Republic (11) and Slovakia (4).

European institutions

There are lots of leaflets and information available both in hard copy and online from European institutions.

The European Commission

The European Commission (http://europa.eu.int) publishes lots of background information related to all issues of the EU. It provides lots of advisory material that can be used to inform your strategy. Its four main roles are to:

1. Propose legislation to the European Parliament
2. Manage and implement EU policies and the budget
3. Enforce European law (with the Court of Justice)
4. Represent the EU in negotiations with the rest of the world.

The European Parliament

The European Parliament (www.europarl.eu.int) is made up of citizens from all the 25 member states and has three main roles:

1. To pass European law
2. To exercise democratic supervision over the other European institutions such as the European Commission
3. To jointly decide the EU budget with the Council of the European Union.

The Council of the European Union

The Council of the European Union (http://europa.eu.int) makes the main decisions of the EU and has meetings between the member state officials who are from each of the national governments of the EU. The Council has six responsibilities:

1. To pass laws
2. To coordinate the broad economic policies of member states
3. To sort out international agreements between the EU and elsewhere
4. To approve the EU budget together with the European Parliament
5. To develop the EU Common Foreign and Security Policy
6. To coordinate cooperation between the national courts and police forces across the EU.

European Investment Fund

The European Investment Fund (www.eif.eu.int) is owned by the European Investment Bank and provides information and resources that can be used by small to medium enterprises growing within the EU or for early stage companies that are developing advanced technologies. The EIF publish leaflets and information on business life in the EU.

European Social Fund

The European Social Fund (www.esf.gov.uk) also provides information about business and employment within the EU. Their main aim is to strengthen economic and social cohesion within the EU. Between 2000 and 2006, ESF will provide Great Britain with £4.5 billion for a range of projects including:

* helping unemployed and inactive people enter work
* providing opportunities for people at a disadvantage in the labour market
* promoting lifelong learning
* developing the skills of employed people
* improving women's participation in the labour market.

Improving women's participation in the labour market

The ESF can provide funding for training and development for businesses wishing to expand in the UK or EU but the business must fulfil one of three objectives:

Objective 1   To develop regions where the economy is lagging behind most of Europe

Objective 2   To renew industrial, urban, rural and fisheries areas that are in decline

Objective 3   To improve people's skills and employment prospects.

If your UK business is likely to cover any of the objectives outlined above as part of their launch in to Europe, then ESF funding as part of that strategy should be highly recommended. The ESF also publish information on the latest development in projects all over the EU.

Primary research

Primary data is very important because it gives you first-hand information for two main purposes: to find out more general information about what is happening in a market and to focus on the likelihood of success for your new product or service including the best way to promote it. Your primary research will be useful in three main ways:

1. To work out whether or not there is a place for a new product or service in the EU market
2. To collect information on what kind of promotional features attract customers in the business you are studying in the UK for your EU strategy
3. To collect information on the way that marketing works in your chosen business at first hand.

Gathering information on customer tastes and needs for a new product or service

Primary research is often the best way of gathering information on whether or not a customer will want to buy a product or service. Primary research, therefore, can be used to identify any gaps in the market that may provide opportunities for launching a new product or

service. It might also be used to gauge whether or not there is a demand for a specific product or service. Remember, you will need to analyse your own data so the quality of that data will influence the results.

It is unlikely that you will be able to visit the EU member state that you will want to launch to as part of this project so you will need to collect as much first-hand information as possible from the business you are studying in the UK to help you consider options for the future. Your choice of method will influence the type of data that you will be able to collect. You may also be able to get in touch with EU citizens who have experience of living or working in that member state to tell you about it.

Questionnaire or survey

A popular and relatively easy method of collecting data is to use a questionnaire. You may wish to use a questionnaire to ask UK businesses in the same market as your business about their product and service availability in Europe to help inform your strategy or to gain specific information from individuals with experience of that country. You will need to consider the usefulness of quantitative information (facts and figures) and qualitative information (judgements and opinions) to help you. More information about how to design questionnaires for this purpose is available in Unit 13 on pages 161–3.

Remember you will be expected to analyse the effectiveness of your strategy to launch the new product or service and your conclusions should be supported by the collection of appropriate and relevant data. If your questionnaire is flawed then it is likely that your results will also be flawed so checking that your questionnaire is working effectively is time well spent.

Discussion with individuals in your chosen business

It may be possible, even in the medium- or large-sized business that you have chosen to study, to interview and have a discussion with a representative from the business about what they feel attracts customers to their current products and/or services and any plans that they may already have for expansion in to other EU member states. If this is not possible face to face you may be able to contact them via telephone or online (remember to check this with your teacher first). You will need to carefully plan how the discussion should take place as they are likely to be very busy and therefore may not have a lot of time to spare.

You will need to have a set of open ended questions that will help guide the discussion. For example, you could discuss existing products they offer in the UK that they feel have been successful or you might even be able to ask their opinion about the ideas you are currently working on. In addition, by looking at the results from your questionnaire you could ask them to comment on the data that you have collected so far.

Visits to your chosen business

A visit to your chosen business can also be a really useful way of collecting primary research material. Many large businesses have visitor centres or education officers who may be able to answer any questions that you have. Again, like the questionnaire or discussion, make sure you are prepared and know exactly what information you are looking for and why. It will be useful to collect background data on the business you are studying and where it currently trades in Europe so that you can ask specific questions that will inform your strategy. You may wish to use a survey in individual departments of the business as part of your visit to find out information about how European expansion would impact on their day-to-day working practices.

Discussions with agencies

There are a number of different agencies both general and specific to help your UK business with its expansion into the EU market. Using websites of such agencies or visiting them to get information will help to inform your strategy. Agents such as the Euro Info Centre (www.euro-info.co.uk), Business in Europe (www.businessineurope.nu) and Business Linx Slovakia (www.businesslinx.sk) provide information services for businesses wishing to expand into Europe.

Considerations to take into account

There are many wide-ranging considerations to be taken into account when launching a new product or service in European markets including:

* logistics
* promotional activity, including branding
* ICT provision
* transport and distribution networks
* training and development of workforce
* skills of workforce
* financial context – sources of finance and budgeting
* communications both internal and external to the business
* language, culture and custom
* regional assistance
* monetary framework
* trade policy
* management resources.

You may be able to think of other considerations but the list above will help you to start researching and understanding your UK business now and as a result of the launch. **You will need to consider those that relate directly to your chosen business context.**

Logistics

Logistics refers to the operation and movement of goods and services in the business. You will need to consider how the business is going to operate in the EU market. Will it be based there? Will goods be made there or exported to the other country? Who will manage the venture in the EU market?

Promotional activity

What kind of promotional activity already takes place in the EU market? Which are the most common and well-known methods of media to be used for advertising and promotional purposes? Are offers such as 'buy one, get one free' common? Are promotional methods such as sponsorship or leaflet drops the most effective or would email and website promotions be better? You may find it useful to revisit Unit 13 on page 153 to reconsider the promotional methods that are available to businesses in general. You will also need to take into account differences in the type of promotional activity and the use of media in different member states. Italy and Ireland, for example, both have strict advertising codes designed to protect children.

You may find it useful to revisit Unit 13 on page 153 to reconsider the promotional methods that

CASE STUDY

The Children's Advertising Code in Ireland

In Ireland, the Children's Advertising Code was implemented on 1 January 2005. This code seeks to control the way that advertising is promoted to children in terms of the products or services that children may want to buy and at the times that the advertising is broadcast such as between children's programmes. The code sets out a number of guidelines that must be followed by businesses wishing to advertise in Ireland including that advertising must:

- respect human dignity and not discriminate on the grounds of gender, marital status, family status, sexual orientation, religion, age, disability, race or membership of the Traveller community
- not deceive or make false claims
- make clear what parts, elements or accessories are included as part of a purchase and which ones are only available at extra cost
- provide information for a sufficient amount of time for children to read or be explained clearly for children under the age of six
- give an indication of the size of the product and whether or not batteries are needed/supplied
- provide assembly instructions
- not encourage children to pester adults to buy the product or service for them

- include children wearing appropriate safety equipment, e.g. helmets when cycling
- not show children using the Internet without an adult being present
- not show children displaying anti-social behaviour, e.g. bullying, taunting or teasing unless the advertising is designed specifically for that purpose
- only show fast food with a warning message, e.g. 'should be eaten in moderation as part of a balanced diet'
- not show celebrities or sports stars being used to promote food or drink products unless the advert is part of a health or education campaign
- only show advertising for confectionery products with a warning message 'snacking on sugary foods and drinks can damage teeth'.

These points represent just some of the Children's Advertising Code that must be followed by any business considering trading in Ireland so more care needs to be taken when advertising products to children there. Ireland isn't the only member state to place restrictions on children. Italy does not permit children under 14 to be used in TV commercials or promotions.

✓ 1. Why do you think Ireland introduced an advertising code for children?

✓✓ 2. What are the advantages and disadvantages to children and parents of having such a code?

✓✓ 3. What are the advantages and disadvantages to producers of products and services aimed at children of having such a code?

✓✓✓ 4. Give a judgment based on the evidence you have already collected, as to whether or not such a code is likely to be effective or desirable throughout the EU member states.

ICT provision

There are still wide differences between access to ICT in the UK and other EU member states in terms of access by businesses to ICT and access by individuals. Both may affect the promotional methods and communication channels used by UK businesses planning to launch a new product or service. Figure 15.15 below shows the differences in Internet access between the EU member states. A UK business launching a new product or service in Greece, Italy or Poland may decide not to use Internet promotion for their product or service as so few members of those populations have regular Internet access.

The use of broadband connections also has implications for businesses moving into the EU (see Figure 15.16). This is because high-speed communication may be an essential part of trading efficiently to let potential customers know what the business has to offer. If Internet connections are slower than broadband speed then communication devices need to be able to be adapted so that potential clients are not lost.

Transport and distribution networks

You will need to consider how the product or service is to be launched within the EU market – with products you will need to analyse whether

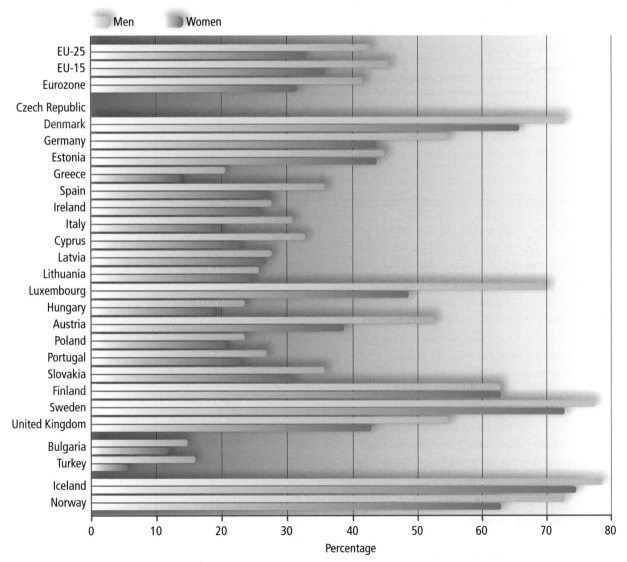

FIGURE 15.15 *Individuals regularly using the Internet in 2004*

Source: Europe in Figures Eurostat Yearbook 2005

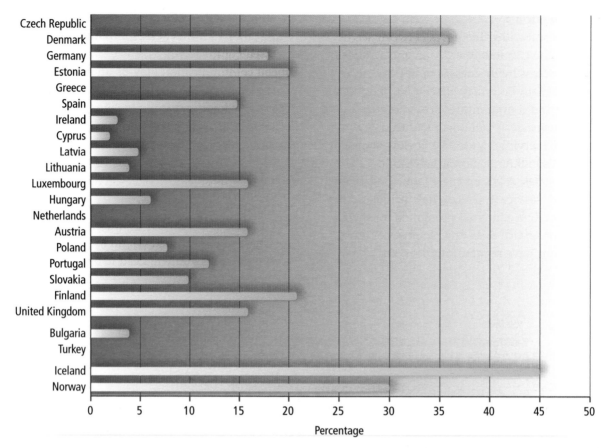

FIGURE 15.16 *Households with a broadband connection in 2004*   Source: Europe in Figures Eurostat Yearbook 2005

they should be made in the UK and be exported or whether a new factory should be set up in the new EU market. It is important to take into account currency differences and additional costs. Bratislava in Slovakia is 848 miles away from Southampton in the UK and the average pay per year in Slovakia for a full-time worker was €4,500 or £3,000 (at a rate of £1= €1.50) in 2002. If this pay level were to continue to be this low it may be cheaper to make the products in Slovakia than it would be to export them there.

Transport will also need to be considered within the EU member state itself. For example, there are around 800 miles to travel from Cherbourg in Northern France to Nice in the South. The further the distance that a product has to travel, the higher the final price the customer will need to pay in order to make a profit for the business.

The choice of appropriate distribution network should also be considered – retailer, agent,

wholesaler, direct to customer are all options that could be chosen. You will need to analyse the implications of the methods that you choose for your launch. It will depend on the type of product or service that you are offering and how perishable or difficult that good or service is to offer.

Training and development of workforce

You will need to consider the training for the workforce that is available in the EU country that you are going to launch in. The level of education needed to sell the product or service will also depend on how technical a product or service actually is. If you are selling a technical product, specialist knowledge and skills may be needed in the language of that member state but if it is more simple then only the packaging may need to be translated into the appropriate language. If the product or service is being launched by an agent or other third party, how much communication do you need to have with that agency and what level of English is required for the business to be able to communicate with them? Should employees be trained in the EU member state's language or new additional staff employed who are able to speak the language already? Remember there may be ESF or other funding available to help with any training needed if the business is supporting one of the ESF objectives.

Skills of workforce

The skills of the workforce are really important as already outlined in the section on training and development as the workforce can make the difference between success and failure in an EU member state. Local knowledge of the EU member state should help the business to understand what consumers want and to target the appropriate audience. IT skills may be an issue in countries where Internet usage is low and training may be needed to update the skills of new employees from those member states. If the product or service is technical there will need to be an assessment of the workforce available in that member state to see if there are workers already skilled or whether new employees need to be trained to the appropriate level. The skills of the current workforce that is employed by the business will also be important and their capability to work in the EU market. The business should do some kind of skills-gap analysis to find out the level and type of skills that already exist within the business before they consider recruiting new people. For more information on how to do this see Unit 16 of this book on page 326.

Financial context

You have already learned in section 15.2.2 about different sources of finance and the availability of special funds to expand into Europe with government and EU support. The business should also consider asking its bank or shareholders for extra funds to expand or even ways of working with businesses already operating within the EU member state to launch the product. Different regulations and banking/accounting principles that are trying to be standardised across the EU are still very different so the business will need

to consider the amount of money available and the amount of tax or other business costs that might need to be payable to the EU member state. When setting budgets the business will need to take into account any special challenges that may affect the business trading in the EU, for example the implications of a peak in trade due to holiday makers in the summer months and a decline in the winter. Budgets need to take into account such peaks and troughs to avoid cash flow problems.

Communications

Once trading in the EU, decisions will need to be made about how communications should take place within the business such as the use of ICT for email communication, business website or mobile phone exchange. Having powerful IT equipment may allow the tracking of goods or instant reporting of business deals so that the UK business can keep up to date with progress from the UK. Communications external to the business relate to how the business communicates with its suppliers, distribution network and indeed customers. Decisions will need to be made about promotional material and the extent to which English may be used together with the EU member state's own language including regional languages such as those spoken in countries like Spain. The style of the communications should very much represent the image and style of the business so must be managed carefully. For more information and ideas on promotional messages see Unit 13.

Language, culture and custom

You have already been made aware of the 20 official languages in the EU and the need for any UK business seeking to expand to take such differences into account. Getting local advice will help with any subtle changes that happen when translating phrases from English into another EU language. Traditional phrases such as 'raining cats and dogs' make sense in UK but if translated literally into another language may seem very confusing! Being sensitive to cultural differences should also avoid citizens of other EU states being offended by inappropriate campaigns or products being promoted. The more citizens feel that the business is for them, the more they are likely to buy from it.

The British butcher abroad

Christopher Robertson moved to Prague in 1995 to set up a butcher's business selling traditional English products to English people living in the Czech Republic. He took a big risk by selling cuts of English-style meat that were produced by Czech butchers under licence. He took a loan from his brother to help him, but luckily was able to pay it off.

Robertson made a profit from the beginning by selling to restaurants and building up his own retail customers by offering a home delivery service. He operated with very few overheads until 2003 when he took over an existing butcher's shop that was modernised to comply with EU standards. By selling to restaurants and to former UK citizens living in the Czech Republic he was successful. Twenty per cent of his trade is now former UK citizens and 40 per cent to hotels. The rest of his trade is sold to Czechs for whom he supplies both English and Czech products, partly because he is able to offer products in a highly competitive market at up to 20 per cent cheaper than his rivals.

✓ 1. What was the unique selling point that made Christopher successful in the Czech Republic?

✓ 2. What helped him to establish his business?

✓✓ 3. What effect would keeping overheads low have on any business moving to an EU member state and what are the problems or benefits associated with this?

Regional assistance

Regional assistance, as you have already learned within this chapter, may be available in certain areas of the EU as part of ESF or EIF funding. There may also be support from the chamber of commerce that operates in that EU member state to help UK businesses to invest or promote their products or services in that member state. There are also often trading relationships between member states and the UK to provide further regional assistance such as the British-Estonian Chamber of Commerce that specifically makes links between Great Britain and Estonia (www. becc.ee). You will need to investigate these types of regional assistance and their availability within the EU market that your business will launch into.

Monetary framework

You have already become aware that part of the EU trades within the eurozone and part of it is outside the area. There are implications for UK business trading with the EU as a result of the changes in currency that take place on a daily basis. Businesses entering into a contract with another EU member state must be sure that they are not going to suffer as a result of currency fluctuations.

Trade policy

The WTO was set up in 1995 and developed from GATT (General Agreement on Tariffs and Trade). The World Trade Organization (WTO) and General Agreement on Tariffs and Trade (GATT) have already been described within this chapter and it will be up to you to investigate any trade restrictions or policy arrangements that may affect your business launching its new product or service into the member state. The latest up-to-date information can be found using the resources listed in the bibliography and looking back through section 15.2.2.

Management resources

Management resources can be looked at from two perspectives: physical resources including access to people and finance and intellectual resources such as the planning, organising and co-ordination needed by a UK business to move into another EU member state. You will need to make decisions about whether or not your business can move into other European markets unaided or whether they should take over or merge with another European competitor to work on the project together.

If a business commits to a sell in another currency and then the value of that currency weakens, the UK business will lose out. For example, the business contracts to sell a pot of jam for €1.50 when the euro rate is €1.50 to the £1.00. If that rate then changes to €1.75 to the £1.00 (the euro is weaker) the business will lose out because the amount that it will receive when converted back is lower. This is demonstrated in the table below.

SELLS FOR	RATE	AMOUNT IN £
€1.50	€1.50 to the £1.00	£1.00
€1.50	€1.75 to the £1.00	£0.88

This means that the UK business has to sell for 12 pence less per jar which could run into many thousands of pounds. It is likely, though, that UK businesses will not be able to avoid trading in other currencies as those other EU member states will not want to trade in £ sterling so they may need to set up bank accounts that are traded exclusively in euros or the currency of the appropriate member state. Banking is also an issue as there may not be a British bank trading in the member state that they are going into so the UK business will need to make arrangements for how banking and payments should be made.

There is a common trend for businesses wishing to trade in the EU to buyout and run subsidiaries within the member state. Even large American businesses have tried to do this. eBay bought Skype (an Internet-based communications company) trading in Luxembourg and Estonia for $2.6 billion in December 2005 as they felt that Estonian talent had significantly helped the progress of Skype in the 225 countries that it is present in throughout the world.

CASE STUDY
Marks and Spencer

In October 2005, Marks and Spencer announced its intention to start opening shops in Tallinn, the capital of Estonia, and it has already found the right premises. It believes it has the appropriate resources and management expertise to also open additional stores in other cities in Estonia including Riga and Vilnius. Marks and Spencer has been a European enterprise from its very beginnings as Michael Marks, one of the original founders of Marks and Spencer was from Poland! Marks and Spencer, however, have had a difficult history in Europe so trading with Estonia is hoped to be the start of new beginnings and careful management expertise will be required to take the project forward.

In France its enterprises were sold off and in Belgium and Germany subsidiaries were shut down as a result of big losses up until 2001. The losses that it made in Europe caused legal proceedings between Marks and Spencer and the UK government when Marks and Spencer claimed the losses against its tax bill in the UK. This resulted in legal action that went before the European Court of Justice who ruled that this was indeed possible and that Marks and Spencer could offset losses from other EU member states against its profits made in the EU. This was a reclaim of over £30 million. Reclaiming such a loss was bad for the UK government who want to use the tax money as part of its budget but is good for the company who said it is perfectly acceptable to make such reclaims as they are now free to set up their shops in any EU member state that they wish.

✓ 1. Why might Marks and Spencer see Estonia as a good place to start trading in the EU again?
✓✓ 2. How did the European Court of Justice ruling affect their task burden and what are the problems associated with this?
✓✓✓ 3. Give a judgement as to what this might mean for other companies trading over the whole of the EU and why might EU governments be worried.

To check that you have completed all the research that is necessary to produce your plan of action use the checklist below to help you make sure that you have collected a lot of the data you will need.

Researching your market checklist

1 The potential market

a) What are the characteristics and type of customers likely to buy from you including age, gender, income etc?

b) Where do competitors of your business in the UK export to in the EU?

c) How much competition do you have in the EU member state(s)?

d) How do your competitors promote their service or product in that member state?

e) What are the strengths and weaknesses of your competitors?

2 Demand

a) How many people are likely to want to buy products from you – number of people and value of sales?

b) Is demand for this product or service increasing or decreasing?

3 Product or service

a) Are there any legal restrictions on the selling of this product or service?

b) Are there any differences between the UK and the other member state(s) in terms of the actual product itself, e.g. Cyprus, Ireland, Malta and the UK all use square three-pin plugs on electrical products whereas the rest of the EU only have two-pin plugs.

c) Are there any other ways that the product needs to be adapted to make it more accessible to the EU market?

d) Does the name translate well from English to another language?

4 Distribution and payment

a) Which is the best way to sell this product or service, e.g. website, retailer, wholesaler?

b) What is the climate in the country and distance from the UK – will this affect distribution?

c) Can the product be made in the UK and be sold in the EU market or will it need to be made or offered in the member state that it is being launched to?

d) Is it easy to get to the country from the UK at short notice?

e) How many extra costs will be needed to be covered, e.g. transport or insurance?

f) How will payment be made and what will the payment terms be? Is it possible for customers to buy products on credit with you and what will the interest terms be?

g) Which guarantees and warranties are applicable?

h) Can you speak the language(s) spoken in that member state and if not do you have access to translation facilities or agents to help with this?

You may also find it useful to produce a SWOT analysis at this point to gather your thoughts on the key strengths, weaknesses, opportunities and threats that your UK business has when launching a product or service in European markets. For more guidance on how to do this see Unit 10 on pages 66–7.

15.2.5 Production of a plan of action

You will need to produce a plan of action for your business including a summary of how the business will deal with the many issues it needs to consider when launching a new product or service in European markets. The summary needs to come out of your research and analysis that you have collected as part of the unit and will include the issues that relate to your chosen business context from the list below:

* **Promotional activity** – how the business will promote the new product or service taking into account methods it currently uses and those that would be appropriate in the European market. Remember to consider advertising differences between member states and the effect of cultural and language differences. You may also wish to consider strategies for pricing and the type of image that you want to be used as part of promotion based on the potential demand and characteristics of your target market. Use information from Unit 13 on pages 154–6 to help you.

* **Transport and distribution networks** – how the business will transport and distribute the new product or service including any constraints or transport issues relating to that member state such as size, population density, availability of distributors and need for local knowledge.

* **Production of a new product or service** – whether production can be carried out in the UK and then be transported across to the European member state or if a production plant or service centre will be opened there to lower costs. You will also need to take into account any manufacturing changes that need to take place before a UK product can be exported to the EU including the use of a two-pin instead of three-pin plug.

* **Legal and workforce issues** – you have learned about different skills, training and pay differentials between the member states. You will also need to take into account usual working life and national holiday differences that may affect your workers. You will need to consider the effect of these and the likely income of potential consumers who may want to buy your product. From a legal perspective you should also consider the different ways that member states operate and which products are legal in differing member states.

* **Customer service** – you will need to provide details of the customer service levels that you are expecting to provide and how these will be organised. You will need to consider different languages that may be appropriate, different levels of service and payment plans as well as policies for returns and guarantees as part of after sales service.

As part of your plan of action you will need to give clear summary guidelines for your UK business including timescales as applicable. You may find it useful to use a table like the one provided below or to make one of your own. Using a summary table like this will help you to focus your ideas clearly.

Action needed	Resources needed for achievement or additional notes	Date for achievement

15.2.6 Evaluation of the strategy

With the strategy complete and the action plan drawn up the last part of this unit asks you to evaluate the likely effectiveness of your strategy. There are a number of considerations that you should take into account.

Different approaches

You will need to consider whether or not the launch of your new product or service will require different approaches in different EU member states including the UK based on issues such as language, cultural and social differences.

Aims and objectives

You should think about what your strategy will mean in terms of your business' current short-term and longer-term aims and objectives. It may help you to consider expansions into Europe by companies such as Marks and Spencer, Ebay and Cadbury. By launching a product or service in Europe the business will need to invest a lot of time and resources so it will need to be sure it is the right move for them.

External influences

How will external influences such as changes in market conditions in the UK or in Europe affect your chosen business' strategy? At this point you should consider the effect of the World Trade Organization (WTO) and any possible increase or decrease in tariffs, quotas or bans on imports to the EU. There is the possibility that more countries will join the eurozone and that may include the UK at some future date which may affect the strategy.

Any events that happen in the world may also have an influence on the strategy including acts of terrorism or natural disasters and these may increase or decrease the effectiveness of your strategy. Changes in the way that consumers purchase products or bad publicity about health effects can all change the effectiveness of a planned strategy. You may find it useful to consider the external influences section of Unit 13 on pages 187–91, which gives further details on external influences that may change market conditions in the UK or Europe including:

* social, cultural and economic
* ethical and environmental
* legislative and regulatory
* pressure groups
* competitors
* technology.

Theory into practice

Produce a PEST analysis of the key external influences that you think may affect the likely effectiveness of your strategy. What might happen in the near or longer term future that may affect your strategy? More information on how to do this is found in Unit 10 on pages 67–8.

The effect on the home market

Any business moving abroad will also need to consider the effect on its operations in the UK and the possible damage that such a move might make as operations and management are neglected and the disruption that might be associated with it. If a business is concentrating on resources abroad it may lead to uncertainty for employees still based in the UK and cause them to feel demotivated if they feel time and resources should be spent improving their working lives and products.

There is always a limit to what can be done by a business so inevitably there will be an opportunity cost for the business of launching a product or service into a European market. The business will need to be sure that the costs of such a move do not outweigh the benefits of moving abroad. The business should also take into account issues associated with diseconomies of scale. This is when a business starts to get too big so that the price to make an individual product starts to go up rather than down like economies of scale. Diseconomies of scale commonly occur as a result of demotivation in staff so they become less productive and problems of communication, co-ordination and control between one branch of the business and another occur or increased costs.

There are cultural issues for the business of expanding from the UK to Europe as working culture in the UK may be very different to that of the EU member state. This means that trying to work in the same way abroad may not be possible and therefore changes in the UK may need to happen for this to take place.

Some top tips for writing your strategy and evaluating it

* You will need to explain, analyse and make judgements about the characteristics of the European market as a whole and include specific reference to the EU member state that you are considering for the expansion and its impact on UK businesses. You will need to clearly explain the evidence that you present in detail. The higher the level of detail and breadth within your work, the higher the likely grade you should achieve.

* Your launch strategy needs to contain appropriate aims and objectives through which you strategy is written. You should use background information on the various types of activity that are currently in place within the business in the UK, with the EU as a whole and in particular the member state that you are examining to help you decide on an appropriate strategy.

* You must promote a new product or service for a medium- to large-sized business into a European market and have a choice of 24 member states from which to choose. Investigate the market of the member state very carefully to ensure that your business does not already operate there.

* You will need to include appropriate research material of a primary and secondary nature including references – you may find it helpful to include some of this material as appendices at the back of your portfolio.

* You will need to critically evaluate and draw logical conclusions by making judgements about the likely effectiveness of your expansion strategy. Your arguments must be clearly based on the research and analysis that you have collected.

* Produce a set of recommendations including improvements and future updates for the strategy.

* You will be assessed on your grammar, punctuation and spelling so ask a friend to proofread your work for you to spot any typing errors.

Knowledge check

1. What are the four stages of the strategic planning cycle?

2. What is meant by the EU-15 and EU-25?

3. In which year did the EU-15 expand to become the EU-25?

4. What percentage of the world's population did the EU represent in 2004?

5. Name two problems associated with an ageing population in the EU?

6. Outline one benefit to a business of setting up in a densely populated member state?

7. The EU exports more than it imports – true or false?

8. What are the advantages and disadvantages to businesses of different EU member states having different levels of income, e.g. in 2002 Danish full-time workers were receiving 9½ times as much as full-time workers in Slovakia?

9. How could a UK business benefit from high levels of unemployment in another EU member state?

10. What was the purpose of setting up the Single Market in 1992?

11. Name one other market, other than the airline market, that has significantly benefited from EU expansion.

12. What is meant by the eurozone?

13. Give two advantages and two disadvantages of the UK joining the eurozone.

14. What is meant by a European Directive? Give examples of two.

15. Why was the European Social Charter introduced?

16. What is meant by tariffs and quotas?

17. How do fluctuations in exchange rates between UK and eurozone member states affect UK businesses trading there?

18. What is meant by the ESF and what does it do?

19. Name three benefits to a UK business of taking over a business trading in another EU member state.

20. How many official languages are there in the EU and what are the implications for businesses trading in Europe of having to work with those languages?

Resources

Books

Artis, M.J. and Lee, N. (1997) *The Economics of the European Union (2nd Ed) Policy and Analysis*, OUP

Dyker, D.A. (1999) *The European Economy (2nd Ed)*, Longman

Healey, N.M., ed. (1995) *The Economics of the New Europe*, Routledge

Hill, B. (2001) *The European Union (4th ed)*, Heinemann

Welford, R. and Prescott, K. (1998) *European Business*, Pitman

Journals

Business Review

Websites

www.europa.eu.int
Official European Union site and source of the Eurobarometer Survey 54 – Europeans and Languages

www.eubusiness.com
EU independent trading advice site

www.prb.org
Population reference bureau

www.uktradeinfo.com
HM Revenue and Customs Statistics

www.fedtrust.co.uk
Federal Trust for Education and Research

www.euractiv.com
EU news and policy online

www.dti.gov.uk/ewt
DTI's website for Europe and World Trade

www.ambafrance-uk.org
French embassy in the UK

www.theeconomist.com
The Economist site

www.europarl.eu.int
European Parliament

www.dti.gov.uk/er/europe/directives.htm
DTI site with employment related EU directives

www.europeanlawmonitor.com
European Law Monitor

www.ecic.ie
European Consumer Centre (Dublin)

www.euroconsumer.org.uk
Euro Consumer

www.european-voice.com
European Voice – independent website view of
the EU

www.spain-info.com
Information about Spain

www.the-backpacking-site.com
Backpacking site describing EU and world
countries

www.anyworkanywhere.com
Site giving details about working throughout the
world

http://myeurope.eun.org
My Europe

www.eurolang.net
European languages site

www.wto.org
World Trade Organization

www.cec.org.uk
European Commission in the UK

www.eu2005.gov.uk
UK Presidency of the EU 2005 (useful source of
background data on the 25 EU member states)

www.eurochambres.be
European Chambers of Commerce

www.chamberonline.co.uk
British Chambers of Commerce

www.britishchambers.org.uk
British Chambers of Commerce

www.uktradeinvest.gov.uk
UK Trade and Investment website

www.link2exports.co.uk
Export Zone website

http://mkaccdb.eu.int
Gives a Market Access Database and Trade
Barriers Database for EU businesses selling across
the world

www.bized.ac.uk
Business Studies website with lots of detailed
information

www.emcc.eurofound.eu.int
European Monitoring Centre on Change

www.euromonitor.com
Euro Monitor site

http://news.ft.com/home/uk
Financial Times website

Training and development

This unit contains six elements:

16.2.1 **Devising a strategy**

16.2.2 **The business context within which the strategy will take place**

16.2.3 **Planning the strategy**

16.2.4 **Research of the strategy and analysis of the information that is collected**

16.2.5 **Production of a plan of action**

16.2.6 **Evaluating effectiveness**

Introduction

This optional unit allows you to combine knowledge that you have already acquired through your AS studies (Units 2 and 4) and during A2 (Unit 10) and put it into the context of training and development. To build upon and explore this knowledge further you will need to construct a training and development strategy for two functional areas that relates to a business you have chosen and the context within which it operates. Common examples of functional areas that you could choose include production, finance, sales, marketing or human resources. You will need to select two functional areas from a chosen business that will allow you to research and analyse their training and development practices.

As part of the unit you will consider why organisations train their staff, different training methods and initiatives that are available and the constraints that there may be on any plans. You will need to conduct research into the business itself and collect data on the current skill levels in your organisation by producing a skills-gap analysis and be able to critically evaluate the provision of training and development that is offered.

16.2.1 Devising a strategy

Devising a strategy is an essential part of any plan and like any other part of the business that needs to be planned for, training and development needs a strategy too. For this process to happen there are a number of steps that must be worked through and these include the gathering of relevant information and its analysis. The key areas that need to be considered when gathering information for the planning phase are:

* understanding the business environment within which the strategy will take shape

* planning the strategy

* researching the business environment to inform strategy development

* analysing the gathered data to inform the development of the strategy

* producing a plan of action based on research and analysis

* monitoring and evaluating various aspects of their strategy with a view to recommending improvements and future updates to the strategy.

Each of these areas will be explored in detail in this unit so you will be able to build up a clear picture of training and development in the organisation and specifically within your two chosen functional areas. Remember that you will need to collect background data for both of these areas.

You will need to consider what is meant by strategy and the strategic process itself. A strategy develops as a result of you considering the longer-term training and development needs of the organisation and the practicalities of working towards the achievement of that strategy. This means you will be involved in producing a long-term training and development strategy for each of your functional areas. To do this you will need to consider the strategic planning cycle (Figure 16.1).

The strategic planning cycle allows you to consider where you are now in terms of what they are doing and the training and development they offer. By thinking about what is to happen in the future gaps can be identified and plans made to fill those gaps. The secret to any planning cycle is of course to have a review of progress and as a result of the review the cycle starts again.

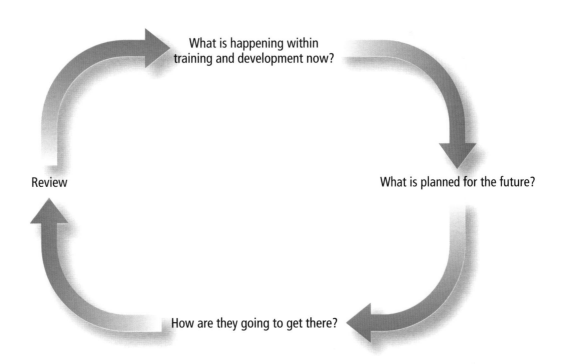

What is happening within training and development now?

What is planned for the future?

Review

How are they going to get there?

FIGURE 16.1 *Strategic planning*

16.2.2 The business context within which the strategy will take place

A successful business is one that has access to well-maintained and controlled resources such as finance or materials. Human resources are one type of resource and like any other, need careful planning in order that the business has the *right people* with the *right skills* at the *right time* in order to meet its objectives. There are lots of ways to make sure that this happens including excellent recruitment procedures and giving people training to make sure they are able to give their maximum effort to the working environment. Training can be something as simple as giving someone time to work through a training manual whilst doing their job. This is known as on-the-job training. Or it can be off-the-job training such as attending a degree or professional course in subjects like accounting or engineering. Both forms of training require resources and planning.

There also needs to be a structure to the development and training of staff to ensure that the money spent on training and its outcomes are managed and used to the maximum efficiency. It would be wasteful to send five people on the same training course if only one person needs to go. By sending one person and asking that person to share the information they have learned, an organisation can benefit from training and development in a way that suits both individual and organisational needs. The organisation will be happy because everyone will be suitably trained, the individuals happy as they have received training and the person who attended the training and then shared their knowledge may be able to gain extra responsibility and recognition as a result.

There are a number of important reasons why businesses train their workforce and these include:

* meeting departmental and overall business objectives
* increasing productivity
* helping introduce new technology
* improving health and safety
* creating a more flexible workforce
* helping employees take on new job roles
* improving job performance and motivation
* satisfying UK and European legislation in areas such as employment and equal opportunities.

Meeting departmental and overall business objectives

You have already learned about aims and objectives throughout your applied business course but they are repeated briefly below.

The terms 'aim' and 'objective' are often used interchangeably as if they mean the same thing. However, they actually mean different things! The aim of the business is the overall purpose of the business, for example to make a profit or expand. Many large organisations write their set of aims in a formal statement known as a Mission Statement. Mission statements can often be found on an organisation's website or in the company report.

To achieve the overall aims of a business you also need a set of objectives. You can think about aims and objectives like a shopping trip! An aim is the trip itself, e.g. to go shopping for food and the objectives are how you are going to get there, e.g. buy a bus ticket, take a list, go to the shop and pick up the items. The overall aims and objectives will be cascaded down to the relevant functional areas within businesses so they can be considered and practical steps taken to achieve them.

A small local window cleaning business might have the aim to expand the business, so the owner needs to think about how they are going to do this by drawing up a list of plans (objectives). Within the context of training, the window cleaner might consider the objective of recruiting and training a new employee to work for the business or providing existing employees with additional training in order to use new equipment and be able to do more work.

As part of your training and development strategy you will need to consider the following aims and objectives:

* aims and objectives of the organisation as a whole

* objectives given to each of the functional areas

* objectives amended into action points for training and development within those areas.

You will also remember that a judgement of how useful a set of objectives actually is will depend on how SMART they are. SMART means Specific, Measurable, Agreed, Realistic and Time-constrained. A SMART objective will contain all these elements and be able to be easily measured within an appropriate timescale, for example for the window cleaning business outlined above:

Aim: To expand the business

Objectives

1. To recruit and train one new member of staff by May 2007.
2. To provide basic health and safety training for the new member of staff on their first day of starting work.

Think it over...

Remembering what is meant by SMART and using your knowledge from AS and A2 so far, apply a SMART judgement to the overall business aims and objectives within the business you are studying. How does training fit within these aims and objectives? Which are the aims and objectives related to training and development?

CASE STUDY

SCOUTS

The Mission Statement for the Scouts is:

'The aim of the Association is to promote the development of young people in achieving their full physical, intellectual, social and spiritual potential, as individuals, as responsible citizens and as members of their local, national and international communities.'

The method of achieving the aim of the Association is by providing an enjoyable and attractive scheme of progressive training, based on the Scout Promise and Law, and guided by adult leadership.

For more information, see www.scouts.org.uk.

1. ✓ Using the mission statement, write a set of objectives that the Scouts may have in order to provide their 'progressive training' to achieve their aims.
2. ✓✓ What kind of training do you think scout or youth club leaders might have to undertake to perform their role? Analyse its impact.
3. ✓✓ Consider the issues that the Scouting Association may need to take into account when planning training for their scouts and scout leaders.

Training in the Scouts is about helping leaders to lead and training them to become better citizens for the future. Training is also an essential part of working towards objectives in industry because it helps employees to do their jobs as well as they possibly can.

If an organisation has the objective of being more profitable, training may be used to improve levels of customer service. This will increase repeat business and profits should go up as customers tell their friends and relatives about how good the organisation really is.

The same is true of the objective to expand. If people are able to do their jobs better it should be easier for the business to take advantage of expansion opportunities more quickly than it might have done otherwise. If the aim of the business is to expand, the different functional areas (such as sales, human resources or production) will have their own set of objectives. Departments that are given **devolved objectives** can benefit from training in their own specialist area, e.g. finance may need their staff to undertake professional training in order to complete their jobs.

If the aim is to expand, these are the objectives that go with that aim:

1. The objective for the sales department might be to increase sales by 10 per cent each year

2. The human resource department might have the objective of increasing staff numbers by 5 per cent over three years.
3. The production department might have the objective of becoming 20 per cent more productive (meaning being able to make more products in the same amount of time).

This is likely to mean that each of those departments will need to have training on offer in order to make these things happen. The sales department might need to train staff on new selling techniques in order to increase sales. The human resource department may need to provide training on the latest legal changes in recruitment when interviewing new staff and the production department may give training on new working methods to help staff produce more products per hour whilst retaining the same quality levels.

Another objective assigned to every department may be to retain staff. This means to keep them working within the organisation for as long as possible. Training is one way to do this because if employees feel that an interest is being taken in them, they are more likely to feel motivated and stay in their jobs. You will learn more about this in the section on training and motivation.

Key terms

Devolved objectives are objectives that have been passed down (cascaded) to departments from more senior management and implemented within functional areas.

Increased productivity

Productivity is the measurement of how much work an employee is actually doing in the time they are employed. A very simplistic example of this is to compare how many pairs of slippers different employees make in a factory in one week. The one who makes the most slippers in that week, in the same number of hours as the others, has been the most productive.

Training can help employees to become more productive as it can make them more efficient in terms of the quality and speed that they are able to carry out their work. A well-trained employee is likely to be one who is productive. This is because they are aware of the best procedures and methods to get the job done.

Think it over...

Consider your skills at report writing when you first started AS Applied Business. You were able to write essays but you have received further training during both the AS and A2 courses that should mean you are now more productive. The quality and number of words you write are likely to have increased and you should be able to produce more work in the same amount of time.

Training employees may also make it possible for them to multi-task to the point where fewer employees are needed as each employee is able to deal with a wide range of tasks. **Multi-tasking** means that employees are able to do a number of different tasks that are required by the organisation. By encouraging multi-tasking the business can become more efficient as people can be deployed to do jobs as and when necessary depending on levels of demand. It can also make the business more flexible as they can take on different types of work. For example, in a restaurant the person clearing tables may also be trained to prepare drinks, operate the dishwasher or even take orders.

Training is also likely to increase productivity from a motivational point of view as a well-trained employee is more likely to be satisfied in their work. If an employee feels satisfied in their work it is less likely that they will take time off due to illness or be away for other reasons. Reducing both sickness and general absence will make the organisation more productive.

In 2005, training was regarded by the government as so important that the Department of Trade and Industry produced a report on 'People, Strategy and Performance' (2005) that outlined the importance of training to make the UK more competitive in the future. Within the research survey it was outlined that there were training needs in the construction and health industries in order to make up skills-gaps.

Learning techniques such as time management and decision-making can help employees to organise themselves better and manage their time and workload more efficiently. Training in these areas can have a positive effect on employee performance.

Time-management training

Time-management training involves teaching employees how to prioritise their time and balance their workload. Employees are taught various techniques such as:

* how to organise their day
* how to prioritise tasks
* how to avoid interruptions
* how to manage stress and fatigue to save time
* how to plan telephone calls
* how to say no to too many tasks.

By learning how to manage these types of issues within the workplace it is possible to improve the time-management skills of employees.

Decision-making training

Decision-making training helps managers to use planning and decision-making tools to assist with critical path analysis or project management. Financial techniques may help managers to make decisions more quickly so this should help the company improve. You may have come across some decision-making techniques such as mind mapping or brainstorming or cause and effect diagrams. These are all aids to decision-making.

Introducing new technology

Training is an essential part of the modern business world across most organisations as a result of constantly changing technology. You are likely to have seen several changes in software that you have been using over the past few years and can recognise the difficulties that even small changes make to how something is done. Minimal training may be required for software changes but further training may be required if new systems are installed to make sure that they are used as efficiently as possible.

Training may also be required to help employees make greater use of software they are already using and in doing so increase the number of processes that they are able to carry out. It is suggested that packages such as Microsoft Word or Excel have a huge number of functions that are never accessed by users. Some people will use around 90 per cent of all the possible functions, others may use only 60 per cent. Using fewer software functions means that an employee may be missing out on being able to do their job more quickly and efficiently. Training can help employees make greater use of information technology and in doing so they should be able to make their jobs easier to do.

Training for technological change can also be important when considering jobs that may cease to exist as a result of changing technology or have been so changed that they are completely different to how they were before. Fewer front-of-house staff are needed now in banks and insurance companies as customers are able to buy their services online. As a result, this means more training is needed for employees supporting online services or in other areas of the workforce completely. Home shopping has taken off so employees may need to be trained in how to select and pack shopping to be delivered to homes rather than working on the tills.

With greater emphasis on the balance between working and home lives, employees may need to be trained on how to use technology to work from home using IT services such as web cams, email or online chat.

Training may also need to be offered to help employees prepare to cope with redundancy if their job no longer exists. Jobs that no longer exist in certain industries, such as manufacturing, have required employees to be retrained in other types of employment when their jobs have gone.

Theory into practice

Now consider the organisation you are studying and consider the following points for both of the functional areas you have chosen.

- Has any new technology been introduced recently or is there likely to be some technological updating soon?
- What training has been offered or will be offered to support this change?
- What are the consequences for your business if training is not adequately given in order to support the business?

You will need to consider such technological changes within a section of the justification for your strategy.

Improving health and safety

Some training such as basic health and safety is a legal requirement as part of the Health and Safety at Work Act 1974. This Act states that training must be given to employees to ensure they know what to do in the event of an emergency and how to make the workplace safer. It outlines that health and safety is not just the responsibility of the employer but is also the responsibility of every employee. In order to comply with the law, training must be given by the employer to make sure that employees know their responsibilities.

Health and safety training is also extremely important in organisations to ensure that employers try to reduce the amount of time each year that is lost to work related illness or injury. Every year, according to the Health and Safety Executive, 200 people are killed in accidents at work, over 1,000,000 people are injured and over 2,000,000 suffer illnesses caused or made worse by the type of work that they do. Empowering people to be responsible for their own health and promoting ways that they can look after themselves through training can have a very positive effect on employees from a physical and mental health point of view. Providing health and safety information and training can help the organisation to:

* prevent illness or injuries to employees therefore maintaining high productivity levels

* develop a culture where safe and healthy working is expected from everyone which can lead to an enhanced reputation for the company

* protect the health and safety of employees as part of the organisation's legal duty

* reduce the financial costs of accidents such as lost working time, fines or litigation

* reduce the number of damaged or substandard quality products being made.

All owners, managers and employees need health and safety training within the business, so there must be a clear health and safety policy implemented with training available to support it. The training needs to be delivered in a way that is accessible to the level and type of employees that the organisation deals with based on their experience and capabilities.

Basic induction training must be provided for new employees including first aid or evacuation in the event of a fire. Training that is given to existing employees to update them is known as **refresher training**.

FIGURE 16.2 *The training gap*

When considering health and safety training it is important to work out the skills and knowledge that are needed by employees to work in a healthy and safe way. These skills and knowledge should then be compared to those that the employee already has and the identified gap is the training that is needed to fill that gap (Figure 16.2).

Risk assessments (Figure 16.3) are an essential part of health and safety training as employees need to be trained to recognise the risks in their workplace and help to control those risks. You may have already seen a risk assessment that was given to you when you went on trips or work experience at school. Your teacher will have completed a risk assessment of any possible risks to your health or safety before you were able to go.

In addition to health and safety training, organisations may also offer additional training as part of contingency planning. This allows the organisation to fully plan for what to do in the event that there is a very serious incident that may need the business to move premises or even country in order to continue operating. Such planning has been used in incidents such as 9/11 (the Twin Towers in New York being blown up), earthquakes in Asia or the floods in New Orleans.

Think it over...

Consider the type of heath and safety training information available in the business and the two functional areas you are studying. Think about relevant health and safety issues within the workplace including which notices are on walls and access to information such as risk assessments?

What are the strengths of the training offered in the workplace?

How could it be improved?

You may find it useful to try to conduct some kind of mini survey amongst employees (ask your teacher first) to get an idea about how employees view health and safety training within the organisation.

HAZARD IDENTIFIED	PERSON AT RISK OF HARM	INITIAL RISK OF SERIOUS HARM	CONTROL MEASURES TO BE USED	FINAL LEVEL OF RISK
Fire	All staff	Medium	Staff to be made aware of fire evacuation procedures and be able to follow them	Low
Medical treatment	All staff	Medium	First aider to be present on the trip and a first aid box is to be carried. Mobile to be carried to call emergency services if needed	Low

FIGURE 16.3 *A risk assessment table*

Training for awareness of issues including mental health is an important part of health and safety provision. It is estimated that 16 per cent of adults of working age have a mental health problem (according to Richard Layard of the London School of Economics). Training within the workplace can help employees to recognise mental health problems and to try to reduce the chance of them occurring. This may be by trying to reduce stress in the workplace or by enhancing the home and work life balance. The same is true for other health issues such as drug taking, smoking or obesity. Training employees to cope with their own lives more adequately can lead to happier and more successful employees with lower absence rates.

Theory into practice

Some organisations use tools like quizzes to help employees identify their own issues in relation to stress or time management. By working out their level of stress from such a quiz they are able to identify whether or not they have a training need in this area. A mini non-scientific test has been designed for you below so you can see how such a test might work.

Review each of the statements and answer either True if the statement applies to you or False if it doesn't.

STATEMENT	TRUE?	FALSE?
It usual for me to have five portions of fruit and vegetables each day.		
I never drink more than three cups of tea, coffee or cola per day.		
I find it easy to relax and see the humorous side of life.		
I earn enough to satisfy my needs.		
I have good support from my family and friends or neighbours		
I enjoy working to deadlines and producing my college work.		
I take regular exercise.		
I always have time to relax and be myself.		
If I am feeling under pressure I know how to help myself unwind, for example by talking to my friends.		
I often find myself laughing and smiling because I see the funny side of things.		

Count up the number of times you answered false to the statements and work out your level of stress in this fun quiz accordingly.

6 or more
You are very stressed You need to chill out and take more time to be yourself.

3–5
You can suffer with stress at times but seem to be able to cope with it. Keep working on your relaxation techniques to try to make sure that you are as calm as possible.

1 or 2
You are so calm you are practically horizontal. Make sure that you are able to keep up with what is happening around you but maintain your relaxed attitude to study and home life.

This is not a scientifically tested quiz but it does give you an idea of the sorts of quizzes that may be used by organisations to help their employees.

Creating a flexible workforce

Creating a flexible workforce is important to any organisation because being able to adapt and change to new customer needs is a crucial driver for success. If an organisation cannot adapt and be flexible they are likely to struggle in the future as competitors may be able to adapt their ideas more quickly to gain **competitive advantage**. Keeping employees aware of the latest developments by training them makes it much easier for those employees to be flexible.

> ### Key terms
> *Competitive advantage* is something that one organisation has that makes it better than its competitors for example higher quality or better pricing.

CASE STUDY

An absence of training puts off shoppers

It is estimated that over 85 per cent of shoppers according to a National Opinion Poll survey in 2005 would leave a retail store if staff are not fully trained about the products that they are selling. This is a high number and reminds retailers how important training actually is, especially for staff dealing with customers face to face.

In spite of this, retailers often don't invest enough time or money into formal training as they want to save money by cutting training costs to keep their prices low in order to beat competition. However, if retailers invest in training in order to make staff more productive, it is likely that they will want to stay working for the organisation as they are likely to feel satisfied in their jobs, better trained and happy. Well-trained and happy staff are more likely to increase sales which helps to cover the cost of the training in the first place and therefore may be cheaper in the long run!

✓ 1. Why would a lack of training encourage 85 per cent of customers to leave a store?

✓✓ 2. Analyse what encourages retailers to cut training budgets rather than invest money in training.

✓✓✓ 3. To what extent might staff training lead to some retailers being more successful than their competitors?

Flexibility can also be applied to the ability to cover another employee's work. For example, if an employee is absent from their job due to illness, it is important that other employees are already trained in how to do that job so that the organisation does not have to disappoint customers or allow work to build up while they are off.

The same could be true of helping the organisation be able to cope with fluctuations in demand. If employees are trained in more than one area of the business they can be more flexible about where they are able to work.

Theory into practice

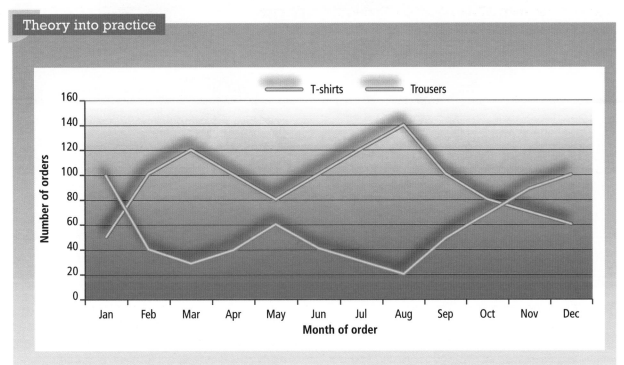

The above graph shows differing output levels expected for T-shirts and trousers by month. By making staff flexible so they are able to work in either section of the factory, the business is able to cope with changes in demand. In August, more employees will be needed to work in the T-shirt department and in December more staff are needed in the trouser section.

Consider the level of production for services or products that are produced within the two functional areas you are studying. Are there times in the year when these areas are very busy or very quiet? How flexible are staff in terms of covering each other's jobs?

It may also be possible to make the job itself more flexible by introducing techniques such as job rotation. This means that employees are moved around the organisation or along the production line to do different jobs at different times. For example, an employee on a cake production line might be working on packaging one day and on another with the ingredient loading section. This can make employees feel happier at work because they get more variety during their working week. A theme park may also use such techniques when considering their employees as they may choose to train employees to be able to work as ride operators of a number of rides, provide refreshments, keep the park clean or help customers with their parking. They will be **deployed** in whichever area of the park needs them on a rotational basis.

Job rotation increases flexibility

Helping employees take on new job roles or responsibilities

Making a job more interesting by including additional tasks and responsibilities is known as job enrichment, for example a junior hairdressing assistant in a salon who is usually responsible for sweeping the floors, making tea and answering telephone calls is given responsibility for the reception area and bookings. These are additional higher-level tasks that will challenge and motivate the employee.

As much as it is important to give these extra tasks to employees, it is also important to make sure that they feel adequately trained in order to be able to carry out these tasks and do them well. There is a saying that 'people are promoted to their level of incompetence' but this should never be allowed to happen. If someone is getting a promotion or increasing their responsibility, a good employer will seek to give them as much training and support as they need. Unless they get this support, they may feel stressed which could lead to illness and time away from their employment, which could ultimately lead to lower productivity and damaged profits. In November 2005, the Health and Safety Executive realised the seriousness of training for stress prevention and devoted a training conference to managing stress in the workplace.

CASE STUDY

Carole Nash Insurance

Carole Nash of Carole Nash Insurance demonstrates how an organisation can train an employee so successfully that they are able to take that training and develop it into a successful business of their own. Carole returned to work after she had brought up her children and was given a job looking after motorbike insurance. She was trained in how to do this and soon developed a level of competence.

Her employer then decided that this part of their insurance business was making a loss and that she was to be made redundant after four years of training. Rather than just give up, she took on the policy in her own name and started to trade as her own company. She built up the business by using the skills she had developed and has now turned it into a multi-million pound business. Carole's success was due to a lot of self-motivation but the skills that she developed with her employer also helped her to be in a position where she was able to develop her own business success.

Carole was extremely lucky that her employer provided training and opportunities for her that developed into such a success story. Spending four years on training and then for the business to decide it was making a loss and making Carole redundant could be seen as a poor use of resources and training from an organisational point of view, but an excellent investment in Carole herself.

For more information see www.carolenash.com.

✓ 1. How did Carole benefit from job enrichment?
✓ 2. Carole became good at her job as a result of training. What other personal quality helped her to be successful in her work?
✓✓ 3. What are the advantages and disadvantages for a business of giving training?
✓✓✓ 4. Give a judgement as to whether training was the key factor in Carole's success story.

Improving job performance and motivation

Making employees feel more motivated is likely to mean that they will want to stay working for that organisation for longer than they would have done otherwise, so they will be retained for longer. **Retention** levels within companies can be calculated by working out the labour stability rate for that organisation.

If a high percentage of employees are still working for the company a year later, they must have been retained and therefore be putting their skills and experience to good use.

Improving job performance and motivation can be achieved through training. This is because an employee who feels they have had interest taken in them and received time or money spent on training is more likely to be able to do their job better and be motivated to try their hardest.

It is based on the work of theorists such as Maslow, Mayo and Herzberg.

$$\text{Labour stability} = \frac{\text{Number of employees still in employment and were 1 year ago}}{\text{Number of employees in employment a year ago}} \times 100$$

Key terms

Retention means keeping employees at the workplace for as long as possible to benefit from their experience.

Training and Maslow

Maslow devised the notion of the hierarchy of needs which demonstrates the needs that need to be satisfied in order for an employee to start towards being motivated. The lower levels of the hierarchy are about fulfilling basic human needs and those needs become more complex the higher up the hierarchy an employee goes (see Figure 11.4 on page 116).

The lower needs relate to basic human needs such as eating, drinking and then on to feeling safe and secure. The higher up the hierarchy you go the more difficult the needs can be to satisfy and this is where training and education can help to satisfy those needs more fully.

From a motivational point of view, training is able to help satisfy the need for safety and security as trained employees are more likely to feel secure in their ability to do their jobs. For example, being trained to lift boxes properly or knowing what to do if there is a fire in the workplace.

Training can also be applied to social needs as trained employees are likely to mix and associate with others and therefore have those needs satisfied. They may need to work in teams and make contacts throughout the business or on a course outside the business. They may also be able to network and help themselves to progress with their career.

Self-esteem needs can be met by the achievement of a qualification that makes a trained individual feel that they are looked up to or well thought of.

Self-actualisation may be more achievable by training employees as they may be more open-minded about work methods and feel more satisfied with all aspects of their working life. Qualifications such as degrees or professional exams such as CIMA for management accountants may make them feel more prestigious.

Theory into practice

Produce a diagram of Maslow's hierarchy of needs and apply it to your experience of being a student or part-time worker. How easy is it to satisfy your basic and safety needs and what opportunities are there for social and self-esteem needs?

Now consider the organisation you are studying. Find out as much as you can about their working methods, training opportunities and the extent to which they cater for such needs. Write up your findings using notes from your diagram.

Training and Mayo

Mayo's theory devised from the Hawthorne Studies can be applied to motivation and training as training means that employees have an interest taken in them. Mayo's studies showed when lighting or heating were changed in the Western Electric Company's Hawthorne plant in Chicago, United States, workers worked harder. He concluded that this was because the interest that was taken in them made them feel more motivated to try to perform as well as they could and that they were working as part of a group.

One of the reasons for this, Mayo concluded, was that being motivated and productive at work involved people being able to have a say and influence over what they did in the workplace. Training can help achieve this by empowering employees to take more control over their working lives and to give people skills that will allow them to be able to make a difference in the workplace. Training employees to help them be more motivated may result in further benefits, such as suggestions for ways to improve work procedures and therefore higher quality. Employees can also be trained to work better in teams and therefore feel more satisfied.

Training and Herzberg

Herzberg believed in the idea that there are two types of influences on motivation in the workplace: hygiene factors and motivators. He based his findings on a study in the United States of 200 accountants and engineers. The different factors are outlined below.

Hygiene factors have to be met before employees can feel motivated:

* adequate pay
* safe working conditions
* fair management
* company policies and procedures
* relationships with other employees.

Motivators could only really be aspired to if those hygiene factors were met first:

* a sense of achievement
* opportunity for promotion
* challenge
* interest in the work
* being recognised for good work
* personal growth.

For example, employees will not feel a sense of achievement or challenge if they do not have safe working conditions. Training needs to be given for both the hygiene factors and the motivators. Training needs to be given to ensure employees feel safe in terms of what their job actually involves (their working conditions). Training also needs to be given from the point of view of advancement, progression and recognition to motivate.

Theory into practice

Using the data shown in the table below, answer the questions that follow.

	NUMBER OF EMPLOYEES EMPLOYED IN 2005	NUMBER OF EMPLOYEES WHO WERE EMPLOYED IN 2006 AND ARE STILL EMPLOYED IN 2006
Record company	500	350
Sandwich café	10	8
Mobile phone store	20	10

* Work out the labour stability rate for each company.
* Rank the companies in order of the best.
* Based on the information presented above, what effect might the size of a company have on their ability to retain staff?
* Consider the organisation you are studying and the two functional areas. What are the labour stability rates for each area and how do they compare? What is responsible for the differences and how could they be improved?

Hilton Hotels

In 2005, Hilton Hotels conducted a survey of over 1,800 Hilton International employees to find out their views on training and development at work. Thirty-seven per cent of employees surveyed said that being offered development opportunities was the most important factor in helping them to stay at Hilton. Fifty per cent said that professional development was very important to them even though it wasn't the deciding factor as to whether or not they stayed. This means that 87 per cent of staff thought that development influenced their decision to stay with Hilton in some form or other.

Further information from the survey also showed that 95 per cent of employees found they appreciated the chance that Hilton gave them to gain additional knowledge and that the skills learned in training activities could be used at work. Ninety per cent of employees found the e-learning programme offered by Hilton useful in relation to their professional development. This programme includes the Hilton University where you can study for many different types of courses whilst working for Hilton.

For more information see www.hilton.co.uk and visit the Careers and Development section of the Corporate Information page.

✓ 1. What is the key influence that makes people stay working for Hilton?

✓ 2. How does Hilton benefit when staff are retained for longer?

✓✓ 3. Analyse the benefits and costs involved when training staff.

✓✓✓ 4. Determine how important e-learning is to businesses like Hilton.

Job performance

When considering job performance it is important to recognise that different sectors provide different levels of training. According to the report from the Institute for Employment Studies in September 2004, public sector organisations and those involved in energy, utilities and finance are much more likely to provide training than those in textiles, manufacturing or retail. This is likely to affect the performance and motivation of employees within those sectors.

Job performance is also important when the organisation is being compared to others. There are lots of different ways for this to be done but a very popular method is **benchmarking**. Benchmarking seeks to provide data so that competitors within an industry can see how they are doing against the best possible performance in that industry. The best organisation in that industry is a standard that all other competitors should aspire to. Benchmarking can be used to compare many industries, for example the performance of universities using performance league tables and the manufacturers of parts for fridges and freezers by comparing the number of products made and their sales volume.

Training is a valuable tool when working to improve target benchmarks as employees are more able to cope with the demands of their jobs. Sometimes this is linked into performance related pay whereby employees are rewarded for undertaking training or gaining a qualification that is likely to enhance their performance in the workplace.

Training may also be used in the workplace to help areas of the business that are underperforming in comparison to other parts. For example, a sales team in one part of the country may not be performing as well as one in another part of the country, so training could be used to help the underperforming team do better. If the training is provided by an outside agency, one member of the team may go to a training event and then share what they have learned with other members of their team. This is known as cascading training. This training gap may also be met by allowing one of the successful sales team to help the other team by training them.

In terms of business performance, training is also important when considering skills needed for the future. Training is needed to prepare the business for the future so that it can move into new areas. A double glazing company may consider providing training in how to fit garage doors in order that they can expand into this complementary service at a later date.

Job performance is also likely to improve as employees gain recognised qualifications as their skill levels increase as well as their sense of commitment. This leads to a further increase in retention as trained and qualified employees are less likely to leave the organisation and work elsewhere.

Satisfying UK and European legislation in areas such as employment and equal opportunities

Training is essential for businesses to comply with both UK and European legislation. For example, health and safety training is essential as part of the Health and Safety at Work Act 1974, both when the employee starts their job and regularly during their employment. Training may be needed to ensure that employees understand and comply with policies related to issues such as equal opportunities in order to make sure that discrimination does not take place. Training needs to be given to both employees directly and to those supervisors and managers who are looking after them in the workplace.

CASE STUDY

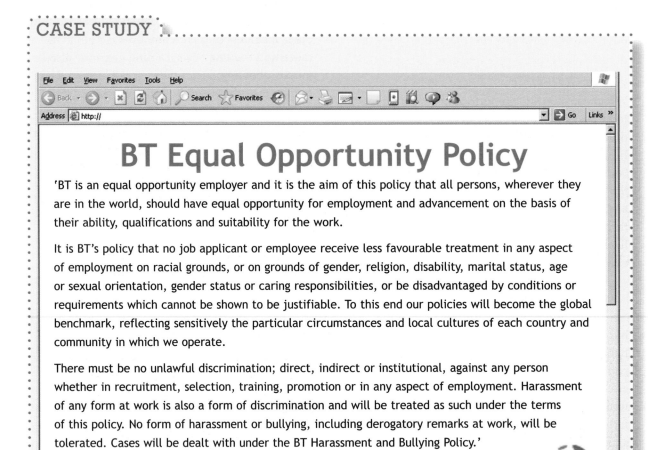

BT Equal Opportunity Policy

'BT is an equal opportunity employer and it is the aim of this policy that all persons, wherever they are in the world, should have equal opportunity for employment and advancement on the basis of their ability, qualifications and suitability for the work.

It is BT's policy that no job applicant or employee receive less favourable treatment in any aspect of employment on racial grounds, or on grounds of gender, religion, disability, marital status, age or sexual orientation, gender status or caring responsibilities, or be disadvantaged by conditions or requirements which cannot be shown to be justifiable. To this end our policies will become the global benchmark, reflecting sensitively the particular circumstances and local cultures of each country and community in which we operate.

There must be no unlawful discrimination; direct, indirect or institutional, against any person whether in recruitment, selection, training, promotion or in any aspect of employment. Harassment of any form at work is also a form of discrimination and will be treated as such under the terms of this policy. No form of harassment or bullying, including derogatory remarks at work, will be tolerated. Cases will be dealt with under the BT Harassment and Bullying Policy.'

Source: Extract from www.btplc.com

✓ 1. Within BT's policy it is also important that training is given to promote equal opportunities and that equal access for all is given to it. Within your organisation what type of training is offered as part of promoting equal opportunities and who provides that training?

✓✓ 2. How are employees able to access any type of training at BT? Discuss the strengths of providing training in this way.

✓✓✓ 3. Evaluate the importance of equality of opportunity for training in an organisation like BT.

The main sources of legislation are outlined in Unit 17 of this book. A very brief reminder of what each Act sets out to achieve is given in Figure 16.4.

The table outlines some of the relevant Acts that managers, supervisors, owners and employees need to be aware of when dealing with employees. Training needs to be given in how to recruit employees correctly in the first place, to ensure that training opportunities and promotions are allocated fairly and that any disciplinary or grievance procedures are handled in the right way. If an employer does not adequately train their staff they risk being taken to an **industrial tribunal**. This is a place where an employee can try to get compensation from their employer if they believe they have been treated unfairly at work. Failure to follow disciplinary procedures correctly can also lead to an increased award by as much as 50 per cent being made to an employee.

Employment Equality (Sex Discrimination) Regulations 2005 Sex Discrimination Act 1975 & 1986	Ensures that all sexes are treated equally in employment situations, e.g. opportunities for promotion. The 2005 regulations now prohibit 'sex-based', (e.g. comments such as all women are …) and sexual harassment which is unwanted physical, verbal or other conduct which is sexual in nature.
Race Relations Act 1976	Ensures that people are not discriminated against on the basis or colour, creed or religion.
Equal Pay Act 1970	Ensures that all sexes are treated equally in employment situations, e.g. same pay for the same job regardless of gender.
Rehabilitation of Offenders Act 1974	Makes sure that if a person has a minor criminal conviction they are not discriminated against. More serious or certain offences are exempt from this Act.
Disability Discrimination Act 1995	Ensures that reasonable adjustments must be made in order that people with disabilities can be employed on an equal basis as far as possible.
European Working Time Directive	Restricts the number of hours employees are allowed to work.
Employment Act 2002	Is responsible for a number of employment requirements to be followed including employees receiving contracts of employment, paternity pay, maternity pay, employees on fixed-term contracts being treated the same as permanent employees and so on.
Data Protection Act 1998	Places restrictions on the processing of personal data in terms of access to it and the amount of time it is stored for.
National Minimum Wage Act 1998	Ensures that a minimum amount is paid per hour to employees aged 16 and over.

FIGURE 16.4 *Employment and equal opportunities legislation*

Training is also important from a legislative point of view in terms of updates. The employer and employee will need to make sure that relevant registrations and update training are received at appropriate times in the workplace. For example, all organisations must have a trained First Aider with an appropriate certificate. Professions such as nursing or medicine also require employees to be registered with appropriate professional associations. If they are not registered they may not be insured.

Training for managers is also important to ensure that they provide appropriate support for flexible working arrangements as required by law. Some managers may initially be resistant to such methods of working as they are relatively new. Training them to operate successfully using such methods may be needed.

> ### Key terms
>
> An *industrial tribunal* is a form of court where an employee can make a claim for unfair dismissal or treatment and try to gain some kind of compensation.

16.2.3 Planning the strategy

Like any other plan, aim or objective, training needs to be approached from a strategic point of view – it must be planned for and implemented in line with the rest of company aims and objectives. When you devise a strategy for the two functional areas you have chosen, you must ensure that your planning stage involves:

* setting the aims and objectives which fit within the framework of departmental objectives and overall corporate objectives

* targeting research at the appropriate audience, e.g. the workers within the two functional areas

* types of research which are most suitable for generating the required information.

Aims and objectives which fit within the framework of departmental objectives and overall corporate objectives

You have already been reminded about the role of aims and objectives within organisations as a whole (see page 300) and now you need to consider how those aims and objectives fit into the departmental and overall corporate objectives from a training perspective. You will need to consider the Mission Statement or overall aims of the organisation. Your teacher may be able to provide them for you including the objectives that have been set from those aims for the individual functional areas to achieve. Once you are aware of what the organisation is aiming for you will be able to support the relevant objectives with a training strategy that can be implemented and reviewed.

Figure 16.5 shows the overall aim of the organisation is to expand the business into France, with knowledge being passed down to managers and employees for information and training purposes. The overall aim means that objectives are set to recruit ten French speaking employees by 2007, to obtain finance in order to buy premises in France in August 2007 and to integrate the IT systems in the UK and France in order to communicate effectively by August 2007. The objectives for the Production and Human Resources functional areas could be broken down again and their implications for training are shown in Figure 16.6.

This explanation of how aims and objectives drive training needs has been very simplified for you to understand it at the most basic level. You will need to research the aims and objectives of your organisation and two functional areas before considering a strategy that you think will be appropriate to use.

You will also need to consider the review cycle as part of the planning of the strategy – how often are you going to check on your progress and which methods will you use to help you? Firstly, you will need to consider how often you think it is necessary to review your progress.

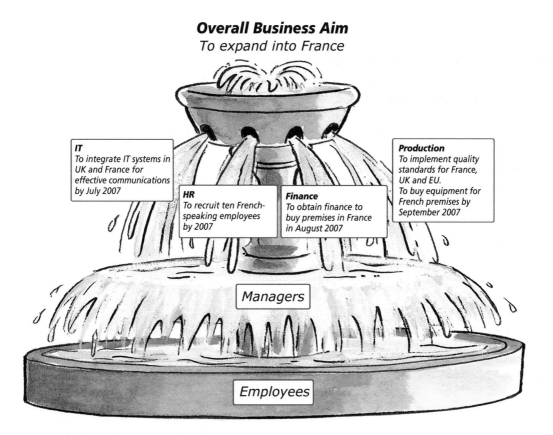

Overall Business Aim
To expand into France

IT
To integrate IT systems in UK and France for effective communications by July 2007

HR
To recruit ten French-speaking employees by 2007

Finance
To obtain finance to buy premises in France in August 2007

Production
To implement quality standards for France, UK and EU.
To buy equipment for French premises by September 2007

Managers

Employees

FIGURE 16.5 *Devolving corporate aims and objectives to departmental level*

OBJECTIVES	TRAINING IMPLICATIONS
Production	
To implement quality standards as appropriate to France, the UK and EU.	To introduce staff to French and EU legislation in order to integrate production in France by training them in latest developments and cultural differences.
To buy and operate French machinery and equipment for the premises by September 2007.	To provide basic training including health and safety when operating the new French equipment.
Human Resources	
To recruit or relocate ten French-speaking members of staff to work in France by July 2007.	To research recruitment options in France and train staff on the implications. To consider relocation packages and train staff in how to explain them to existing staff.
To learn and put into place working arrangements and legislation as specified in France.	To train staff in the day-to-day working differences between French and UK arrangements taking into account French and EU directives.

FIGURE 16.6 *Training implications for Production and Human Resources*

Some organisations might consider reviewing their training strategy monthly, bi-monthly, quarterly, six monthly or annually or even a combination of more than one. The choice of review period will depend on the type of training needed and its importance and relevance to the organisation.

Think it over...

Consider your aims and objectives and how they link to the training strategy for your chosen organisation. Ask your manager or supervisor how often the organisation reviews them. How often do you think they should review them?

Targeting research at the appropriate audience

It is important when planning a training strategy to make sure that it is based on the aims and objectives of the organisation that are coming from the top downwards but it should also be influenced by the needs and interests of functional area workers. This is because the implementation of the training strategy needs to take place at the functional level and if employees do not feel it is something that is being done for their benefit they will not make the most of the training offered.

The way you collect your research, therefore, must be targeted to both the aims and objectives of the organisation and to the type of workers that are likely to be influenced by the training and development strategy. As part of your research you will need to collect your targeted data from within the two functional areas and collect information about the type of training that is needed for employees depending on their level in the department, for example manager or supervisor, the length of time they have been working there, their work experience level and skills to date.

You should also consider that by targeting the research at the appropriate audience you should gain a better understanding and idea of the type of training and development strategy that should be implemented. This means that your research will be specific to the training needs of those two functional areas rather than the business as a whole. By being more specific the strategy and plans implemented as part of that strategy are likely to be SMART.

Again, remember that you will need to get permission from the organisation before you conduct any kind of research.

Types of research which are most suitable for generating the required information

As you already know there are two main types of research that can be collected: primary and secondary. Primary research can generate excellent brand new research data and will potentially help you to gain a deeper understanding and analysis needed to plan your strategy effectively. This is because it will specifically relate to the two functional areas that you have chosen within the organisation.

The way research can be collected will have implications for you and will influence your choice of research method. Research amongst managers could involve a one-to-one interview or in-depth questionnaire in order to get highly detailed thoughts and feelings about future training needs. However, it may be impossible to conduct such a lengthy exercise in a retail or factory environment with lower-level staff. This may mean a short survey or brief interview for data collection may be important for junior-ranking staff.

You will also need to consider the wording of the research method used – long, complicated questions may be difficult for employees to answer easily within their working day and you will need to make the research process as simple as possible in order that you are able to collect enough data. Figure 16.7 gives you some key issues that you should consider when collecting research.

Time available for data collection	It is likely that the employees in each of the functional areas will be extremely busy. You will need to choose research methods that allow you to gain the maximum amount of information with minimum disturbance. This may mean collecting research data at a time that is suitable to the employee rather than you, for example by using email or online forms.
Relevance to the strategy	It is important from the outset to choose research methods that will actually generate information that you need to help with the strategy. It is easy to collect too much information and then not be able to sort out what is important and what is not important.
Accuracy	If you use the wrong research method and then collect the wrong data your planning strategy will be flawed from the start. If you are using primary research methods, test them before you use them. Ask a friend to answer them as part of a mock interview or fill in a questionnaire if you are going to use one.
Access	Some information is sensitive to the organisation and to the employees themselves. Don't include personal information within your research such as age or marital status for employees if it's not relevant. Is it important to name those people you have worked with (as long as they give their permission) or whether you would prefer your data to be anonymous. This will affect the method you use and how you present your results.
	Company information that is already published may be available from larger companies but more difficult to access in smaller companies. You may need to adapt your research methods to take this into account.
Supervisor influence	Your teacher or other employees may have information about the role and ideas of a supervisor. Use these ideas but remember to consider them as objectively as possible. Remember a supervisor is likely to be working within the environment or have close contacts there and may be trying to influence what you might find out.
Organisational influence	It is important to recognise that any information that you research and write about may be read by the organisation themselves. You will need to remain objective in your writing and if you do need to make any criticisms of the methods used in the organisation or data you collect, you should do so with constructive criticism.

FIGURE 16.7 *Key issues when collecting research*

One of the key issues when collecting research is accuracy because if the information is not collected properly you may get the wrong results and your analysis and strategy planning may also be done incorrectly. You will need to collect data from a variety of sources to help you see data from more than one perspective but make sure you keep reviewing and rechecking your methods and data to check that is it appropriate and accurate. This should help you to check your ideas through to see if the same ideas are being repeated or question an idea if it is presented by one group of employees in one way and in a completely different way by another group of employees.

An example could be taken by comparing the reactions of senior managers, middle managers and junior staff to how important they thought training was viewed within the organisation. If all three groups of employees agreed that it was important on an equal basis, this helps to confirm the priority of training from everyone's perspective. However, if senior managers and middle managers saw it is a priority but junior staff did not see it as important this should be investigated to try to work out why. Comparing different groups and their reaction to training could give you lots of material in order to prepare your strategy.

16.2.4 Research of the strategy and analysis of the information that is collected

You have already considered a number of the issues involved in choosing your research methods. To make sure that your research is both clearly targeted and focused with a clear training and development strategy, you will need to carry out both primary and secondary research. Some suitable methods for collecting such data are outlined for you, taking into account issues associated with those methods. Remember to keep looking back to the Figure 16.7 to remind yourself of the tips for choosing the right method.

Primary research

There are four main methods of carrying out primary research within the context of training and development. These are:

* questionnaires and surveys
* discussion interviews with senior managers
* visits
* discussions with workers.

The choice of method may change depending on the level of the member of staff that you are working with and the number of people working within the functional areas. If there are different numbers of staff including supervisors or managers working in the two functional areas it is likely you will need to adjust your research method or **sample size** to take this into account.

Questionnaires and surveys

You have already come across questionnaires and surveys during your AS studies and are familiar with some of the issues involved with using them to collect data. A reminder of the key points is given in Figure 16.8.

At this stage you will need to consider the sample size that you are going to use and the method for sampling. It may not be practical or possible to interview everyone who works in each of the functional areas so you need to consider whether you are going to pick the people to answer your questions at random from within those areas or whether you are going to give out questionnaires to the first quota of people you are able to.

Open or closed questions?	Open: How do you feel about training at Bright Sparks plc?
	Closed: Are you satisfied with training at Bright Sparks plc? Yes or No
Use of scales within questions?	**Likert scaling**: My training is managed well • Strongly Agree • Agree • Have no opinion • Disagree • Strongly disagree Please tick.

Semantic scaling:

My training is well organised

	1	2	3	4	5	6	
Agree							Disagree

Use of ranking? When considering your own workplace, rank which of these factors would influence you the most to undertake training:

	Rank 1 to 5
To gain better understanding of my job	
To improve the amount of work I can achieve	
To help with my career progression	
To impress my supervisor or colleague	
To network with other colleagues and share experience	

FIGURE 16.8 *Methods of data collection using questionnaires and surveys*

Theory into practice

Produce a mind map considering the key areas of research that you wish to investigate. Produce a set of questions for each section, making use of the question techniques that you have learned about.

Put the questions into the most appropriate order and produce a copy that could be given out to employees.

Give a copy of the questions to other members of your class and ask them to answer your survey or questionnaire. Ask them to comment on questions they found easy or difficult to answer and suggestions for improvement. Make changes to your questionnaire and test it again with one employee from the workplace you are studying and make changes after reviewing their comments.

Now give out your questionnaire or survey in the workplace using the sampling technique you have chosen.

Discussions with senior management to gain a second perspective on the training and development needs of staff

It is good practice within your research to get a variety of sources of information. For example, if you are considering using questionnaires to get data from more junior employees, you are likely to find it useful to consider training and development needs of senior management using a different method. Discussion in an interview situation can be a useful way to do this.

Using prepared questions

You will need to carefully plan how the discussion should take place as senior managers are likely to be very busy and therefore may not have a lot of time to spare. You will also need to have a set of ideas of open ended questions that can help guide them to the areas of training and development that you wish to research. An example might be 'How important is the role of training and development within your organisation?' This type of question will allow the manager to give more general information to start with and as the researcher you could follow up with additional questions. By looking at the results from your questionnaire or survey you could consider the views of managers and employees separately in order to see if there was a link between the two.

Using previously collected results

Within the discussion you may wish to use the results that you have already gained from more junior employees to use as talking points. If the questionnaire results indicate that training is viewed highly you could ask the senior manager to reflect on this and consider why they think this is the case. Alternatively, if there any problems such as lack of investment in training, this would be an opportunity for the senior manager to consider and make comments about this.

Remember to make sure the results of the questionnaire or survey do not link back to individual employees so that they are freely able to comment. Any negative points should also be approached with sensitivity so that the manager does not feel you are just being critical of the organisation but that you are looking for ways to improve it by suggesting the implementation of your own strategy.

Visit to the business to hold a meeting with the HR department and explore their role in promoting training and development

Larger organisations will tend to have a separate department that will oversee all aspects of training and development. This may be done by the human resources department as part of their duties, by a training officer or administrator or in very large organisations there might be a separate training department. Some organisations will refer to the human resource department as the personnel department. Smaller organisations might not have a department at all so a manager might be responsible for looking at the staff working in the organisation and all their training and development needs, or function managers may be responsible for training in their department, for example the marketing manager.

The way that training and development is organised within the organisation you are studying may give you useful clues as to how to plan your strategy and the type of people who will be key drivers in terms of its implementation. If most training takes place and is organised within the functional areas it would be important to consult the managers working within these areas. If most training is centrally organised and administered by a training department it would be useful to speak to the training department and relevant HR staff.

Discussions with workers on what they consider to be the most effective forms of training programmes

You may also find it useful to consider other techniques such as a focus group or individual interviews with employees. Focus groups are when employees sit together and discuss and share their different individual views, for example towards training and development which may provide useful ideas to consider as part of your strategy. When using focus groups it is important to consider they may be biased and so what is important to one focus group in terms of their attitudes, needs and personal development may be influenced by stronger members of the group than others.

Talking to individual members of staff may also be useful but remember to make notes or

Focus groups are useful for sharing ideas with a number of employees

record the discussion if permission is given. You will also need an outline or some kind of framework for the discussion to make sure you get all your questions answered.

Secondary research

Secondary research is research that has already been published by someone else. This can be a very useful source of information to help you learn more about training in the workplaces of competitor organisations. Research is published on websites, in journals and newspapers and books. It is important to try to collect as much information as possible about how training is delivered in those organisations including:

* the type of training offered

* perceived importance of training

* qualifications held by employees

* training programmes offered

* the level of accreditation by agencies such as Investors in People

* the resources available for training

* awards and ratings given to the business by external bodies, e.g. The Times Top 100.

Skills-gap analysis

It is also important when you are collecting your research to produce a skills-gap analysis. A skills-gap analysis measures the skills that the business has at the moment within their current workforce and then measures the skills that they are likely to need in the future. The gap is the difference between the two. Producing a skills-gap analysis has three main stages to the process:

* analysing the short-, medium- and long-term business objectives

* analysing existing knowledge and skills available

* identifying training needs to achieve the necessary knowledge and skills.

Analysing the short-, medium- and long-term business objectives

The aim of the organisation might be to expand, so an objective of that aim could be to recruit and train a further 20 new staff by 2010 (longer term). Part of the expansion may also be to produce additional goods and therefore the objective might be in the medium term to implement a training update programme for the production department by 2007. The alternative of course is the organisation might need to reduce staff by 2020 if new technology is to be implemented and in terms of training, staff may need additional support to move on to different roles or even different employers in the event of redundancies.

Finally, it could be that in the short term there is a problem in a specific area of the business. It may be necessary to try to implement training as a result of an issue such as a reduction in quality or customer service. This may mean that emergency training is needed for all staff in the sales department within the next six months.

Theory into practice

You will need to investigate the short-, medium- and long-term objectives in order to relate them to the training needs of the business. More information about this area of research can be found in Unit 10 on pages 55–7.

Analysing existing knowledge and skills available

In order to use existing knowledge and skills available, you could make use of the questionnaire data that you have already collected but there are also a number of additional sources of information that are useful:

* staffing records, e.g. number of staff, average age of staff, length of service

* qualifications held by staff

* skills held by staff

* training records

* company newsletters and statistics

* staff turnover (number of staff leaving known as the wastage rate) calculated by:

$$\frac{\text{Number of staff leaving in a time period}}{\text{Average number of staff employed in that time period}} \times 100$$

* sickness and absence rates.

Identifying training needs to achieve the necessary knowledge and skills

By examining the objectives of the organisation in the short, medium and long term and then the skill and knowledge levels of the organisation, it is possible to identify a gap between what the organisation has at the moment and what they want to have. This gap in the skills and knowledge needed for the future leads to the identification of training needs. This is the training that the organisation needs to offer in terms of its future objectives.

One example of an objective in the medium term might be to plan for a new manager to take over in the marketing department in 2008. The marketing department already contains ten employees, two of whom are supervisors and have some management skills. The organisation could choose to recruit someone external (outside) of the business or alternatively they could do some **succession planning** in that the two supervisors could be given further training to

Training for future job roles motivates employees

fill that gap. Identifying a skills-gap and training existing employees for future job roles can be an excellent way to motivate employees and also keep experienced employees working within the business.

Theory into practice

Produce a skills-gap analysis by completing the following table. Remember to look back over section 16.2.2 to help you.

What are the aims and objectives of the business in relation to training?	
What are the current skills and knowledge levels within the business?	
What are the immediately identifiable gaps between what the organisation has now and what is needed in the future?	

16.2.5 Production of a plan of action

Now that you have identified the skills-gap, you are aware of what the business needs to do in terms of increasing the skill and knowledge levels for the short, medium and longer term. Remember that within your training and development strategy you will need to cater for the two functional areas that you have chosen to study and some of the skills required might be needed for both areas but others will be more specific and only relate to one. You will have gathered a lot of information on the background to the organisation, staffing levels, how training has been done in the past, what staff think about training and the strengths and weaknesses of that training.

Remember training can be something as simple as giving someone time to work through a training manual whilst doing their job (on-the-job training) or it could be off-the-job training such as attending a degree or professional course in accounting or engineering. Both forms of training require resources and planning.

When you have refocused your thoughts, it is important to consider the way that the training to bridge the gap between what is in place and what needs to be in place is to be offered. There is a wide range of training opportunities that can be used and the success of your strategy and its plan of action will depend on you conducting research into what is available in order to analyse and make judgements about its usefulness. These opportunities are divided into two main categories: training programmes and training initiatives.

Training programmes

These consist of six main types of programme:

* job shadowing
* coaching
* computer-based training (CBT)
* in-house courses
* simulations
* external courses.

Job shadowing

You may have already experienced some form of job shadowing during your time at school or college. The purpose of allowing someone to job shadow is to see what it is like to do the job of the other person by actually following them for a day, week or month and seeing exactly what they do. Job shadowing might be able to offer an insight into a career for people who are thinking of joining an organisation or it might be useful as part of succession planning in that more junior employees can see what it is like to

Theory into practice

You may find it useful to complete a SWOT analysis of training and development at this point in order to gather your thoughts.

Strengths	Weaknesses
These are the positive aspects of training and development at your organisation in the functional areas.	Which areas did you find would benefit from improvements? Which gaps appeared between the current level of skills and future needs?

Opportunities	Threats
What future opportunities are there for the business in terms of training; awards, accreditation, better organisational image, higher productivity or even expansion?	What are the organisation's competitors doing in terms of training? What are levels of training like within that industry in general – shortages?

spend the day as a senior manager or director of the organisation. This can be a huge motivator for employees as it can make them think seriously about their future career development.

Coaching

This is when a coach is put in place to help employees to develop themselves and set targets for their own training and development. Coaches may be recruited inside the organisation, for example senior employees are asked to help coach more junior employees or there are schemes where external consultants may be employed to provide assistance. These consultants may be specifically trained for this purpose or may be working in a similar industrial sector so that they can offer specific industrial and networking advice. A senior accountant, for example, in one organisation may offer coaching to a newly qualified accountant working in another town, city or even country. This help and advice may be face to face but more commonly is now offered using the Internet such as email, website or chat forum.

Computer-based training (CBT)

There is a huge variety of computer-based training programmes. You have already learned about Hilton Hotels and its use of e-learning programmes to train, support and retain their staff. Many organisations will offer computer-based training that might be available on their Intranet site (this is the site that is only available to employees working for the organisation) so that employees can access courses at their own pace and when they need them.

CASE STUDY

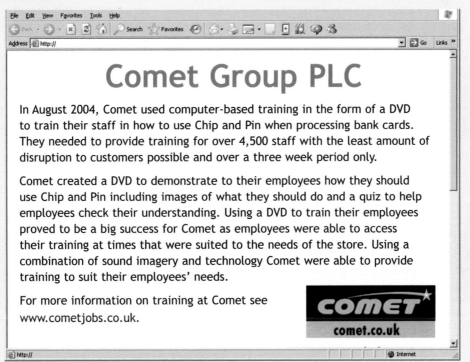

Comet Group PLC

In August 2004, Comet used computer-based training in the form of a DVD to train their staff in how to use Chip and Pin when processing bank cards. They needed to provide training for over 4,500 staff with the least amount of disruption to customers possible and over a three week period only.

Comet created a DVD to demonstrate to their employees how they should use Chip and Pin including images of what they should do and a quiz to help employees check their understanding. Using a DVD to train their employees proved to be a big success for Comet as employees were able to access their training at times that were suited to the needs of the store. Using a combination of sound imagery and technology Comet were able to provide training to suit their employees' needs.

For more information on training at Comet see www.cometjobs.co.uk.

COMET*
comet.co.uk

✓ 1. What is meant by computer-based training?

✓ 2. Give two reasons why Comet needed to provide this kind of training.

✓✓ 3. Using Figure 16.9, analyse two advantages to Comet of using computer-based training specifically outlining issues that relate to Comet and its business.

✓✓✓ 4. Based on the evidence from the case study and Figure 16.9, do you think Comet chose the best method of training in this case? You will need to give arguments for and against this method of training for Comet before drawing conclusions.

Computer-based training is not just about learning how to use a computer, it is about studying a subject or area using a computer. It must be approached carefully because the usefulness of the training will depend on how often employees are able to access training, how comfortable they feel using computers to train and the level of support and additional assistance they may need to train this way. There are a number of institutions that offer computer-based training in this way including the Open University, Open College and learndirect. There are now courses including degrees that are available to study only online.

Figure 16.9 gives a summary of some of the main advantages and disadvantages of using computer-based training.

ADVANTAGES	DISADVANTAGES
Allows employees to study in their own time if they want to.	Employees need to be highly motivated to complete a course if they use online distance learning to study.
Employees are encouraged to teach themselves using the computer.	The results will only be as good as the package itself and like any course there can be good and bad computer-based training.
In some systems the learner can easily build on what they have already learned rather than having to start at the same point as everyone else in a class or seminar.	The software that is used to run the training may change very rapidly and therefore become out of date very quickly.
Employees can study at their own pace rather than at the pace of the whole group.	People who are scared of technology may not enjoy this type of learning and may find it too difficult unless they are given lots of support.
The learning materials can provide a huge variety of information as graphics, video clips, sound and images to help employees learn using computers.	Employees will need to be given access to enough computers at work and/or home and this may be very expensive to provide.
There are no travel costs for employees to access an online course and training costs can be kept low as organisational resources and computers are used.	Computer-based training materials can take a long time to produce and may be too expensive.

FIGURE 16.9 *Advantages and disadvantages of using computer-based training*

learndirect

learndirect offer a way of accessing both off and online courses using computer-based material. It is possible to be referred to a local centre where computer-based training can take place or a course can be taken entirely online including enrolling on the course, making payment, studying the material and even gaining credits towards recognised qualifications.

learndirect also offer a scheme known as Learn Through Work. This scheme allows employers to give their employees training opportunities through the World Wide Web as employees can log on and take courses either in the workplace or at home but all the payments and details are passed on to their employer. Training using computer-based methods means that employees can fit in the training to suit them rather than the other way round and by using Learn Through Work the employer can also be made aware of the progress being made.

✓ 1. Name one benefit of studying using computer-based training.
✓✓ 2. Analyse three possible barriers that might prevent employees being able to access training that they would like to have in the workplace?
✓✓✓ 3. Give a judgement about how useful you feel services such as learndirect might be to individuals, organisations and the country as a whole.

Theory into practice

Using the Internet, conduct a search into the different types of computer-based training that could be used as part of your plan of action. You will need to analyse the usefulness of these programmes in relation to your training and development strategy including how they can support the strategy and their limitations.

In-house courses

Some organisations, especially larger ones, will have their own training department and may offer their own in-house courses. These are courses that are designed and delivered by employees within the company. Smaller organisations may also offer courses that have been designed by experienced staff to train employees in the working methods used by the organisation. Some in-house training will result from an employee going on an external course and bringing back the information they have learned to share with their colleagues.

In-house courses are likely to be cheaper than external courses as the training is carried out in the workplace and is specifically targeted to the needs of that organisation. The downside to offering training in this way is that it may not be viewed as important as external training and therefore not taken as seriously.

Simulations

In some industries simulations are an extremely important way of training employees. Simulations take a variety of forms such as trainee pilots doing training and tests in flight simulators or simulations such as those carried out by the police, fire brigade and ambulance staff in the event of a major incident. Even within the office environment simulations may be used to plan what is going to happen as part of health and safety training. Simulations also allow employees to practise in a safe environment something they will have to carry out for real at a later stage, for example a presentation, meeting or even an appraisal with their line manager. The feedback given to the employee as part of the simulation can help them to improve when they are in the real situation.

External courses

External courses come in several different forms. These can be online using computer-based methods as you have already learned or in person at training providers such as schools, colleges, training agencies or universities. External courses may be offered for a day, a week, weekly, twice weekly, monthly or even annually. Some of the courses may provide the employee with a certificate from the training provider to show they have attended. Other courses will lead to recognised qualifications such as the OCR Applied Business A Level.

The advantage of sending employees on external courses is that they will mix with other employees from different organisations and therefore may bring new ideas back into the company. Receiving recognised qualifications may also help employees with their career development and therefore make them more motivated at work. The disadvantage of such external courses, though, is that they can be expensive and it may be difficult for employees to transfer the skills and knowledge they acquire into their workplace directly.

Training initiatives

Training initiatives are designed to encourage employers and employees to view training and development seriously. They may provide opportunities for accreditation such as Investors in People or offer advice or incentives to participate more in training. Rewards such as improved company performance, image and help with funding can all encourage employers to consider training and development as something that is seriously viewed and supported within their organisations. There are three main training initiatives you need to study:

* Investors in People
* appraisals/performance reviews
* Learning and Skills Council.

Investors in People

Investors in People (IIP) is an award that was developed in 1990 by a partnership of leading businesses to improve the management and development of people in the workplace. Organisations work towards IIP status by following the IIP framework. The three main areas are plan, do and review. IIP requires organisations to plan their training as part of the overall strategy, aims and objectives of the business, to take action to improve the performance of the organisation and finally to review the impact of that performance on the organisation as a whole. There are lots of benefits to an organisation of having IIP status including:

* more satisfied customers as their input is measured as well
* more satisfied and motivated staff as their training and development needs are catered for which leads to increased retention
* lower absence/sickness and improved productivity
* lower costs and wastage as people take more interest in their work and therefore suggest ideas for ways to improve the business.

For more information on Investors in People see www.investorsinpeople.co.uk.

INVESTORS IN PEOPLE

Many businesses aspire to Investors in People status

Appraisals and performance reviews

Appraisals and **performance reviews** are used within organisations to set targets for employees. They can be used with both individuals and teams. At an appraisal, an employee is asked to look at what they have done since their last appraisal and whether they have achieved the targets they set out to achieve. Once this has been agreed the manager and employee then agree the set of targets the employee needs to achieve by the next appraisal.

Appraisals and performance reviews are really useful tools to help any organisation coordinate and implement its training and development strategy. This is because an appraisal or performance review provides an opportunity to discuss what is going well within the workplace or not so well. It also allows the training and development needs of employees to be linked in to both the aims and objectives of the functional area and the company as a whole. This can be done by introducing a version of the relevant objective into the appraisal or review procedure and then making this one of the employee's targets.

Learning and Skills Council

The Learning and Skills Council (LSC) is responsible for the funding and planning of education and training for people over 16 years of age in England. Its purpose is to increase the number of learners aged 16 and over to make the UK one of the most knowledgeable and skilled countries in the world. In 2003–4 its budget was £8 billion!

The Learning and Skills Council works to increase the amount of education and training in the workplace for adults, by making business links and in colleges and school sixth forms.

It seeks to work with employers, education providers, community groups and individuals to try to develop and meet training and education needs. Over the years the LSC has supported a number of campaigns including EMA (Educational Maintenance Allowance) which is a means-tested allowance that is paid to 16–18-year-old students in return for attending full-time courses. In 2005 students received up to £30 per week. For more information about the LSC see www.lsc.gov.uk.

Proposed training programme

As part of your training and development strategy you will need to produce a proposed training programme for each of the functional areas that you have chosen. An example of a very simplified training programme is shown in the following exercise. You will need to include a variety of activities and programmes in order to meet the training and development needs of those functional areas as a whole.

Theory into practice

The following programme for job shadowing is an example of the kind of programme you will need to write. You will need to consider the gaps in training and then write clearly detailed programmes that relate specifically to the two functional areas you have chosen. There may be some opportunity to introduce programmes that are applicable to both areas but it is essential to introduce specific programmes that must be carried out independently.

Senior management work shadowing programme

The overall purpose of the training programme is to allow Grade 2 employees to experience what it is like to be a Senior Manager working within the organisation. The work shadowing programme will take place over five days and these can be taken during the course of one working week or over five days to be agreed by the Senior Manager and member of staff.

Aim: To complete a five-day Senior Management work shadowing programme for Grade 2 employees.

Objectives: To understand the role of a Senior Manager.

To participate in Senior Management meetings.

To understand the structure of a Senior Manager's day.

To increase awareness of organisational procedures.

To write a career action plan.

As a result of each day spent with the Senior Manager, the Grade 2 employee is expected to keep a learning log detailing what they have learned and the implications for them in their future career.

On the afternoon of day five the employee is to have a review meeting with the Senior Manager when progress is to be discussed and a career action plan put into place with regular dates for review.

---

1. Using the training programme devised above – *take one of the objectives outlined* and write a draft of what you think an employee should cover in such a training programme within your chosen organisation.

2. Which resources would they need?

3. Where should the training take place?

4. When should the training take place?

16.2.6 Evaluating effectiveness

The last element of training and development is the review process. Training and development is an ongoing process in any organisation and needs to be constantly reviewed and updated. As the aims and objectives of the functional areas and organisation as a whole need to be adapted to the changing needs of the business, so too do the skills and expertise required.

It is important, therefore, to consider the effectiveness of your chosen strategy in meeting the departmental and organisational aims and objectives and in doing so you need to consider:

* how the effectiveness of a training strategy can be affected by internal and external constraints

* the problems associated with one-off training rather than ongoing initiatives

* a radical change to a business' aims such as expansion causing a revision of training initiatives.

How the effectiveness of a training strategy can be affected by internal and external constraints

There are four key constraints on the training strategy from either an internal or external business point of view and these are: legislation, competition, physical resources and cost implications.

Legislation

The legal process has huge implications for training as new laws are being passed each day and statutory guidelines mean that new working methods may need to be introduced. This is common within areas such as health and safety where new requirements are brought in on a regular basis and updates and procedural changes must happen by law. In October 2005, the Sex Discrimination Act was updated and new laws were brought in relating to sexual harassment, which means that employees need to be trained in how to work within this new legislative framework. You will need to consider employment law whilst planning your strategy and the implications of any changes.

Competition

Competition can either help or hinder your training activity by their lack of activity or inactivity. If other employers within your sector are offering better training for their employees they may be able to attract the best employees to work for them and therefore your organisation may struggle to recruit. Alternatively, some competitors fail to train employees at all and rely on other organisations to do the training. Then they poach the trained employees once they have the appropriate qualification and experience by offering a slightly higher salary or benefits. Organisations who 'poach' employees in this way do so because they save both time and money on training but this can mean that employers may feel reluctant to train within that sector for fear that they will lose employees anyway. If this starts to happen it is known as labour market failure.

Physical resources

The physical resources that are available to the organisation may also help or hinder training in the organisation. This is because there may only be a limited number of resources that can be used for training, e.g. hours available per week for training or money available in the training budget. There may also be a limited number of trainers or the person running the functional area may also be responsible for training and therefore may be trying to balance the daily requirements of the business with the longer-term training needs.

The availability of physical space for training can also be an issue and whether or not there is space within the organisation to take people away from their desks, if necessary, to train in new methods or working techniques.

Cost implications

The final area of constraint is the cost of training. Any organisation will have a limited amount of money that they expect to spend on training each year and it is important to make the best use of that money. This may mean sending only one employee on a training course and then asking them to share what they have learned with the rest of the organisation.

One of the best ways to evaluate the positive effects of training is to conduct a cost-benefit analysis. A cost-benefit analysis examines the cost of the training and the expected benefits as a result of that training before the training has taken place. This way training can be planned for and the money used to the maximum benefit.

Theory into practice

Raafi and Rajesh have been asked to produce a cost-benefit analysis of a training day on presentation skills. The course costs £150 including lunch.

Its aim is: to improve presentation skills in the workplace.

Its objectives are:
- to understand what makes a presentation effective
- to outline and provide strategies to avoid common mistakes
- to introduce presentational aids such as software and prompts
- to overcome fears and survival techniques.

COSTS	BENEFITS
• £150 training cost. • Opportunity cost of not being able to work that day and needing the job to be covered.	• Improved sales techniques for external customers. • Better satisfaction leading to increased motivation and productivity. • Improvement in in-house training. • Greater self-confidence and self-awareness.

1. What is meant by opportunity cost?
2. How important are aims and objectives when considering a cost-benefit analysis?
3. What is meant by productivity?
4. Using motivation techniques you have learned within this unit on pages 311–14, how might this course lead to increased motivation?
5. Judge whether or not Raafi and Rajesh should both go on the course – what other factors might be relevant in this decision, for example do they both need to go or could one of them go and then share the information?

The previous exercise looks at one course in one functional area but there will be a cost benefit for a number of courses both within the functional area and the organisation as a whole. There may also be implications for training in terms of costs depending on the level of demand for the products or services that the organisation offers. If demand is high and sales are good then training is likely to be offered more readily. If demand is declining then the organisation may have to cut back and training is an area that is often reduced first. This can in turn have devastating consequences for the company as not only are they likely to be losing trade but their productivity levels are likely to suffer as well.

The problems associated with one-off training rather than ongoing initiatives

It is important to consider training as part of constant updating and improvement. One-off training is training that is offered in isolation, e.g. a training course at a hotel on assertiveness that isn't followed up again afterwards. In terms of training it is good practice to have some kind of follow-up to any kind of training even if that only consists of a review six months later. This is because unless there is follow-up after a training

event the positive benefits of that event are not likely to be carried forward. Employees need training to be reinforced regularly at later dates or they will forget the skills that they have learned.

Think it over...

Consider a one-off training event or workshop that you attended with your school, college or part-time job in the past three years.

Did you review that training at a later date and if so when?

How much of that training event can you remember?

How much of the information have you included in your day-to-day method of working?

It is likely that unless you have reviewed that training event at some later stage, you will have forgotten most of it and will not have transferred the skills that you have learned into the workplace.

Even if a training event only takes place on one occasion, the best way to ensure that it is followed up and implemented in the workplace is to follow what is known as the training cycle. This cycle has four stages as shown in Figure 16.10.

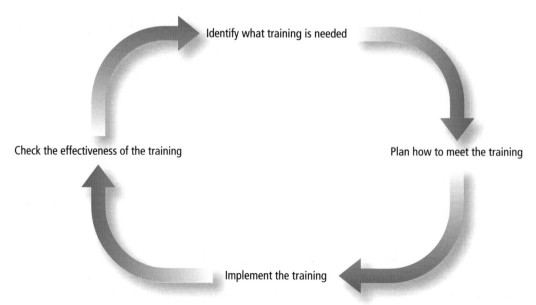

FIGURE 16.10 *The training cycle*

By identifying what the training is and then planning for it, implementing and then reviewing it, the training is more likely to be taken on board and transferred from the training event by the person attending to the workplace. For example, time-management training skills would actually be used at work.

Employees may also be encouraged to bring their training outcomes back in to the workplace by completing evaluation sheets when they return to the organisation detailing how the results of the training event can be put into practice at work. They may also be asked to share their experiences as part of a training event for other staff. Both of these methods require one-off experiences to be used to good effect, for example an employee sent on a time-management training day would then tell their colleagues how to implement those techniques so they can benefit and provide extra help with time management on an ongoing basis.

A radical change to a business' aims causing a revision of training initiatives

As you have already learned within this chapter a business' aims are the key driver for training within the organisation. Therefore if these aims

Virgin Trains

In October 2005, Virgin Cross Country Trains suffered as a result of not having enough trained drivers to operate new full speed tilting trains. The new trains needed drivers to undergo extra specialist training in order to operate them at full speed. The effect of the training programme taking a long time to deliver was that train journeys were longer than they were expected to be. The consequences of this late training affected the aim of Virgin Cross Country Trains as a business in that journey times were longer leading to less efficiency and potential customer dissatisfaction. When an organisation decides to implement the steps in order to achieve the aim of a better service or greater customer satisfaction, they need to make sure that training is provided in order to make sure that it happens.

✓ 1. What was the consequence of lack of training for Virgin Trains?
✓✓ 2. Consider the effect of this lack of training on the efficiency and reputation of Virgin Trains.
✓✓✓ 3. Give a judgement on whether this situation could have been avoided.

are changed or amended there are likely to be implications for training and development. If the organisation decides to work towards an expansion plan it is likely that additional money may need to be spent on the induction training of new staff or existing staff may need to have additional new training such as management training in order to take on more responsibility including supervising subordinates in the future.

There may also be a training need in terms of the number of potential employees in the labour market who are trained in the relevant industrial skills. This may mean that training needs to be provided now ready for expansion to take place in the future. Plumbing has been an industry where too few employees were trained in the past which led to a skills shortage. If employers know such a shortage might occur in their industrial sector, they can plan to train their own staff. The consequences of not doing this might affect the performance of the business, as shown in the case study on page 339.

There may also be training implications if the organisation has decided to reduce the number of staff that they have. Responsible employers will try to give employees new opportunities to train for employment after they leave the organisation. Reducing the workforce is known as contraction and happens when workers are made redundant, leave of their own free will or retire. Training is needed to help them adjust for their own personal situation. The Job Centre provide a service to employers who are going to have to make significant numbers of workers redundant. They offer training and advice to employees to help them find work with other employers or to retrain in a different career. This service is known as the Rapid Response Service. More information about the services offered by the Job Centre is available from www.jobcentreplus.gov.uk.

You will need to consider these kinds of issues and whether or not they relate to your organisation and the two relevant functional areas. Part of your training strategy may be to help put in place training for people to prepare them for redundancy or even to cope with retirement.

Some tips and reminders for writing your training and development strategy

Some final reminders to help you produce your strategy are given below:

* Always ask permission from your teacher before you access people or data working at your chosen organisation.

* Remember to ask an employee's permission before you quote them at all as they may prefer to remain anonymous.

* If you do need to be critical of the organisation make sure you are constructive about it, giving suggestions if possible of ways things could be improved.

* Make sure all your information is clearly presented and easily understood.

Use a mixture of primary data and secondary data with suitable references to back up your analysis and evaluation – you need to show clear, justified thinking throughout.

Get as much advice and opinion as you possibly can from as many different groups of people within the organisation as you can. This will help to confirm ideas and opinions about training and development within the organisation.

1. What is the difference between on- and off-the-job training?

2. Give two benefits to a business of providing training.

3. What is meant by the term productivity and how is it measured?

4. What effect does technological change have on training?

5. Compare two different induction training programmes that you are aware of. How do they differ? Are there any common elements?

6. How can training create competitive advantage?

7. Explain the difference between job enrichment and job rotation.

8. Explain how benchmarking may be used to compare businesses and its importance for training.

9. What is meant by cascading training and what are the possible problems associated with it in the workplace?

10. Consider the influence of legislation on training.

11. What is the role of the Human Resources Department in relation to training?

12. What is meant by succession planning?

13. Discuss the strengths and weaknesses of face-to-face versus computer-based training.

14. Describe the role of Investors in People in industry.

15. Judge the role of work shadowing in business.

16. Name two internal constraints that affect training levels.

17. Analyse two external constraints that may affect training levels.

18. Assess the impact of a lack of training in the plumbing industry.

19. To what extent does training improve retention levels in the workplace?

20. To what extent does training lead to better profitability?

Resources

Books

Gillespie, A (2002) *Business in Action*, Hodder & Stoughton

Lockton, D (2003) *Employment Law*, LexisNexis UK

Martin, M and Jackson, T (2002) *Personnel Practice (People and Organisations)*, Chartered Institute of Personnel and Development

Journals

Personnel Management
Personnel Review
Personnel Today

Websites

www.bized.ac.uk
Business Education on the Internet

www.bitc.org.uk
Business in the Community website

www.hse.gov.uk
Health and Safety Executive website

www.employment-studies.co.uk
Institute for Employment Studies contains Research Report, 5 September 2004

www.investorsinpeople.co.uk
Investors in People

www.trainingreference.co.uk
Resource for training developments including relevant articles and information

www.lsc.gov.uk
Learning and Skills Council

www.cipd.co.uk
Chartered Institute of Personnel and Development

www.businesslink.gov.uk
Support on all aspects of business including training and development

www.bbctraining.com
Free online resources to consider as part of online training

www.trainingmag.com
Training resource and news site

www.dti.gov.uk/training_development
Government supported training and development resources

www.skillbasetraining.co.uk
Training supplier

www.impactfactory.com
Training provider specialising in communication

www.personneltoday.com
Provides information on training and personnel issues

www.trainingzone.co.uk
Articles, news and features to do with training

www.trainingjournal.com
Articles, news and features offered on a variety of training and development issues

www.trainingpages.com
Provides training courses

www.huthwaite.co.uk
Business coaching website

www.projectalevel.co.uk/business
Business Studies related materials

www.tuc.org.uk
Training and development materials from a union perspective

www.times100.co.uk
Useful list of top companies to work for giving details of training and development that they use

www.bestcompanies.co.uk
Best Companies website giving awards to companies displaying excellence

www.cbi.org.uk
Confederation of British Industry

www.managementqualifications.co.uk
Management Qualifications website giving advice

www.statistics.gov.uk
National statistics published by the government

http://education.guardian.co.uk
Education Guardian website

Business law

17.2.1   Sources of law

17.2.2   Law of contract

17.2.3   Business formation

17.2.4   Business dissolution

17.2.5   Employment protection

17.2.6   Health and safety legislation

17.2.7   Consumer protection legislation

17.2.8   Intellectual property rights

This unit describes the rules of business law and how they affect the operation of the business. It adds insight into the rules and procedures and legal concepts required for day-to-day running of businesses. The unit will draw on ideas that you may be familiar with from your previous business studies and add to your knowledge to form a solid basis for understanding business law.

This unit provides an overview of the way English law has developed and where UK law comes from. There is information on contract law including the rights of consumers under contract law and how business contracts are formed. The unit also provides details on employment legislation and health and safety legislation in the workplace.

Finally, this unit ends by considering the impact intellectual property legislation has on organisations, particularly the way businesses deal with copyright, designs, patents and trademarks.

The unit is assessed through an external assessment. The mark that you get for the external assessment will be your mark for the unit.

17.2.1 Sources of law

Modern businesses exist within an ever-changing legal framework. In the UK the legal framework that businesses must operate under is the English legal system. This legal system controls virtually every aspect of the running of a business including the creation of the business, the employment of staff, the selling of products and the ending of the business itself.

It is important to understand where the law relating to businesses comes from and in particular the way different types of law such as **criminal** and **civil law** affect the organisation.

> ### Key terms
>
> *Criminal law* is the type of public law where the state punishes individuals for crimes against the state.
>
> *Civil law* is the type of private law concerned with disputes between individuals.

This developing legal system has created a system of law that can be classified into two distinct groups, both of which have an important part to play in the way businesses operate.

The law in the UK can be split into **public law** and **private law.** The main type of public law that will affect businesses is the operation of the criminal law, for example if a business produces faulty and dangerous products or breaks health and safety law. The majority of law that will affect businesses is the private area of civil law.

> ### Key terms
>
> *Public law* is the body of law concerned with matters of public importance.
>
> *Private law* is the law relating to private matters concerning businesses or individuals.

Criminal law

Criminal law can be used to punish offending businesses and possibly deter other businesses breaking the law. A criminal case is heard in the criminal courts: either the Magistrates' or Crown Court, depending on the seriousness of the case. Less serious cases can be heard in the Magistrates' Court with more serious cases being tried in the Crown Court. In court, the business is called the **defendant** and the person trying to prove the case is called the prosecution.

It is up to the prosecution to prove their case **beyond a reasonable doubt**. This is known as the **standard of proof**. This is a very high burden of proof because the punishment that a person can face if found guilty under the criminal law can be severe including imprisonment and fines.

> ### Key terms
>
> *Beyond a reasonable doubt* is the burden of proof in criminal cases.
>
> *Standard of proof* is the level of proof required to prove a case.

Civil law

An example of private law that will affect businesses is civil law. Unlike criminal law, civil law is concerned with the law between individuals, for example, where businesses involved in contracts fail to stick to the agreement made (a breach of contract) and employees claiming unfair dismissal against their employers. There is little state involvement.

The purpose of civil law is to give a remedy to the individual or business that has suffered loss. There should be no idea of punishment. The parties to the action are called the **claimant** (the person bringing the action) and the defendant (the person defending it). The action will be heard in the civil courts which are called the County Court and High Court depending on the monetary value of the claim. The standard of proof is much lower in civil law because the claimant must prove their case merely on the **balance of probabilities** (more than 50/50). In the event of being successful, the winning claimant (proving liability against the other side) can expect to receive remedies to right the wrong they have suffered to include damages and other remedies to put the person back to the position they would have been in before the action arose.

Common law

The different types of law seen above are the result of a long historical journey through the common law that can be traced back nearly one thousand years to the times of the Norman kings of England who established the first legal system in the UK.

The kings' representatives began to deal with all aspects of criminal and civil disputes with the help of local people who sat as the first judges and juries to help decide cases by virtue of the kings' fairness or **equity.**

These courts established a system of law based on equity, common law and customs. Many of these laws still exist today:

* the rights of property ownership
* laws relating to business contracts
* the remedies of specific performance (forcing a person to complete a contractual obligation) and injunction (stopping a person completing such an obligation).

One of the most important developments under common law was the development of an organised court system where parties in dispute could have their disputes heard and settled fairly. Over time, this common law system has evolved and embraced the civil law particularly (but not exclusively) so that businesses faced with legal problems will be looking for resolution and justice based on this ancient common law approach.

Statute law (Acts of Parliament)

Alongside the common law, another important source of law has developed. **Statute law** is law that is created by Parliament, usually by the government reflecting the wishes of the electorate (those of us who vote at a general election). There are many important pieces of legislation that Parliament has passed over the years many of which have an important part to play in the business world.

Parliament is responsible for creating around 50 to 70 new pieces of legislation each year. Each Act that is created has to go through strict procedures in both Houses of Parliament: the **House of Commons** and the **House of Lords**.

The procedures for creating a new Act in the Houses of Parliament are as indicated in Figure 17.1.

Firstly, the Act starts as a **Bill.** This is the Act in its earliest form and is a draft or outline of the legislation that is to be created. When the Bill has been drawn up it will then be entered into the House of Commons where its journey will begin.

Once the Bill enters the House of Commons, it will be given its first reading. This is where the name of the Bill and its main aims are read out in the Commons usually by the government minister who is sponsoring the Bill. There is no debate at this stage but there will be a vote by the Commons to see if the Bill is to progress any further. This can be informal (measuring the vocal support for the Bill) or formal via a formal vote. If this vote is successful the Bill will go onto the next stage which is the second reading.

The second reading is a very important part of the legislative process as the whole Bill is debated by the Commons. This debate will usually be

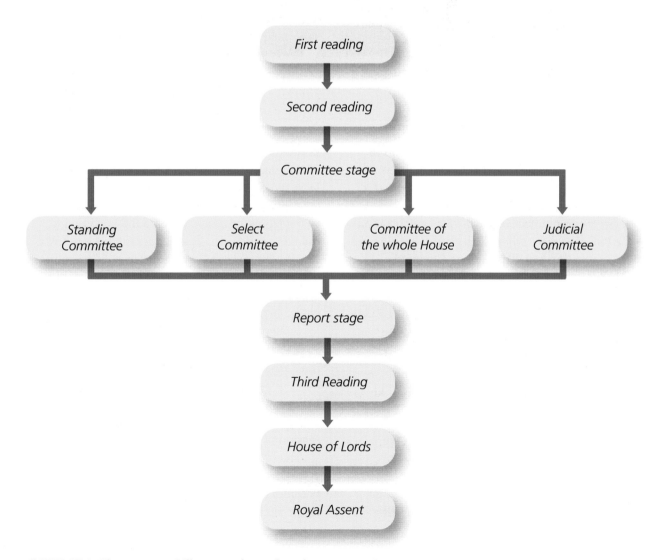

FIGURE 17.1 *The stages a Bill passes through to become an Act*

House of Commons in debate

about the main principles of the Bill rather than concentrating on smaller details. At the end of the debate a vote is taken and there must be a majority in favour of the Bill for it to proceed to the next stage which is the committee stage.

At the committee stage a detailed examination of the Bill takes place where each clause is scrutinised by a committee called a Standing Committee of between 16 and 50 Members of Parliament. It is almost certain that the committee will amend the Bill in some way and when amendments are made a vote will have to be passed. In this case, the committee report back to the Commons at the next stage which is the report stage.

The report stage is where the committee report back any amendments they feel necessary to the Bill. These amendments will be debated by the Commons and voted on. This is seen as a necessary safeguard against the possible tampering of the Bill by the committee. Once the amendments have been agreed the Bill will go onto the next stage which is the third reading.

The third reading is usually the final opportunity for the Commons to vote on the Bill and is usually little more than a formality because a Bill that has passed all of the previous stages is unlikely to fail at this point. Mostly, there is not even a debate on the Bill at this stage (unless at least six MPs request it).

A Bill that begins in the Commons is now sent to the House of Lords. When a Bill is passed to the House of Lords for consideration it will follow exactly the same route as it did in the Commons. Their Lordships can amend the Bill and it is then sent back to the Commons as agreed or they could, in theory, reject the Bill.

It should be noted that the power of the Lords to vote against Bills is severely weakened by the Parliament Acts 1911 and 1949. These allow a Bill to become law even if it is rejected by the House of Lords provided the Bill is introduced and passes all stages in the Commons at the next session of Parliament.

The final stage in the legislative process is formal approval to the Bill from the monarchy and it then becomes an Act of Parliament. This **Royal Assent** is never refused and is a mere formality. Its procedure is governed by the Royal Assent Act 1961. All the monarch will know is the title of the legislation. She will not even know the details of the legislation.

The last time this Royal Assent was refused by the monarch was in 1707 when Queen Anne refused to give Assent to a Bill to take up arms against Scotland.

European Union Law

Along with common law and statute law, another very important source of English law is European Union law. The UK has been a part of the European Community since the passing of the European Communities Act 1972.

There are four major institutions of the European Community responsible for the creation of European law.

* Council of Ministers
* European Parliament
* European Commission
* European Court of Justice.

Council of Ministers

The Council consists of one minister from the government of each member state. For general debates, this may be the Foreign Minister but on most occasions it is the minister most closely associated with the subject of the meeting. The Council is the ultimate law making body of the Community.

European Parliament

The Parliament has a supervisory role. It approves the appointment of the President of the Commission. Most primary legislation is now enacted under the co-decision procedure in which the Council and the Parliament must each approve the proposed measures before they become law.

European Commission

The Commission is led by its President and supervises the day-to-day administration of the Community, acts to enforce European law (by taking action against member states in the Court of Justice if necessary), presents legislative proposals for the consideration of the Council and of the Parliament and exercises limited legislative power delegated to it by the Council of Ministers.

European Court of Justice

The Court of Justice is based in Luxembourg. It consists of 15 judges and nine Advocates-General, appointed by the agreement of the national

governments for a period of six years. Each is meant to represent the legal traditions of their home state whilst upholding the principles of European law.

The European Court of Justice hears cases that refer to civil law but plans are being drawn up to allow it to have powers to deal with criminal matters in the future.

European Union law as a source of law

As European laws sit at the top of the English legal system, decision on new legislation in Europe and new case law becomes an important source of law in its own right.

The main sources of European law are:

* treaties (primary legislation)
* regulations (secondary law)
* directives.

Treaties

Treaties are the fundamental piece of law within the European Community. Treaties are attended by the political leaders of the Community where key policies and laws are drawn up which change the shape of Europe.

> **Key terms**
>
> *Treaties* are the highest form of European law.

Examples of EU treaties include:

* the Treaty of Rome Treaty establishing the European Community in 1958
* the Maastricht Treaty of 1991 creating the single European currency and the commitment by the UK government to the scrapping of the pound in favour of the euro
* the Treaty of Accession 2003 which increased the EU to 25 members with the inclusion of the Czech Republic, Estonia, Cyprus, Latvia, Lithuania, Hungary, Malta, Poland, Slovenia and Slovakia.

As treaty legislation is the most important type of law within Europe, all community governments must implement new law by changing their own national law. If a country fails to do this then a person living in that country can take legal action against that country to enforce it.

Regulations

Regulations made by the Council or the Commission have general application. They are binding in their entirety and are directly applicable in all member states. Regulations may deal with matters of minor detail or with fundamental issues. Council regulations for example have dealt with:

* promoting the free movement of workers
* abolishing discrimination as regards employment.

An individual can rely on the provisions of a regulation before a domestic court, either against his government or against another individual.

An individual or business may be prosecuted for violating a regulation, without the need for separate domestic legislation.

> **Key terms**
>
> *Regulations* are European law that should be implemented by member states.

Directives

Directives are issued by the Council with the consent of the Parliament or occasionally by the Commission under delegated powers. They are binding as to the result to be achieved, but leave the choice of form and method to the individual member states. For example, the Product Liability Directive was implemented in the UK by the Consumer Protection Act 1986. Directives are binding on member states but not on individuals and cannot generally be relied upon in English courts.

> **Key terms**
>
> *Directives* are European law issued by the Council.

Marshall v Southampton Health Authority (1986)

Mrs Marshall was forced to retire at the age of 62 from her employment with the National Health Service. This was a breach of the Equal Treatment Directive created by the European Community in 1976. The Sex Discrimination Act 1975 passed by the UK government excluded matters related to retirement from its provisions.

The Court said she was entitled to succeed and could use the provisions of the directive against her employers because the UK had not properly implemented the directive.

✓ 1. Explain how directives protect citizens of Europe.
✓✓ 2. Discuss whether citizens are treated equally across all European states.
✓✓✓ 3. Evaluate the effect of European law on the English legal system.

Where a member state has not implemented a directive within the time laid down, the European Court of Justice has developed the legal concept of 'direct effect'.

The purpose of a directive is to grant rights to the individual. They may be enforceable by an individual against the state if the state has failed to implement it or has implemented it in a defective way. The only person who may bring an action is the person who is affected by the failure by the state to implement the directive. This is known as vertical direct effect.

The 'direct effect' of an unimplemented directive can be relied upon only in an action against the responsible government, not against another individual through the idea of horizontal direct effect.

For more information see www.europa.eu.int.

Case Law

Over time, many aspects have helped create the English legal system. We have already discussed the common law, how Parliament makes law and the influence of Europe as a source of law. Finally, it is important to consider the role of the judges in law-making through the use of **case law** or **judicial precedent**.

> ### Key terms
>
> *Case law* is the body of law made by judges.
> *Judicial precedent* is the binding case law made by judges.

On page 346 we discussed the way statute law is created by Parliament. Parliament is not the only law-maker in the English legal system. Often the judges who sit in courts will be asked to pass judgment on new situations perhaps not covered by legislation. The decision of the judge will create a precedent for subsequent judges to follow in later cases.

There are two types of precedent:

* Binding precedent is a precedent from an earlier case that must be followed by subsequent judges even if the judge does not agree with the legal principle decided.

* Persuasive precedent is a precedent not considered binding on lower courts but the judge may consider it and decide that it is a correct principle so will be persuaded that he should follow it.

Donoghue v Stevenson (1932)

In this case, the claimant went to a café with her friend who paid for her to have a bottle of ginger beer. After consuming nearly all of it she found the remains of a decomposing snail at the bottom of the bottle. Having drunk the beer she became very ill. She could not sue the café for her illness as she had no contract with the café, so she decided to sue the manufacturer of the beer.

The House of Lords said the manufacturer had a duty of care to the consumer of their product and had been in breach of that duty and she was awarded damages.

In this case, Lord Atkin in the House of Lords laid down the general principles of negligence. He quoted his now famous neighbour principle:

'You are under a duty to take reasonable care to avoid acts or omissions that you can reasonably foresee might injure your neighbour. Your neighbour is someone so closely and directly affected by your actions that you ought reasonably to have them in mind as being so affected when considering those actions.'

✓ 1. Identify the key issues in this case.
✓✓ 2. Consider whether or not comments made by judges should become rules of law.
✓✓✓ 3. Assess the advantages and disadvantages of judge-made law.

17.2.2 Law of contract

The modern business world is based on individuals and organisations trading with each other. The English legal system has developed a sophisticated legal framework to deal with these business agreements. It is a mixture of common law, statute law, European law and case law. That is the law of contract.

Clearly contracts are all around us. They affect all of our daily lives from buying a sandwich worth a few pence to buying a new house or car. Certainly without contracts modern businesses would not be able to operate effectively. It is important to understand what is meant by a contract.

A contract is a binding agreement made between two or more persons that is enforceable by law. A contract is certainly more than a vague promise that is not meant to be enforceable.

How contracts are formed

There are various things that must be in place before a person or business can rely on the protection of a contract. The following legal concepts must be in place before a contract can be formed.

Offer

An **offer** is a declaration of agreement to make a contract, made with the intention that it becomes binding upon the person making it (**offeror**) as soon as it is accepted by the person receiving it (**offeree**).

> **Key terms**
>
> *Offer* is an attempt to be bound by a contract.
> *Offeree* is the person who receives an offer.
> *Offeror* is the person making the offer.

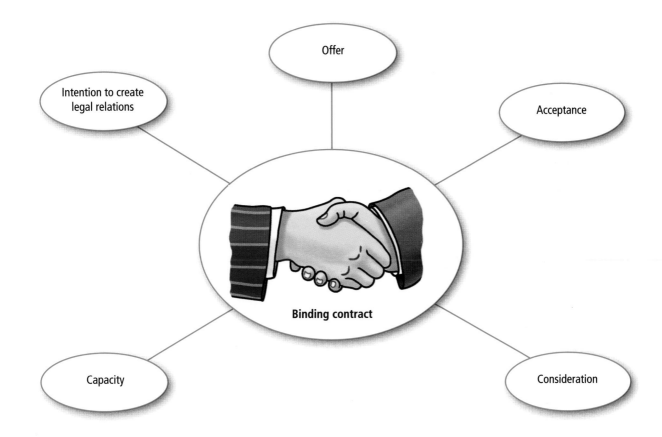

FIGURE 17.2 *Elements of a contract*

Common law rules have been established over time with regards to the validity of the offer.

✳ The offer must be communicated to the person who is to receive it. If the other person does not know that they have had an offer made to them how can they accept it?

✳ The wording of the offer must be certain and not be open to misinterpretation.

✳ The offer will normally be made verbally or, more normally in business contracts, in writing.

✳ An offer can be made to specific people or organisations but sometimes be made to anyone who might want to accept it.

Invitations to Treat

It is important particularly when dealing with business contracts to distinguish between what are genuine offers and what are known as **invitations to treat.**

> ### Key terms
>
> *Invitation to treat* is a statement in contract law that a person will be open to offers for sale.

An offer will be the start of the agreement between the parties but an invitation to treat is not enforceable because a person or organisation will be in the position to receive offers to purchase that can either be accepted and a contract formed or rejected, ending the matter. The following matters are all termed invitations to treat and are not enforceable as valid offers:

* the display of goods with a price ticket attached in a shop window or supermarket as the shop owner can accept or reject a customer's offer to buy products at the price stated

* advertisements, catalogues and brochures which can include Internet catalogues and advertisements

* a company prospectus which is a document issued when a company is selling its shares showing the type of price per share that the company might be willing to accept from purchasers.

The common theme with all of these points is that these are not real offers. They are merely guides to tell prospective purchasers or parties of the type of price that they might be expected to pay if a contract is formed but the person or organisation who makes the invitation to treat can refuse to do business at any time up to the point a valid offer is accepted.

Acceptance of the offer

A valid offer must be accepted by the offeree.

Several important factors should be considered when looking at **acceptance.**

* Acceptance of the offer must in normal circumstances be communicated to the offeror, so that silence to an offer will not be acceptance of that offer.

* Acceptance of an offer must be in the form (if any) specified in the offer.

* There is a presumption that if the offer is silent as to the method of acceptance then only written or oral acceptance will suffice.

* Acceptance need not necessarily be in the specified form as laid down in the offer as long as the method of acceptance used satisfies the offer and the offeror is not prejudiced in any way.

> ### Key terms
> *Acceptance* in contract law means the accepting of an offer.

CASE STUDY

File Edit View Favorites Tools Help

Back · · · Search Favorites · · · · Links »

Address http:// Go Links »

A bargain TV

In August 2005, Argos mistakenly advertised a Bush 28 inch TV/DVD player on its website for the amazing price of £0.49p. The retail price was actually £350. The website was overloaded with customers with over 10,000 orders being taken. The company realising that a mistake had been made refused to honour any of the orders leaving thousand of customers angry and disappointed.

http:// Internet

✓ 1. Explain why Argos were able to refuse to sell the TVs at this low price.
✓✓ 2. Consider if this is an unfair bargain.
✓✓✓ 3. Determine whether invitations to treat protect the buyer, seller or both.

* Acceptance of an offer must be absolute, unqualified and without condition. A change in acceptance will have the effect of cancelling the original offer. It creates a counter offer.

There are issues that may arise regarding acceptance. Particular difficulties have arisen in business law when companies deal with one another. Often they use their own contracts called **standard form contracts**. These contracts will be drawn up for the organisation and will be tailor-made for its own needs and requirements. When businesses contract with each other they may make an offer and acceptance on their own contracts. These standard form contracts often contain terms that conflict with each other. In the event of a dispute, the courts have to decide which standard form contract applies to the transaction, which is not an easy decision to make.

> ### Key terms
> *Standard form contracts* are pre-written business contracts.

Consideration

The mere agreement between the parties will not in itself create a legally binding contract. The law of contract is concerned with bargains and not the enforcement of gratuitous promises made between parties who have given no value or **consideration** to the agreement.

> ### Key terms
> *Consideration* in contract law is the value attached to the promises made between the parties.

Consideration is defined as 'something given, promised or done in exchange' by each side in the agreement.

There are certain rules relating to consideration that should be followed.

* Consideration can never be past. So something already completed by one side of the party can never be deemed to be consideration for a promise later made by the other.

CASE STUDY

Butler Machine Tool Co. Ltd v Ex-Cell-O Corp. (Eng) Ltd (1979)

The claimants offered to supply machinery to the defendants for £73,535. The quotation included a term in a standard form contract called a variation clause that would allow the sellers to increase the price of the quotation. The defendants accepted the offer on their own standard form contract that was silent as to variation clauses. An agreement was made and on delivery the claimant had increased the price by £2,892. The defendant refused to pay this.

The Court of Appeal decided that the defendant's form had been accepted by the claimant so the defendant's terms governed the agreement and the claim to recover the extra money failed.

✓ 1. Explain why businesses use standard form contracts.
✓✓ 2. Consider how the courts decide which standard form contract should be used.
✓✓✓ 3. Can you propose a better way of dealing with such disputes?

For example X is away on holiday and Y, without being asked paints X's house for him. On his return X promises to pay Y. The promise is not enforceable as there was no consideration between the parties. Past consideration is no consideration at all.

(There is an exception to this rule where a person is *asked* to perform a service which is completed and later a promise is made to pay for it.)

✳ Consideration must move between the parties.

If a person X makes a promise (the promisor) to Y (the promisee), Y must also show consideration for that promise.

✳ Consideration cannot be one-sided.

✳ Consideration must not be illegal.

A contract will not be valid if the consideration involved is illegal or considered immoral.

✳ Consideration must be sufficient but does not have to be adequate.

In all valid contracts consideration must have some value and be sufficient but there is no requirement for that consideration to be adequate. The value of consideration is agreed by the parties and the court will not help parties who agree consideration and then complain of making a 'bad bargain'.

There are circumstances when the law may regard a promise as valueless and the promises involved will not amount to valid consideration.

✳ A promise to perform an existing duty.

A promise to perform existing duties will not be consideration as the promisor is only giving that which he is bound to give.

✳ A promise to forego a debt.

The long established rule from Pinnel's Case (1602) is that an agreement to accept a lesser sum in a contract is *not* binding *unless* supported by fresh consideration.

✳ **Promissory estoppel** 'rules of equity'.

Equity (or fairness) will help a person who has relied on the agreement to pay a lesser amount. For example, Josh owes Ava's company £1,000

for a delivery of wine to his off-licence. Both businesses are struggling financially and Josh tells Ava that he can only afford to pay £800. Having problems with cash-flow, Ava agrees to accept the lower sum of money. A while later she hears that that Josh's business is doing better and tries to claim the other £200. Rules of equity or fairness would not allow her to do this through what is known as promissory estoppel.

Theory into practice

As part of a promotional campaign, a sweet manufacturer called Sweetworld offered to supply a DVD to consumers who sent in a cheque for £5 plus three wrappers from its leading bar of chocolate.

1. What is the consideration between the parties?

2. Do you think that consideration should have to be more than 'sufficient'?

Intention to create legal relations

Even if all other elements of a contract are present, in law there will be no binding contract between the parties unless there is an **intention to create legal relations.** Each side must be trying to create a legally enforceable contract.

If there is a clear intention there is no problem but if there is doubt then certain presumptions are brought into play allowing the law to decide what the parties *actually* intended to be bound upon.

These presumptions can be divided into business agreements and social agreements.

* In business and commercial agreements, there is an automatic legal presumption that parties in business transactions always intend to create legal relations and create legally enforceable contracts. This presumption in law exists *unless* there is a definite statement to this effect in the agreement.

* Agreements of a domestic, social or friendly nature raise a very strong presumption that no legal relations were intended between the parties.

Most domestic or social arrangements are never intended to form legally binding agreements. However, in cases between husbands and wives who are splitting up the parties can make binding agreements under what are called separation agreements which can lead to a divorce settlement. The reason for this is that unlike most social arrangements these types of agreements have the backing of the court and must be followed.

Capacity

Under English law there is a presumption that all are free to enter into and negotiate contracts. The ability for a person to have legal capacity to enter into an agreement is vital if a valid contract is to exist between the parties. It is important for businesses to understand exactly who can and cannot make contracts with them.

Minors

Minors are young people under the age of 18. Generally there are two types of contract that will bind a minor when dealing with adults or organisations.

* Contracts for necessities: contracts for the supply of necessary goods and services and beneficial contracts of service are binding on the minor. 'Necessities' are defined as:

'goods suitable to the condition in life of the minor and to his actual requirements at the time of sale and delivery'.

Here the definition will be looked at by the courts in the context of the social and financial background of the minor involved. Items that might be considered necessities to life include food, shelter, heating, clothing and education. Luxury goods are generally excluded as are items or services that the minor already has. Duplicate items and services are not seen to be necessities of life.

* Contracts of Employment/Education/ Apprenticeship for the minor's benefit: a minor is also bound by contracts of employment, apprenticeship and education as long as the contract taken in totality is for the benefit of the minor.

CASE STUDY
Roberts v Gray (1913)

Roberts was a professional billiard player who agreed to take Gray (a minor) with him on a world tour. The tour had cost a lot of money and time to organise and at the last minute the boy refused to go. The boy was sued for breach of contract.

The Court of Appeal held that this tour was an instructional tour for the benefit of the minor so it was held he was liable for breach of contract.

✓ 1. Explain why contracts with minors are generally not valid.
✓✓ 2. Justify how you think this type of tour could be considered educational or instructional.
✓✓✓ 3. Assess whether all contracts made by minors can be enforceable against them. If so, why?

The Minors' Contracts Act 1987 states that contracts agreed by minors at 18 do not now require the need for fresh contracts to be drawn up. The contract is enforceable in its own right.

Incapacitated persons

People who are incapacitated fall into one of two categories.

Mentally ill people

People suffering from medically diagnosed mental health conditions cannot enter into a valid contract as they do not have sufficient mental capacity to understand what they are doing.

However, under the Mental Health Act 1983 the court may enter into valid contracts on the patient's behalf and continue contracts entered into before the illness came to the person and before the person was sectioned under the above Act.

Temporary incapacity

If a person is suffering from a temporary insanity or a drink or drug-related problem, any contract made by that person during that time will be voidable by the person. It will be voidable as long as it can be proved that at the time of negotiation he or she had no understanding of what was going on. It must also be proved that the other party to the agreement knew about the incapacity or should have known about it.

If this is the case, the afflicted person can reject any contract entered into provided he does so within a reasonable time of him recovering from the temporary condition.

Contracts made by business organisations

It is quite common for businesses to enter into contracts with each other, so it is necessary to know if they have capacity to enter into a valid contract.

Registered companies

Companies are created by registration under the Companies Acts 1985. The company in law has a legal identity of its own and can sue and be sued on contracts made in its name.

A company has no legal power before it is **incorporated** (legally formed) to enter into binding contracts. Any person 'acting on behalf of the company' before the date of incorporation will be personally liable on the contract. For example, Faye and Shamilla are in the process of forming a fashion design company. The company has not yet been incorporated. Faye agrees to purchase two cars for the company on hire-purchase. After the company has been formed, payments are not kept up to date and the company receives default notices from the finance company demanding payment. In this type of situation it would be Faye who would be responsible for the payments not the company.

Under the Companies Act the company's power or capacity to contract is by those powers in its **Memorandum and Articles of Association** (a guide to the general powers of the company). The capacity of the company is normally limited to those powers in that document. Any contract entered into that was outside this power and can be held to be what is known as *ultra vires* ('beyond the power of') and void.

However, the Companies Act 1989 has amended the 1985 Act allowing a company to change its **objects clause** in the Memorandum and Articles of Association clause so that it can carry on 'any trade or business whatsoever'. This effectively allows a business to enter into any contract it likes and means that a contract formed by a company having such a clause in its Memorandum cannot now be automatically challenged on the grounds that it went beyond the objects clause of the company.

As a result, to decide whether or not a company has capacity or not to enter into particular contracts it will be necessary to look at its objects clause and decide whether or not it has changed that clause under special resolution.

Key terms

Incorporation is the legal process of forming a company.

Memorandum of Association is a document which sets out the company's name, registered office and what it will do.

Articles of Association are the rules for the running of the company's internal affairs.

Ultra vires is to go beyond an authorised power.

Objects clause can be found in a company's memorandum of association setting out what the company will do.

Unincorporated associations

These are groups of people joined to further a common interest such as a sporting, social or political group. In general terms these groups are not considered legal entities and capacity to contract belongs to members jointly and not with the group or association in its own right.

Partnerships

Many **partnerships** are in fact associations formed for business purposes and are governed by the Partnership Act 1890. Under this Act, each partner has capacity to contract and therefore each is liable on any contract entered into on behalf of the partnership. In this case, it is not the partnership that has legal capacity but the individual partners themselves.

How contracts are brought to an end

A contract can be terminated or ended in four ways.

Discharge through performance

Complete performance of the contract will of course bring that particular contract between the parties to an end.

The parties must carry out exactly what they agreed under the contract, so that if one of the parties does something less than or different to what he has agreed then the contract will not have come to an end. However, certain exceptions to this rule have developed:

Substantial performance

If the court decides that the person has substantially carried out the terms of the contract, they may recover for the work already completed.

Acceptance of partial performance

If one of the parties only partially carries out his side of the bargain, and the other side accepts this partial performance then the contract will be deemed to be completed and the there will be an obligation to pay for the partial work carried out.

Partial performance caused by one of the parties

If one of the parties prevents the other from completely carrying out the contract the other party will be able to claim for the work done.

Divisible contracts

We have already seen that some contracts can be regarded as entire so that a party is not entitled to payment until the full performance of the contract has taken place. However, some contracts can be divisible in that obligations can be split up into parts or stages where payment can be claimed for completion of each stage. A common example of this is a building project where payments are made for each stage of the work.

Discharge by mutual agreement

It is possible for the parties to agree to allow the contract to come to an end. This is known as discharge by mutual agreement and usually occurs in one of two ways.

Specific contractual provision

Parties may include in the contract any term which will end the contract providing both parties agree. A common example is a contract that will come to an end by a fixed time. For example, contracts for lease or hire or fixed-term employment contracts.

New contract

This is where a new contract is substituted for the old one through a process known as **novation.**

Key terms

Novation in contract law is where a new contract is substituted for an old one.

Discharge by frustration

Frustration involves the parties to a contract being unable to complete the contract. This has the effect of bringing the contract to an end.

Traditionally the law has always imposed strict burdens on parties, imposing on them absolute duties to carry out their obligations under the contract. Gradually courts began to relax this very strict application of this rule and developed the idea of frustration to help parties whose performance of a contract is prevented because of events beyond their control.

Frustration occurs where for whatever reason it becomes impossible to complete the contract. For example, a farm business might be supplying organic crops to supermarkets and their farm is hit by disease or perhaps flood. The contracts between themselves and the supermarkets would not be able to be completed. They would be frustrated.

All common law frustration will bring the contract to an immediate end. The rights and liabilities of the parties are frozen and monies payable before frustration are recoverable whilst those waiting to be paid cannot be recovered.

The doctrine of frustration will not apply in the following situations:

* where the parties have foreseen the likelihood of such an event occurring and express provision has been made for it

* where one of the parties is responsible for the frustrating event.

There are several circumstances where frustration will apply.

Physical impossibility

This is where someone or something necessary to carry out the contract ceases to be available. Death or illness of one of the parties or one of the parties becoming unavailable may also frustrate the performance of the contract.

Illegality

A subsequent change in law may make the contract illegal and impossible to perform.

The main part of the contract has been destroyed

If the main purpose of the contract cannot take place the doctrine of frustration may apply.

Discharge by breach of contract

A breach of contract can occur in a number of ways and may bring a contract to an end. There are two main types of breach of contact.

Repudiatory breach

A repudiatory breach arises as a result of or a consequence of one of the parties to refuse, fail to perform or be incapacitated to perform their side of the contract. In this case, the innocent party can either end the contract or can accept the contract as it stands.

Anticipatory breach

An anticipatory breach is where one of the parties announces in advance that he does not intend to carry on the contract or he puts himself in a position where he is unable to carry on with the contract.

In this case, the party who has been let down has the choice to either sue for breach of contract immediately or wait until the time of performance of the contract to arrive to see if the other party will carry out the contract or not.

Theory into practice

Speedforce, a courier firm, were employed by MN who are a men's clothing company. MN employed Speedforce to act as a courier to deliver its parcels in Europe. The contract was to begin on 1 June that year.

On 11 May 2005 MN wrote to Speedforce to inform them that their services were no longer required. Speedforce started an action for breach of contract on 22 May 2005.

Although the date for performance had not yet arrived it was agreed by the court that that MN's letter was sufficient to represent a breach of contract and Speedforce were awarded damages.

1. Explain the different types of breach of contract.

2. Why were Speedforce successful in the above case?

Difference between express and implied terms

A contract is a set of mutually agreed promises made between the parties with the intention of creating a legally binding agreement but it is important to analyse exactly what it is that the parties are agreeing to do.

To do this we will examine those things that the parties are bound to do under the contract which are called terms of the contract. It is important that a person knows exactly what it is they are agreeing to in a contract.

CASE STUDY

In September 2005, the Advertising Standards Agency (ASA) investigated Jamster, the producers of the 'Crazy Frog' ringtone for making misleading advertising by not explaining fully the terms of the agreement that users were signing up to. The ASA claimed that Jamster did not explain that this was a subscription service rather than a one-off payment agreement.

See www.asa.org.uk for more information about this case.

✓ 1. Suggest why it is important to have terms in a contract.

✓✓ 2. Should parties be free to put whatever terms they like in a contract?

✓✓✓ 3. What proposals could you suggest to ensure terms are not misleading?

There are two broad types of term found in a contract:

* express terms

* implied terms.

Express terms

Express terms of a contract are statements actually made by the parties either by word of mouth or in writing. They can be either conditions or warranties.

Conditions

A condition is a fundamental part of the agreement and is something which goes to the root of the contract. For example, if the parties agree to buy and sell a brand new car and the actual item supplied is a motor-bike then there is a clear breach of contract as the supply of a car was a condition of the contract.

A breach of condition will entitle the injured party to repudiate the contract (treat as an end) and claim damages.

Warranties

A warranty is a less important term that does not go to the root of the contract.

A breach of a warranty will only give the injured party the right to claim damages. The contract cannot be rejected.

For example, consider the issue of buying a new car. You agree with the supplier that it will be fitted with a particular model/brand of DVD player. The car arrives, so the supplier has completed the main condition of the contract which is the supply of the car. However, it has been fitted with the wrong type of DVD player. The DVD player is not the vital part of the contract and will be seen as a warranty. This failure although annoying for the person buying the car will still allow them to sue the supplier for damages but it will not mean the contract can automatically be ended.

Implied terms

Implied terms are not actually stated in a contract but are introduced into the contract by statute, custom and common law.

Terms implied by statute

Terms are implied into a contract by virtue of legislation that protected early trading agreements. The best example is the Sale of Goods Act 1979 (see page 386) which is implied into contracts for the sale of goods.

Terms implied by custom

An agreement may be made subject to customary terms not actually specified by the parties. These could be historical and a person making a contract should try to find if any such terms are in existence.

It should be noted however that such a custom will be overruled by any express clause to the contrary.

Terms implied by the common law

The courts will be prepared to imply a term into the contract in order to give effect to the obvious intentions of the parties. This may be a point that has been overlooked or may not have been clearly stated by the parties. In such circumstances the court will imply such a term in the interests of 'business fairness' so that the contract makes commercial common sense.

Remedies for breach of contract

In law, every breach of contract will give the injured person the right to recover damages.

Other remedies are available such as specific performance and injunctions. These are equitable remedies granted at the discretion of the court.

Damages

When things go wrong in a contract it is quite normal for the injured side to want to gain damages from the other party. These damages can take two forms.

Liquidated damages

In the business world it is quite common for parties to agree in advance the amount of damages that will be paid in the event of a breach of contract. These are known as **liquidated damages.**

> ### Key terms
>
> *Liquidated damages* in contract law are when parties agree in advance the amount of damages that will be paid in the event of a breach of contract.

Unliquidated damages

Unliquidated damages are those damages awarded for breach of contract where there is no prior agreement between the parties as to the amount of damages to be awarded.

The aim of unliquidated damages is to restore the person to the position they would have been in had the contract been carried out correctly.

The damages are designed to compensate only for loss suffered so if no loss has been suffered damages awarded will only be nominal to recognise that there has been a breach of contract.

Awarding damages

Courts use the following guidelines when awarding damages:

* the damage can include sums for financial loss, damage to property, personal injury and distress, disappointment and upset caused to the claimant

* an injured party cannot necessarily recover damages for every kind of loss.

Breaches of contract can cause a chain of events. There has to come a point in law after which the damage becomes too distant from the original damage to be recoverable:

* provided that the loss is not too distant, courts have to decide how much is payable by way of damages

* once a breach of contract has occurred, the innocent party is under a duty to mitigate or lessen his loss.

A victim of a breach of contract cannot simply stand back and allow his losses to get worse. For example, a seller whose goods have been rejected must attempt to get the best price for them elsewhere.

Equitable remedies

There are some situations where damages are neither adequate nor appropriate. Equity has developed other forms of help to ensure that justice is done.

Specific performance

Specific performance is an equitable remedy granted instead of damages in cases in which damages are not considered an adequate remedy. A decision of specific performance requires the party in breach of contract to carry out his contractual obligations. However, specific performance will not be available where damages are adequate.

This in reality means that specific performance is a limited remedy in ordinary commercial transactions or sales of goods as damages will normally be available to buy similar goods elsewhere.

Injunction

This an order of the court requiring the party at fault not to break the contract.

Its main use is to enforce negative promises in certain contracts such as employment contracts restraining employees working in a similar capacity for rival employers.

Theory into practice

Advent Builders have secured a contract to build a new sports centre for a local council. The contract has strict guidelines regarding time for completion. Penalties have been included for late completion. For every day the job is late the builders lose 1 per cent of the total contract value. If the delay is more than one month the damages the council can claim is 50 per cent of the original contract price. The job has been delayed by 20 days and the council are suing the builders for breach of contract.

1. What type of damages are the council claiming?

2. What factor will the court consider in a case like this?

Theory into practice

Music promoters Star Enterprises have booked a famous singer to perform as the main act in a large concert. The venue and the supporting acts have been booked and all of the tickets have been sold. The singer has a row with one of the producers of the show and is refusing to perform. Star's lawyers have gone to court to gain a remedy.

1. What is the contractual position between the parties?

2. What remedy will Star Enterprises be trying to get?

3. Are damages suitable here?

17.2.3 Business formation

Many people run their own business. There are many different types of business organisation that can be formed. They vary in complexity and size and vary considerably in law in terms of the owner's liability to pay debts when things go wrong. This section looks at the different legal frameworks that business organisations can work within.

Sole traders

A sole trader is probably the simplest form of business. A sole trader is the sole owner of a business. The business is often quite small in terms of size measured, for example, by sales generated or number of staff employed. However, the number of these businesses is very large indeed.

Examples of these businesses can be found in most industrial sectors but particularly in most service sectors, for example electrical repair, picture framing, photography, diving instruction, retail shops. It may well be a good starting place for a person to begin their business enterprise. However there are certain considerations that should be considered before setting up as a sole trader.

Many small businesses operate as sole traders

Liability of sole traders

As the name suggests, a sole trader has full responsibility for receiving any profit the organisation might make but is also fully and personally liable (responsible) for the debts of the business including income tax and VAT. In the event that the debts are unpaid, creditors could apply for a declaration that the sole trader be made bankrupt.

Ability of a sole trader to raise finance

The sole trader is responsible for raising all of the finance for the business. This means that they are responsible for personally raising the capital to begin trading, either from their own personal wealth, through investment or by raising a bank loan with their own property being used to guarantee the finance.

Tax implications of the sole trader

As a very simple business structure the sole trader will incur tax liabilities very similar to an individual. A sole trader will pay income tax at similar rates to an individual which is up to a maximum of 40 per cent of profit. However, under schedule D of the government's rules on taxation a sole trader can offset certain business expenses. These expenses can include such things as lighting, heating, machinery and equipment. The current schemes allow for self-assessment of liability to pay tax on the completion of an annual self assessment form.

Class 2 **National Insurance** contributions are payable by anyone who is self-employed. National Insurance payments are deductions made to cover the sole trader's contributions to things such as the National Health Service. If the person earns from the business more than £4,345 per annum they will have to make a contribution. This is a fixed weekly amount, paid by monthly direct debit or quarterly bill. The current figure for the tax year 2005–06 is £2.10 per week

The sole trader will incur further National Insurance contributions by having to pay a more substantial amount under Class 4 contributions. The starting point here is that the first £4,895 of profit per annum is exempt with a maximum limit for assessment purposes being £32,760 per annum. The rate between the lower and upper limit is 8 per cent of that figure and anything above that figure is an extra 1 per cent of that figure.

Theory into practice

Nadira decided to become a sole trader and has made £21,000 profit for the year.

1. What would her total National Insurance contributions be?

2. How would this figure change if she made £75,000 profit?

3. What would happen if Nadira only made £3,000 profit this year?

The sole trader may also be liable to pay Value Added Tax (VAT). To be registered for VAT the business must have a turnover of more than £60,000 per annum.

If a sole trader employs staff then they may be liable to paying part of their National Insurance contributions as well. At the moment if an employee earns over £4,895 per annum the employer will pay 12.8 per cent of that figure to the government as National Insurance.

See www.hmrc.gov.uk and www.hm-treasury. gov.uk for more details of tax liabilities.

Legal formalities for sole traders

The sole trader is a relatively simple business structure and requires little formality to be undertaken. There are however certain conditions that have to be fulfilled.

* If the sole trader is going to trade under a name different to their own personal name they must display the name of the owner and an address where documents can be served on all business stationery and at their premises.

* The sole trader will also need to be careful about choosing a name since the wrong name can cause legal problems. Certain words and expressions like 'international', 'federation' and 'registered' are protected and restricted under the Business Names Act 1985 and the Company and Business Names Regulations 1981. Details of restricted names can be found at Companies House.

See www.companieshouse.gov.uk for details of business names.

* The business name cannot be the same or too similar to that of another business, trademark or company. If it is a new business you could face legal action from its owner. Thorough checks should be taken to ensure these problems are avoided.

* The sole trader must also be registered with the Inland Revenue for tax purposes and if necessary registered for VAT as well.

Theory into practice

Derrick is trying to think of a name for his business and comes up with the idea of Microsoft International.

1. What are your views on the choice of name for the business?

2. How can a person check to see if a name is restricted or protected?

The role of the sole trader as stakeholder

The owner of a sole trader business can decide the way in which the business is to be conducted and has the total flexibility to restructure or dissolve the business whenever it suits. The law does not recognise the sole trader as being separate from the owner and so the business will cease on the death of the owner.

For many, the great advantage of being a sole trader is having this complete control over the business and its profits; the owner is able to use any money the business brings as they think fit without having to justify their actions. Department of Trade and Industry figures estimate that over 60 per cent of all business organisations operating within the UK in 2006 were sole traders.

A sole trader should always remember that they are liable financially for the business and the need for the business to examine the implications and consequences of bankruptcy or loss of personal possessions due to the individual accepting unlimited liability should be considered.

Partnerships

After the sole trader, the next most common form of business is the partnership. A partnership is a business with two or more owners who share in the control, management, profit and loss of that business. The partnerships are often small businesses where partners want to work together for a common goal such as firms of lawyers, doctors, accountants and dentists but partnerships can be very large organisations in their own right.

Liability of partners

There are two types of partnership that can be created and the liability of the partners depends on which type is formed.

The full partnership

Under the Partnership Act 1890, two or more people can join together to make a partnership. Under the Act, the maximum number to own the business is 20 (there are exceptions such as solicitors and accountants where there is no limit).

The financial liability of such partners is that they are jointly and severally liable for the debts of the firm. This means they are jointly responsible when things go wrong. Partners can be sued as a collective group but a partner should also be aware that they can be sued individually for liabilities owed by the partnership. This liability can extend into the partners' own personal assets as well so a person intending to go into partnership should understand the very serious nature of the agreement.

The limited partnership

It may be that a full type of partnership is not acceptable and the partners want to put a limit on their individual liabilities. They can do this by forming a limited partnership. The legal status of these partnerships is governed by the Limited Partnerships Act 1907. The partners can put a financial limit on their own personal liability but at least one of the partners must have unlimited liability to cover all the losses and debt of the partnership should things go wrong.

CASE STUDY

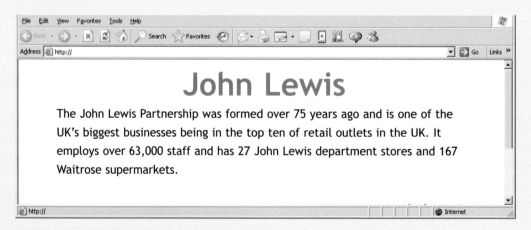

John Lewis

The John Lewis Partnership was formed over 75 years ago and is one of the UK's biggest businesses being in the top ten of retail outlets in the UK. It employs over 63,000 staff and has 27 John Lewis department stores and 167 Waitrose supermarkets.

✓ 1. Explain the purpose of forming a partnership.
✓✓ 2. Comment on the positive impact for John Lewis of forming a partnership.
✓✓✓ 3. Determine whether a firm like John Lewis should be a public limited company.

Suzy has set up an IT consultancy with James which is a full partnership. The partnership is being sued for £10,000 by a builder who has refurbished their offices. The partners are refusing to pay and Suzy has received a letter from the builder's solicitors demanding the money from her alone.

1. Explain Suzy's liability for the debt.

2. How could she have avoided such liability in the first place?

The partners' ability to raise finance

Partnerships are no different from any other business in that they need finance to operate effectively so the partnership will need to raise money to do this. It is unlikely that a bank will lend a new partnership 100 per cent of the capital needed to begin operating and to continue trading until profit is made. The advantage of a partnership (compared to a sole trader) is that there is more scope to raise money privately as up to 20 people can be allowed to become partners and it is very common for new partners to bring with them to the business private capital to effectively buy into the partnership.

The tax implications of a partnership

As with all businesses the aim of the partnership will be to produce income. That income when it comes attracts taxation from the government in the same way as sole traders under Schedule D of the tax rules.

There are however some differences in the tax liability of the partnership. It is the income of the partnership that is taxed and all the partners will be jointly liable for the for tax. Profits of the partnership are usually split in a way that has been agreed in the partnership agreement and partners will be assessed individually on that share of the profit they receive. This assessment will take into account the partners' individual circumstances so that they can deduct allowances that are owed to them. The partnership figure and the partners' individual liability is then added together to make a total tax bill that is owed to the revenue. Partners should be aware that they may be liable for the tax bills of other partners should they become insolvent and be unable to pay it.

Many partnerships allow for partners to be paid a salary by the business. If that is the case, the partners will be taxed individually as employees and pay tax under Schedule E of the taxation rules. This means that the person's first £4,895 per annum is exempt from tax but earnings above that will be taxed in the following ways:

* the starting rate of 10 per cent for earnings between £1 and £2,900

* the basic rate of 22 per cent for earnings between £2,901 and £32,400

* the higher rate of 40 per cent for earnings over £32,401.

See www.hmrc.gov.uk for more details.

Emma, Angus and Louise have formed a partnership and have received their tax bill. It is £25,000. Louise is a salaried partner and has earned £36,000 this year from the business and receives no other allowances.

1. Explain the tax position of the partners.

2. How much tax should Louise be expecting to pay?

Legal formation of a partnership

Unlike the sole trader, the partnership is regulated by a statutory framework. The Partnership Act 1890 lays down guidelines that should be followed:

* The partners must be carrying on a business.

* The partners must act in common to allow all partners to have a say in the management of the business.

* The partnership must be formed to try to make a profit and there must be provision made to share that profit.

The essence of the partnership comes from contract law in that there is an agreement between the parties to carry on a business. This agreement can be informal and unwritten but it is very common to draw up a partnership agreement which legally binds the partners to the promises they have made. Although no formal guidelines are needed the following points should be covered in any partnership agreement:

* the name of the business
* the names of the partners
* date the partnership started
* the nature of the business the partnership will be dealing with
* the address for the business
* the set-up investment of the partners
* the personal contributions of the partners (if any)
* details of ownership of the partnership property
* the role of the partners
* how decisions will be made
* how profits and losses will be shared
* liability of the partners
* bank account details
* accounting procedures
* partners' holidays
* the effect of illness, incapacity, retirement or death of a partner
* how new partners are brought in
* the dismissal of partners
* expenses
* how the partnership can be ended
* signatures by the parties.

There are more formal registration procedures in relation to accounts and reports filing needed for a limited liability partnership and the rules relating to choosing the firm's name must follow the guidelines already discussed for sole traders.

Theory into practice

In small groups, imagine that you are setting up a partnership. Think of a business idea and using the list above draw up a partnership agreement for it.

The role of the partner

The partner in a firm can have many roles and functions. The most usual type of partner in any firm is the general partner who is equal to all of the other partners in the firm in terms of management and day-to-day control. This type of partner will be jointly responsible for the losses and debts of the firm and will share equally in the profit. They will usually have full power to contract and negotiate on behalf of the firm.

There are also sleeping partners who although they are a full partner in the firm will have little if anything to do with the running of the firm. Instead they will invest in the firm and draw on the profits.

The final type of partner commonly found in partnerships is the salaried partner. This type of partner will usually have made no contribution financially to the capital investment of the business but will have authority to say how the firm is run. The key difference here is that the salaried partner will receive a salary instead of sharing in its profits.

Limited companies

Limited companies exist in their own right, distinct from the shareholders who own them. This means their finances are clearly separated from the personal finances of their owners. There are many types of limited company but the main two to consider are:

* Private limited companies can have one or more members (shareholders). They cannot offer shares to the public on the stock exchange. Examples of private limited companies are Macmillan Publishers Ltd and Rowntree and Co. Ltd.

* Public limited companies (plcs) must have at least two shareholders and can offer shares to the public. These are the most famous business names and include Vodafone, Shell and Tesco.

The liability of shareholders

The formation of a company creates a separate legal entity that is capable of existing in its own right. This means that it has shareholders as members who can limit their liability to the amount of their shareholding.

Shareholders are not generally responsible for the company's debts. However, they may lose the money (up to the value of their shareholding) they have invested in the company if it fails.

More specifically in certain situations members of companies may incur personal liability.

Firstly, any contract made by a director before the company is formed will mean that the director making it will be personally liable for it. Likewise, if a company falls into debt and the company continues to trade then directors may become personally liable for those debts provided that the company is unable to meet them.

Company directors and members can also be liable for personal guarantees that they might make in respect of the company for things such as bank overdrafts. In the event of the company failing to honour such debts the directors or members making such guarantees may be forced to honour the debts.

Ability of the company to raise finance

A company as a business concern must have the finances in place to be able to operate effectively. This can be achieved in a number of ways.

At the outset the most common way for the company to raise finance is by way of personal contribution by those directors who are creating the company. Those directors will then receive **shares** in the company up to the value of their investment and the investment will become the company's **issued capital.** A public limited company must have an authorised share capital of £50,000.

The initial capital may not be enough to run the business and it is common for a company to borrow money from a bank or other lending institution. This may take the form of a loan or an overdraft facility which will allow the company to spend money over the amount it has in its bank account. In the event of the company being liquidated the lender will be able to recover their money as a creditor of the company. It is normal for banks and other lenders to ask the company to give a paper **guarantee** that the loan will be re-paid. This type of guarantee is called a **debenture.** This guarantee will often be backed up by a personal guarantee by the directors that they will be personal liable for the debt if the company cannot pay it.

From time to time the company may raise finance by allowing new shares to be purchased in it. The public limited company can have as many shareholders as it wishes and in theory can issue as many shares as can be purchased by members of the public up to their stated authorised share capital.

However, a private company is not allowed to issue new shares to the general public but is allowed to issue new shares to its existing members as long as all current shareholders agree to whom they are being sold.

Company tax implications

As well as the liability for personal taxation of members of the company, the company itself will incur liability for tax. Members of companies, such as directors who are classed as employees will incur normal income tax and have to pay Class 1 National Insurance contributions.

The current income tax levels have been discussed on page 367 and the National Insurance contributions for members of companies is 11 per cent for earnings below £32,760 and 1 per cent for additional earnings over that.

Companies may be liable to VAT and all companies are subject to a specific type of tax called corporation tax. This is a tax based on the profits made by UK based companies and under the Companies Act 1985 (as amended) a company must file its accounts for tax purposes at the end of each financial year. The current rates of corporation tax are as follows:

* the starting rate of 0 per cent for profits between £0 and £10,000 (as long as profits are distributed to existing shareholders)

* a rate of 19 per cent for profits between £50,001 and £300,000

* a rate of 30 per cent for profits above £1.5 million.

For profits between £10,001 and £50,000 and £300,001 and 1.5 million, corporation tax will be levied at a gradual level called marginal relief to allow companies to make allowance for the changes to higher rate tax.

See www.hmrc.gov.uk for more details.

Theory into practice

Nicola and her friends have an IT consultancy company called ITbiz. It has been trading for a year and must file its tax return. The company has traded well and has made profits of £65,000.

1. What is ITbiz's corporation tax liability?

2. Are Nicola and her friends liable for the tax?

Company legal formalities

The formalities for setting up a company (called incorporation) are far more complex and detailed than other types of organisations and have to comply with rules laid down by the Companies Act 1985 (as amended by the Companies Act 1989).

The Companies Act allows one or more persons to form a company for any lawful purpose but there are certain formalities that must be complied with when forming a company. Both public limited companies and private limited companies must complete the following legal paperwork which must be sent to Companies House.

Memorandum of Association

This is document which sets out the following:

* the company's name

* where the registered office of the company is based (in England, Wales or Scotland)

* what it will do (its objects).

Articles of Association

This document sets out the rules for the running of the company's internal affairs. Model articles (Tables A–F) are provided by Companies House for new companies to use and the majority of new companies opt to follow articles that are already drawn up.

Form 10

Form 10 (Figure 17.3) is a form that must be completed by new companies. It gives details of:

* the first director(s) and secretary

* the intended address of the registered office

* the names and addresses of the company's directors, their date of birth, occupation and details of other directorships they have held within the last five years.

Each appointed person must sign and date the form.

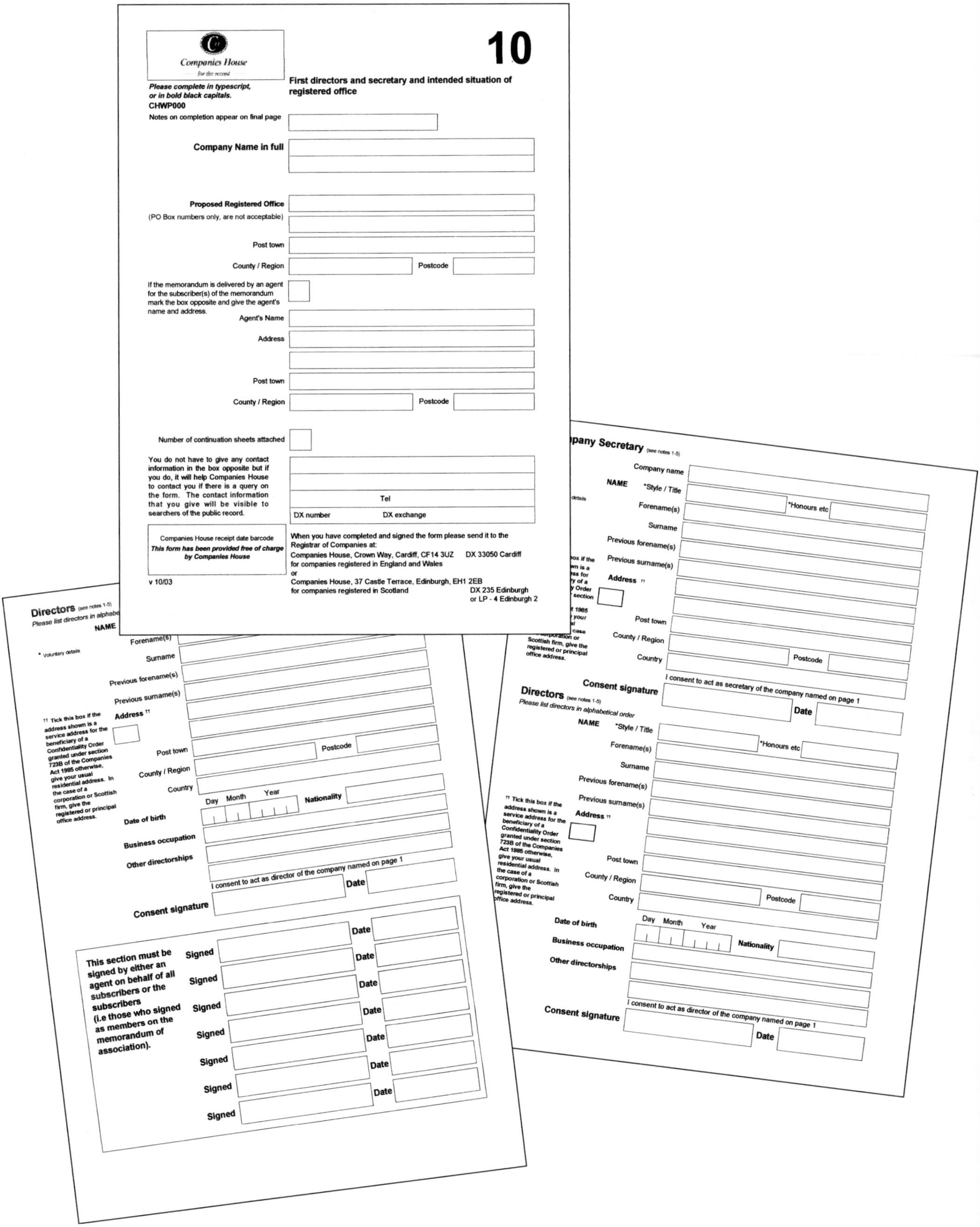

FIGURE 17.3 *Form 10*

Form 12

Form 12 is a statutory declaration that all the legal requirements relating to the formation of a company have been completed. It must be signed by a solicitor who is forming the company or by one of the people named as a director or company secretary on Form 10. It must be signed in the presence of a professional legal person such as a justice of the peace or a solicitor.

See www.companieshouse.gov.uk for more information.

Company name

The new company will of course require a name to trade under and as before there are rules relating to the names that can be used:

* A company cannot register the same name as another company, for example it would be illegal to form a new company and call it Tesco.

* The use of certain words is restricted such as 'Royal' and 'Government'.

* Names likely to cause offence or discrimination are not allowed.

Special formalities

As well as rules that are common to all companies there are specific formalities that apply to different types of companies.

Public limited companies

* The company must state in all paperwork that it is a public limited company by using 'Public Limited Company' or 'PLC'.

* The company's memorandum of association should follow Table F as far as possible.

* The company must have authorised share capital of at least £50,000 which must be given (allotted) to shareholders before it can start trading.

* A public limited company must have at least two members and at least two directors and a professional person who can act as company secretary.

Private limited companies

* The company must state in its paperwork that it is a limited company by the use of 'Limited' or 'Ltd'.

* The company must have at least one director and a company secretary. A single person cannot run a private limited company.

Stakeholders in a company

A company will have a diverse set of stakeholders who are affected by its operation. They include the following.

Shareholders

The most common form of stakeholder is the person who buys shares in the company (the shareholder). The amount of power that a person has within the company at any one time will depend on the type of shareholder they are. The most common types of shareholders are:

* private shareholders

* large corporate shareholders

* holding companies, a company which normally holds the majority shares in one company but controls the shareholding in another (it's subsidiary).

Other groups of stakeholders that can affect and influence the company include:

* employees

* customers

* suppliers

* government agencies

* bankers

* stock markets.

It is only the shareholder who is entitled to vote on company matters and the other stakeholders can influence company decisions but play no part in making them.

Manchester United FC

Manchester United football grounds

During 2004-05, the famous football club was the subject of a takeover bid from American billionaire Malcolm Glazer who wanted to purchase the club. At first the club was hostile to the takeover bid but gradually over the year Glazer began to purchase shares in the company.

Despite strong and often violent opposition by fans and some shareholders Glazer acquired enough shares in Manchester United to force remaining investors to sell their shares to him. By 2005, he had acquired 98 per cent of the shares in the club and therefore took total control of the club.

✓ 1. Explain what a hostile takeover is.
✓✓ 2. Discuss the advantages and disadvantages of the Glazer family having sole control of Manchester United.
✓✓✓ 3. Assess whether or not you think it fair that minority shareholders should be forced to sell to powerful shareholders like Glazer.

Charitable organisations

Charities are lawful organisations that provide a social benefit to various groups or countries. They are usually called not-for-profit businesses such as Amnesty International or Oxfam.

Often charities are set up as companies limited by guarantee which means the same rules apply as for a limited company so that they cannot incur liability beyond a certain level.

Charities will employ staff and are subject to the same rules as other companies. They are regulated by the Charitable Regulation Authority and if they have an income of over £10,000 they must be registered. If they have an income of over £1million per year they must file a set of accounts to the Authority detailing the extent of the fundraising work and where the money has gone.

Contributions made to charities now qualify for Gift Aid so are exempt of tax. Charities are also generally exempt from income tax and corporation tax.

See www.charity-commission.gov.uk for more details.

Think it over...

Think of the advantages and disadvantages of each type of organisation. If you were setting up a new business, which factors might influence your final choice?

17.2.4 Business dissolution

According to the British Chamber of Commerce, the number of companies failing in 2005 was 13,599 and as many as one in two of all new businesses will fail in the their first two years of trading. See www.britishchambers.org.uk for more details.

Having spent time and effort in setting up a business the question has to be asked why do businesses cease to exist? There are numerous reasons why a business might fail. Some of the more common include:

* poor marketing
* cash flow problems
* poor business planning
* lack of finance
* failure to embrace new technology
* poor choice of location
* poor management
* poor human resource management
* lack of clear objectives.

Theory into practice

Choose a business that you know has failed, for example 'Red Letter Days'

1. Why did the business fail?

2. What other reasons might there be for a business to fail?

Having looked at some of the main reasons for business failure it is important to look at the procedures involved when a business becomes **insolvent** or unable to operate. The law relating to this topic is found in the Companies Act 1985 (as amended) and the Insolvency Act 1986.

The Insolvency Act is the main piece of legislation controlling the way a business can be dissolved and the effect this has on the creditors of the business. It also addresses the qualification and appointment of insolvency practitioners to oversee the process.

Key terms

Insolvent is when a business cannot operate due to financial reasons.

Liquidation of companies

When a company is ended the process is called liquidation or winding up. The ending of a partnership is called dissolution. It is a complex and often expensive process and is far more difficult than actually forming the business in the first place! Company liquidation can take one of two forms.

FIGURE 17.4 *Many types of business are affected by insolvency*

Compulsory liquidation

Compulsory liquidation of a company is when the company is ordered by either the County Court or the High Court to be wound up or liquidated. The most common reason for this is that the business has over-stretched itself financially and cannot pay its debts.

A company is regarded as unable to pay its debts if a person who is owed money (the creditor):

* is owed more than £750 and

* presents a written demand (known as a statutory demand to the company) and

* the company fails to pay, secure or agree a settlement of the debt to the creditor's reasonable satisfaction within 21 days of the statutory demand.

The court may also order the company to be wound up by:

* the company itself or

* the company's directors or

* one or more of its members.

Before the court can order the liquidation of a company, the application to have the company wound up (called the petition) must be placed in a publication that deals with statutory/legal matters called *The Gazette*. See www.gazettes-online.co.uk for more details.

If the petition is successful, the company must send the winding-up order to the Registrar of Companies at Companies House and it will be placed on the company's public record so that any potential traders with the business will know the business is about to cease trading.

When the company has been liquidated, the court will appoint a person called the **official receiver** to deal with the winding-up process. Along with the issue of dealing with creditors of the business the official receiver has a duty to investigate the company's affairs and the causes of its failure. Only upon notification from the official receiver that all of the company's matters have been concluded will the company be officially dissolved at Companies House.

Voluntary liquidation

It is not only the court that can force a company into liquidation. There can also be what is known as **voluntary liquidation.** There are two kinds of voluntary liquidation.

Members' voluntary liquidation

Members' voluntary liquidation means at least 75 per cent of the directors have made a statutory declaration of solvency but want the company liquidated. The statutory declaration will state that the directors have made a full inquiry into the company's affairs and that, having done so, they believe that the company will be able to pay its debts in full within 12 months from the start of the winding-up.

Creditors' voluntary liquidation

This means that the directors have not made such a declaration of solvency and that the company cannot pay its debts.

Process of voluntary liquidation

To begin the process of voluntary liquidation, members of the company will hold a general meeting and pass a resolution called a **special resolution** to wind up the company voluntarily.

Notice of this resolution must be given to the general public by placing an announcement in *The Gazette* within 14 days of the meeting. A copy is also sent to Companies House.

A meeting of creditors must be held in the next 14 days after passing the resolution so they can try to recover their losses.

A person called a **liquidator** will be appointed to wind up the company's business affairs. The liquidator does this by calling in or recovering all the company's assets and distributing them to its creditors usually in accordance to the size of the debt with the biggest creditors being dealt with first. If anything is left over, the liquidator distributes it among the members of the company.

The process will be completed after a final meeting of creditors has taken place and a final account is returned to Companies House and the company will be dissolved.

Dissolution of partnerships

We have already seen the nature of partnerships on page 366. As with all types of businesses inevitably some partnerships will end. When partnerships end, they are dissolved.

Dissolution can occur in a variety of ways.

* Dissolution by agreement when all of the partners simply agree to end the partnership.

* Automatic dissolution of the partnership by the passing of a fixed time limit, for example if the partnership was only for five years or by the completion of the project if the partnership was created for a particular project. Automatic dissolution will occur upon the death or bankruptcy of a partner although partnerships today tend to treat the affected partner as 'retired' to allow the business to continue.

* Dissolution by notice occurs when a partner in a partnership that has been created with no end date (a partnership at will) serves notice on the other partners that they want the partnership to end.

* The court can order the dissolution of the partnership. The likely reasons for this are:
  * a partner's mental or physical incapacity
  * a partner's conduct is damaging the business
  * where the partner has broken the partnership agreement
  * when the business can operate only at a loss
  * when the court using its equitable jurisdiction believes it fair to do so.

* A partnership agreement can also be dissolved when a person has been misled into signing the agreement by fraud or misrepresentation by the other partners.

The effect of the dissolution of a partnership is similar to that of when a company is liquidated. The firm's assets are collected together and the liabilities of the firm will be repaid including the repayment of any loans or capital to the partners if there is sufficient funds and finally giving any surplus funds to the partners. One of the most important assets the partnership might have is its **goodwill**. Goodwill is the value of the partnership's reputation and business connections and this can be sold as part of the value of the partnership.

It is usual to make a public announcement that the business has been dissolved to inform other businesses and creditors and to warn them that the partners no longer have the authority of the business to act.

Administration

To avoid the necessity of liquidation, companies can go into what is known as administration. Due to its poor financial position an administrator (an expert in insolvency) is appointed to manage its affairs, business and property for the benefit of the creditors. Administration orders can be made by the court, by the company itself or by a person who has a hold on the company's assets such as a loan or mortgage.

The reason for administration is to:

* keep a company as a going concern

* get a better price for the company's assets for the creditors as a whole than would be likely if the company were wound up

* realise the value of property in order to make a distribution or pay out to one or more creditors.

The effect of an administration order is to suspend any winding up orders so the company cannot be liquidated. Again notice of the administration order must be placed in *The Gazette* and notice of the appointment of an administrator must be sent to Companies House.

The administrator will request a statement of the company's affairs from relevant people to ascertain the true financial position of the company.

The administrator will then make a statement setting out proposals for achieving the purpose of the administration or explaining why they cannot be achieved. This will usually involve a compromise being reached between the company and its creditors about the company's debts.

If the administrator is unable to provide the necessary rescue remedy the company will be forced to wind up using the creditor's voluntary liquidation process and the business will end.

Cessation of trading

When a business is wound up and its affairs have all been concluded, it legally ceases to exist. The consequences of this are as follows:

* The business stops trading.

* The business will no longer be able to enter into contractual negotiations.

* Any directors' powers will cease with the end of the business.

* Any further share transfers will be void.

* Provision will have to be made for the payment of creditors and arrangements made for the now-redundant employees.

* The cessation of trading will be publicised and it may be necessary under the Insolvency Act to launch an investigation into why the business failed.

The steps involved

We have seen that creating a business can be a complex process, but the procedures for ending one are no less problematic and many steps must be completed before the business is concluded. These include the following:

* Resolutions are passed at company meetings to indicate that the liabilities of the business are too great to allow it to carry on. This can happen either through a special resolution (see above) or an extraordinary resolution passed by at least three quarters of the members entitled to vote.

* A statutory declaration is then made, in which three quarters of the members of the business agree that, having started the process of liquidation, the business will be able to pay its debts within twelve months.

* Orders are passed by the court to allow an administrator to oversee the winding up of the insolvent business. Before such an order comes into force the court will have to be satisfied that conditions contained in the Insolvency Act are fulfilled. These include the following:

  * That the company is unable to pay its debts;

  * That the order will either promote the survival of the business as a whole or in part, or that the assets of the company would be best used by being sold now rather than after liquidation.

* The next stage is that the assets (for example buildings, equipment and cars) of the company will be liquidated, which means they are sold and the proceeds used to pay creditors.

* The final stage in this process is ideally that creditors are paid. Creditors of a business are ranked in order of priority: appointed liquidator's costs, preferential creditors (for example National Insurance and Income tax contributions, wages and salaries), secured creditors whose loan is secured against an asset of the business, and finally unsecured creditors such as suppliers and deferred creditors (those who are owed through unpaid share dividends). When the final assets of the company are liquidated there may not be enough money to pay all of the debts and it is common for creditors to settle for less than that owing to them.

17.2.5 Employment protection

Businesses employing staff must be aware that their employees are protected at work in a number of ways. These are discussed below.

Equal opportunities legislation

Disability Discrimination Act (1995)

Employers must be aware that they have duties placed on them where they employ disabled workers. The law is governed by the Disability Discrimination Act (1995) to prevent discrimination that many disabled people face in areas of their life including employment.

Since December 1996 it has been unlawful to treat disabled people less favourably in businesses and organisations than other people for a reason related to their disability. Since October 1999, businesses and organisations have had to make reasonable adjustments for disabled people, such as providing extra help or making changes to the way they provide their services and since October 2004 they have had to make reasonable adjustments to the physical features of their premises to overcome physical barriers to access.

For example, a business employing people who use wheelchairs must allow ramp access to its building and lifts to enable them to have the same access to the building and work environment.

See www.dwp.gov.uk/employers/dda for more details.

Race Relations Act (1976)

Under the Race Relations Act (1976), it is unlawful for a person to discriminate on racial grounds against another. The Act defines racial grounds as including race, colour, nationality or ethnic or national origin.

To bring a case under the Race Relations Act, the victim must show they have been discriminated against in one of the following ways.

* Direct racial discrimination occurs when a person is able to prove they are treated less favourably on racial grounds than others in similar circumstances. Racist abuse and harassment are forms of direct discrimination and are unlawful under the Act.

* Indirect racial discrimination falls into one of two categories. The first is on grounds of colour or nationality, under the original definition in the Race Relations Act. This happens when there is a non-discriminatory requirement which applies to everyone and the proportion of the victim's racial group is considerably smaller than the size of the group who can comply. The requirement must be unjustified irrespective of race and it must be to the victim's disadvantage that they cannot comply with it. The second is on grounds of race, ethnic or national origin. This was introduced by the Race Relations Act (Amendment) Regulations 2003. This is broadly the same as under the Act but takes into account a broader approach as it outlaws discrimination on the basis of ethnic origin as well.

See www.cre.org.uk for more details.

Sex Discrimination Act (1975 and 1986)

Under the Sex Discrimination Act 1975 (as amended) employers should not discriminate on grounds of sex, marriage or because someone intends to undergo, is undergoing or has undergone gender reassignment or sex change. This can take the form of direct discrimination where an individual is treated less well than another person on the grounds of their sex or indirect discrimination where a whole group of people is discriminiated against on the basis of their gender.

Sex discrimination covers all aspects of employment including recruitment, pay, training and termination of a contract. It also includes applying conditions which, though applied equally to all, have a bad effect on one sex or on married people and which cannot be shown to be justifiable.

There are limited exceptions: the 1986 Act permits employers, under certain conditions, to train employees of one sex in order to fit them for particular work in which their sex has recently been under-represented or if the job requires a particular sex, for example a female community worker being employed to look after women in refuges.

CASE STUDY

British Airways

A female pilot Jessica Starmer won a sex discrimination case against her employers, British Airways in April 2005. The reason she was discriminated against was that she was refused the right to work part-time to look after her baby. BA denied sex discrimination on two grounds.

Firstly, its decision was made on safety grounds as it requires pilots with less than 2,000 hours flying time to work at least 75 per cent of a normal rota. Starmer had completed about 1,100 hours.

Secondly, it said it would be too expensive to have two part-time pilots covering Starmer's duties.

✓ 1. Identify the basis of the pilot's discrimination claim.
✓✓ 2. Justify how you think the pilot had been discriminated against.
✓✓✓ 3. Evaluate whether British Airways objections were reasonable.

Equal Pay Act (1970)

One of the oldest employment rights is the right to equal pay between men and women. Legislation has existed since 1970 with the Equal Pay Act extended by the Equal Pay Directive which states that employers must give men and women equal treatment in the terms and conditions of their employment contract if they are employed on work that is the same or broadly similar, or work found to be of equal value.

FIGURE 17.5 *Do you know anyone who is discriminated against in this way?*

Contracts of employment

The main rights and duties of both employers and employees will be found in the contract of employment. These rights are specified in the terms of the contract, which will include the job title, location, date of beginning of employment, rate of pay, number of working hours, entitlements such as breaks, benefits such as pension schemes and notice period.

The contract of employment exists to protect both the employer and the employee so that each party to the contract knows what is expected of them.

The Employment Rights Act (1996) states that all employees should receive a written contract of employment within eight weeks of the start of their employment.

The contract itself will contain key terms. These terms can be either express terms or implied terms. Express terms are the main part of the individual contract and will have been discussed at an interview and confirmed in writing. They will include: pay, hours and holidays. Other terms in the contract, the implied terms are provisions in the contract that are not included as written terms as they are understood to be included automatically. These will include terms such as the right to equal pay and the right not to suffer discrimination. Some terms may be included in a contract through custom or tradition, for example the business might close every Wednesday afternoon but be open every Saturday morning and those times form part of your contract of employment.

Common law duties

The majority of the provisions found within the contract of employment embrace old common law duties laid down through the master–servant relationship such as the duty of the employer to look after the employee, provide safe working conditions and pay the employee for work done. In return, the employee will agree to do the work required and to obey all reasonable instructions.

Employment protection legislation

Fair dismissal

Inevitably there will come a time when employers will have to discipline employees. The ultimate disciplinary sanction is to dismiss an employee.

The main types of dismissal are summary dismissal where a person has been found guilty of gross misconduct, for example violence towards a customer or staff member or a serious theft. A person dismissed in this way will receive an instant dismissal in that they will be given no notice and have to leave immediately after the disciplinary hearing.

The other main type of dismissal is dismissal with notice and will be for such things as persistent lateness, poor performance or failing to follow instructions. Here, the person dismissed will be given a paid notice period and will leave after that has finished.

The Employment Rights Acts (1996) and the Employment Relations Act (1999) lay down guidelines that should be followed. Failure to follow the statutory guidelines could lead to the former employee claiming unfair dismissal.

A potentially fair reason for dismissal is known as the statutory restriction. In this case, the employee can no longer work in the job he has without breaking the law. For example, a driver who has been banned for drink driving would be fairly dismissed if no other job could be found for them.

Procedure for dismissal

There is now a standard statutory procedure for dismissal. If an employer is contemplating dismissal or action short of dismissal, such as loss of pay or seniority, they must follow a three-step disciplinary procedure. This statutory procedure involves:

* a statement in writing of what it is the employee is alleged to have done
* a meeting to discuss the situation
* the right of appeal.

If an employer fails to adhere to these procedures the dismissal may be classed as unfair.

Unfair dismissal

Other automatically unfair reasons for dismissal include dismissing an employee because they are pregnant, have taken maternity or parental leave, are proposing to join a trade union, are seeking to claim their employment rights such as equal pay, have disclosed wrongdoing in the workplace (whistleblowing), have been unfairly selected for redundancy or are involved in a grievance claim against the company. It would be classed as an unfair dismissal to dismiss an employee who cannot work due a physical or mental incapacity without full medical investigation and the opportunity for the employee to 'recover'.

If the dismissal is seen as unfair the wronged person may be able to take out a claim for unfair dismissal at an employment tribunal where it may be ordered that the person is re-instated back to their old job, re-engaged back into the business but at a different job or be given financial compensation by way of damages.

Redundancy

Redundancy is an unfortunate aspect of employing staff. Legally, redundancy is classed as a dismissal of staff. In the event of redundancy employees have certain rights over their employers contained in the Employment Rights Act (1996) and Employment Relations Act (1999).

Where the redundancy is through the closure of the business the employer has little more to do other than ensure that redundancy payments are made correctly.

Where an employer shuts part of the business but continues the business as a whole the employer must try to find suitable employment for the employee in the existing company but this has to be reasonable for both sides.

The most problematic redundancies are in areas where rationalisation of the workforce takes place. The biggest problem for an employer is selecting who is to be made redundant and who stays. The best practice is to involve the organisation's trade union from the start to help manage the process. This involves explaining the situation to staff and perhaps asking for voluntary redundancy first which may be attractive to some workers and then to advise in the drawing up of an objective list of employees to make redundant. The employer must not draw up this list in a discriminatory way as that would be unfair dismissal.

Constructive dismissal

Constructive dismissal occurs when an employee resigns as a result of a breach of a fundamental term of their employment contract by their employer. This in effect gives the employee the right to claim unfair dismissal from their employer.

Breaches of contract that may give rise to unfair constructive dismissal claims might include anything which makes it impossible or intolerable for the employee to continue doing the job.

Examples include breaches such as:

* cutting an employee's wages
* transferring an employee to a different job or location
* failing to provide a safe place of work.

Employees must normally begin a grievance procedure before bringing an unfair constructive dismissal claim or the complaint will be rejected by a tribunal.

Legal rights after dismissal

When a person has been dismissed it may well be that they may feel that they have the right to claim unfair dismissal. The dismissed person may apply to an employment tribunal where the employer will be asked to justify why the decision was made to dismiss them.

There are many reasons why a person might bring a claim in an employment tribunal. These can include:

* breach of contract
* discrimination or victimisation on grounds of race or ethnic origin
* discrimination or victimisation on grounds of religion or belief
* discrimination or victimisation on grounds of sex, marriage or transgender.

It is a relatively simple process to apply to a tribunal although many people will employ a solicitor to represent them. The tribunal may award a successful person damages to compensate them for the loss of their job. See www.employmenttribunals.gov.uk for more details.

One thing the tribunal will try to do is try to make the parties negotiate a settlement without the need for a legal process to take place. They will advise the involvement of trade union representatives to reach an agreement and failing that, the involvement of trained negotiators such as the arbitration service ACAS to try to bring the parties together. Both ACAS and trade unions have a major role to play in this area. ACAS tries to negotiate an agreement between the parties without the need to go to a tribunal. The role of the trade union is seen as more of a help to the employee as they provide advice on disciplinary procedures and ultimately can provide legal help and representation in the tribunal hearing. Unions can also play an important role in agreeing redundancy procedures with employers to help with redundancy and to stop unfair procedures being used. See www.acas.org.uk for more details.

Wages

Employees rates of pay will be an express term in the initial contract of employment. The rate could be any maximum amount but cannot fall below what is known as the national minimum wage, which as of October 2006 will be as follows (under the Minimum Wage Act 1998):

* adult workers £5.35 per hour
* workers aged 18–21 £4.45 per hour
* workers aged 16–17 £3.30 per hour.

Trade unions have a role to play

Working time regulations

The EU Working Time Directive has set out a detailed framework for all workers in Europe to be subject to the same types of work patterns, break and rest periods and length of work allowed.

Break period and rest periods

All employers are entitled to breaks and rest from work. All employees who work more than six hours a day are entitled to a rest break. This can come from the contract of employment but if not then the rest period must be at least 20 minutes uninterrupted break away from their work. Ideally this should be taken during the six-hour period and not at the start or end of the shift to allow workers a real break from work.

Adult employees are also entitled to a complete rest period of not less than 11 continuous hours in any 24 hour period. There are longer periods of rest that should be given to night workers and younger employees.

Maximum working week

There are rules that exist that protect workers from working too many hours each week. The Working Time Regulations 1998 state that an employee should not work more than 48 hours on average in each week.

This is not as straightforward as might appear. An employee at the moment has the right to opt out of this arrangement and can work as many hours as they wish. Also the calculation is complicated by the fact that the 48-hour guide is an average so it is possible for an employee to work over the 48 hours on occasions as long as the overall average does not exceed that figure. See Unit 15 on pages 269–70 for workers' rights under the social charter.

17.2.6 Health and safety legislation

Health and Safety at Work Act (1974)

In the UK we are very fortunate to have a very strict set of legal rules in place under the Health and Safety at Work Act (1974) to ensure our workplaces are as safe as possible. However, accidents do happen and according to the union the GMB there were around 170,000 industrial accidents in the UK workplace in 2004 and 31,000 of these were classed as major incidents or resulted in death.

Every business has legal responsibilities to ensure the health and safety of employees and other people who come into contact with the business, including environmental issues such as pollution.

The responsibility for health and safety is embodied in Section 2(2) of the Health and Safety at Work Act (1974). It provides specific duties on employers which are as follows:

* the provision and maintenance of plant and systems of work so that they are safe and without risk to health

* the making of arrangements for the use, handling, storage and transportation of articles and substances

* the provision of information, instructions, training and supervision

* the maintenance of places of work under the employer's control in a safe condition with safe and risk free means of access and egress

* the provision and maintenance of a safe, risk free working environment with adequate welfare facilities and arrangements.

The Health and Safety Executive provide detailed guidance for businesses to achieve their legal duties under the legislation. For details of this guidance see www.hse.gov.uk.

Think it over...

There are many ways in which an employer is protected whilst at work. What other employee rights should be protected? Why do they need protecting?

Common law duties of employer and employee

The relationship between an employer and his employee is one that is found essentially

B&Q

DIY chain B&Q plc was fined £550,000 following a horrific accident in which a careless forklift driver reversed into an elderly shopper. Pamela Hinchliffe, 68, was crushed against metal shelving at B&Q's Poole store in Fleetsbridge and later died from internal injuries.

✓ 1. Identify the law that B&Q had broken.
✓✓ 2. Consider why B&Q were punished for the death of the customer.
✓✓✓ 3. Analyse whether or not companies should face criminal action in such cases.

in common law which has been embodied in contract law (see page 352) and provides that both employer and employee should as far as possible look after each other and make sure that:

* employers provide a safe place to work
* employees work in a safe way.

This is what the Health a Safety at Work Act seeks to do as its overriding aim is to provide safe working practices for all. This backs up the common law idea of equity or fairness between the parties.

Theory into practice

Janine is working at a factory when she sees sparks coming from the back of the machine she is working at. She does not really want to cause any fuss and by the time her shift has finished the sparks have stopped. The next day she hears that the factory has been destroyed by fire and that two of her colleagues have been badly injured.

1. In what way is the owner of the factory responsible for the fire?

2. Should Janine have done more when she saw the sparks coming from the machine?

Contributory negligence

When something goes wrong at the workplace and an employee is injured or killed it is very common for the injured person or their surviving relatives to bring an action in the civil courts against the employer for damages because the employer has been negligent in some way. If successful, the injured person will receive a monetary sum to help them with their injuries. However, lawyers for the employer will sometimes try to persuade the court that this level of compensation should be reduced to lower the perceived level of blame attached to the employer because the employee themselves were in some way to blame for the accident or the injuries received through what is known as contributory negligence.

The following are examples where courts have reduced the amount of damages awarded:

* failing to use appropriate eye goggles resulting in eye injury
* not following correct training instructions on a slicing machine causing loss of a finger.

Occupiers Liability Act (1957/1984)

Occupiers (owners or tenants) of, amongst other things, business premises have a special duty of care towards those who visit their premises. They must ensure that the condition of the premises is safe as far as is reasonably possible so that visitors do not come to harm. This area of law has been covered by the Occupiers Liability Acts of 1957 and 1984.

The Acts provide that any lawful visitor to the premises must be protected from harm. A lawful visitor to the premises is anyone who is invited onto the property by the occupier or who can enter the property legally without the occupier's consent. These sorts of visitors are those people who have a legal right to enter premises through their profession for example, a police officer, a VAT inspector and a court bailiff. All have power to enter property without the owner's consent. These people must be given the same protection as all other visitors.

A person who goes beyond the scope of their permission to enter becomes a trespasser and is not protected under the legislation unless an occupier put deliberate hazards in the way of that person to harm them.

An occupier should take special care to ensure that the property is safe if it is to be used by special categories of users, for example, the very young or old.

It is a good idea to put up warning signs to alert visitors of particular hazards but there is no general duty to do so and such signs will not necessarily help reduce the occupier's blame for harm unless they can be clearly communicated to the visitor and would make the visitor

Vicarious liability

Vicarious liability makes employers liable in civil law for the negligent actions of their employees. An employee, for example who whilst delivering goods for a company crashes into another car damaging it, will in the majority of cases not be sued by the other driver. Instead the driver will sue the owner of the delivery van instead.

There are many valid reasons why an injured person might want to claim off an employer rather that the employee:

* Financially it makes more sense to sue the employer as they will usually have more money.

* Employers will be insured against such losses.

* Companies will want to avoid bad publicity so may settle claims more quickly.

* To sue the company will perhaps ensure that safety systems are tightened up to avoid repetition.

An employer will only be liable for the acts of the employee whilst they are being carried out in the course of the employer's normal business and an employer will not be liable unless:

* the act in question is authorised, or
* the employer has failed to instruct the employee correctly.

An employer can still be liable for the acts of the employee even if the act is expressly forbidden by the employee so long as it is within the course of the employer's business. This would be an authorised act carried out in an unauthorised way and would make the employer liable. For example, an employer who forbids employees driving their delivery vans above 60 mph on any road would be liable if the driver crashed at 65 mph whilst making a delivery.

The employer however will not be liable for the actions of the employee when the action is not in the course of the employer's business or is considered a mere 'frolic'.

Theory into practice

Josephine worked for a company that stripped paint from metal and wood products at customers' homes. She had been told by her employer that under no circumstances should she carry out these procedures whilst the customers were near unless they were given protective clothing to wear. One day Josephine visited a customer and they were injured by the chemicals she was using without giving the customer protective clothing.

When Josephine got home she stole some chemicals from her van for her own use but as she lifted them out of the van they fell and damaged the paintwork of a neighbour's car?

1. Who would you advise the customer in the first example to sue and why?

2. Who could Josephine's neighbour sue?

17.2.7 Consumer protection legislation

Contract law is an important subject not only to protect businesses but also to protect us as consumers when we purchase products. Without really knowing it consumers enter into countless contracts everyday for the purchase of items ranging from bars of chocolate to the purchase of cars and computers. Even though these contracts are diverse, one thing that is certain in all of them is that consumers in the UK are protected by law when things go wrong with the products purchased.

For example, if an MP3 player purchased from a high-street retailer fails to work properly the purchaser can expect to have that product replaced or have their money returned. The reason for this is that there is a powerful set of legal guidelines to ensure that businesses do not as far as possible get away with selling inferior (or at worse dangerous) products to consumers.

Sale and Supply of Goods Act (1979/94)

Fitness and satisfactory quality

There is no general duty placed on sellers who sell in private ensuring that the goods sold are of correct quality and suitability. This preserves the principle of 'caveat emptor' or 'let the buyer beware' so if you buy a camera from a friend and it does not work you will have little remedy available. However, if your friend was selling the camera in the course of his business the legislation implies two conditions:

1. that the goods are of satisfactory quality
2. that they are fit for a particular purpose.

Satisfactory quality as amended by the Sale and Supply of Goods Act 1994 provides that where a seller sells goods in the course of his business there is an implied condition that the goods supplied are of satisfactory quality, except to the extent of defects which are brought to the buyer's attention before the contract is made, or ought to have been noticed by the buyer if he has examined the goods.

State and condition of goods

Fitness for the purpose for which goods of the kind in question are commonly supplied, in terms of their appearance and finish, means that they are safe, free from minor defects and durable (longer lasting).

It does not impose absolute standards of quality with which all goods must comply but goods must be satisfactory to a reasonable person. This means that goods do not have to be absolutely perfect but satisfactory in the usual run of events.

Where the seller sells goods in the course of a business there is an implied condition that they will be reasonably fit for the purpose that the buyer had expressly or impliedly made known to the seller. It is vital that a seller is told if a particular product is to be used for a particular purpose as this will offer them a degree of protection under the legislation.

Supply of Goods and Services Act (1982)

The sale of goods legislation only applies to contracts where goods are sold for a money consideration. It does not cover other methods of obtaining goods by means other than money purchase nor does it cover the provision of services such as hire-purchase services.

Legislation has been passed to protect commercial transactions that are not covered under the sale of goods including: contracts for work and material (building work, car repairs, installation work such as central heating and double glazing, hairdressing and gardening), contracts where no money changes hands (exchange or barter), contracts for 'free gifts' (where a buyer is given a free product if they buy another) and contracts for hire of goods (including the hire of cars, machinery and clothing).

The Supply of Goods and Services Act 1982 requires traders to provide services to a proper standard of workmanship. Also, any material used or goods supplied in providing the service must be of satisfactory quality.

Section 4 of the Act provides that where goods are transferred in the ordinary course of business there is an implied condition that the goods are of suitable quality and fit for the purpose. For example a gas engineer who is called to repair a boiler would be legally bound to fix the boiler with materials that are of appropriate quality and fit for the purpose.

Trade Descriptions Act (1968)

The Trade Descriptions Act makes it a criminal offence to mislead a consumer by a false description, so a description of goods that is sold or hired must be accurate. The description could be:

* in writing
* in an advertisement
* in an illustration
* given orally, for example in a sales pitch.

The description itself covers a range of factors, including:

* quantity and size
* composition
* method, place and date of manufacture
* fitness for stated purpose
* endorsements by people or organisations.

When offering to supply services, accommodation or facilities, it's a criminal offence to make a statement that is known to be false or misleading or 'recklessly' make a false or misleading statement about the provision, nature, manner, location or approval of the services, accommodation or facilities.

If a person is guilty of an offence under this Act they could receive an unlimited fine or up to two years' imprisonment.

Consumer Protection Act (1987)

The Consumer Protection Act establishes a 'general safety requirement' that all goods for domestic use must be reasonably safe. This can include many different types of consumer products such as toys, pushchairs, bicycles, helmets, babyseats, cosmetics, tyres, furniture, gas cookers and electrical equipment. Powers under the Act allow suspect goods to be 'suspended' from sale for up to six months while checks on safety are conducted. If found to be faulty, the goods may be destroyed.

Under Part 1 of the Consumer Protection Act, a claimant who is injured by an unsafe product will be able to sue the manufacturer of the product without the need to prove the tort of negligence.

Section 5 of the Act also gives the person injured by a defective product the ability to claim damages from the manufacturer.

Under the Act, liability is strict in that in the absence of one of the defences listed in the Act consumers injured by a product will always gain damages from the producer of the product. The producer of the product is defined as:

* the manufacturer of the product
* the extractor of raw materials
* industrial processors of agricultural produce
* own branders who add their own label to products which they do not produce.

The Act gives the right to sue to any person who is injured by a product, 'the safety of which was not such as persons generally are entitled to expect'. Products include not only finished product but also component parts of another product and raw materials. For example a new car is a product, but so are all its component parts such as radios, batteries, rubber for the tyres and so on.

The court will consider all the circumstances of the case in deciding whether or not the standards of care that the Act expects have been broken or not. Factors will include:

* the way the product was marketed
* any instructions and warnings with the product
* what is expected to be done with the product
* the time at which the product was supplied so that if new versions of the product are produced older versions are not necessarily considered unsafe.

Theory into practice

Explain how consumers are protected when they buy products.

Consumer Credit Act 1974

Businesses that offer credit to customers have a number of regulations governed by the Consumer Credit Act 1974. The rules apply to specialist credit businesses such as credit card providers or moneylenders, shops and mail order businesses that offer credit facilities.

Businesses have to apply to the Office of Fair Trading (OFT) for a consumer credit licence. This also shows consumers that the business is considered fit by the OFT to provide credit. A consumer credit licence will be required for a business that:

* sells on credit
* hires or leases out goods for more than three months
* lends money
* issues credit cards or trading checks
* arranges credit for others
* offers hire-purchase terms
* collects debts for lenders
* helps people with debt problems
* advises on people's credit rating.

Credit businesses must provide consumers with a written agreement setting out their rights and duties, containing clear information on the terms of the agreement before it is signed.

It must be clear the total charge for the credit, the rate of interest and any information explaining how the interest charges are worked out, so that customers can compare different deals.

Consumers have a cooling-off period when they sign agreements anywhere other than on your premises. The length of the cooling-off period depends on the type of transaction. However, if the consumer signs an agreement on the credit company's premises it cannot be cancelled.

The customer must be given clear information about how they can pay their account off early. For more details on consumer credit legislation see www.dti.gov.uk.

Weights and Measures Act (1985)

There are very strict rules in place to make sure that business that sell goods by weight or by measure do not short change the public. These rules are regulated by Trading Standards officers who will carry out spot checks to see if businesses are complying with them and in extreme cases take court action against businesses. A brief summary of some of the main regulations are as follows:

✳ Goods sold by weight or measure must normally be sold in metric quantities apart from a few exceptions, for example draught beer and milk can still be sold in pints.

✳ Goods packed by weight should either state the goods as a minimum quantity or as an average quantity – no individual package may be significantly short.

✳ The weight mustn't include the weight of the packaging.

✳ Businesses must check and keep records to show they follow the guidelines by carrying out their own tests of packaged products and weighing them.

✳ Weighing equipment must use suitable equipment. Scales must be tested for trade use or tested every day with officially stamped weights.

See www.tradingstandards.gov.uk for more details.

> **Think it over…**
>
> In which other areas should consumers be protected, in terms of safety and quality? What factors would the business need to take into account to comply with these laws?

Data Protection Act (1984/1998)

The 1998 Act came into force on 1 March 2000 and aims to protect individuals' rights to privacy with respect to the processing of personal data. Personal data does not just mean data of a personal nature such as medical information, it means any data relating to a living individual. For example, a business will keep personal data about its employees covering such things as address,

FIGURE 17.6 *Goods sold by weight must normally be sold in metric quantities*

dates of birth, bank details, personnel issues such as pay, pension and discipline.

This is a large job within any organisation and businesses that hold data must appoint a person known as a data controller who is the person who manages the accuracy and validity of information held. This person must be registered with the Information Commissioner (a government body responsible for data protection). Businesses should be aware that it is a criminal offence for a person to hold data without permission of the Commissioner.

This information can only be stored if an individual has consented to the data being stored or it is necessary for the performance of the individual's job or to protect the individual in some way (such as sensitive medical information).

The Data Protection Act seeks to provide a balance between the interests of an organisation that holds data and the individual. The individual has certain rights under the Act as well. The main ones are as follows:

* the right to access the information

* the right to stop information being held

* the right to prevent the information being used for marketing purposes (passed to third parties)

* the right to compensation for mistakes made and the ability to ask the data controller to rectify errors.

See www.informationcommissioner.gov.uk for more details.

17.2.8 Intellectual property rights

Intellectual property concerns the idea of the ownership of ideas, designs, inventions and trademarks. When a person or business comes up with an idea, product or design, who is it that owns it and controls how it is used? The answer is found in intellectual property rights. There are many different ways such rights exist.

Copyrights

Copyright is protection over creative work published by an author. Creative work is a broad category that covers:

* literature (articles in journals, books, poems and song lyrics)

* art (photographs, logos, paintings, architecture)

* websites

* music

* broadcasts

* sound recordings

* films.

Such creative work can be protected under the Copyright, Designs and Patents Act 1988. It provides safeguards for the creator in the following ways:

* Copyright protection means that other people cannot produce the work without the owner's prior permission which may be rejected or may be allowed for free or for a fee (called a royalty).

* Copyright can be sold or given away but although the ownership has changed the work may not be used without the permission of the new owner.

* Copyright material is marked by displaying a © symbol next to, or close to, the work.

The recommended way of displaying a copyright mark is as follows:

© Owner of copyright, Date of publication. Example: © Neil Richards 2006

In the UK, displaying the above is not a legal requirement, but it may support a legal case in the event of copyright infringement or dispute. In the United States, displaying the symbol is a legal requirement and a person seeking protection must clearly mark all of their work with it.

Once the work is marked and dated it should be protected and it is usual for first works or original copies of the work to be lodged at banks or similar types of building or signed and dated by a legal representative (a solicitor).

Also, a copy of the work could be sent to the creator of the work via recorded delivery and left unopened on receiving: the packaging would display a stamped date proving when the creative work was sent.

A copyright lasts during the author's life plus an additional 70 years after death. For sound recordings and broadcasts, it only lasts for an additional 50 years after the death of the author.

There are circumstances when the copyright will not belong to the author of the original work:

* work created for a company the author works for, copyright belongs to the company

* student's university projects belong to the university and not the student.

The legislation allows the right to take legal action if copyright has been infringed. This would involve court action that could result in the guilty person having to pay damages to the copyright owner. However, more serious copyright issues on a larger scale such as copying and distributing CDs will be dealt with by the police and the criminal courts.

For more information please see www.patent. gov.uk.

Designs

Copyright deals with the creative work but part of that might be the actual design of the work itself which also requires protection. This can include the following points of design of the product to be protected:

* lines

* contours

* colours

* shape

* texture

* materials.

The legislation that is concerned with protecting designs is the Registered Designs Act 1949. It provides the following guidelines.

* To be protected, the design in question must be new and original and have an individual character that makes it different from any design that is currently available to the public.

* Design that by law cannot be registered are designs concerned with only how the product works, designs for complex products that are not in normal use or designs for products contrary to the law or moral code.

* Application to register a design is made to the UK Patent Office and currently costs £60 to do so.

CASE STUDY

X factor v Pop Idol

In 2005, the X factor creator, Simon Cowell and the creator of Pop Idol, Simon Fuller, were involved in a very high profile case involving the alleged infringement by Mr Cowell of the Pop Idol format for his own programme.

This was a very important case worth somewhere in the region of £100 million to the winning side. As it turned out, both men settled their differences before the case went to court.

✓ 1. Identify what the parties were trying to prove.

✓✓ 2. Consider how Simon Fuller could prove that Pop Idol was an original idea.

✓✓✓ 3. Can you think of any other types of show or entertainment format that appear very similar? Could you develop a criteria to protect original ideas?

* Registration can last for a maximum of 25 years and is a property that, like any other business right, may be bought and sold by the owner.

See www.patent.gov.uk for more details.

Patents

A patent is protection for an inventor preventing anyone else from using that idea. The law relating to patents is covered by the Patents Act 1977 and allows the invention to become the property of the inventor, which the inventor can deal with in any way they please. The important thing is that it is protected from others using it.

Again, the application for a patent like designs is made to the UK Patent Office but this process is much more rigorous and will take several years (average four years) and can cost several thousand pounds as a search has to be made of all patents. Also there are more involved standards applied under the legislation that must be fulfilled before a patent is granted.

A patent granted in the UK only protects the invention in the UK so for full protection a worldwide patent would be required costing even more money and taking even more time.

To satisfy the legislation an invention will be patentable if:

* it is new, in other words, it has never been seen before
* it involves an inventive step forward in a product or process that is already known
* the product is capable of industrial application so that it can be made and used in some way and not in an excluded category. Excluded categories include:
  * a discovery
  * a scientific theory or mathematical method
  * a creation such as a literary, dramatic or artistic work
  * a scheme or method for performing a mental act, playing a game or doing business
  * the presentation of information, or a computer program
  * an invention if it is a new animal or plant variety

* a method of treatment of the human or animal body by surgery or a method of diagnosis.

See www.patent.gov.uk for more details.

Trade marks

One of the most important things for a business to do is to register its trade mark for either its business or its products. A trade mark is a badge used so that customers can recognise the product of a particular trader.

The trade mark can distinguish the goods and services of one trader from those of another. It includes words, logos, pictures, or a combination of these.

Coca-Cola products are immediately recognisable

The trade mark can be registered and protected under the Trade Marks Act 1994 and again the application is made to the UK Patent Office.

The trade mark must be:

* distinctive for the goods or services which the business is trying to register it for

* not deceptive, or contrary to law or morality

* not similar or identical to any earlier marks for the same or similar goods or services.

There are of course many benefits for a business in registering its trade mark.

The trade mark is a vital piece of the business and vast sums of money go into the imaging and branding of the product using the trade mark or logo to promote that image. Indeed the trade mark or symbol of the business in organisations such as McDonalds, Coca-Cola, Apple and Mercedes-Benz have become multi-million pound assets of the business and of course are highly protected.

Unauthorised use of a mark means the rightful owner may lose business and goodwill and may sue for infringement under trade marks law. The burden of proof for this to succeed is relatively low as the owner of the trade mark only has to show that another business is using a mark that is the same or similar to the mark that is registered. The civil courts will deal with this type of infringement but if the trade mark has been used on goods to mislead customers into thinking that they are dealing with the genuine product then a criminal offence has been committed and the criminal courts will be involved.

An application to register a trade mark costs £200 for the first application and £50 for any subsequent applications. It is not a worldwide application but a business may ask for an EU trade mark at the same time providing more detailed protection under the Madrid protocol which many countries of the world have signed to offering greater trade mark protection. The trade mark will then be protected for ten years which is renewable upon application to the Patent Office.

For more details see www.patent.gov.uk.

Recent developments

European Union anti-competitive licensing directives

The European Union has been trying to stop anti-competition practices within its member states since it was created. Article 81 of the EC Treaty prohibits agreements that restrict competition between businesses.

The UK government has followed this ethos by passing the Competition Act in 1988 following EU law. This created a highly centralised procedure wherby the EU controlled all competition law procedures.

Over time many had tried to get around this system by forming oligopolies particularly in industries such as energy supply, postal and telecommunications. Lack of member state intervention was producing a system where one or two large organisations were dominating industries. To counter this, the EU has passed the EU Regulation 1 2003 which became law in May 2004 in an attempt to end this situation.

The original framework still exists but now allows the member states to investigate and challenge anti-competitive practices. The UK government has embraced the changes and amended its 1988 Act giving power to the Office of Fair Trading to investigate such practices.

See www.oft.gov.uk and www.europa.eu.int for more details.

Internet transmissions

In October 2003, the Copyright and Related Rights Regulations 2003 came into force. The effect on UK copyright law is to amend the Copyright, Designs and Patents Act 1988.

The effect of the legislation is as follows:

* a performer has the right to consent to or prohibit a recording of their performance being made available by electronic transmission, including the Internet.

New criminal offences are created for a person who:

* makes illegal copies of a work and communicates them to the public

* makes available illegal recordings of performances, infringing a performer's right.

It is also unlawful to remove information provided which identifies the work, author, the copyright owner or the holder of any intellectual property rights.

An injunction may be obtained against an Internet Service Provider if it has actual knowledge of another person using its service to infringe copyright. Duration of copyright protection is 50 years from when it was published.

There are some exceptions that apply to the UK:

* Temporary copies are permitted in certain circumstances and provided there is no independent economic gain to be made.

* Businesses will now have to review whether they need licences for their copying activities as they were previously exempt.

* Library copies are now only allowed for research for non-commercial purposes or private study.

Theory into practice

Analyse the impact of these new EU directives on UK businesses over the course of your studies.

Knowledge check

1 What is the difference between public and private law?

2 Describe how Statute Law is created.

3 What elements are required for the formation of a valid contract?

4 Explain the difference between limited and unlimited liability.

5 How is a partnership formed?

6 Describe how businesses can be brought to an end.

7 How are employees protected at work?

8 What duties does the Health and Safety legislation place on an employer?

9 Explain how consumers are protected when they purchase goods.

10 Explain how trade marks can be protected.

Gourmet on the Go

For the past two years, Sid has been running a mobile ice-cream van called 'Mr Chocci'. It is a reasonably successful concern and Sid is happy with how his sole trader business is going, but he is always looking at ways to improve things.

His friend Nancy has been watching a national TV soap opera where one of the characters buys an ice-cream van and sets up a mobile gourmet catering and entertainment business from it. Inspired by this, Nancy believes this is a potential gold-mine and begins to persuade Sid that he should branch out and diversify.

Sid is more practical than Nancy and soon realises that, whilst this is a good idea, it would take a lot of financial risk to change the van, buy new stock and advertise the new business. Nancy says that she is willing to come into partnership with Sid, invest in the new business and become business partners. They agree to call the partnership 'Gourmet on the Go'.

1. Read case study 1.

   a. Gourmet on the Go will be a partnership created under the Partnership Act 1890. Describe **two** main provisions of this Act that Sid and Nancy must comply with. (4 marks)

   b. When Sid and Nancy draw up the Partnership Deed, explain **four** of the main provisions that it should contain. (8 marks)

   c. Discuss the advantages and disadvantages of Sid giving up being a sole trader and forming a partnership with Nancy. (8 marks)

Nancy is keen to begin trading but she is a little apprehensive about the new venture as she has no real business or legal background. Her friend John, who is a barrister, has warned her about the potential legal problems that she might face. Worried by what John has said, Nancy looks into the matter further.

She does some research into the law and realises that both she and Sid face responsibilities in both civil and criminal law. In particular she is drawn to a case reported in the newspapers of R v Express Shopping (2004) where a mobile entertainment business was fined in the court for selling defective DVD players under the Consumer Protection Act 1987.

2. Read case study 2.

   a. Explain how businesses are responsible in both civil and criminal law. (3 marks)

   b. The case of R v Express Shopping (2004) raises the issue of consumer protection legislation. Explain briefly **three** legal principles covered in this area of law, either in civil or criminal law. (6 marks)

   c. Nancy realises that she will have serious responsibilities under civil and criminal law if she goes into partnership with Sid. She realises that consumer protection and safety will be an important issue for them. Assess how these areas of law might influence the business now and in the future. (14 marks)

Gourmet on the Go is set up and begins to trade. Sid and Nancy realise that they should invest some money on advertising and they employ an agency to create some flyers to be inserted in local newspapers. They also want to have a website to advertise their products.

Sid realises that they do not have the funds to have a professional develop the website, so he has a go at it himself. The result is pretty good, but unfortunately Sid makes a huge mistake on the price of a bottle of champagne they sell. Instead of the selling price of £125 they normally charge for it, Sid advertises it as priced at £1.25. Not surprisingly they are bombarded with customers who want this bargain.

Nancy consults her friend John who tells them not to worry as they do not have to sell the champagne at that wrong price.

3. Read case study 3.

   a. Explain why Gourmet on the Go are not legally bound to sell the champagne at price stated on the website. (5 marks)

   b. Assuming that the price of the champagne is now correct, describe **two** elements required for a contract between Gourmet on the Go and its customers to be legally binding. (4 marks)

   c. Explain **two** ways either the business or its customers might bring a contract to an end. (4 marks)

After a few months of very successful trading, Sid and Nancy assess how they are doing and are interested in a couple of potential investors who have come to them with exciting ideas for expansion.

Whilst keen to expand their business, they are unsure how to go about changing their business status.

4. Read case study 4.

   a. Sid and Nancy are considering changing their business to a private limited company. Describe how this can be done. (5 marks)

   b. Evaluate whether changing the business to a private limited company will be an advantage or a disadvantage to Sid and Nancy. (10 marks)

Sid and Nancy decide not to change their business status and carry on as a partnership without any new investors. They believe that they will be more successful on their own. Unfortunately, a few months later a new much larger organisation doing the same thing as Gourmet on the Go takes much of the business away from them.

Reluctantly, Sid and Nancy have to undercut the opposition and their profit margins begin to suffer. In a bid to beat the opposition, they recruit a couple of new workers, Paulo (21) and Marianna (23), who have just arrived in the country and are looking for work but have little knowledge of English employment law. The two are employed on a very casual basis, paid cash in hand with no contract of employment.

Sid tells them that he will pay Paulo £3.00 per hour and Marianna £2.75 per hour and for that he expects them to work seven days a week and at least 15 hours per day with half an hour break each day.

To help the two new recruits, Sid buys a van from a friend of his. He knows that it is an MOT write-off and a danger to have on the road but it is very cheap. Sid has also managed to secure a consignment of cheap laptop computers that he knows have been sent back to the manufacturer because they have a wiring fault in the plug and are prone to overheat. He gives the laptops to Paulo and Marianna and tells them to sell the lot.

After about two weeks of working almost non-stop, Marianna asks for a day off and is refused by Sid who sacks her on the spot. Paulo continues to work and one evening, whilst making a delivery to a customer, loses control of the van and crashes into a group of pedestrians injuring two of them.

The police visit the business premises of Gourmet on the Go and explain what has been going on to Nancy. She is deeply shocked. When the police finish with Sid, she tells him that she wants to dissolve the partnership. In the meantime, the two pedestrians injured by Paulo have spoken to a solicitor who has advised them to sue the partners.

5. Read case study 5.

Sid and Nancy have to consider the consequences of their actions. They face a variety of legal actions from the pedestrians, Paulo, Marianna and customers who have bought the faulty laptops. They also have to resolve their own internal problems. Legal issues involve health and safety, consumer safety, vicarious liability, employment law and partnership law.

a. Explain **three** legal issues raised by this case.   (9 marks)

b. *Quality of written communication is assessed in this question.*

Illustrating relevant areas of law, assess the likely outcome of this case. (20 marks)

Total 96 marks

Resources

Abbott, K. (1994) *Business Law*, DP Publications

Beale, H., Beatson, J. et al. (eds) (1994) *Chitty on Contracts*, Sweet & Maxwell

Dransfield, R. et al. (2004) *BTEC National Business*, Heinemann

Keenan, D. and Riches, S. (2002) *Business Law*, Longman

Lockton, D. (2003) *Employment Law*, Palgrave

Sparrow, A. (2001) *The E-Commerce Handbook*, Fitzwarren Handbooks

Cases used

Butler Machine Tool Co. Ltd v Ex-Cell-O Corp. (Eng) Ltd [1979] 1 All ER 965

Donoghue v Stevenson [1932] AC 562

Marshall v Southampton & SW Hampshire Health Authority (Teaching) [1986] 2 All ER 584

Pinnel's Case [1602] 5 Co Rep 117a

Roberts v Gray [1913] 1 KB 520

Websites

www.acas.org.uk
Dispute resolution organisation

www.asa.org.uk
Standards in advertising

www.britishchambers.org.uk
British Chamber of Commerce advice for businesses

www.charity-commission.org.uk
Guidance for charities

www.cre.gov.uk
Campaigning group to promote racial equality

www.companieshouse.gov.uk
Company formation and regulation body

www.dwp.gov.uk/employers/dda
Government advice on disability discrimination

www.dti.gov.org
Government advisory body for trade and industry

www.employmenttribunals.gov.uk
Employment tribunal website

www.eoc.org.uk
Equal opportunities advice group

www.europa.eu.int/
Official European Community website

www.gazettes-online.co.uk
London Gazette journal where company information is published

www.hm-treasury.gov.uk
Official site of the Treasury department

www.hmrc.gov.uk
Her Majesty's Revenue department dealing with taxation

www.hse.gov.uk
Health and Safety Executive dealing with work related safety issues

www.informationcommissioner.gov.uk
Data protection controller

www.oft.gov.uk
The Office of Fair Trading

www.patent.gov.uk
The government department dealing with copyright, designs, patents and trademarks

www.tradingstandards.gov.uk
Government agency protecting consumers

Glossary

Acceptance   In contract law, the accepting of an offer

Accounting rate of return   A measure of the average return on an investment

Accruals   Outstanding revenue, such as rent receivable, if due at the year end is considered to be an accrual. A business must record the total value of all expenses consumed within the financial year. If expenses have yet to be paid they are considered to have accrued. A business must also record all revenue due even if it has yet to be received

Acquisition   Taking over another business enterprise

Added value   When something is either physically made better within a product or service to add perceived value to the product, e.g. by association with a brand – the Nike brand has added value as people are prepared to pay more for their products

Aim   The overall purpose – a superordinate goal or a plan for an organisation to work towards

Ansoff's matrix   A marketing tool to help a business plan for growth by setting out the positions that it can take to fit its strategy to the business environment

Appraisals   The opportunity for the manager and employee to agree targets for the future

Articles of Association   The rules for the running of the company's internal affairs

Authorised share capital   The total number of shares a business can issue as outlined in its Memorandum of Association

Authority   Having permission to carry out something

Autonomy   Having the ability to self-manage, commonly used with autonomous work groups who manage, check and improve their own working practices

Average capital employed   The average value of the capital employed in a business over a period of time

Bad debts   Sales that are made on credit for which payment is never received

Balance of probabilities   The burden of proof in civil cases

Bank loan   An agreed sum of money lent to a business over a set period of time, usually longer than one year. It can be repaid with either fixed or variable interest rates

Bank overdraft   When a person or business spends more money than they have in their bank account. Interest is only charged for the days that the account is overdrawn. If the overdraft has not been agreed with the bank in advance, there is usually a fixed penalty fee and a higher rate of interest might be charged

Bank   In a balance sheet, the bank column shows the balance of the money that is currently in the bank. If the bank is overdrawn, it is a current liability not a current asset

Bankrupt   Where a person is unable to pay their debts

Benchmarking   The process whereby industries compare themselves with one another to try to reach best performance levels, possibly in terms of customer service or productivity

Beyond a reasonable doubt   The burden of proof in criminal cases

Bill   Document going through Parliament before it becomes an Act

Binding precedent   A decision made by a judge in a higher court which must be followed by lower courts

Boston matrix   A tool used to manage product portfolio development

Bottom line   The profit made on the bottom line of a profit and loss account or income statement

Breach of contract   Going against the terms of a contract

Break-even point   The point at which the revenues earned by a business exactly match the costs

Call centre   A customer service centre where calls are handled by telephone operators

Capacity utilisation   The extent to which a business makes use of the maximum amount they can produce (capacity)

Cascading   Passing something down or on to another employee, e.g. skills learned at a training event or objectives that need to be implemented

Case law   The body of law made by judges

Cash flow   The money flowing in and out of a business. The balance is the difference between the money that comes into a business after total expenditure has been deducted

Chain of command   The communication path that goes from the most senior manager down to the most junior employees. A long chain of command means that the message may get altered on the way down

Civil law   Private law concerned with disputes between individuals

Claimant   In civil law, the person bringing an action against another

Company prospectus   A document issued when a company is selling its shares, showing the type of price per share that the company might be willing to accept from purchasers

Compensating errors   Errors that cancel one another out. These errors occur when two separate errors of the same amount occur in the ledgers

Competitive advantage   Advantages that one business has over its rivals, usually related to having lower costs or more exciting and different products and services

Competitors   Other businesses in the same market that are trying to attract the same customers

Complete reversal of entries   These errors occur when the entries have been made on the wrong side of the accounts. The debit has been made on the credit side, and vice versa

Consideration   In contract law, the value attached to the promises made between the parties

Contingency planning   Drawing up plans and giving training to employees for what to do in the event of an emergency; also referred to as back-up planning

Continuous improvement   The ability across the organisation to make improvements to the way things are done, including working practices and customer service. Each employee is responsible for their own small set of changes that builds up a culture of improvement (Japanese version: Kaizen)

Contract   A legal agreement made between two or more individuals

Contribution   The amount that an item sold contributes to paying off fixed costs. The contribution is the difference between the sales revenue earned from an item and the variable cost of that item

Contributory negligence   Where a person can be blamed in some way for their own accident

Copyright   Protection given to original literary, dramatic, musical and artistic work

Corporation tax   Tax paid by companies

Credit purchases   Goods that have been purchased and received. Payment will be made by an agreed date – usually 30 days

Creditors' voluntary liquidation   In business dissolution, when the directors have not made a declaration of solvency and the company cannot pay its debts

Creditors   Other businesses or people the business has purchased goods or services from with the promise of payment at a later date

Criminal law   Public law where the state punishes individuals for crimes against the state

Critical path analysis   A means of identifying the critical path of activities that need to be completed to finish a project on time

Critical path   The sequence of the most important activities involved in executing a plan. They are critical because they need to be completed in sequence and on time

Culture   The typical pattern of relationships and ways of doing things in an organisation

Current assets   Items that can be quickly turned into cash. They consist of stock, debtors, bank and cash

Current liabilities   These are debts that the business has with other organisations. This includes creditors

Data controller   The person in an organisation responsible for keeping data accurate and who has to comply with the Data Protection Act to protect personal data

Debenture   Loans made to a business by other businesses or individuals. They usually carry a fixed rate of interest and a set repayment date

Debtors   People that owe the business money for goods or services received

Decision tree   A diagram setting out the expected outcomes resulting from alternative decisions that a business can make (usually in terms of financial outcomes)

Defendant   The person who is accused of something in court and who must defend that claim

Delayering   Taking out a management layer in an organisational structure. This most commonly happens with middle management and results in the organisation becoming much flatter

Delegation   Handing down responsibility for tasks to others but not accountability

Deployment   Moving someone to do a task in an effective way, e.g. moving someone from one department to another as they are needed to work there more

Depreciation   The fall in the value of a fixed asset over time

Development   Processes designed to help an individual to meet their potential in the workplace

Devolved objectives   Objectives that have been passed down (cascaded) to departments from more senior management and implemented within functional areas

Differentiated   Made to stand out as being different, through offering a different level of quality, branding or extra services. It is what gives the business a unique selling point

Directive   European law issued by the European Council

Discounts allowed   The amount deducted by a customer when making prompt payment

Discounts received   The amount deducted by the business when making prompt payment to a supplier

Dissolution   Bringing a partnership to an end

Diversification   Broadening out to produce a variety of goods and services rather than engaging in narrow specialisation

Dividend   The percentage of the profit paid out to shareholders as a reward for their investment in the business

Drawings   The money the owner of a sole trader business takes out for personal use

Earliest start time (EST)   The earliest time that an activity can start

Economies of scale   The process whereby individual unit costs decrease as production goes up

Efficiency   Using resources in the best possible way so as to cut out waste; gaining the highest possible returns from a given basket of resources

Empowerment   Making workers feel responsible for, and able to make changes to, their working environment

Entrepreneur   Someone starting their own business that is often risky

Equity   Common law idea of fairness

Error of commission   This kind of error means the posting has not been carried out correctly. The debit and credit entries have both been made on the correct side of the account, but the wrong account has been used. The most common is a posting to the wrong personal account

Error of omission   This error occurs when the whole of the entry has never been made

Error of principle   This is caused by a mistake being made in the principles of bookkeeping. The entry is made in the wrong class of account, e.g. a fixed asset being posted to an expense account

EU-15   The states that made up the EU in 1995: France, Germany, Belgium, Italy, The Netherlands, Luxembourg, UK, Ireland, Denmark, Greece, Spain, Portugal, Austria, Sweden and Finland

EU-25   The states that made up the EU in 2004: France, Germany, Belgium, Italy, The Netherlands, Luxembourg, UK, Ireland, Denmark, Greece, Spain, Portugal, Austria, Sweden, Finland, Cyprus, Czech Republic, Estonia, Hungary, Latvia, Lithuania, Malta, Poland, Slovenia and Slovakia

European Commission   The group of people made up from all EU states that advises the European Parliament

European Parliament   The group of members of parliament (MEPs) from all the EU member states who pass legislation affecting all member states

European Union law   The body of law that all EU member states must follow

Eurozone   The area of the EU where the euro is used

Expected value   The expected return from making a decision, often expressed in financial terms

Express terms   Parts of a contract definitely agreed by the parties

Fixed assets   Items that are used within the business and are not for resale. They will have a life expectancy of greater than one year

Flexible working practices   The ability to make work fit in with an employee's needs, e.g. flexi-time, where employees can choose when they work as long as they do the right number of hours in a week

GDP   Gross Domestic Product; the amount of output in goods or services that a country produces

General partner   A partner who is equal to all of the other partners in the firm

Goodwill   The value of the partnership's reputation and business

Grapevine   The informal communication channel that can work in organisations usually based on gossip and heresay

Grievance procedure   The procedure whereby employees can officially complain about their treatment at work

Gross profit   The profit the business has made getting its goods to the customer. It does not take into consideration the costs of running the business. Sales – Purchases = Gross profit

Guarantee   An undertaking that a loan will be repaid

Holding company   A company that gains controlling interest over other companies through purchasing and holding majority shares in those companies

Horizontal direct effect   Under European law, citizens are able to rely on the provisions of Treaties to make claims against other individuals in national courts

House of Commons   The elected representatives of the UK Parliament whose job function is to debate and pass laws

House of Lords   The upper chamber of the UK Parliament who review, amend and may reject the work of the House of Commons

Implied terms   Parts of a contract not agreed by the parties but included through implication or statutory guidelines

Income tax   The main tax paid to the UK government by people who earn money from their jobs or investments

Incorporation   The legal process of forming a company

Industrial tribunal   A form of court where an employee can make a claim for unfair dismissal or treatment and try to gain some kind of compensation

Inflation   The general increase in prices measured in the UK by the Consumer Price Index looking at increases in prices for a set number of goods

Insolvent   When a business cannot operate due to financial reasons

Intellectual property   The ownership rights of unique concepts, such as designs and original works

Intention to create legal relations   In contract law, the intention to form a contract

Interest rates   The amount that borrowers must pay and savers receive on money placed in a bank or building society

Investors in People   An award given to organisations demonstrating that they have reached specified levels in terms of staff development and training

Invitation to treat   In contract law, a statement that a person will be open to offers for sale

Issued capital   Directors receive shares in a company up to the value of their investment and the investment will become the company's issued capital

Issued share capital   The total number of shares that the business has currently issued

Job enlargement   When employees are given additional tasks to do at the same level

Job enrichment   When employees' jobs are redesigned to give them more difficult tasks to do such as increased responsibility

Job rotation   When employees are able to move round (rotate) within the workplace to do different jobs of the same level. This helps to avoid boredom by adding variety and increasing employee flexibility

Job security   The feeling that your job is safe

Job share   When two employees share the hours of one full-time job

Judicial precedent   Binding case law made by judges

Just in time (JIT)   Goods are only ordered as they are needed

Labour stability index   A measure of how long employees stay with their employers, or how stable the labour retention rate is in a particular workplace

Labour turnover   The regularity with which employees leave their jobs

Latest finish time (LFT)   The latest time that an activity can finish if a project is to be completed on time

Liability   The extent to which a person or business is responsible for debts

Likert scaling   Scaling that is used within questionnaire design to gauge opinions, e.g. strongly agree, agree, have no opinion, disagree and strongly disagree

Limited company   Businesses in their own right, distinct from the shareholders who own them

Limited partnership   A partnership where partners want to put a limit on their individual liabilities

Liquidated damages   In contract law, parties agree in advance the amount of damages that will be paid in the event of a breach of contract

Liquidator   The person who is appointed to wind up a company's business affairs

Liquidity   Measures the amount of money a business has available to meet its immediate debts. It is usually measured by deducting current liabilities from current assets

Manager   Someone who does the planning, organising, motivating, monitoring and directing, problem solving, training and mentoring and appraising of employees that work for them

Market leadership   Having the biggest share of the market as measured by value or volume of sales

Marketing bias   Results that reflect a way of thinking that may not be truly representative of the whole sample

Marketing plans   A total strategic plan for all of the marketing activity in an organisation

Mass market   A market that has a wide audience and products or services become everyday items

Media   The term used for different forms of promotional channels such as television, newspapers and radio

Members' voluntary liquidation   When at least 75 per cent of directors of a company have made a declaration of solvency but want the company liquidated. A statutory declaration is made that all debts will be paid within 12 months of the start of the winding up

Memorandum of Association   A document which sets out the company's name, registered office and what it will do

Mentee   The person who receives advice from a mentor about their ideas and ways to go forward

Mentor   Someone who is given someone more junior to support and look after with a similar background or type of experience

Merger   Joining together with another company so that it is jointly managed and resources are shared in the new company structure

Methodology   The way something is done or collected, e.g. research

Mission statement   The purpose of an organisation set out in writing

Multi-tasking   Being able to do more than one task at one time, e.g. being able to do typing and answer the phone

National Insurance   Payable by anyone who is self-employed or employed. National Insurance deductions are made to cover contributions to things such as the National Health Service

Net present value   The total of all cash flows restated in today's money terms

Net profit   The profit made after all the expenses of the business have been deducted. Gross profit – Expenses = Net profit *or* Sales – Total expenses

Niche market   A specific market segment that has characteristics that can be targeted as part of marketing and promotion

Node   A point in a critical path diagram showing the earliest and latest times that particular activities can start and finish

Novation   In contract law, where a new contract is substituted for an old one

Objectives   The list of plans that a business uses to achieve its aims. SMART objectives are specific, measurable, achievable, realistic and time-constrained

Objects clause   In a company's memorandum of association, setting out what the company will do

Offer   An attempt to be bound by a contract

Offeree   The person who receives an offer

Offeror   The person making the offer

Official Receiver   Person appointed to oversee the winding up of a company

Off-the-job training   Training away from the workplace, such as a college course or computer-based training package completed in the training room

On-the-job training   Training that takes place whilst the employee is working, e.g. being trained how to use a computer package in an office whilst the work is actually being performed

Opening capital   The money or goods that are put into the business when it first starts to trade

Opportunity cost   The cost to the business of investing money in one area of a business and then not being able to spend that money somewhere else

Ordinary shares   Receive a dividend agreed by the business – this might be high, low or even nothing depending on the profit of the business. Each share has one voting right

Original errors   This is an error made with the initial entry into the accounts, e.g. an invoice has not been posted in the accounts

Partnership   A group of two or more people joining together to do business

Patent   The protection of technological inventions

Payback period   The length of time required to pay back an original investment, assuming that the investment is depreciated in a straight line

Performance review   When a manager and subordinate meet in order to discuss how well the employee has completed their work and what improvements can be made

Personal development plan   A plan designed by an individual and agreed with a mentor or supervisor to enable the individual to achieve personal goals

PEST analysis   A business tool that looks at external influences on a business

Piece rate   When someone is paid per item that they produce or service performed, i.e. you are paid according to how much you have actually done

Porter's generic strategies   Typical competitive positions that businesses can take to win market share. These positions are based on either seeking to be the low-cost producer or the provider of products that are different from those of competitors

Positioning map   A diagram comparing the competitive position of a business with that of rivals – often using two dimensions such as price and perceived quality

Preference shares   Have a fixed rate of interest, no voting rights and are paid out before the ordinary share holders

Prepaid   Expenses that have been paid in advance are known as prepaid. Only expenses consumed within the financial year can be deducted against next profit. The prepayment must be deducted from the total before transfer to the trading account. If revenue received has been paid in advance, this figure must also be adjusted so that the figure recorded in the trading profit and loss account truly reflects the money received for services supplied within the correct financial year

Primary research   Research collected at first hand, also sometimes called field research

Private law   The law relating to private matters concerning businesses or individuals

Private limited company   A company that can have one or more members. It cannot offer shares to the public

Proactive approach   A planned approach anticipating change; doing something rather than waiting for a change to happen before taking action

Probability   The likelihood of a particular outcome occurring given a number of alternative outcomes

Productivity   The measurement of how much work an employee (or employees) is actually doing in the time they are employed

Promissory Estoppel   In contract law, equity will prevail to support a person who has relied on the agreement to pay a lesser amount being made to pay a higher amount

Promotion   Making customers aware of the products and services that your business offers including any special deals

Promotional strategy   The goal or purpose of any activity that you take to increase awareness or sales of a product or service

Public law   Body of law concerned with matters of public importance

Public limited company   A company with at least two shareholders; it can offer shares to the public

Qualitative research   Research based on judgements, opinions and feelings so it attempts to give reasons for why customers behave, e.g. what do people *think* of an advertising campaign or how do people feel about advertising targeted at children under the age of five

Quantitative research   Research concerned with facts and figures that can provide statistical judgements, e.g. counting the number of times or yes/no answers

Reactive approach   Responding to change rather than planning for change – sometimes referred to as 'fire-fighting

Refresher training   Training that needs to be carried out to update existing staff in working methods or new practices such as health and safety or changes in legislation; a reminder or renewal of existing training

Regulations   European law that should be implemented by member states

Residual value   The remaining value of an asset after it has been fully depreciated

Respondents   The people who answer questions as part of primary research, e.g. those that answer questionnaires

Retention   Keeping employees at the workplace for as long as possible to benefit from their experience

Retrenchment   Cutting back to focus on what you do best; concentrating on your best lines

Royal Assent The Queen's permission to pass an Act of Parliament

Sample size The number of respondents you have used to collect your research data

Secondary research Research that has been collected by someone else, also sometimes called desk research

Shareholders People or businesses that invest money into a business. The percentage of the business they own will be reflected by the total number of shares owned

Shares Part-ownership of a company up to the value of the shares held

Skills auditing The process where employers look at the types and levels of skills of the people that they have working for them

Sole trader A business owned and controlled by one person

Span of control The number of employees that a manager has working for them – wide means there are a high number and narrow means there are few

Special order A one off non-recurring order

Special Resolution A decision made at a general meeting of the company's members

Specific performance A remedy for breach of contract requiring the person in breach to carry out the contract

Stakeholder society A society in which everyone who has an interest in decision-making is able to take part in making decisions

Stakeholders Individuals, groups, organisations or businesses who are affected by or have an interest in a business

Standard form contracts Pre-written business contracts

Standard of proof The level of proof required to prove a case

Start-up capital The amount of money that is needed to start up a business

Statute law Law created by the UK Parliament

Statutory restriction Where a person can be fairly dismissed due to their conduct; keeping them employed might break the law

Stock Items that the business has in their storeroom waiting to be sold

Strategic decision A major decision affecting the whole of an organisation and its resources

Strategic planning The process of working out a vision (future idea) of where the business wants to be and how it is going to get there, including reviews

Subordinate An employee lower down the organisation's structure

Succession planning When a business plans to train junior employees to take over more senior roles within the business when staff retire or leave

Supervisor Someone who watches over a person or activity to make sure everything is done accurately and safely

SWOT analysis A tool that examines influences on a business with strengths and weaknesses (internal) and opportunities and threats (external)

Synergy The measurement of power that is gained by group working which is higher than the same number of individuals working separately

Target segment A specific part of market that has been chosen to be the target of marketing

Terms The clauses and content of a contract

Trade mark The protection given to ownership of a logo or symbol

Treaties The highest form of European law

Trespasser A person who enters your property without permission

Triple bottom line The results that an organisation seeks to achieve stated in terms of three results areas – profits, social benefits and environmental performance

Ultra vires To go beyond an authorised power

Unions Groups of workers who join together to negotiate pay and working conditions, e.g. National Union of Teachers

Unique selling point (USP) What makes a product or service different from others

Unliquidated damages Damages awarded for breach of contract. The amount is not agreed beforehand and is decided by the court with the effect of putting the injured party in the position they would have been in before the breach took place

Value Added Tax (VAT) The tax a business pays on its purchases and charges on its sales

Venture capitalist An investor who is prepared to put money into high-risk ventures

Vertical direct effect The effect of European law that creates individual rights against the state

Vicarious liability The idea that employers will be responsible in civil law for the negligence of their employees if the negligent act occurs whilst in the course of the employer's business

Vision A future directed statement setting out what an organisation is and what it is trying to achieve

Voluntary liquidation When a company is wound up by its members

Whistleblowing Where a person informs the relevant authority about their employer's bad practices

Work and home life balance The ability to combine working and home lives so that neither dominates the other. This allows the employee to work to their best within the workplace

Working capital Current assets less current liabilities; the amount of money the business has available to meet its immediate debts

Index

absence rate 39
accounting rate of return 24, 27-8
accounts 211-14
    accruals and prepayments 224-7, 232
    balancing 209-10
    errors 227-31
    limited company 235-9
    suspense accounts 230-1
acid test ratio 243
action planning 111
Acts of Parliament 346-9
administration order 374-7
advertising
    email 176-7
    internet 174-5, 177, 178
    media 170-9
    search engine 178
    sponsorship 180
aesthetics 164-5
AIDA 169, 170
aims and objectives 3-6, 7, 108, 148, 279
    business plan 55-7
    departmental 300-3
    and human resources 33, 37-8
Ansoff matrix 8-11, 69, 73
appraisals 130-2, 334
appropriation account 237
Articles of Association 358, 370
average capital employed 24, 27

bad debts 218-21
balance sheet 214-21
    limited company 238-9
    start-up 90-1
bank loans 202
benchmarking 78, 315
Bill (legislation) 347-9
board of directors 236
Boston matrix 72-3
bottom line 6-7
breach of contract 362-3
break-even analysis 28-30, 87-9
budget
    sales 81-4
    start-up 81-3
    summary 84
business law 343-97
    administration 376-7
    case law 351
    civil, common and criminal law 345-6
    contracts 352-63
    contributory negligence 384
    dissolution of business 374-7
    employment protection 378-83
    ending contracts 359-61
    European Union law 349-51
    express and implied terms 361-2
    intellectual property 390-4
    private and public 345

    remedies 362-4
    sources of 345-51
    statute law 346-9
    and types of organisation 364-74
business plan 53-103
    aims and objectives 55-7
    constraints 99-103
    financial plan 81-91
    human resources plan 91-5
    information within 58-96
    marketing plan 60-75
    preliminary information 59-60
    production plan 75-80
    quantity and resources 75-6
    reasons for 55-8
    templates 97-8

call centres 76, 123
capacity (contract law) 357-9
capacity utilisation 75
capital 201-2, 206
case law 351
cash-flow forecasts 85-6
cause and effect diagrams 126
charitable organisations 373-4
common law 346
competition
    analysing 65-6
    legislation 393
    and promotion 191
    training and development 336-7
competitive advantage 8, 308
    strategies for 7, 12-14
competitive forces 102
computer-based training 329-30
constraints 94
    business plan 99-103
    training 336-8
Consumer Credit Act (1974) 189, 388
consumer protection legislation 386-90
contingency planning 44-8, 112-13, 306
    template for 46
contingency theory 141-2
continuity planning 44
continuous improvement (kaizen) 122
contract law 352-63
contracts of employment 380
contribution 29
contributory negligence 384
copyright 390-1, 393-4
cost benefit analysis 32, 125
credit 202
credit note 204
creditors 199, 244
critical path analysis 19-23, 127-8
culture of organisation 107-8
current ratio 243

DAGMAR 170

damages (contract law) 362-3
Data Protection Acts 317, 389-90
debenture 369
debtors 199, 244
decision trees 15-18
decision-making 30-1
delayering 118, 119
demand, factors affecting 65
demographics, Europe 252-6
depreciation 24, 221-4
designs, registering 391-2
devolved objectives 303
differentiation 12, 191
direct mailing 182-3
directives, EU 265-8, 270, 350-1
Disability Discrimination Act 317, 378
discounts 212
dismissal 380-2
dissolution of businesses 374-7
distribution 75
diversification 7, 8, 9
dividends 200, 236
documentation, buying/selling 203-4
double-entry accounting 205
drilling down 127
Drucker, Peter 11

e-mentoring 130
eBay 68, 175-6, 289
economies of scale 67, 76
efficiency 10
efficiency ratios 243-4
employees 303-4
    and contingency planning 306
    employer relations 145
    empowerment of 118-19
    flexibility 308-10
    motivation 311-15
    see also labour; training
employment, contracts of 380
employment protection 378-83
    common law duties 380
Employment Rights Act (1996) 380
entrepreneurs 54
environmental constraints 101-2
equal opportunities 33, 315-18
    legislation 317, 378-9
Equal Pay Act (1970) 317, 379
equity 346, 356
ethical business 187-8
European Commission 264, 265, 281, 349
European Council of Ministers 349
European Court of Justice 349-50
European Parliament 264-6, 281, 349
European product/service launch 249-93
    business context 252-79
    devising strategy 251-2
    evaluation of strategy 292-3
    issues to consider 283-90
    plan of action 291
    planning the strategy 279
    primary research 282-90
    production of plan 291
    research and analysis 280-90
    secondary research 280-2
    tips for writing strategy 293
European Union
    anti-competitive legislation 393
    assistance to businesses 277-9, 288
    customs 270-4, 287

demographic profile 252, 254-6
directives 265-8, 270, 350-1
impact of EMU 261-4
impact of single market 259-61
income levels 257-8
institutions 281-2, 349-50
labour skills 258-9, 287
legislation 264-70, 315-17, 349-51
map 253
regulations 268-9, 350
Social Charter 269
trade 256-7, 275-7
eurozone 261-4
expenses 202, 208

Fiedler, Fred E. 141-2
finance, sources of 81
financial planning 23-32, 81-91
    appraising investment projects 23-8
    break-even analysis 28-9
    decision-making 30-2
financial records 198-200
financial strategy 195-247
    accruals and prepayments 224-7
    bad debts 218-21
    balance sheet 214-21
    bank loans 202
    business context 198-200
    capital 201-2
    depreciation 221-4
    devising 197
    division of ledgers 205-9
    documents used 203-4
    double entry accounting 205-12
    errors 227-31
    evaluation of financial data 244-7
    fixed assets 202
    limited company accounts 235-6
    planning 200-39
    purchases 203-4
    ratio analysis 239-44
    sales and credit 203
    strategic research 239
    trading profit and loss 214-21
    trial balance 210-11, 231-5
flexible working 118, 308-10
Form 10 370-1
Form 12 372
formation of businesses 364-74
    legal formalities 370

Gantt charts 126
general ledger 205, 206-8, 209, 212
gross profit 214, 242
growth strategies 8, 9-10

Handy, Charles 142
Harrison, Rosemary 36
Hawthorne studies 312
health and safety 305-6, 307
    legislation 383-6
Herzberg, F. 116-17, 313
human resource planning 32-41, 91-5
    evaluating strategy 39-41
    matching demand and supply 36
    and organisational objectives 37-8
    planning cycle 32

incorporation 358
industrial tribunal 317, 318